DETECTING MEN

THE **SUNY** SERIES

CULTURAL STUDIES IN CINEMA/VIDEO

WHEELER WINSTON DIXON | EDITOR

DETECTING MEN

Masculinity and the Hollywood Detective Film

PHILIPPA GATES

STATE UNIVERSITY OF NEW YORK PRESS

Published by
State University of New York Press, Albany

© 2006 State University of New York

For information, address State University of New York Press,
194 Washington Avenue, Suite 305, Albany, NY 12210-2384

Production by Marilyn P. Semerad
Marketing by Susan M. Petrie

Library of Congress Cataloging-in Publication Data

Gates, Philippa, 1973–
    Detecting men : masculinity and the Hollywood detective film / Philippa Gates.
       p. cm — (SUNY series, cultural studies in cinema/video)
    Includes bibliographical references and index.
    ISBN 0-7914-6813-5 (hardcover : alk. paper) — ISBN 0-7914-6814-3
(pbk : alk. paper).   1. Detective and mystery films—United States—History and
criticism.   2. Masculinity in motion pictures.   I. Title.   II. Series.

PN1995.9.D4G38   2006
791.43'6556—dc22

                                                                    2005024123

ISBN-13: 978-0-7914-6813-5 (hardcover : alk. paper)
ISBN-13: 978-0-7914-6814-2 (pbk : alk. paper)

                    10 9 8 7 6 5 4 3 2 1

CONTENTS

ILLUSTRATIONS

ACKNOWLEDGMENTS

The author gratefully acknowledges that financial support for this research was received, in its first stages, by the Bill Douglas and Peter Jewell Charitable Trust and, later, from a grant partly funded by Wilfrid Laurier University (WLU) Operating funds and partly by the SSHRC Institutional Grant awarded to WLU. I would like to thank Susan Hayward, Lee Grieveson, Nadine Wills, Duncan Petrie, and Frank Krutnik for their insight, advice, and guidance. A special thank you also to James Peltz, Interim Director at SUNY Press, and Wheeler Winston Dixon, the series editor, for their support of this book and seeing it come to light. I would also like to thank my Hollywood detective film class of Winter 2005 for their enthusiasm and ideas—especially Jillian Harrington who encouraged me to reconsider the contributions of the female detective comedy.

Finally, I would like to dedicate this book to Micaela and Philip Gates, without whose love and support this project would never have been realized. I would like to thank my mother for her exhaustive editorial assistance through the evolution of this project and my father, who ignited my passion for the detective genre with an introduction to Perry Mason through re-runs of the original television series. I am sure it was my parents' own addiction to detective fiction that led me to Agatha Christie in the first place and then beyond. This is for you.

The author is grateful for the kind permission to reproduce selections from the following copyrighted material:
- An earlier version of Chapter 7—Investigating the "Other": Race and the Detective—appeared as "Always a Partner in Crime: Black

PART I

The Crime Lab

*Theorizing Masculinity
and the
Detective Genre*

CHAPTER ONE

Introduction:
The Case

From William Powell to Humphrey Bogart—or debonair to tough; from Bruce Willis to William Petersen—or wisecracking to wise: the celluloid detective has evolved over time, processing society's fears about crime and articulating debates about law enforcement and justice. The 1980s saw cinematic justice exacted by muscle and firepower; today it is pursued with science and brainpower—or what Agatha Christie's sleuth Hercule Poirot called using "the little grey cells." In the mid-1980s, William Petersen starred as detective Will Graham in *Manhunter* (Mann 1986), the first film adaptation of Thomas Harris's novel *Red Dragon* (1981), which introduced the world to Dr. Hannibal "The Cannibal" Lector. The film was ahead of its time, bringing the criminalist and that which he hunts—the serial killer—to the big screen several years before the genre became pervasive in the mid-1990s. Today William Petersen produces and stars in one of the most popular television drama series in the world, airing in 100 countries: *CSI: Crime Scene Investigation* (Cole 3). Like *Manhunter*, *CSI* centers on the investigations of its detectives, including Gil Grissom (played by Petersen), who are criminalists—detectives who specialize in the analysis of physical evidence.

The criminalist is a modern-day incarnation of the classical sleuth first envisioned by Edgar Allan Poe in the 1840s with C. Auguste Dupin, the hero of a handful of "tales of ratiocination," and popularized by Sir Arthur

FIGURE 1. Basil Rathbone as Sherlock Holmes. The classical detective:
Popularized by Sir Arthur Conan Doyle's Sherlock Holmes, the sleuth is
perhaps most identified with actor Basil Rathbone, who played Holmes in
film and radio from 1939 to 1946. Photo from author's collection.

Conan Doyle's famous detective Sherlock Holmes in the late 1800s. "I always watched Sherlock Holmes movies on Saturday afternoons," says Petersen. "I think it's fascinating to deal with people who are smart at something" (qtd. in Dickson 11). And being smart is the defining characteristic of the criminalist: he *or* she (and often, unlike in previous eras of the fictional detective, the criminalist can be a woman) is a well-educated professional whose most powerful weapons against crime are intelligence, observation, and deduction. In between the classical sleuth and the contemporary criminalist, however, is a long history of change and development in the kinds of heroes that have populated the genre. The genre's codes have adapted and altered with the changing society that consumes it and the industry that produces it, forming trends or subgenres specific to the social, historical, economic, and political moment. The first type of detective, the classical detective or sleuth, was introduced by Edgar Allan Poe in the 1840s with his hero Dupin, and was present on movie screens in the 1930s and 1940s in detective series. In American detective fiction of the 1920s and 1930s, the sleuth gave way to the private detective of the hardboiled variety, created by authors like Raymond Chandler and Dashiell Hammett, who made it onto the screen in softboiled versions in the 1930s and hardboiled in the 1940s *film noir*. The street-wise, solitary detective of the hardboiled story, however, was replaced by the police detective of the procedural by the 1940s. The 1950s saw the hero as neurotic and often corrupt; the late 1960s into the 1970s, a violent vigilante hero; the 1970s into the 1980s, a return to a *noir*-hero; the 1980s, a cop-action hero; and the 1990s and 2000s, an educated, intelligent, middle-class criminalist. Although other kinds of detectives existed during each of these moments, these were the dominant trends within the overarching genre of the detective film. At the center of each trend, however, has been a preoccupation with investigating the hero and—as the vast majority of detective films have focused on male heroes—with the masculinity of that hero. This study is an exploration of the detective film over the course of the genre's history in film and its representation of the men of detection.

THE CRIME SCENE KIT

Detecting the Genre

Feminist criticism has exposed the constructedness of femininity in cinema and also explored the relationship of the female spectator to the image, which has, subsequently, inspired the exploration of cinema's relationship to other marginalized subjects. Homosexual, African American, and other types of marginalized masculinities have been addressed by critics but the construction of normative masculinity in the cinema has only more recently been the focus of critical debates about cinematic representations of masculinity.[1] Similarly, although genre studies is a vital topic within film studies, there have been few studies that have addressed the detective genre and those that do tend to focus on one specific moment of the genre—*film noir*.[2] With a focus on *noir*, film critics have often neglected to address the detective genre in film as a whole, especially detective films prior to the arrival of *noir* and those classical detective films that ran concurrently to *noir* in the 1940s.[3] Moreover, the discussion of masculinity in the detective genre has been almost totally ignored by critics.[4] This study is an attempt to redress this gap in scholarship with an examination of the evolution of the detective film—*noir* and otherwise—and its representations of masculinity.

Gender has been a dominant focus of film scholarship because of popular cinema's preoccupation with the construction of ideal images of femininity and masculinity. Film studies, thus, is a logical perspective from which to address the question of masculinity in the contemporary era. In this study, I explore the relationship of gender and genre, engaging with feminist criticism and theories of performance, the body, masquerade, and spectacle to examine the construction of masculinity in Hollywood film. The construction of heroic masculinity is also affected by the actor who embodies it, and a star's persona and career trajectory can shift as social attitudes toward masculinity and heroism shift. In contemporary film, Bruce Willis portrays detective-heroes with different connotations from those portrayed by Morgan Freeman; but a star's persona is modified through the roles that he plays, and those roles are sensitive to changes in social conceptions of heroism and masculinity. Thus, Willis played cop action-heroes in the 1980s and early 1990s but now plays less physical, more sensitive detectives that are still considered heroic. The studies of masculinity over the past decade or so have attempted to de-universalize the male subject by highlighting the way that the masculine "norm" can be seen as fragmented, changing, and contradictory (Lane et al. 1). Popular film reacts to changing social conceptions of masculinity in an attempt to re-imagine those fragmented, changing, and contradictory notions of masculinity into a unified and unproblematic image of masculinity for its audiences.

In order to offer a cohesive study on how the conception and valuation of masculinity has changed in American society, this book focuses on popular, mainstream American film—more specifically, Hollywood film. Hollywood cinema is pervasive and exerts an influence not just in American culture but also around the world, where American popular cinema is predominant. Film is a powerful medium through which social values can be exported and emulated through cultural imperialism; however, it also offers a specific processing of American culture as a mainstream and popular entertainment. As a commercial entertainment that is produced with mass audiences and greatest box-office return in mind, Hollywood film presents mainstream rather than radical or controversial attitudes. This uniformity of mores and values in the fictional Hollywood world creates a consistency in representation across the films it produces. Although no longer a cohesive industry as it was during the Studio Era under the influence of the Production Code, which dictated cinematic content through a regulatory framework of self-censorship, Hollywood film production, nonetheless, still focuses on many of the elements that defined the Classical Hollywood style that dominated the studio era: genre films with goal-oriented and character-driven narrative, strong closure and often happy endings, and a visual style that strives to clarify narrative, character motivation, and theme.[5]

The focus of this book, however, is not Hollywood film as a whole but a single genre—films that can be defined as detective films. According to Christine Gledhill, genre is a particularly useful concept, filling the gap left by the fragmentation of grand theory by providing the conceptual space where certain questions can be pursued through the intersection of texts and aesthetics with industry and institution, history and society, culture and audiences (221). Genres are fictional worlds but they do not remain within the bounds of fiction; instead, their conventions cross over into critical and cultural discourse and can be seen as an alternative public sphere (ibid. 241). Popular film is such because it resonates and has cultural currency with audiences through its reflection—or, just as often, deflection—of social concerns and anxieties with heroes who overcome every problem with which they come face to face, whether finding love or bringing to justice international villains, problems that are easily resolved by the end of the narrative.

The detective genre has traditionally been a male-centered one based on the social assumption that heroism, villainy, and violence are predominantly masculine characteristics. Although there has been a proliferation of the female detective in recent decades in films, television series, and literature of the detective genre, the vast majority of protagonists throughout the history of the genre have been male.[6] Not only is the genre male-centered, it is also hero-centered, tending to adhere to a structure of binary oppositions—good/bad, civilized/uncivilized, law/crime, order/chaos, and heroes/villains. This book is concerned with the representation of masculinity in popular film; therefore, the detective genre's tendency to delineate character, narrative, and thematic concerns in terms of oppositions allows for a confident examination of positive and negative conceptions of masculinity. Not all detective films make absolute distinctions between these oppositions, and the examination of the indeterminate, "gray" area between heroism and anti-heroism also proves illuminating in terms of the social mores and attitudes toward crime and law that it can reveal. This book explores the changes in the conventions of the detective film in terms of how the genre processes changes in social conceptions and expectations of masculinity. As Harry Brod asks: "What do changing styles in genres such as adventure and detective stories tell us about masculinities?" ("Case" 43–44). The Western, the gangster film, and the war film are also male-centered genres; however, these genres exist only in occasional and intermittent cycles, whereas the detective genre has existed consistently in Hollywood film since its conception.

The genre of the Hollywood detective film has continued to be popular with, and relevant to, audiences for two main reasons: first, because the issues and themes explored in the genre are central to contemporary American society; and second, the genre is infinitely flexible in adapting itself to changing social and cultural conditions (Shadoian 1). A genre is a body of films that share a set of conventions, including formal elements such as themes, types of action, and character types; and visual elements such as settings, costume, and props (Buscombe 14). Thus, a detective film can be identified by a narrative that follows an investigation and a protagonist that functions as a detective-figure. As Rick Altman states, for a group of films to constitute a genre they must share a common topic and a common structure (23). In the detective film, the common topic is the investigation of a crime and the common structure is the detective as protagonist driving the narrative forward to a resolution of the investigation.

Beyond those two fundamental elements, however, detective films can cover a wide range of films and their content and conventions can crossover into other genres, making the attempt to define the group of films as a genre difficult. In fact, many critics regard the detective film as a subcategory of the overarching genre of the crime film along with the gangster film, the thriller, and the social-problem film. The detective film has much in common with the gangster film because of the shared setting of a contemporary urban milieu and the similar address of the conflict between social order and anarchy, between individual morality and the common good (Schatz 26). The detective film's concern, however, with crime is most often an oppositional one: the gangster film aligns audience sympathies with the criminal while the detective film does so with the law. This inclination to champion one side of the law or the other is dependent upon the type of protagonist that occupies the center of the film. Narrative film functions to offer the audience a point of identification with the protagonist and thus align the audience's sympathies with him/her: the gangster film has a criminal as its protagonist and, thus, the audience's sympathies will be marshaled to his quest for personal fulfillment in opposition to the law; on the other hand, the detective film with its representative of the law (whether an official one or not) as the protagonist allies the audience's sympathies to the side of law, justice, and order.

Nicole Rafter argues that the overarching label of the crime film should not be regarded as a genre because the various films that make up its subcategories—for example, detective films, gangster films, courtroom dramas, and cop and prison movies—are too diverse in their features and concerns to be united under one genre heading. Instead, she suggests that the crime film should be seen as a category that encompasses a number of genres, including the detective genre (Rafter 5). Thomas Leitch holds the opposing view—that the overarching category of crime film should be regarded as a more cohesive genre than critics have considered it heretofore, one that includes gangster films, detective films, and the much-ignored crime-comedy (289). He argues that an investigation of the connections between these subgenres rather than their differences illuminates why certain subgenres are popular at specific times as the product of specific factors—from the economic imperatives of the film studios that produce them to the changing attitudes toward the culture of the audiences that consume them (295–96). Leitch states that every crime film has three main roles—the criminal, the victim, and the avenger or detective—and that the different subgenres of the crime genre focus on different angles of the triangular relationship between villain, victim, and detective; thus, the gangster film is firmly aligned with the criminal, the "wrong man" film with the victim, and the detective film with the investigator. While I agree with Leitch that specific subgenres of the overarching crime genre have been dominant at specific times in the course of film history, my interest is in the detective genre (or detective subgenre of the crime genre, according to Leitch) because of its focus on heroic masculinity.

There are many ways to group films into genres: by their emotional effect on viewers (for example, the horror film or the weepie), by their content (for example, the science-fiction film or musical), by their themes (for example, the social problem film), by their setting (for example, the Western), or by their protagonist (for example, the gangster film and the detective film). Genres can also be determined by the labels that the film industry places on its films, such as the musical, the Western, or the gangster film, and labels that critics place on films, often retrospectively. For example, feminist and psychoanalytic critics in the 1980s applied the term "melodrama" to films of the Classical Hollywood period that were considered, at the time of their release, woman's films and "weepies" when the term melodrama was applied to action-adventure films.[7] The label *film noir* was also one applied retrospectively by French critics to describe a body of Hollywood films produced during and after World War II that Hollywood itself had defined as detective films, crime melodramas, or thrillers at the time of their release. Critics have argued whether or not *film noir* is a genre at all or whether it is merely a style or movement in film—and then debated its parameters.

Film noir has proven a difficult genre or category of film to delineate and different critics include different films in their definitions of *noir*. For example, in Charles Higham and Joel Greenberg's 1968 book *Hollywood in the Forties*, the films that are now seen as exemplifying the genre of *noir*— such as *The Maltese Falcon* (Huston 1941), *The Big Sleep* (Hawks 1946), *The Blue Dahlia* (Marshall 1946), *Murder, My Sweet* (Dmytryk 1944), *The Glass Key* (Heisler 1942), *Dark Passage* (Davis 1947), *This Gun for Hire* (Tuttle 1942), *The Big Clock* (Farrow 1948), and *Gilda* (Vidor 1946)—are not listed in their chapter on *noir* (entitled "Black Cinema") but in the chapter on melodrama. Similarly, the films that are now regarded as melodramas, like *Ivy* (Wood 1947) and *So Evil My Love* (Allen 1948), are instead described as *film noir*. As James Naremore points out, the use of the term *film noir* was not widespread until the 1970s and was a creation of postmodern culture in a belated rereading of Classical Hollywood (14). According to Paul Schrader, *film noir* is a group of films defined not by setting and conflict but by tone and mood; it is not a genre at all but a style and a time period (169–70). The period of *film noir* is generally considered to have run from 1941, with the release of John Huston's *The Maltese Falcon*, to 1958, with the release of Orson Welles's *Touch of Evil*.

There has been much debate since the supposed return of *noir* as to what actually constitutes *noir* and whether it existed beyond the 1950s. While some critics argue that a new group of films appeared a decade after

Touch of Evil that attempted to replicate or reference classic *film noir*—for example, Leighton Grist argues that *Harper* (Smight 1966) is the starting point of "modern" *film noir* (267)—others suggest a continuation of *noir* rather than its termination in the late 1950s—for example, Foster Hirsch ("Detours" 15–18) and C. Jerry Kutner (287–88). The idea of *film noir* as a genre rather than a style (*chiaroscuro* lighting) or theme (social critique) seemed increasingly justified as neo-*noir* emerged in the 1960s and 1970s and was regarded as commonplace by the 1980s. Contemporary film's use of *noir* elements to evoke *noir* associations helps to solidify what originally constituted *film noir* in the postwar period.

The labeling of *film noir* is problematic as genre critics rarely agree on what genres exist and to which genre specific films belong. Complicating this, as Steve Neale argues, is the tendency for individual films to participate in several genres at once (*Genre* 25). This hybrid nature of films is more the rule than the exception as film producers/directors borrow from other genres to differentiate a film from its generic predecessors and to make it innovative and interesting. For example, rarely are the films that I discuss referred to as detective films. The label "detective film" seems to have become a pejorative one, evoking the image of a sleuth sporting a deerstalker and magnifying glass in a predictable plot of investigation and solution through examining minutely important clues and interviewing witnesses—in other words, the classical mystery that one's parents (or grandparents) would have read. There are no audience thrills, social relevance, or brave heroes in this conception of the genre. Instead, many of the films I discuss, despite having detective-heroes who investigate crimes, tend to be labeled as thrillers, dramas, or crime films. For example, on the Internet Movie Database *L.A. Confidential* (Hanson 1997) is described as belonging to the genres of crime, drama, mystery, and thriller; *The Sixth Sense* (Shyamalan 1999) to thriller, drama, and horror; *Sleepy Hollow* (Burton 1999) to horror, mystery, and romance; *Devil in a Blue Dress* (Franklin 1995) to crime, thriller, and mystery; *The Bone Collector* (Noyce 1999) to mystery, drama, and thriller; and *Memento* (Nolan 2000) to drama (www.imdb.com). On the official Web site for *The Bone Collector*, the film's director Phillip Noyce describes the film: "It's a love story. It's a thriller. It's a detective story" (www.thebonecollector.com). This demonstrates not just the hybridity of individual films, but also the difficulty in categorizing them or assigning them to one genre.

This inability to readily delineate the detective genre or separate it from broader and related genres is indicative of the critique of generic labels as straightforward. For example, technically *Citizen Kane* (Welles 1941) can be defined as a detective film with a narrative that revolves around an investigating-figure—the reporter Thompson—and a mystery to solve—"Who is Charles Foster Kane?" Although the reporter's investigation may be the driving force behind the narrative, Thompson is an almost invisible figure (his face is quite literally hidden in shadow and is never revealed to the audience) and in the end it is Kane who fulfils the role of protagonist rather than the detective. Similarly, the spy, such as James Bond, often plays "detective" as his missions involve solving a mystery; however, with the spy there is greater emphasis on action—as when Bond attempts to elude the villain and his minions—than on the skills of detection. Genre is also affected and determined by industrial and cultural factors more so than the seemingly organic evolution of a specific kind of narrative. Altman describes a genre as multifaceted: a blueprint, a structure, a label, and a contract (14). Therefore, the idea of genre can be seen as a tool used by the industry to "pre-sell" a film to audiences: as a blueprint and a structure the idea of genre can be used to develop a film along pre-established lines that have proven successful with audiences; then the generic label that can be attached to the film functions as a contract between the producers and audience that the film will deliver the expectations audiences have of that generic label.

The continual presence of the detective genre throughout cinematic history and its popularity with contemporary audiences is due, in part, to the pleasure that the genre offers audiences—although the specific kind of pleasure can vary among subgenres. Classical detective films of the 1940s offered a reassuring picture of the restoration of order and a nonviolent and bloodless image of murder whereas the *noir*-detective films of the same period offered a much darker and more violent image of urban society, offering a critique of its social moment that was left almost unexplored in Classical Hollywood films. Although contemporary neo-*noir* films echo the former with a particular *noir* look, they rarely explore the latter, offering little substantial criticism of present-day society. Instead they offer audiences the pleasure of narratives concerned with anti-heroes or criminal protagonists and the spectacle of violence, as well as an acknowledgment of the generic structures that neo-*noir* self-consciously plays with. What the various trends of the detective film have in common are particular kinds of pleasure—although in differing quantities and relationships: audience participation in the construction of the narrative, identification with both sides of the law, and the lack of ambiguity of the classical narrative structure.

Narrative and the Detective Genre

Tzvetan Todorov argues that the classical detective story, or whodunnit, consists of two different narratives: the story of the crime and the story of the investigation (44). In *Murder on the Orient Express* (Lumet 1974) the action of the film is literally brought to a halt until the story of the crime has been reconstructed through the investigation of the famed Belgian sleuth, Hercule Poirot (Albert Finney). A snowfall blocks the railway tracks shortly after the murder occurs and brings the train to a standstill; the investigation then proceeds. It is only at the precise moment of Poirot's revelation of the identity of the murderer that the snowplow reaches the train, clears the tracks, and the train whistles and shudders forth once again on its journey. Although such a literal halting of action is rare in detective stories, there is always a sense that the characters cannot resume their normal lives until the story of the crime is reconstructed and the criminal is brought to justice. The narrative of the crime in the classical detective story tends to occur in the present, usually a retelling of the events as the memoirs of a character who was present at the scene, often in the capacity of the assistant or companion to the sleuth who investigates; but this narrative of the investigation is separated in time from the narrative of the crime that occurred at some point in the past. There is, therefore, a temporal gap between the events of the story and the telling of the story. Todorov argues that this gap disappears with the advent of the second form of the detective novel, which peaked in America around World War II: the thriller, or what the French referred to as *série noir*, or what is now more commonly referred to as the hardboiled detective novel (47). The thriller sets the story at the time of its occurrence, rather than as a retrospective, and suppresses the first story—the story of the crime—while highlighting the second—the story of the investigation.

Both these types of the detective story survive today in literature and film; however, the pure form of the whodunnit as established by Edgar Allan Poe, popularized by Arthur Conan Doyle, and continued by Agatha Christie has not survived except in rare instances.[8] Even the contemporary adaptations of the classical novels—for example, the *Agatha Christie's Poirot* television series (1989–) starring David Suchet—abandon the framing structure of the memoir to recount the narrative of the investigation. Todorov further argues that, whereas the classical detective novel functions to create a curiosity in the reader by beginning the narrative with an effect (the crime) and looking for the cause (the perpetrator), the thriller instead creates suspense for the reader following a more direct cause-and-effect relationship between events (47). Rather than establishing a mystery that needs to be solved like the whodunnit, the thriller follows the investigation and capitalizes on the thrills and fears induced in the reader as the narrative questions whether or not the criminal will be brought to justice before he/she commits further crimes. In this sense, both the classical and the thriller traditions have survived in contemporary detective stories but most often are married to one another. The goal of many contemporary detective films remains the discovery of "whodunnit," although they are rarely the "locked room" variety of crime story with a sleuth as the investigator. But the contemporary detective film does combine the original intentions of both forms of the detective story—to instil curiosity and to evoke thrills in the consumer. As David Bordwell indicates, the detective genre aims to promote three emotional effects: curiosity about the past, suspense about upcoming events, and surprise with respect to unexpected disclosures (65). To promote all three emotional states the narration must limit the viewer's knowledge by restricting it to that of the investigator's.

The detective genre illustrates how in film the *syuzhet* (plot) manipulates the *fabula* (story). The *fabula* is the story from which the plot is derived, and is a chronological, cause-and-effect chain of events; the *syuzhet*, on the other hand, is the actual arrangement and presentation of the story in the film (Bordwell 49–50). Like Todorov, Bordwell agrees that the detective tale is composed of two stories: the story of the crime—which is composed of the cause of the crime, the commission of the crime (indicating the identity of the criminal), the concealment of the crime, and the discovery of the crime—and the story of the investigation—which is composed of the beginning of the investigation, the phases of the investigation, the elucidation of the crime, the identification of the criminal, and the consequences of the identification (64). In the detective genre, the telling of the story of the crime followed by the story of the investigation in chronological order would erase any sense of suspense and much of the mystery. It is the withholding of crucial events of the story of the crime by the *syuzhet*—i.e., gaps—that promotes curiosity, suspense, and surprise in the detective film. The basic structure of the detective film narrative begins with the crime and its concealment, and then the majority of the story follows the investigation and the resolution of the mystery surrounding the crime. As the story progresses, facts and clues are revealed, but they are revealed sporadically and among other information that may or may not be relevant to the detection of the crime ("retardations"). As Bordwell states, the detective film "justifies the gaps and retardations by controlling knowledge, self-consciousness, and communicativeness," thus these delays in information are justified by the degree of subjectivity of the narration (65).

A purely objective and omniscient narrator could reveal all to the reader at the beginning of the story, his/her knowledge of the events being complete; but this would ruin the suspense of the detective story and the pleasure for the reader that the suspense supplies. It would go against one of the original "rules" of the detective story: the rule of "fair play"—that the story should provide readers with enough clues to solve the mystery them-selves (Waugh 160). All classical detective stories, therefore, are told to the reader by a subjective narrator whose knowledge of the events is limited: the "Watson-figure," inspired by Sherlock Holmes' companion Dr. Watson. In the literary versions of the classical detective story, the subjec-tivity of the narration is defined by the Watson-figure's recounting, in the form of a memoir, the events of the investigation of the detective. In the film versions and in later literary incarnations of the classical detective story, the literal subjectivity of the narration is abandoned for a more subtle, over-the-shoulder mode of narration; but there is still a restriction to the reader/viewer's access to the workings of the sleuth's superior intellect, and identification is often established with the companion rather than the de-tective him/herself. The knowledge of the reader/viewer is similarly re-stricted to that of the private detective of the hardboiled narrative, since he tends, despite the accompanying voice-over in the film versions, to keep his elucidations to himself. The subjective narration of the detective story does not necessarily mean that the novel is told in the first person, nor are there necessarily point-of-view shots in the film attributed to the detective or a voice-over narration spoken by the detective. However, the narration of the story and the relaying of the information are attributed to a specific charac-ter who is the center of consciousness for the story. It is his/her presence in the story that defines the quantity of information relayed to the reader/viewer as he/she is the character with which the reader/viewer is asked to identify. This narrational position in the novel or film is actualized in an over-the-shoulder point of view that follows the character who acts as the center of consciousness for the enunciation of the narrative. Some de-tective novels and films do have first-person narrators and point-of-view shots. In the case of film, however, this is not typical for the genre.

Two *films noirs* that did attempt such an explicit identification are *The Lady in the Lake* (Montgomery 1947), in which the camera offers the subjective point of view of the detective for the duration of the film, and

Dark Passage (Davis 1947), in which the camera is positioned for an extended sequence at the beginning of the film so that the heroes (Robert Montgomery and Humphrey Bogart, respectively) are rarely shown in front of the camera but rather as the driving force behind it. However, these experiments in visually representing the subjective point of view of the detective-hero were unsuccessful and not repeated. Narrative cinema is propelled by the actions of a film's protagonist, and that need for action relies on the physical presence of that character/star in front of the camera, which also establishes a visual identification for the spectator with that character. In *The Lady in the Lake* and *Dark Passage*, the absence of the protagonist as the subject in front of the camera constitutes the lack of a center of consciousness for the narrative and a lack of identification for the spectator. For film audiences, it would appear, the presence of the star in the role of the detective as a visual point of subjective identification was very necessary as part of the appeal of the genre.

Every trend of the genre has been very much concerned with narrative—namely, the reconstruction of the story of the crime—and heroes that restore order to the social disorder incited by criminal behavior specifically through the construction of a cohesive narrative of the crime. The construction of a cohesive narrative was essential to the classical detective story with the climax of the film being the "scene of revelation" in which the sleuth reconstructed the story of the crime—the story revealed literally through a flashback sequence in which all the missing pieces of the puzzle are filled in and put in their proper place. Suddenly the detective not only puts all the clues—the pieces of the puzzle—together but puts them together in the proper sequence/pattern that clears up the mystery surrounding the crime and also identifies the perpetrator of the crime. *The Usual Suspects* (Singer 1995) was the first of contemporary crime films to play with these generic conventions and exploit audience expectations in an obvious and meaningful way, garnering critical acclaim and popularity with audiences because of it. Contemporary audiences are overly familiar with the "rules" of the detective genre, and *The Usual Suspects* offered a challenge, playing with viewers' expectations and predetermined knowledge. As the film's star Kevin Spacey explains:

> This was the experiment that Bryan Singer and Chris McQuarrie did on an audience with *The Usual Suspects*. They said: "Let's see if audiences are as smart as we think they are. Smarter than most people treat them. So let's use an audience's intelligence about movies. They

know movies, they go to movies, they watch movies over and over again, they know dialogue from movies, they know archetypes, they know plotlines, they know storylines, they know where movies are going. Let's take all this incredible intelligence that an audience has about movies, and use it against them." (Southam 98)

The detective-hero, Agent Kujan (Chazz Palminteri) presents his "scene of revelation" after interrogating Verbal Kint (Kevin Spacey) based on the information supplied to him in Verbal's recounting of the events leading up to the heist and his own interpretation of that information. But while the revelation of "whodunnit" seems logical from the facts as they were told to Kujan and the audience, the facts on which the deductions are drawn prove to be fabricated. The audience believes the narrative because of the preconception that seeing is believing: we are shown, rather than merely told, Verbal's narrative in a series of flashbacks and, therefore, we assume that the events narrated have, in fact, occurred. At the end of the film it is revealed that Verbal's narrative was partially or wholly fabricated, but the film does not necessarily break the rule of "fair play." This is achieved through the alignment of the camera wholly with Verbal as the narrator, a relationship of oral and visual narration made explicit in the film's flashback sequences. The film does not obscure but instead highlights that the camera reveals specific events and conceals others.

In the first scene, the events of the heist at the harbor are shown: Dean Keaton (Gabriel Byrne) meets Keyzer Soze and is killed by him. Although the camera seems to suggest that it shares Keaton's point of view, it only reveals Soze's hand and parts of his body—but not his face—despite the fact that Keaton can see much more; therefore, the point of view belongs to someone other than Keaton. The scene ends mysteriously, with a close-up of rope and tackle, a shot that is held for an atypically long period of time. In the second telling of the same scene near the end of the film, the significance of the rope and tackle is revealed: it is Verbal's hiding place at the moment of Keaton's murder. Therefore, it was his point of view that the camera revealed in the first instance—not Keaton's. In the re-showing of this scene, certain discrepancies in Verbal's narration are made apparent, which, mirrored by inconsistencies in the cinematography, suggest Verbal is lying in at least one of the versions of the story.[9] It is revealed in the end, however, that he is, in fact, Keaton's murderer and that both versions were false. Some viewers may feel cheated in watching *The Usual Suspects* because all that is shown is not "the truth." But because of the explicit connection drawn

FIGURE 2. Will Petersen and Marg Helgenberger in *CSI*. Male and female, black and white, young and old, middle-class and educated: *CSI*'s heroes like Gil Grissom (Will Petersen) and Catherine Willows (Marg Helgenberger) reassure contemporary audiences that catching criminals is a science. Photo from author's collection.

between Verbal's spoken narration and the camera's visual narration—and the fact that both contain discrepancies—the film can justify its "trick" ending. *The Usual Suspects* began a trend that marked the beginning of a new cycle of detective films in contemporary Hollywood: a cycle of films that not only acknowledged and exploited the audience's accumulated knowledge of films and the detective genre, but that also gave equal importance to the puzzle of the narrative—and the gruesome spectacle of violence that is a distinguishing feature of the new era of the genre.

The classical detective gathered all the suspects into one place and revealed to them the identity of the killer; but this scene of revelation was a recounting of the facts as they occurred rather than an attempt on the hero's part to identify with the perpetrator of the crime and experience the crime through his eyes.[10] The contemporary criminalist is able to enter into and/or manipulate the literal space of the crime in an attempt to occupy the position of the criminal or—in the case of *Crossing Jordan* (2001–)—the victim, or—in the case of *CSI* (2000–)—the murder weapon. In the first few seasons of television's *Crossing Jordan*, the solution to the mystery would be, in part, arrived at through a game played between Jordan (Jill Hennessey) and her father, the ex-cop (Ken Howard), whereby one of them would pretend to be the victim and the other the killer. What followed was an imagined flashback sequence to the crime in which Jordan and her father replace the real participants; if the scenario did not seem to be correct, then another scenario would be reenacted until a logical conclusion was reached. In *CSI*, the "reading" of the cadaver and/or crime scene leads to an oral—accompanied by a visualized—reconstruction of the crime in which the cadaver is seen alive and then killed again. These sequences are done with digital effects; for example, the camera—and viewer—follows the passage of a bullet through a wall and into the head of a sleeping child.

Mark Seltzer nicknames the criminalist "the mindhunter" who, like Poe's sleuth Dupin, tries to get into the mind of the killer he seeks and tries to simulate the killer's experience in performing his murders. In the detective film, this entering of the space and sharing the criminal's perspective is literalized. In *Under Suspicion* (Hopkins 2000) Victor Benezet (Morgan Freeman) uses Henry Hearst (Gene Hackman) and his account of the discovery of the crime scene to enter the space of the crime—literally. Henry sits in Victor's office as he begins his account of how he came to find the body of a young girl. The camera moves into a close-up of his eyes as his flashback will offer his point of view of the incident. The flashback reveals him jogging with his neighbor's dog up the path by his house. Jump cuts and the repetition of various moments of the sequence highlight the patch-iness of Henry's recollection of the event. The camera cuts back to the police station as Henry details his actions that day. As we re-enter the flashback, Henry—in the flashback—speaks the words that Henry—in the police station—is speaking. He says, "We took the path by my house like always." The jump cuts and the dialogue bridges collapse time and space, allowing the present to enter into the space of the past. It also pre-pares the audience for the moment when Victor, the detective, appears in the flashback next to Henry. As Henry jogs past the bottom of the stone steps, Victor appears in the bushes and watches the dog run off the path when it smells the corpse in the woods. Back in his office, Victor stands behind Henry as he tries to share the man's point of view. In the flashback, as Henry kneels beside the girl's body, Victor also materializes on the other side of the victim and asks Henry questions about his discovery. It is as if the two men have returned to the scene of the crime, as it was when it was discovered, to discuss the physical evidence. The camera then takes up the position of Henry, and Victor confronts the camera and the audience in a direct address intended for Henry.[11]

The contemporary detective film takes advantage of the popularity of films, such as *Pulp Fiction* (Tarantino 1994), that disrupt or obviously ma-nipulate the realist narrative with jumps in time, space, and logic to relate the detective story in a more dramatic way. However, just as in the classical detective story, firm narrative closure is necessary. If the criminal attempts to construct a false narrative—i.e., like Verbal Kint—with misleading clues or the lack thereof, the detective offers the reader/viewer the "truth"—the "real" story of what occurred. In *Along Came a Spider* (Tamahori 2001), a decoy kidnapper, Gary Sonjei, is used by the real criminal, Jezzie Flanagan (Monica Potter), to keep Detective Alex Cross (Morgan Freeman) off her scent as she pursues her intended victim. In *Murder By Numbers* (Schroeder 2002), the two young killers (Ryan Gosling and Michael Pitt) attempt to commit the perfect murder with a trail of false clues that point to a different kind of killer. In *The Bone Collector* (Noyce 1999), the killer (Leland Orser) is recreating the illustrations from a book on Victorian murders—literally, from a narrative. The detective's organization of facts, clues, and testimony—whether seemingly significant, random, or misleading—into a cause-and-effect, linear, and logical story brings a sense of conclusion to the mystery but, more importantly, a sense of comfort to the audience that, as civilized beings, we retain a mastery over the world in which we live no matter how complex, violent, or chaotic it seems.

Detecting Social Change

The genre's continued presence on screen and popularity with audiences, however, is also due, in large part, to its specific ability to change with the times. As social attitudes toward policing, law, and crime have altered, the detective genre has engaged these changes. As Michael Ryan and Douglas Kellner state: "Genre films have been some of the most powerful instruments of ideology. [. . .] But the close tie between genre films and social ideology means as well that genre films are among the most fragile forms, the most vulnerable to the effects of social change" (76). The longevity of a genre depends not so much on the repetition of the conventions of the genre as on the differences—the innovations—that make each film new and exciting. As Altman argues, change must occur within a genre; otherwise it would go sterile (21). The issues of law and order, crime and its detection, are ongoing social concerns and will always have relevance to audiences, especially when packaged in films that offer a certain kind of social commentary at the same time as pleasurable entertainment. Social and historical factors alter the emphasis, themes, and protagonists of the detective genre, leading to new subgenres and cycles of the genre and also to new interest for audiences.

Genres do evolve over time, but they also tend to adhere to the more global codes of Hollywood film in general: cause-and-effect logic, character-driven narratives, self-effacing cinematography, narrative closure, emotional identification with protagonists, evil punished and innocence rewarded, and heterosexual coupling. As Ruth Vasey explains, "[I]f the movie is a product of Hollywood we know that the fiction will be governed by a set of narrative and representational conventions that will override the social, geographic, and historical characteristics of its nominal locale" (3). As well, broader cultural myths about heroism can also remain relatively unaffected by social change: the frontier hero was the inspiration for the hardboiled private eye and also retributive heroes like "Dirty" Harry and Rambo. As contemporary critics of genre have argued, genre is less an organic evolution of film narratives than a result of negotiation between producers and consumers of film to ensure that the popularity and success of one film will lead to others like it in an attempt to mimic its success.[12] As certain trends do well at the box office, more films will be produced within that trend; similarly, if audiences enjoy one film, they will undoubtedly go to see another film that purports to be in the same vein.[13] However, a film cannot be seen as belonging to a genre without containing some of the elements associated specifically with that genre: in the detective film a crime must be committed, a mystery must surround that crime, and a protagonist must investigate the crime and solve the mystery.

That said, one of the aims of this study is to problematize the notion of genre in terms of looking for a category that can contain a wide variety of films over a long period of time. Narratives that contain the preceding list of conventions—a crime, a mystery, and a detective—can all be seen as falling under the umbrella of the detective genre; however, the detective genre has undergone many cycles of development over the decades, and each cycle of films can be seen, more or less, as an autonomous subgenre or trend—films that have much more in common with other kinds of film from that social moment than with detective films from another decade. As John Cawelti explains:

> A formula is a combination or synthesis of a number of specific cultural conventions with a more universal story form or archetype. [. . .] But in order for these patterns to work, they must be embodied in figures, settings, and situations that have appropriate meanings for the culture which produces them. (6)

Thus, although all detective films may deliberate themes of law and order, heroism and villainy, the commitment to one side of the debate or the other will change over time in relation to shifting social opinion. For example, the gangster film of the early 1930s offered a sympathetic image, if not a glorification, of criminal behavior by aligning the audience with the criminal as the "hero" of the film, while the G-Men pictures of the mid- to late-1930s firmly aligned audiences with the detectives who brought those criminals to justice. Similarly, the mid-1990s saw a resurgence of sympathy for, if not veneration of, villainy with the popularity of screen villains like Hannibal Lecter, John Doe, and Keyser Soze. While different and conflicting representations of masculinity and heroism will exist in different films at the same moment and often even within the same genre, most often one specific trend within a genre will be predominant. Similarly, the presence of particular stars in the role of the detective-hero affects the construction of that protagonist's heroism and masculinity as certain stars carry with them specific associations of masculinity. Thus, both these factors—the social moment and the star—affect a film's characters, themes, and plot. For example, the prison film *Lock Up* (Flynn 1989) starring Sylvester Stallone has much more in common with the 1980s cop-action film and Stallone's previous roles as Rocky and Rambo than with a prison film of the 1990s like *The Shawshank Redemption* (Darabont 1994) starring Tim Robbins, which itself has more in common with the "sensitive men" films of the early 1990s.

Thus, in this study, rather than search for cohesion across the decades of detective films, my aim is to highlight the individual dominant trends—those trends that were most prolific and more popular at a specific time. It is my contention that a film's thematic concerns are determined less by a genre's conventions and more by contemporaneous social concerns, and that by examining the cohesive trends within a genre—trends defined by specific thematic concerns—the development of that genre in relation to social shifts can be identified. My interest in the detective genre, thus, is not to explore the genre as a cohesive corpus of films and generate a list of films that can "count" as detective films—in other words, explore the similarities of the films I discuss—but rather to highlight their differences. According to Nick Browne, film genre criticism has often only attempted to regulate, classify, and explain film through genre; instead, he argues it should consider film genres as gravitating toward "specific assemblages of local coherencies—discreet, heterotopic instances of a complex cultural politics" (xi). Increasingly, film genre scholarship has attempted to explore genres as products of specific historical, economic, political, and industrial moments rather than as a cohesive body of films that extends over great periods of time. For example, Vivian Sobchack takes up Marc Vernet's point that *film noir* is not easily definable as a genre and instead she explores *noir* as a cultural mode related to changes in American culture around World War II (129). Similarly, my aim in this study is to investigate the dominant trends or cycles that, in themselves, offer a cohesive treatment of masculinity in relation to good and evil/law and order as the hero, but in comparison with one another demonstrate shifts in social conceptions of masculinity.

In doing so, I will challenge the idea of a cohesive genre as each trend/cycle has arisen from a specific moment as a result of cultural circumstances and, as such, differs from the trends that precede and succeed it. The erudite and upper-class Nick Charles as played by William Powell in *The Thin Man* (Dyke 1934) differs greatly from vengeful and violent Harry Callahan played by Clint Eastwood in *Dirty Harry* (Siegel 1971), and Eastwood's portrayal of Terry McCaleb in *Blood Work* (Eastwood 2002) differs from his earlier role. The question to address then is, "Why were these trends dominant and why at those moments in time?" The answer is that each trend offered a processing and negotiation of the social change and upheaval of the time, although not necessarily in a direct reflection. Shifts in politics, economy, gender relations, race relations, and important events have an impact on how a society views itself and, in doing so, this view colors and informs the cultural products of that society. Each type of fictional detective has a different relationship to the law and the crime committed: some are official investigators, others amateur; some are paid to investigate, others get involved for personal reasons; some have special skills or experience in investigations, others are just average people with no investigating experience; some are clearly defined as moral men, others as almost indistinguishable from the criminals they pursue. These differing relationships between the protagonist and the law—between masculinity and heroism—reflect the themes of the specific trend to which they belong and process the specific social concerns and attitudes toward masculinity and crime of their time.

The genre is about containment and closure: the detective film presents a problem—the mystery—to be investigated and resolved by the end of the film. The detective film not only wraps up the case by the conclusion of the film but also the issues it raises, including questions of gender, race, law and order, heroism and villainy. No matter how gray these issues may seem at the beginning of the narrative, the majority of Hollywood detective films firmly identify good with the law and evil with the villain who transgresses it. As Barry Keith Grant says of the success of films like *Thelma and Louise* (Scott 1991) featuring "other" kinds of heroes, "The essentially monolithic construction of white masculinity in genre movies has been fractured by the emergence of other voices, other representations," including women, black men, and the working class ("Strange" 188). However, the detective film tends to offer conservative messages about race, class, and gender—bringing closure to anxieties raised in the course of the narrative about white masculinity's place in today's society. The white hero's masculinity is validated and confirmed; the black hero's race is rarely an issue and he could just have readily been portrayed as white; and the femininity of the female detective and that of the victim is realigned with social expectations—the former through marriage and/or motherhood and the latter through death. Lastly, the genre also offers closure in terms of social fears about crime, as the villains—no matter how seemingly unstoppable—are eventually brought to justice. The detective offers the ultimate line of defence for society from evil and, thus, the detective film offers fantasies of resolution for society's anxieties concerning crime and gender. Through an investigation of the evolution of the detective film—and its relationship to changing social conceptions of masculinity—perhaps we can detect men.

CHAPTER TWO

The Myths of Masculinity

THE MUTABILITY OF MASCULINITY

Feminist critics have tended to regard the category of masculinity as a monolithic, stable, unproblematic, and hegemonic idea, against which the representations of women have been measured. For example, Laura Mulvey in her seminal 1975 essay "Visual Pleasure and Narrative Cinema" argues that there is only one dominant type of subjectivity in narrative film and that subjectivity is inherently male. Feminist studies have since argued for the existence of female subjectivity and also for the possibility of multiple points of view for spectators differentiated along the lines of race, ethnicity, class, age, and sexuality. As Harry Brod argues, the treatment by traditional scholarship of a generic man as the norm systematically excludes what is unique to men and male experience, just as women's experience was formally excluded by the same assumption ("Introduction" 2). The impact of feminism over the past two decades has affected social conceptions of both masculinity and femininity and indirectly incited a pro-feminist men's movement that aimed to expose the diversity of masculinities and men's real experiences in a reaction against the assumed hegemony of masculinity. Just as feminism attempted to reconfigure the place of female subjectivity, so too did the pro-feminist men's movement attempt to redefine masculinity as victimized by patriarchy rather than as monolithic and dominant. As Jonathan Rutherford explains: "The myth of masculinity is its attempt to pass itself off as natural and universal, free of problems" ("Who's" 32). The first step in this recovery is to demystify the traditional notions of masculinity as natural, universal, and unproblematic and to expose masculinity as a construction and a myth.

Masculinity, like femininity, is a product of culture, not of nature: it is constructed and performed. There remains an assumption, even in contemporary society, that gender differences are innate and reflect an underlying dichotomy between men and women based on sexual difference. The assumption arises from conflating biological sex with gender: sex—male/female—is biologically determined; conversely, gender—masculinity/femininity—is a social construction. There is a cultural assumption that the qualities associated with each gender—for example, power with masculinity and emotionality with femininity—are biologically determined; but this ignores the influence of culture on the social subject. According to John MacInnes, the terms gender, masculinity, and femininity are products of an ideology used in modern-day societies to imagine the existence of difference between men and women on the basis of their sex—where none necessarily exists (1). Masculinity is not a collection of attributes possessed by a male subject from birth but a set of expectations that society deems appropriate for a male subject to exhibit.

According to Rutherford, the reality of men's heterosexual identities is dependent upon an array of structures and institutions, and when these weaken or shift, men's dominant position in society is threatened ("Who's" 23). For example, he notes the changes in the 1980s induced by the shifting nature of work, the introduction of new technologies, high levels of unemployment, and the growing employment of women (among other factors) as contributing to the challenge of assumptions about men's roles. This capacity for change demonstrates that, even within one culture, masculinity is not monolithic or stable and can vary over time and across the different cultural groups that compose that society; indeed, our contemporary ideals of masculinity are not the same at the beginning of the new millennium as they were a decade or two ago. As Ian Craib states: "Whereas masculine qualities were once seen as normal and good they are now seen as politically and morally wrong, as perhaps in crisis, and as damaging for all concerned" (724). Soft feelings like empathy, nurture, and gentleness have been culturally defined as feminine, and the dominant ideals of masculinity have been constructed in opposition to them (Rutherford, *Men's* 70). However, men in today's society are expected to exhibit, to some degree, the qualities associated with traditional masculinity—strength, heroism, virility, and violence—and yet also the qualities previously associated with femininity—emotional vulnerability, parental affection, and romantic tendencies—to be acceptable to contemporary society. These qualities are sufficiently contradictory as to make fulfilling them, in any consistent way, impossible. However, the reality is that masculinity is not homogeneous and consists of an array of multiple masculinities differentiated by class, race, ethnicity, sexual orientation, age, and other social determinants. As Scott Coltrane states, scholarship on masculinity since the 1980s has sought to highlight the multidimensional, mutable, and constructed aspects of masculinity—in other words, *masculinities* or the diversity in masculinity (42). However, contemporary Western society does not necessarily recognize the multiplicity of masculine experience and tends to prescribe a standard masculine role to its male subjects regardless of their individuality. That role is then problematic for individuals to fulfil because it does not necessarily correspond to their actual experiences in society and because it can embody conflicting expectations of the characteristics of masculinity.

Arthur Brittan argues that the assumption in Western culture that masculinity is an essence or characteristic with which one is born is the result of the conflation of two distinct concepts: masculinity and masculinism. According to Brittan, "Masculinism is the ideology that justifies and naturalizes male domination. As such it is the ideology of patriarchy" (53). Thus masculinism determines society's conceptions of masculinity by asserting that sexual difference exists and that masculinity is *naturally* superior; however, this dominant fiction of masculinity is employed to measure not just American masculinity but all masculinities. As Robert Connell argues, contemporary conceptions of masculinity are centered on the ideals of Western society and ignore those of the rest of the world; for example, Latin American masculinity is defined by *machismo*, a different kind of masculinity that is the product of a different history, namely colonialism and an interplay of cultures (198). Susan Bordo also identifies types of masculinity that exist in other cultures but are absent from American or Western culture in general: the *tranvestis* of Portugal are male prostitutes with female clothes, names, and hairstyles, who take female hormones and use silicon injections in order to create a womanly figure but do not identify themselves as women, and the *Knanith* ("effeminate") of Muslim Omar are men who dress as women, perform female tasks, and are accepted by society as female (40). Despite the diversities in cultural conceptions masculinity, the dominant type of masculinity is that which Western culture defines as white, middle class, early middle-aged, and heterosexual. It is this conception of masculinity that occupies the center of Western culture. All other kinds are then regarded as marginal, being perceived as different from, or in opposition to, that dominant masculinity—whether that distinction is based on race, class, or sexual orientation. Dominant masculinity then transfers its problems and anxieties onto others to disavow them and maintain its own centrality. For example, the image of women as compliant, black men as sexual savages, and homosexuals as perverted are conceptions of "otherness" constructed to deflect dominant masculinity's problems onto those who seem to be a threat to that masculinity (Rutherford, "Who's" 23). These negative images of marginalized "others" exist to define normative heterosexual masculinity by contrasting it with the things it is not—or at least not supposed to be: feminine, raced, and homosexual.

FICTIONS OF MASCULINITY

The Myth of the Frontier

Feminist criticism is a response to a patriarchal male position that dominates culture and its texts, exploring a female perspective and subjectivity in regards to that culture. Pro-feminist male critics, inspired by the women's movement and feminist criticism, have explored the fact that, by assuming a hegemonic masculinity, the dominant position also excluded any real male experience. Feminist criticism assumed that masculinity was the privileged position and focused on the recovery of female voice and subjectivity, and only gradually did critics develop the ideas of feminist criticism in regards to masculinity—ideas such as performance, the masquerade, and spectacle—to interrogate the reality of the dominance of male subjectivity. Not only women but also those "other" masculinities that did not adhere to the dominant model of a hegemonic masculinity were excluded from the privileged position of subjectivity. Aligned with this idea of a dominant position is Jacques Ranciére's notion of the "dominant fiction": we conceive of society's ideological "reality" as its dominant fiction, and America's dominant fiction is "the birth of a nation"—the story of national origin as staged through binary oppositions such as white/Indian, North/South, and law/outlaw (qtd. in Silverman 30). Ranciére asserts that the dominant fiction consists of images and stories—such as film, fiction, popular culture, and other forms of mass representation—

through which society figures a consensus and upon which both society and its popular culture draw. Thus, the dominant fiction can shape society as it is recycled through society and its popular culture and is eventually cemented into a seemingly natural meaning.

Mainstream film tends not to be radical; rather than challenging the dominant fiction of American society, Hollywood film tends to aid in its persistence through narratives that focus on lone, white, male heroes who perform heroism successfully—including the detective film. The first popular type of fictional detective—the upper-class British amateur sleuth—gave way in American culture to the tough, working-class private eye, and the social setting of crime shifted from that of a traditional British past—the country estate or picturesque village—to that of modernity—the American city. As Harriet Hawkins argues, because some of Britain's most glamorous national heroes have been poets, British literary and cinematic traditions have allowed for brilliant, witty, cultivated, and sensitive heroes, whereas American cultural traditions have favored the all-American tough-guy (29–30). In golden age British detective fiction, tough manliness was equated with stupidity and the more cultured and androgynous masculinity of Holmes and Poirot that was esteemed (Heilbrun 4). The myth of a tough, uncompromising masculinity in American detective fiction is the urban evolution of the version of masculinity represented by the heroes of the frontier literature of the first half, and the dime novels of the second half, of the nineteenth century.

Richard Slotkin suggests that, from the beginning, American popular culture has provided one of the primary means of mass education: the general public received its knowledge of history and politics through the mass circulation of journals, papers, and popular novels and histories (92). He argues that popular novels were the most powerful of these forms because the didactic intent of the literature is embedded in its entertainment, and the historical and moral concepts offered are linked to appealing personalities. The frontier romance, which was concerned with the conflict between whites and Native Americans, was established in the 1820s with the novels of James Fenimore Cooper. Slotkin argues that if the Native Americans were ever depicted as winning these conflicts, which the reader knows will not happen, the perceived progress of America would halt (93). This idea of a war of races in broader terms is a war of morality—of good versus evil—and there is clearly a transference of the themes of frontier literature into popular culture in general, including the hardboiled detective narrative. If evil were to win the war against the detective-hero, progress in American

FIGURE 3. Daniel Day Lewis in *The Last of the Mohicans.* An "American" hero: Hawkeye in *The Last of the Mohicans* (1992) is white and therefore not a "savage," but he was raised by the Mohicans and is, therefore, more violent than the seemingly impotent British on the eighteenth-century frontier. Photo from author's collection.

culture would halt and crime would predominate. Paul Bernard Plouffe argues that in American popular fiction of the nineteenth-century the United States was seen as the new Garden of Eden, and its heroes—such as Fenimore Cooper's Leatherstocking hero, Natty Bumpo, and Edward L. Wheeler's Deadwood Dick—were regarded as the descendants of Adam (5). Fenimore Cooper's *The Last of the Mohicans: A Narrative of 1757* (1826) offers an image of mid-eighteenth-century America as wild and untamed and shows how a knowledge of, and appreciation for, that wilderness is necessary for survival. Despite British attempts to civilize it, the country was occupied by native peoples, many of whom were violently opposed to the settlers, and violence was seen as an integral part of survival and resistance. Although Fenimore Cooper's hero, Natty Bumpo, is a white man, he was raised by the Mohicans and possesses a knowledge of the wilderness and accepts that violence is necessary: his nickname is *La Longue Carabine* (The Long Rifle) because of his skill with the weapon. Natty is regarded as an *American* hero because his upbringing among the Mohicans differentiates him from the invading imperialist British and his whiteness differentiates him from the "savage" natives, establishing him as the closest manifestation of an American possible in the mid-eighteenth century. As Martin Barker explains, in Fenimore Cooper's novels, Natty is "the site of all virtues: simplicity, honesty, strength, manhood, essential 'Americanness'" (97). The frontiersman's embodiment of American heroism still holds currency in today's society, with the success of films such as Michael Mann's 1992 version of *The Last of the Mohicans*, ironically starring British actor Daniel Day-Lewis as Natty (here called Hawkeye), and the continued appearance of Westerns on the big screen.

Plouffe argues that while some of the nineteenth-century heroes have strengths—such as Deadwood Dick's survival skills and moral fiber—and others have weaknesses—such as Natty Bumpo's use of violence—there is a straightforward progression in the development of the frontier-heroes: although some may show an ambivalence toward the law or women, there is never a complete degeneration into immorality (25). Plouffe remarks that this development of a personal moral code replacing a "code of gentility" follows the descent of the heroes from the aristocracy to the lower classes (25). A similar pattern emerges as the British classical detective of the upper classes is displaced in American literature by the hardboiled private eye of the working class. The substitution of a personal moral code in place of one sanctioned by society is a crucial stage in the development of the American hero as it sets up the opportunity for a conflict between the hero and society at large—a conflict intrinsic to the Adamic myth. William Stowe argues that the hardboiled detective is like the frontier-hero because he has an affinity for the criminals he combats and could have been a criminal himself; his activities are dangerous and he plays an active role in the fight between good and evil; and he is a loner defending his society against evil (80–81). The same could be argued for other versions of the detective-hero, most notably the vigilante cop hero of the late 1960s and early 1970s, as embodied by "Dirty" Harry (*Dirty Harry* [Siegel 1971]) and John Shaft (*Shaft* [Parks 1971]), and the cop-action hero of the 1980s, such as John McLane (*Die Hard* [McTiernan 1988]) and Martin Riggs (*Lethal Weapon* [Donner 1987]). And, like the frontier-hero, the detective must also ride off into the sunset, metaphorically speaking: to remain an effective hero, he must remain an outsider to the society that he attempts to heal. The reason that the *noir*, vigilante, and action heroes are so effective in defeating the enemy is that they think along the same lines and have the guts to use the same methods as those they pursue; these abilities may work in the fight against crime, but they are considered undesirable qualities for the average social citizen to possess. While these men may fight for the preservation of American society, they are not invited to be one of its normal members and, more often than not, the hero finds himself alone and/or living at the margins of society at the end of the narrative. Personal relationships—romantic, platonic, and familial—are potential points of vulnerability for the hero, either for his enemies to exploit or because they make him "soft"; to remain alone is to remain effective. But perhaps the greatest legacy the American detective-hero takes from his frontier antecedents—and what most differentiates him from the British sleuth—is his reliance on violence and firepower to bring criminals to justice. The equation of violence plus heroism is the legacy of the frontier-hero, and it remains relevant for film audiences in the twenty-first century. He is a tough hero.

Tough Masculinity

One of the most pervasive traditions of America's dominant fiction is the tough guy. As Rupert Wilkinson says: "Everybody knows the modern tough guy. [. . .] Writ large on the screen, he is most obviously a Bogart, a Wayne, an Eastwood" (3). The term "tough guy" did not come into general use until 1925, and Wilkinson argues that it maintains its modern ring due to its initial association with gangsters and detectives (3–4). The tough guy tradition was associated with a manly masculinity and used femininity as its opposite—as innocent, fragile, and dependent. Wilkinson argues that the notion of toughness cuts across American culture in contrary strains represented by certain binary oppositions, such as mind/muscle, and that culture is constantly reworking them (11). In other words, the notion of toughness is a dominant myth of heroic, American masculinity but it is one that is fraught with contradictions and is constantly being revised.

The heroes of America's popular culture tend to be tough and independent, challenging conformity or the loss of self-reliance by remaining loners. There is a contradiction in America's democratic and egalitarian traditions with the belief in personal achievement while simultaneously supporting conformity. The tradition of toughness in American society is most obvious in the heroes of popular culture that are constructed as ideals of hypermasculinity; nevertheless, just as there are contradictions within the tradition of toughness, so too are there contradictions in the construction of heroes. The hero of the detective genre struggles between the two opposing forces of social conformity and independence; he must assert his independence as a hero while working within the boundaries of the law and often within the bureaucracy of a law-enforcement institution like the police force or the FBI. He also exposes the contradiction between using his mind and his muscle in the right proportions: he must be smart enough to outwit the criminals but must also prove he is tough through performing violence. For example, the reliance on muscle-power and firepower as the hero's most effective weapons against crime was celebrated in the cop action-films of the 1980s but was seen as a shortcoming by the mid-1990s: today's heroes must employ brains, wit, and cunning rather than rely on gunplay to triumph over the enemy.

The tradition of toughness is exhibited through the body, but more importantly it is seen as possible to *acquire* toughness—an internal quality—through the remodeling of the body—an external one. According to Wilkinson, this attempt to acquire toughness was evident in the exercise and dieting boom of recent decades, but in the 1940s and 1950s toughness was more pronounced and demonstrated through styles of walking (such as strutting) and through acts like cigar-chomping, jaw-working, and squinting while smoking (11). This attempt to construct a manly masculinity internally by donning visible traits externally echoes Judith Butler's idea of performing gender, and indeed Wilkinson's description of the tradition of toughness would suggest that such masculinity is not natural but performed. As Richard Dyer comments, while it is assumed that women's beauty is attainable through cosmetics, diet, and clothes, the masculine ideal is only attainable through hard work in order to create the muscle that defines the beautiful male body ("Don't" 71). But it is not only the ideal *image* of femininity and masculinity that is achieved differently, but also how those ideals are performed and evaluated. Women can *look* feminine but men must *perform* masculinity through activities in order to confirm virility, power, and toughness.

Performing Masculinity

As David Gutterman notes, the metaphor for performance provides an explanatory framework for understanding the contingency of identity, not because identity is necessarily a false construction but because it is something one *does* rather than something one possesses inherently (223). According to Butler, gender identity is a construct determined by culture to enforce the heterosexualization of desire by establishing distinct opposites of masculine and feminine (*Gender* 17). Masculinity and femininity are constructed in opposition to one another by attributing to each gender a list of characteristics that are binary opposites. For example, traditionally, masculinity has been defined as strong, dominating, controlling, confident, powerful, and active, whereas femininity has been defined as weak, submissive, vulnerable, emotional, and passive. While shifting social conceptions of gender have changed over the past decade or so, with men now expected to exhibit what were once seen as feminine characteristics—for example, being demonstrably affectionate with partners and children—these conceptions are still generic and individuals are expected to conform to them just the same. With the cultural definitions of gender being so intractable and hypothetical, as opposed to being fluid enough to allow for real people's individual personalities, it seems inevitable that these fixed notions of gender would become problematic and that individuals would attempt to fulfill those expectations through the performance of a desired gender identity. Gender can then be understood as performative, as individuals are expected to suppress their personal characteristics in favor of exhibiting the ones allocated to their gender and thereby fulfilling their social roles as prescribed by society. Yet gender is not perceived as performative; it is perceived as natural. As Butler states: "Gender is the repeated stylization of the body, a set of repeated acts within a highly rigid regulatory frame that congeal over time to produce the appearance of substance, of a natural sort of being" (*Gender* 33). These acts, gestures, and desires are enacted by the individual in an effort to convince others that the demonstrated and perceived gender identity is authentic or an expression of the individual's "true" self.[1] As Butler states, gender is "a ritualized production, a ritual reiterated under and through constraint, under and through the force of prohibition and taboo, with threat of ostracism and even death controlling and compelling the shape of the production" (*Bodies* 95).

Cinema offers a constructed, performed, and ideal masculinity while promising its audiences that it is a real and attainable one. Despite the fictional nature of narrative film, audience attitudes and perceptions are shaped by the cultural objects they consume; Hollywood film offers fantasies of heroic and romantic success embodied by glamorous stars that can be desired or emulated. Part of the perception of naturalness is achieved through the performance of the masculinity being played out on the body of an actor who plays it convincingly or a star of whom the audience possesses personal knowledge. Despite the fictional nature of narrative film, the presence of a real person on the screen blurs the distinction between reality and fiction, especially when the fiction is placed in contemporary society. However, I am not arguing that the actors are merely performing their characters and, therefore, the male gender because their characters are male, but that the characters, as Steven Cohan and Ina Rae Hark argue, overtly perform their gender in neurotic relationships to it or seek alternatives to their masculinity as society defines it (3).

The Spectacle of Masculinity

Linked to this idea of the performance of gender being played out on the surface of the body is the idea of the body as spectacle. Pat Kirkham and Janet Thumim define the body as containing notions from "the visual representation of the male, to dress, to the spectacle of the male body and the invitation to audience pleasure in this spectacle" but also the actor's presence and his star persona (*Tarzan* 11–12). The body of the male character is, thus, a complex system of signs making up a package of representation from his actions to the persona of the actor who portrays him. The representation of the body on screen invites a reading by the spectator through which assumptions about the character's interiority are made from examining his exteriority. The body then plays a dual role as an image for spectatorial pleasure and also as the site of meaning about character, narrative, and masculinity. However, it is not just the body that contains meaning but also how that body is exhibited in action. As Kirkham and Thumim suggest, "the filmic construction of *being* (the body) and of *doing* (the body in action) are both sites where assumptions about masculinity are made manifest" (ibid. 12). The male body has traditionally been seen as one of action in opposition to that of passive femininity; masculinity in motion, therefore, has a different meaning from masculinity shown at rest or in a state of passivity. However, the male body, whether in motion or at rest, is problematic because of the contradiction between the vulnerable passivity implied by being in a position to be looked at as the site of spectacle on the screen and the dominance that the male is expected to exhibit.

Feminist critics and critics of masculinity in the early 1980s argued that the male body deflects the gaze while the female body is presented for the male gaze. In his 1983 article "Masculinity as Spectacle," Steve Neale states that the male body deflects the gaze because, in our heterosexual and patriarchal society, the male body cannot be marked explicitly as an erotic object of the male look, and, therefore, some other motivation other than eroticism must be offered to justify the display of the male body (13–14). One example of an alternative motivation is to offer the male body in action: by fragmenting the body through close-ups and displaying it in action—running, leaping, and shooting—the motivation for the body to be a spectacle is the action of violence. Neale argues that the male body, like Rock Hudson's in Douglas Sirk's melodramas or the male stars of musicals, can also be offered on display in more passive moments but argues that the eroticism of the body is contained because it is feminized (ibid. 18–19). Neale agrees with Mulvey that in mainstream cinema the spectatorial look is implicitly male and that this is the reason why the eroticism of the male body must be disguised, repressed, and disavowed (ibid. 9). However, I would argue that in the case of melodrama or other films intended for a female audience, the display of the male body for the heterosexual female viewer is not necessarily problematic. Nor is homoerotic desire necessarily an effect of the male body put on display that must be disavowed in the action film or the musical, as the male body functions as a spectacle of action and motion and is more likely put on display to enact an ideal to be emulated rather than desired.

Since the late 1980s, a second wave of masculinity critics has argued that the male body does not necessarily deflect the gaze and that it can be spectacular—to male and female audiences. Peter Lehman argues against Mulvey's assertion that only the female body is driven to be looked at

(6–7). Many feminist scholars like Miriam Hansen, Sandy Flitterman-Lewis, Gaylyn Studlar, and Chris Holmlund have analyzed the sexual appeal of male stars for female spectators, and other scholars such as Richard Dyer, Steve Neale, and Tom Waugh have looked at the appeal of the male body for gay spectators. Studlar argues against Neale's supposition that only women can function as the object of the gaze and that males who are sexually displayed must be feminized. Instead, she argues that the eroticized presentation of John Barrymore, the 1920s matinee idol, and the construction of his erotic allure seem more complex than Neale's formula allows, since Barrymore's characters were both feminized in some ways and emotionally, physically, or sexually dominating (*Mad* 131–32). Hansen debates Neale's assertion that violence is used only to suppress the eroticism of the male body for heterosexual male spectators; instead, she argues that the films of Valentino demonstrate how violence was used to evoke an erotic response in the female spectator (qtd. in Studlar, *Mad* 136–37). Lehman remarks that even if a case can be made that women, psychoanalytically or culturally, do not derive pleasure from objectifying the male body (implying that this is not likely), this cannot be the case with the cinema; in watching a film, everyone is looking at the representation of bodies in ways that include objectification, and the phenomenon of the star system clearly indicates this (21). Film theory and its critics, he argues, have drastically underestimated the pleasure female spectators receive from looking at the male body but also that of heterosexual men: that it is not only the gay man who finds pleasure in looking at the male body (ibid. 22). As Lehman suggests, I would argue that what film critics and theorists have tended to ignore is the importance of identification with the protagonist as an ego ideal. Spectatorial pleasure is not just derived from the erotic, and the male star is put up on the screen to be looked at as an ideal of masculinity for heterosexual women to desire and heterosexual men to want to emulate. The male star is always good looking, and those looks are to be envied and/or desired; indeed, films are made based on the star's popularity.

For example, Eric Clarke and Mathew Henson argue that action star Jean-Claude Van Damme produced himself as an erotically charged persona and achieved sex symbol status through publicity venues in the late 1980s and early 1990s (134–35). Unlike his major rivals in action film—Arnold Schwarzenegger, Sylvester Stallone, Steven Seagal, and Bruce Willis—Van Damme was nominated by the *National Enquirer* as not only number one on their "Top Ten Sexiest Men in the World" list but also the only action film star even listed. Clarke and Henson argue that Van Damme's sex appeal is a result of his attractiveness to female and gay audiences rather than the intended audience of the action film—the male heterosexual audience (136). On the cover of *Movieline* magazine in August 1994, Van Damme is shown shirtless, crouching down, and flexing his bicep. Next to his picture, the caption reads, "Jean-Claude Van Damme—'If people see me naked to the waist, they can imagine anything they want'" (ibid. 138–39). But who does Van Damme think would do this imagining? Is it women, gay men, or his films' intended heterosexual male audience?

Many industries, especially advertising and film, rely upon same-sex idealization to sell much of its product. The shots of Schwarzenegger in *Terminator 2* (Cameron 1991), Mel Gibson in *Lethal Weapon*, and Van Damme in *Universal Soldier* (Emmerich 1992)—in the nude—are presumably aimed at neither female nor necessarily gay male members of the audience but at the target audience of the action film: young heterosexual males. As Studlar argues in relation to the popularity of Tom Cruise, we might assume that mainstream cinema must "delimit or disavow the dangerous multiplicity of desire (across genders and sexualities) set into circulation by an attention to masculinity as an erotically marked object of attention" and, yet, we cannot ignore the commercial need for mainstream cinema to exploit the star's appeal to the broadest audience base possible, which includes an appeal to both genders ("Cruise-ing" 173). The exposure of the bodies of action stars like Schwarzenegger, Stallone, Gibson, and Willis offers a multiplicity of pleasures to different members of the audience—an appeal that can be an erotic one to desire or an ideal to imitate. These images of "musculinity" are geared toward action cinema's dominant heterosexual male audience not necessarily for the purpose of sexual titillation but to induce admiration and the desire for emulation, evoking the notion of the ego ideal. The display of the male body can be consciously offered by mainstream cinema to attract a male heterosexual spectator but can also offer that spectator pleasure in looking without eroticism necessarily being the primary effect. As I will explore in a later chapter, the male body was put on display in the 1980s action film to articulate anxieties about masculinity and nationalism.

This shift in critical thought concerning the representation of the male body as erotic for spectatorial pleasure has been mirrored in, or can be regarded as a result of, a shift toward a sexualized and passive representation of the male body in the media. According to Dyer, an instability is produced when the man—the bearer of the look—becomes the object of the look ("Don't" 63). The female body has conventionally been regarded as a passive and spectacular body, unaware of the spectator who regards and consumes her image; but the male model, despite being the object of the gaze, must disavow his seeming passivity if he is to remain aligned with the dominant idea of masculinity as a body of action. This is most often achieved by the model performing some kind of activity within the image. Jennifer Craik argues that a change in the positioning of the male body and the male gaze occurred in fashion photography during the 1990s as a new, young, more androgynous male was placed in positions of passivity and unawareness of the spectator's gaze (199)—a mode of representation previously reserved for the female body. A similar change has occurred in the representation of masculinity in contemporary cinema.

The male body of the 1980s in popular cinema tended to be muscular—muscle being the biological advantage that differentiates men from women and allows them to physically dominate women and other men. However, Hollywood's heroes decreased in muscularity in the 1990s, and, consequently, there was a decrease in the differentiation between men and women in terms of physicality. The arrival of female action heroes occurred simultaneously: Sarah Connor (Linda Hamilton) in *Terminator 2* (Cameron 1991), Thelma (Geena Davis) and Louise (Susan Sarandon) in *Thelma and Louise* (Scott 1991), and Maggie/Claudia (Bridget Fonda) in *Point of No Return* (Badham 1993). Similarly, the slimmer, smaller, and uncertain youth replaced the older man as action hero: Jack Dawson (Leonardo DiCaprio) in *Titanic* (Cameron 1997), Johnny Rico (Casper Van Dien) in *Starship Troopers* (Verhoeven 1997), Neo (Keanu Reeves) in *The Matrix* (Wachowski Bros. 1999), Rafe McCrawley (Ben Affleck) in *Pearl Harbor* (Bay 2001), and Sergeant Eversmann (Josh Hartnett) in *Black Hawk Down* (Scott 2001). By the late 1990s onscreen heroism was no longer embodied by a hypermasculine body. Instead, there was a proliferation of other kinds of representations of masculinity and femininity. Positive masculinity is no longer defined as necessarily active and muscular, but can be passive, boyish, spectacular, and more driven by brains than brawn. This shift in the representation of masculinity in contemporary film occurred in reaction to changing social conceptions of masculinity and has been reflected in the detective genre. The detective-hero is no longer defined as a gun-slinging cop action-hero as in the 1980s, but rather as a more average kind of man both physically and emotionally—in other words, a man performing a different kind of masculinity.

FIGURE 4. Josh Hartnett. Masculinity as feminized: Youth actors and pin-ups like Josh Hartnett have come to replace older men as the stars of action films in the 1990s and 2000s, redefining conceptions of Hollywood heroism. Photo from author's collection.

A Masquerade of Masculinity

If gender is a "performance," then it becomes evident that that performance can be a false one—a masquerade—whereby individuals pretend to adhere to their gender while simultaneously being other (Butler, *Gender* 47). The performance of drag fully subverts the distinction between the inner and outer psychic space by assuming the gender performance of the opposite sex, and exposes the three contingent dimensions of gender as read through the body: anatomical sex, gender identity, and gender performance (ibid. 137). Butler suggests that hegemonic heterosexuality in its constant and repeated effort to imitate its own idealizations is as much an imitation as drag and, therefore, holds no claim to being natural (*Bodies* 125). The idea of the masquerade goes against that of masculinity since masculinity has traditionally been conceived of as natural; but masculinity is a performance and that performance can be a false one—a masquerade.

One way to negotiate the effects of changing social roles for men is to ignore them, and this can be accomplished through troubled masculinity masquerading as untroubled. Mulvey argues that the female spectator can only oscillate between the feminine—a masochistic overidentification with the female image—and the masculine—an identification with the male hero of the narrative ("Afterthoughts" 13). Mary Ann Doane argues that this movement between the two positions, one inherently male and the other inherently female, evokes the idea of transvestism, or wearing the appearance of the opposite sex; but there is a possible recourse for the female spectator through the masquerade, or the donning of the appearance of femininity (25). The masquerade presents femininity as a mask that can be worn or removed. Patriarchy positions and constructs femininity as a "closeness"; the employment of the masquerade resists this positioning by constructing femininity at a distance.

Doane tends to conflate the female protagonist with the female spectator in her discussion of the masquerade, not distinguishing which of the two can resist patriarchal positioning through the masquerade. She seems to argue, however, that the masquerade offers the female spectator a recourse by which to construct distance between herself and the image of femaleness that is presented on the screen and viewed through the male gaze; it also offers the female protagonist a recourse by which to maintain the power and "maleness" of the active gaze of a male character—yet conceal it—as her possession of it would be deemed threatening by the male. The masquerade of the female protagonist conceals her possession of the powerful active gaze that allows her to propel the narrative and behold the spectacle—for example, the male as erotic object. The female spectator then acknowledges the masquerade of the female protagonist, constructing a distance between herself and that female image. As Doane explains: "The effectivity of masquerade lies precisely in its potential to manufacture a distance from the image, to generate a problematic within which the image is manipulable, producible, and readable by the woman" (32). The theory of the masquerade is as applicable to the discussion of masculinity in film as it is to femininity.[2] In regards to the female protagonist, the masquerade allows her to use the appearance of femininity to seem unthreatening to the male hero by disguising the innate masculine qualities she may possess, including the power of the gaze. Similarly, in regards to the male protagonist, the masquerade allows him to use the appearance of masculinity to seem more manly by disguising the innately feminine qualities that he may possess.

According to Yvonne Tasker, the representation of masculinity in the 1990s became problematic following the 1980s backlash against feminism and the New Man with the "muscular cinema" (1). The acknowledgment, on the behalf of the male spectator, of qualities that the male character may possess that are perceived as effeminate is a threat of vulnerability that must be disguised from the spectator since the two qualities—male and vulnerable—cannot be openly acknowledged and collapsed into one male image in popular culture today. Tasker argues that this tendency for masculinity to be constructed is a product of the 1980s consumer movement aimed at men: "The invitation extended to western men to define themselves through consumption brings with it a consequent stress on the fabrication of identity, a de-naturalising of the supposed naturalness of the male identity" (110). I agree with Tasker that consumerism aimed at men over the last two decades has encouraged men to construct their masculinity in the most optimum way; however, the notion of the masquerade has always existed in society to maintain a separation of the public and the private, one's innermost feelings and one's exterior appearance. The protagonists of the detective film are constructed as representations of heroic masculinity; even if in the course of the film that heroism is called into question, it is proven at the end by the successful defeat or capture of the villain. But there are many ways in which this demonstration of heroic masculinity is just a performance: a masquerade of manliness concealing vulnerability, emotionality, fear, and other characteristics seen as effeminate and unmanly. For example, the hardboiled detective is presented as epitomizing tough masculinity with his fast talk, fedora tipped forward, unkempt and unshaven appearance, and cigarette dangling from his lip. But his is a divided masculinity, living on the periphery of society, working alone and trying to make ends meet, suffering from postwar disillusionment and displacement, and feeling the guilt from his associations with the evil of the underbelly of society. The masquerade is then employed by the detective-hero to disguise vulnerability and emotionality beneath an *appearance* of tough manliness.

Similarly, the cop-action hero uses a masquerade of hypermasculinity to disguise his inner crisis, either through a pumped-up body or through a uniform of paternal authority. As Tasker explains, the latter masquerade can stabilize the body image as male and is related to "homeovestism," or wearing the garments of the same sex, but those that are associated with paternal authority, especially uniforms (128). Because these men appear to be manly, professional, and authoritarian they can deflect the weakness of emotionality and vulnerability by presenting themselves through the clothes of their profession. This echoes Stephen Heath's discussion of Lacan and the "male parade," or a man's donning the trappings of phallic power to conceal his lack of power and authority (qtd. in Tasker 129). Also, wearing a uniform removes individualism from one's external appearance, making it more difficult for others to "read" one's innermost feelings. The uniform of a job—whether a formal uniform or a business suit—defines the man who wears it not as an individual with distinct characteristics and feelings but as his job. This reinforces one of the common themes of the police-detective film: that the detective is first and foremost a cop and that to do his job he must deny himself a life beyond his duty. Thus the uniform performs a dual function: one, to define the detective as his job; and two, to allow him to conceal personal vulnerability and appropriate the power and authority evoked by the uniform.

THE MYTH OF MASCULINE CRISIS

Susan Faludi argues that each advance of feminism has met with a backlash from men and, thus, each moment of backlash has induced a "crisis of masculinity": the late 1880s, post-World War I, post-World War II, and the 1980s (*Backlash* 84–85). Many critics, commentators, books, and films suggest that men in Western society are again (or still) in crisis at the dawn of the new millennium. In her 1999 book *Stiffed: The Betrayal of the Modern Man* Faludi attempted to demonstrate that American men were experiencing a crisis at the turn of the new millennium in response to the empowerment of women—

from teenage boys competing for "points" (sexual conquests) to grown men frustrated by the recession, unemployment, and low wages of the 1990s (5). These men belong to generations born in peacetime, unable to "prove" their virility through wartime victories as their fathers had done. Similarly, the release of a number of popular films at the turn of the new millennium centered on male protagonists in crisis—*American Beauty* (Mendes 1999), *Fight Club* (Fincher 1999), *Magnolia* (Anderson 1999), *The Sixth Sense* (Shyamalan 1999), *American Psycho* (Harron 2000), *The Beach* (Boyle 2000), *Memento* (Nolan 2000), *Unbreakable* (Shyamalan 2000)—seemed to indicate a broader social concern that at the turn of the new millennium masculinity was, indeed, in crisis.

In *Fight Club*, after laying down the rules of the club to its new members, Tyler (Brad Pitt) explains why each of the men there represents masculinity in crisis:

> Man, I see in Fight Club the strongest and smartest men who ever lived. I see all this potential . . . and I see squander. Goddammit, an entire generation pumping gas, waiting tables—slaves with white collars. Advertising has us chasing cars and clothes; working jobs we hate so we can buy shit we don't need. . . . We're the middle children of history, man. No purpose, or place. We have no Great War; no Great Depression. Our Great War is a spiritual war; our Great Depression is our lives. We've all been raised by television to believe that one day we'd all be millionaires and movie gods and rock stars—but we won't. We're slowly learning that fact. And we're very, very pissed off.

Tyler blames consumerism, television, and the lies of culture for male dissatisfaction; but he also notes that masculine identity is not natural, something that one is born with, but rather something that is born out of masculinity's relationship to culture. The film suggests that masculinity can only be defined through work, war, and economic strife: without conflict to test masculine violence and power, masculinity cannot be proven. Fight Club is a substitution for cultural conflict through which men can reassert their masculinity against the feminization of consumerism. As Tyler explains,

> TYLER: Do you know what a duvet is? It's a blanket . . . just a blanket. Now, why do guys like you and I know what a duvet is? Is it essential to our survival in the hunter-gatherer sense of the word? No. What are we then?

JACK: I dunno. Consumers?

TYLER: Right! We're consumers. We are by-products of a lifestyle
          obsession. Murder, crime, poverty—these things don't con-
          cern me. What concerns me are celebrity magazines, televi-
          sion with five hundred channels, some guy's name on my
          underwear. Rogaine, Viagra, Olestra . . .

JACK: Martha Stewart . . .

TYLER: Fuck Martha Stewart! Martha's polishing the brass on the
          Titanic. It's all going down, man. So fuck off with your sofa
          units and string-green stripe patterns. I say never be com-
          plete. I say stop being perfect. I say let's evolve. Let the chips
          fall where they may.

Tyler blames the consumerism and materialism of society for the masculine
crisis and also for general social decay. He argues that, as a society, we focus
on the fulfilment of personal desires rather than on social needs and he suggests that consumerism feminizes the male (Martha Stewart being the icon
of domestic-oriented consumerism). He says "never be complete" as if consumerism is an attempt to fulfil personal identity and suggests that one can
remain separate from society and, therefore, find true personal fulfilment by
living life according to one's own rules. Similarly, in a rejection of contemporary society, Lester (Kevin Spacey) drops out, smokes dope, and tries to
seduce a high school cheerleader in *American Beauty*; Bateman (Christian
Bale) commits serial murder (or fantasizes that he does) in *American Psycho*;
and Richard (Leonardo DiCaprio) flees to an alternative, hedonistic society in *The Beach*. These films present men who—rather than rising triumphant over their crisis—are defeated and, in being so, debunk the myth
of dominant masculinity that has informed society since the frontier era
and expose men's lack of access to power in American society. The "masculine crisis" film offered audiences protagonists who perform crisis—through
a regression to adolescence—as a backlash against the perceived loss of
masculine power incited by female empowerment and the perceived feminizing effect of consumerist culture.

   Faludi's discussion of contemporary masculinity is based on the
assumption that men are in crisis. But the release of "masculine crisis" films
in 1999 and 2000, while perhaps indicative of popular opinion regarding
the subject of contemporary masculine crisis, is not necessarily proof that

masculinity in society at large is in crisis. Although film as a cultural product is inevitably affected by social and cultural changes, those changes do not necessarily have a direct expression in film because of film's own conventions that override external influences. The aim of popular film is not to record reality but to process it through idealized characters, narratives, and themes into a fantasy that will bring pleasure to its audiences. As Ruth Vasey explains:

> The world according to Hollywood is an exotic, sensual cousin of the realm outside the cinema. [. . .] In Hollywood's fictional kingdom, the desires that viewers project onto characters are fulfilled and regulated by a narrative resolution that reasserts and reestablishes a deterministic moral order, by which the guilty are punished, the sympathetic are discovered to be innocent, and audiences "exhausted with the realities of life" are "improved." (3)

Hollywood does draw from the world outside the cinema and contemporary events. But rather than engage in any serious social criticism, Hollywood tends to exploit "hot" topics and sensational events in order to attract audiences. For example, the revelation by scientists in the mid-1990s that a meteor might hit the Earth spawned two blockbuster films concerned with America's response to such a crisis—*Armageddon* (Bay 1998) and *Deep Impact* (Leder 1998). Similarly, the widespread presence of the Internet by the mid-1990s resulted in films like *The Net* (Winkler 1995) and *Changing Lanes* (Michell 2002), which exploited fears about personal data on the information highway. And the scientific reality of advances in genetic engineering saw films like *Jurassic Park* (Spielberg 1993) and *Gattaca* (Niccol 1997) explore the negative consequences of scientific breakthroughs. Although Hollywood film may explore contemporary social fears or concerns, it does not necessarily do so in a direct—or accurate—reflection. As Murray Pomerance notes,

> the masks of gender in the late 1990s may be less rooted in cultural practice, an expression of hope more than social fact; or a clever deception built and re-built to guide us away from the pathway of equality instead of toward it. Surely, much of the critique in [*Ladies and Gentlemen, Boys and Girls*] seems perceptively to note a conservative, atavistic political abreaction beneath the surface of the appar-

ently renovated society of sensitized men and empowered women we see laid before us on movie screens day after day. ("Gender" 7)

Just because male protagonists in films like *American Beauty* and *Fight Club* are in crisis does not mean that men in society at the moment are. But the presence of such a great number of films focusing on masculinity in crisis that proved popular at the turn of the millennium suggests that it is a topic of concern and audiences want to see films that explore contemporary definitions and conceptions of gender. The pleasure that popular film offers audiences is a fantasy in which social and personal problems can be raised but also, more importantly, resolved—problems that cannot be so readily resolved in reality.

Masculinity is not necessarily in a moment of crisis in contemporary society but rather in a state of fluctuation in its attempt to negotiate social and economic changes that define gendered social roles. As Tim Edwards notes:

> Empirically at least, this claim seems contentious, as there is little evidence to support the claim that men or masculinity are indeed in a kind of crisis; whilst theoretically there is clearly a quantum leap from the impact of feminism upon women's lives to large-scale or generalised changes in men or masculinity. (6)

As some scholarship seems to suggest, masculinity is not *in* crisis but is instead a by-product *of* crisis: "a survival strategy with its payoffs as well as its disadvantages" (Lane et al. 2). Through the cinematic images of heroism and villainy, masculinity—and its discontents—can be explored in meaningful ways for the audience to accept, resist, contest, or celebrate. One aim of *Detecting Men* is to problematize the idea of masculinity in crisis as raised in the writing of both social and academic critics. The *Concise Oxford Dictionary of Current English* defines the term "crisis" as "a decisive moment," "a time of danger or great difficulty," and a "turning point" (319). As Lee Grieveson notes, critics argue that masculinity is in crisis in relation to a previous moment of stability. But this moment of stability is elusive (405). In discussions of masculinity in film—such as, Joan Mellen's *Big Bad Wolves* (1978) and Gaylyn Studlar's *This Mad Masquerade* (1996)—it becomes evident that almost every historical moment of cinema purports conflicting images of masculinity.[3] The cause of crisis for contemporary masculinity has been identified as feminist empowerment, which began in the late 1960s and gathered momentum in the 1970s, but a crisis, by definition, cannot be so long lived. Not every representation of masculinity in Hollywood film depicts crisis, and other representations of masculinity exist alongside those of crisis. For instance, the contemporary criminalist—a stable and confident masculinity—preceded and succeeded the protagonists of the "masculine crisis" films of 1999 and 2000. Thus, through the course of this study, I will demonstrate how masculinity in contemporary society is not in crisis and that contemporary film, with its images of masculine crisis, does not necessarily reflect an *actual* crisis in society but does offer a space in which conflicting conceptions of gender roles can be expressed, negotiated, and, in many cases, resolved in the attempt to offer viewers a fictional solution to their contradictory experiences of power in society.

Hollywood film offers a response to the moments of perceived masculine crisis and backlash. However, as Brittan argues, what is perceived as a crisis is actually just the resistance and confusion that arises in the face of changing conceptions and realities of masculinity:

> Masculinity refers to those aspects of men's behavior that fluctuate over time. In some cases these fluctuations last for decades—in others it may be a matter of weeks or months. For example, if we look at the fashion of men's hairstyles over the past 20 years or so, we find that they range from the shoulder length vogue of the sixties, to the punk cuts of the late seventies and early eighties. During the same period men have experimented with both macho and androgynous types of self-presentation. At the same time, we have been bombarded with stories about role reversals in marriage and the home. [. . .] The speed of these changes, it is sometimes suggested, has led to a crisis of masculinity. The implication here is that the male identity is a fragile and tentative thing with no secure anchorage in the contemporary world. (53)

This tendency to conflate crisis with change is most likely the reason why masculinity is seen to be in crisis at various stages of social history. In order to dispel the myth of masculinity, general society must recognize that masculinity is not a naturally occurring characteristic that the male sex should be born with, but is instead something that is socially constructed and performed. On the big screen, heroes rarely offer real or contradictory experiences of gender and power in society and continue to act out ideals of masculinity. However, those "performances" do alter over time in relation to whatever ideals of masculinity are dominant at any one time, so that the heroes of the 1940s will perform a different kind of masculinity those of today. The following chapters of this book will, thus, examine the various ways in which Hollywood has responded to perceived masculine crisis through the relationship of its male heroes and the law in the detective genre. From the classical sleuth of the 1930s to the hardboiled private eye of the 1940s, from the conservative cop of the 1940s to the vigilante one of the 1970s, from the cop action hero of the 1980s to the criminalist of today, the Hollywood detective has evolved over the years as social ideals of masculinity have changed, but he has also remained very much the same as an icon of American heroism.

PART II

Investigating Masculinity

The 1940s and the 1980s

CHAPTER THREE

Investigating National Heroes:
British Sleuths and American Dicks

In a response to the social changes incited by World War II, Hollywood offered audiences two different types of detective-hero in the 1940s: the soft-boiled transitional detective and the hardboiled *noir*-detective.[1] The 1950s also produced two different responses to the Cold War: the conservative cop of the police procedural and the corrupt cop of what have been identified as late *film noirs*. The hardboiled detective was a twentieth-century incarnation of the American tough-guy tradition that originated in nineteenth-century frontier literature. But his tough masculinity did not arrive simultaneously with the hardboiled novel's translation onto the screen. Even after the arrival of the tough *noir*-hero, many of the more gentlemanly sleuths survived along-side him—even in those films adapted from hardboiled novels. The tough-guy image of the *noir*-detective was, therefore, not the product of hardboiled literature; instead, it was a product of a specific social moment. The private eye of *film noir* was supplanted by the professional in the late 1940s, and the police detective came to be the dominant type of investigating hero. The police detective offered a professional, conservative, and everyday hero that relied on teamwork and procedure to catch the criminals that plagued postwar America. These three trends of detective narrative—the classical, the hardboiled, and the police procedural—established the major conventions of the genre that have been revisited in later incarnations of the detective film, although often in different relationships to myths of heroism, masculinity, and the law—myths often tied to ideas of national identity.

THE CLASSICAL DETECTIVE

The birth of detective fiction coincided with the birth of the modern police force, and both can be traced to the anxieties of the literate, upper classes concerned with the threat to social order posed by the lower classes. Robert Reiner argues that in order to alleviate the concerns of the upper classes, the classical detective[2] was put forth as a "rational and unfailing resourceful individual symbolising a superior ideal of self-disciplined initiative, who is symbiotically related to a well-ordered social organisation" (*Politics* 147). It is generally agreed that American author Edgar Allan Poe became the "father of the detective story" with the publication of his short story "Murders in the Rue Morgue" in 1841 (Waugh 6; Symons 28). Other critics cite English novelist William Godwin as the creator of the detective story with his novel *The Adventures of Caleb Williams*, published in 1804, in which an investigator-figure brings to light a murderer and also the corruption of England's justice system (Rimoldi, *I* 165). In Britain, Charles Dickens is often cited as Poe's parallel with his publication of the first British story featuring a detective—*Bleak House* (1853)—or, more often, Wilkie Collins with his detective novel *The Moonstone* (1868).

It is Poe's amateur detective, Auguste Dupin, however, who is best known and considered the archetypal classical detective, who relies on observation and ratiocination to solve the mystery where the police fail. Julian Symons argues that each of Poe's detective stories anticipates almost every later development in the genre: "Murders in the Rue Morgue" is the first locked-room mystery; "The Purloined Letter" offers the most unlikely solution to the crime; "Mystery of Marie Roget" is the progenitor of documentary crime fiction; and "The Gold Bug" has the puzzle or code at the center of the solution (28). These stories also introduce the omniscient detective and his companion that would remain the basis of the classical detective story. Poe's detective stories established the pattern for the detective novel, which would remain the norm until the development of the hardboiled detective story, including the hermetically sealed room, the wrongly accused man, the solution by unexpected means, the trail of false clues, and the criminal being the least likely person (Karimi 46–47).

The defining feature of Poe's stories was the focus on detection: a mystery surrounding a crime is solved by a detective-figure through the accumulation of evidence that eventually identifies the criminal. Two conventions of the detective story that Poe did not invent, but which would follow as the genre developed, were the ideas of "fair play" and motive. The idea of playing fair—or the author providing enough evidence for the reader to figure out the solution—is an essential ingredient for the classical detective story, but it was not invented until almost seventy-five years after Poe wrote the first detective story (Waugh 22).[3] Also, in "Murders in the Rue Morgue" no motive is given for the crime—the murder of two women—as the killer is an orangutan, not a man. But the idea of motive is also fundamental to the detective story. As Amir Karimi states: "Without purpose, there is no guilt and without guilt, there is no case" (23).

The precursor to the detective story is Vidocq's *Memoires*, published in France in 1828. Vidocq had been a criminal in Paris but was offered the chance to use his knowledge of crime to help catch criminals, and he became the head of France's first police force, *La Sûreté*, in 1811. His *Memoires* were a multivolume account of his success as a detective (although the sheer number of the cases has caused critics to suspect many of the stories were fictional). Although Vidocq's *Memoires* were not necessarily the first fictional detective stories, they do illustrate that there could be no detective fiction before the nineteenth century because there was no detection until the birth of the modern police force. With the birth of policing came the birth of the fictional detective (Karimi 45; Reiner, *Politics* 147). As Symons remarks, Poe's invention of the detective story is most impressive because at the time he was writing there were no detective departments in police forces and the term "detective" was not even in use (28). He invented the detective before it existed in reality.

The birth of the police force occurred in reaction to a major shift in society's attitude toward law and order, crime and criminals. As Michel Foucault argues, public execution and torture as public spectacle disappeared in the late eighteenth century, and the punishment of criminals became the most hidden part of the penal process: "The body as the major target of penal repression disappeared" (7–9). The publicity of crime shifted from the execution to the trial and sentencing, and a double process occurred with the disappearance of the spectacle in punishing the criminal and the elimination of pain and torture imposed upon the body (ibid. 11). The punishment of the body did not wholly disappear with the shift from execution to imprisonment as imprisonment, entailed the control over the body through rationing food, sexual deprivation, solitary confinement, and corporal punishment. But it did represent a shift from the body to the soul, with long-term imprisonment replacing death through execution. The public spectacle of punishment for crimes has not disappeared, nor has it lost its appeal for society. But by the twentieth century the spectacle had shifted to the trial (perhaps, in part, to capital punishment being replaced with life imprisonment in many places) as the popularity of courtroom and lawyer films and television series (and the real-life trials of O. J. Simpson and Michael Jackson) might suggest.

Before the advent of the police force, torture was the means of both punishment and investigation, used to extract vital information concerning crimes and also confessions (Foucault 34). With the Enlightenment came the condemnation of torture as an atrocity, and not long afterward the police force replaced torture with detection and investigation. In 1829 Parliament passed the act that established the London Metropolitan Police—England's first body of professional, uniformed, fulltime police (Weaver 289). This marked the beginning of a comprehensive reform of the criminal code. As Ronald Thomas notes, American policing had a more gradual evolution from an improvised and amateur system of local protection to professional agencies, with the key moment commonly identified as the establishment of the "day watch" in Boston in 1838 (13). The Federal Bureau of Investigation (FBI) was created in 1908 to take over policing responsibilities on a national scale from private agencies like the Pinkertons, thus marking a great delay in comparison to the British in establishing an official police force.

In terms of film, the appearance of the detective did not begin with the first literary detective, Dupin, as Poe's stories only made it to the screen as horror films. According to Larry Langman and Daniel Finn, the earliest crime films focused chiefly on bloodless crimes such as burglary, petty thefts, scams, and prison escapes (*Silent* xi). For example, Thomas Edison's 1897 film *Arrest in Chinatown, San Francisco, Cal.* shows two policemen placing a Chinese man into a horse-drawn wagon labeled "Police Department." There were different types of crime films, many of which focused on the crime, the criminals, or the victims; but there were also films that focused on the detective. The detective gained prominence in early silent cinema with films such as Edwin S. Porter's *Getting Evidence, Showing the Trials and Tribulations of a Private Detective* (1906) and *The Detectives of the Italian Bureau* (1909), and some films even depicted the police as less than honest rather than upholders of the law (ibid. xiii). Around 1915 films became more sophisticated with the industry's shift, in anticipation of greater profits and attracting middle-class audiences, from one- and two-reel films to feature-length films that ran for an hour or longer, which encouraged more complicated plots and character development. In these feature-length films, police officers and detectives served as main characters in crime plots, with the treatment of the police alternating between sympathy and ridicule. The lengthier crime film resulted in better scripting, rounded characters, and higher production values, but it also led to familiar narrative structures and plot devices with stereotyped characters (ibid. xvi).

In 1913 Louis Feuillade directed *Fantômas*, based on the best-selling novels by Marcel Allain and Pierre Souvestre in France. Its success led to a series of crime films (1913–1914) following the exploits of the ingenious master-criminal Fantômas, who managed to outwit his two pursuers—Inspector Juve and newspaperman Fandor (Rubin, *Thrillers* 54–55). This early detective film series was concerned less with a complicated investigation plot and more on the visual pleasures of the cinema. As Tom Gunning notes,

> The approach of the mystery film genre in the early teens seems to rely more on the power of visual transformations than on the un-raveling of carefully crafted enigmas. It remains a genre based on visual effects and attractions rather than intricately crafted plotting. ("Tale" 35)

Gunning suggests that this was due to several factors, including early film's tendency to withhold information from the audience for the purpose of suspense as well as the visual pleasure in having the villain dress up in a va-riety of disguises. The emphasis on mystery was created through the main-tenance of the villain's identity rather than on an intricate plot of suspense and intrigue. Feuillade further explored the crime genre in his next major series, *Les Vampires* (1915–1916), which centered on a flamboyant gang of criminals (les vampires) and its opponents, the Parisian reporter Phillippe Guérande and his sidekick Mazmette.

The detective also featured as the protagonist in American silent crime film—for example, in the feature-length *Traffic in Souls* directed by George Loane Tucker in 1913. The narrative follows the investigation of Mary Barton (Jane Gail) and her fiancé, police officer Burke (Matt Moore), into New York's white slave trade. Burke is not portrayed as a bumbling and inef-fectual cop but as an intelligent and brave detective-hero, and the police force is repeatedly presented as an organized and efficient body of men not unlike the army, with dozens of officers in line, at attention, and ready to be called into action. The screen detective of the Jazz Age in the 1920s developed into "a complex and formidable icon of justice and law," and many detective-heroes were drawn from popular literature, including Sherlock Holmes played by John Barrymore in a 1922 film adaptation of William Gillette's popular play based on Conan Doyle's detective (Langman and Finn, *Silent* xvii). The romantic figure of the ex-thief-turned-detective became a staple in the 1920s, including the detective-heroes Boston Blackie and The Lone Wolf. Detective Charlie Chan also made his first appearance on the screen in the 1920s, as a minor character in *The House without a Key* (Bennett 1926) and then in his first feature film, *The Chinese Parrot* (Leni 1927). However, "the detective as an unruffled observer of human folly"—or the sleuth of classical detective fiction—did not appear until the 1930s (ibid. xiii).

It was the birth of sound film in the second half of the 1920s that made possible the depiction of the classical detective narrative on the screen. The plots of classical detective fiction were often long, convoluted, and based more on dialogue than on action. The detective usually interviewed witnesses, discussed the case with his companion, uncovered clues, and then—in the grand scene of revelation at the end—revealed to the group of suspects "whodunnit." This emphasis on information gathering rather than action meant that the translation of such a story was difficult in silent cinema but perfectly suited to sound film. The 1930s witnessed the proliferation of classical sleuths on the screen and several "B" detective series at the various Hollywood studios.

The British classical detective story is probably the most influential type of story in the mystery genre, having remained popular in fiction for more than a century. In 1887 Arthur Conan Doyle's "A Study in Scarlet" was published and marked the first appearance of the most famous detective-figure of all time: Sherlock Holmes. Conan Doyle followed in the footsteps of Edgar Allan Poe by making his detective one who solves mysteries through ratiocination and observation and is also an amateur rather than a policeman. While the urban tough guy may be the predominant masculine type in American popular culture, the gentleman is a central type in British popular culture, "a product not of modernity and the city, but of tradition, Home Counties' pastoralism and the London club" (Spicer 81). The figure of the gentleman pervades British classical detective fiction: he is a figure of intellect rather than violence.

Walter Benjamin believed the rise of the detective story occurred in response to the redefinition of the body and the mobile transformation of identity in the modern era—as an attempt to reestablish the traces of individual identity that came to be obliterated in the crowd of the modern city. As Gunning notes, both real-life policing and the classical detective story are driven by the need to pin an identity (the criminal's) down to a specific body ("Tracing" 20). A variety of scientific methods were developed in the

Victorian era to aid authorities in the pursuit and conviction of felons, including mug shots and fingerprints. In 1895, criminal anthropologist Cesare Lombroso invented the lie detector with the assumption that, although words might lie, the heart would "betray" the truth through the pulse (R. Thomas 21). Around the same time, the London police began taking fingerprints of suspected criminals, although at the time they were seen less as *the* means of identification than as a complement to the established system of identification called anthropometry or signaletics. Signaletics was a procedure developed by Bertillon whereby a subject's anatomical characteristics were measured and recorded; seven years later Scotland Yard abandoned Bertillon's system and constructed the first fingerprint file (ibid. 201). The mug shot also made its appearance at this time and in conjunction with Bertillon's signaletics system. While photography can be seen as undermining traditional notions of identity through its ability to capture mechanically and reproduce *ad infinitum* the body, in criminology the photograph represented a means of establishing innocence or guilt as the "proof" of identity. Bertillon rationalized the iconicity of the photograph (its function as the "proof" of identity) by supplementing it with his system of recording bodily measurements—transposing the body into a series of signs. As Gunning notes, the modern—especially the criminal or deviant—body became identifiable, classifiable, and distinguishable from the masses ("Tracing" 32).

But Conan Doyle chose to ignore these real-life advances of science in investigative technology, especially fingerprints and ballistics tests. Julian Symons argues that Conan Doyle must have been aware of these technological advances but suggests that he ignored them because Holmes's methods were already firmly established. As Symons explains: "It is more romantically impressive, more appropriate to a superman, to be able to distinguish 140 different varieties of tobacco and be familiar with forty-two different impressions left by tyres, than to be making fingerprint and ballistic tests" (Symons 24–25). Fingerprint and ballistic tests are objective tests that anyone can be trained to do, whereas the skills of observation and ratiocination are not only of a higher caliber but also seemingly more likely for a reader of Holmes to possess. The appeal of the classical detective story is that the reader might be able to solve the mystery as readily as the detective; this is achievable when the solution of the mystery lies in mental gymnastics rather than in scientific findings.

The emphasis on observation and ratiocination as the crime-fighting weapon of choice for Dupin and, subsequently, Holmes, however, was also most likely in a reflection of the idea of the *flâneur*. Indeed, Benjamin saw a distinct correlation between Poe's detective-hero and the figure of the *flâneur*. As James Werner notes, there is considerable disagreement as to the nature and origins of the *flâneur*, but he was a figure associated with the rise of modernity—an aristocrat, or individual without social obligation, that walked through the city, observing and reflecting upon it. His methodology was intuitive, his conclusions based on observation and inference, and he had to preserve his liminal perspective to interpret the city objectively for danger of becoming a window-shopper or consumer of the culture he observed. The *flâneur* may have been strictly an observer of the public life in the modern city, but the detective of early detective fiction was just as knowledgeable and observant of what Benjamin calls the "*intérieur*" of modern life: it is Dupin's knowledge of interior spaces (and people's life and behavior within them) that enable him to solve the mysteries at the center of "The Purloined Letter" and "Murders in the Rue Morgue" (Gunning, "Exterior" 109). Thus, just as the *flâneur* often provided written accounts of his observation of the public sphere, called "physiologies," Poe—according to Benjamin—was the progenitor of the detective tale as a "physiognomist of the interior" (qtd. in Werner). The early detective can be regarded as a *flâneur* that observed, deliberated on, and made sense of the private sphere; an upper-class, intelligent, and rational man that was differentiated from the working-class police with their newfangled tests and theories. Thus, the classical sleuth is a semiotician who observes the clues (i.e., signs)—some meaningful, others irrelevant—left behind at the scene of the crime and pieces them together, like solving a puzzle, into a cohesive and intelligible narrative that identifies its author: the criminal. The detective story plays off two desires of the reader: the desire for mystery and the desire for certainty (D. Lehman 5–6). The puzzle offers readers intrigue through the crime and the mystery that surrounds it, but the solution of the crime assures them that law and justice will prevail because the detective will always arrive at the truth. The classical detective story can be regarded as a modern version of the medieval morality play in the sense that good triumphs over evil (Melling 9; Mandel 42).

Sherlock Holmes—the definitive sleuth—remains the greatest and most famous fictional detective and also one of the most recognized names, real or fictional, in the world (DeAndrea 167). With his international appeal as a character, it is not surprising that he has proven to be one of the most popular detectives on the big screen with more than 200 films and television shows being centered on his character. Holmes has been portrayed by more actors than any other character in the history of cinema (Hawkins 30). Conan Doyle's stories were written in the same era as the birth of cinema, and it was not long until Holmes appeared in early films, making his debut in 1900 and then appearing in the 1910s in twelve British and a handful of American films. In the 1920s and 1930s Holmes was the hero of several series. In British film, Ellie Norwood starred as the sleuth in forty-six films from 1921 to 1923; in American film, Clive Brook starred in a series for Paramount from 1929 to 1932, and Arthur Wontner in five films for RKO from 1931 to 1937 (Everson, *Detective* 7–15). But the actor most closely associated with Holmes is the South African-born Basil Rathbone, who starred in two films for Twentieth Century-Fox opposite Nigel Bruce's Dr. Watson in 1939 and then both actors moved to Universal to make thirteen more films from 1942 to 1946. Sherlock Holmes was also a popular character on broadcast radio, with series based on his character running intermittently from 1930 to 1955; Rathbone and Bruce reprised their roles as the detective duo on the radio from 1939 to 1946 (Harmon 169).

The golden age of the classical detective story was in Britain between the two World Wars in the 1920s and 1930s, with the novels of authors like Agatha Christie, Dorothy Sayers, and John Dickson Carr. The detectives of these novels remained true to the classical sleuth as introduced by Poe's Dupin and developed by Conan Doyle with Holmes. The detective was usually an amateur in the sense that he/she did not work for the police, although he/she was sometimes a former officer. Often the detective investigated the crime alongside the official investigators, working either with them by sharing information or against them by withholding it, and the police were often shown as inept or merely lacking the necessary insight and intellect to solve the crime on their own. The defining feature of the sleuth was his/her superior intelligence or reasoning ability; however, he/she masked these superior qualities beneath a veneer of eccentricity or doddering incompetence so that those characters involved in the mystery were more likely to let down their guards to the sleuth, whether voluntarily or not.

The classical detective, as envisioned by the golden age writers, never flourished on the big screen in the same way that he/she did in literature because stories with labyrinthine plots and an emphasis on ratiocination and observation rather than action or characterization were not easily translatable into film; nevertheless, the 1930s were the heyday of the classical detective in film before the arrival of the American private eye. While the United States in the first half of the nineteenth century had been dominated by notions of expansion—taming the Wild West, "pacifying" the native population, and rapid economic and urban growth—and a frontier-hero to accompany them, by mid-century this image of masculinity—and America—was threatened by industrialization and the spread of political democracy (Kimmel, "Contemporary" 137–38). By the end of the century masculinity was to be threatened by the closing of the frontier, industrialization, and women entering the traditionally male public sphere. The image of masculinity that summed up this movement was a man of the people—physical, not necessarily well educated, and from the working class. Thus, masculinity preceding World War I was defined by a belief in the "strenuous life," a life of action and anti-intellectualism, and male bonding in the face of the threat posed by the "new women" (Pleck and Pleck 24). As Gaylyn Studlar states, in the early decades of the twentieth century there existed a conception of masculinity as instinctual, impulsive, and primitive in opposition to the industrialized, consumer-oriented, bureaucratic, and sedentary society that was seen as feminized (*Mad* 29). This feminization and over-civilization were seen as the antagonists of traditional masculinity—masculinity defined by physical strength, moral action, and individual independence.

With World War I, the turn-of-the-century crisis of masculinity found itself resolved as men had the opportunity to prove their masculinity through patriotism, male bonding, and violence. However, masculinity was once again redefined in the decade following the war. As Michael S. Kimmel states:

> The optimism ushered in by the Roaring Twenties was ushered out by the Great Depression and widespread unemployment in the 1930s. Never before had American men experienced such a massive and system-wide shock to their ability to prove their manhood by providing for their families. (*Manhood* 192)

The Great Depression, which lasted from 1929 to the early 1940s, brought with it a sense of disillusionment to American society as one quarter of American men were unemployed (Hatty 137). The Depression was the American Dream gone wrong; instead of being able through hard work and determination to achieve anything, suddenly it seemed almost impossible even to survive. Hollywood's response to the Depression was to offer, on the one hand, the rebellious gangster and, on the other, the aristocratic and stable sleuth. The gangster and the classical detective flourished at the same time in the 1930s on screen, with the gangster films representing the tension between the working class and Depression-era America and the classical detective film showcasing the nostalgic image of a stable middle- and upper-class society untouched by social and economic change.

The gangster represented the antithesis of the reality of the Depression by fulfilling the American Dream, even though he did so by disobeying the law; the audience, for its part, was encouraged to experience a release vicariously through the "hero." Just as the gangster offered one kind of escape, so too did the glamorous and successful male sex symbols of the 1930s distract unemployed audiences from their troubles, namely the emasculation caused by the Depression (McCann 8). The male crisis incited by the Depression was, therefore, not represented directly on screen in the 1930s but was ignored and escaped by means of two different responses: through the unproblematic image of the male sex symbol and through the tough and lawless gangster. The gangster film offered, as hero, a criminal who struggled to survive and was inevitably defeated. But its narrative focused on the pleasure of the protagonist's exploits against the oppressive law and Depression. By the mid-1930s, self-censorship in the form of the Production Code was instituted in the Hollywood film industry, a code that delineated which representations were deemed appropriate for general audiences and which were not: the gangster as a glorification of lawlessness was deemed the latter.[4] Thus, the gangster-hero of the first half of the 1930s was supplanted by the G-man as the protagonist of the crime film— a shift from the glorification of criminality to that of law enforcement. The pleasure that the toughness and success of the gangster-hero, however, offered its audiences was not lost but merely redirected into the law-abiding figure of the G-man, often played by stars who had previously played the gangster-hero, including Edward G. Robinson. Along with the American G-man, the British sleuth made an appearance in the 1930s, aligning audiences with the side of the law through the detective-hero but also serving as an escape from the realities of the Depression with images of the high life of the upper classes and the myth of a stable society.

Robert Reiner argues that the appeal of the classical detective film on the big screen was the puzzle it offered the viewer but also the escapist form of entertainment it represented, not unlike the musical, with its nostalgia for a never-existent present ("Keystone" 199–200). The classical detective offered a sense of reassurance that, even if the police could not uncover the identity of the criminal, the detective could succeed where the law failed.

This idea of identifying evil was central to the classical detective narrative: once the criminal was identified and eliminated, society could once again return to normal. The sleuth thus brought with him a sense of both nostalgia and security: society was able to return to its state previous to the disruption caused by the criminal. After all, the sleuth did not disappear in the post-World War II period and continued to offer reassurance and escapism for the audience into the 1940s on the screen and radio. This reassurance and nostalgia is most likely the reason for the sleuth's renewed popularity since the 1980s, especially on television. Sleuth television series (produced in the United Kingdom) are set in the past, like those following the adventures of Holmes, Marple, and Poirot, and often focus equally on lavish period décor and costume and on the mystery at hand, offering an image of a supposed untroubled world where murder is an anomaly and society—and the detective— is stable. Similarly, those set in the present (produced in the United States), like *Murder, She Wrote* (1984–1996) and *Diagnosis Murder* (1993–2001), offer a bloodless and often comedic take on murder and an image of the world that is as reassuring as those set in the past. The return of the sleuth to television was part of the same impulse that brought the criminalist to the big screen in the 1990s and to the small screen in the 2000s. The criminalist— like the sleuth—is a semiotician who employs his intellect and experience to read clues and from them identify the criminal that left them behind. The relationship between the classical detective on screen and in literature was always close, with many of the detective films of the 1930s being adaptations of novels. But the detectives that were popular in Hollywood film were not necessarily those of golden age detective fiction—for example, Poirot, Holmes, and Lord Peter Wimsey. Instead it was many of the American detectives that became popular heroes of "B" movie series—the heroes of American hardboiled fiction.

THE TRANSITIONAL DETECTIVE

Just as there were no detectives in fiction until there were detectives in reality, so too the evolution of the crime story echoes the history of crime itself (Mandel 31). With Prohibition, crime spread from the fringes of bourgeois society into the center and became organized. The coming of age of organized crime marked the end of the classical detective story. According to Ernest Mandel, a mass consciousness of crime first came to the surface with the pulp magazines of the 1920s—the prototype for which was *Black Mask*,

first published in 1920 (34). The hardboiled detective story did not immediately appear in American crime writing, and the classical detective story
did dominate the genre, even in America, until the mid- to late-1920s. *Black
Mask* featured a large proportion of English-style classical detective stories
with "thinking-machine" detectives; however, by the end of the 1920s the
magazine was almost exclusively composed of hardboiled-type detective stories (Krutnik 34). The hardboiled tradition was an adaptation of the British
classical detective to the environment and concerns of urban American society. But many critics have argued that the hardboiled detective owed as
much to American frontier literature as it did to previous detective fiction
traditions.[5] The hardboiled detective was a product of urbanized American
society and its fears of growing crime and ineffectual police; he followed in
the footsteps of the frontier-hero with his affinity for the criminals he com-
batted on behalf of society.

Dashiell Hammett is widely regarded as the first hardboiled detective
writer. He had been a Pinkerton detective and his stories were based on his
experiences as a crime fighter. His first short story in *Black Mask* in 1923
featured his hero, known only as Continental Op, and was followed by his
novels *The Maltese Falcon* (1930), *The Glass Key* (1931), and *The Thin Man*
(1934). Raymond Chandler wrote his first story for *Black Mask* in 1933 and
wrote hardboiled detective novels mainly in the 1940s, beginning with *The
Big Sleep* in 1939. His relationship with Hollywood not only included film
adaptations of his novels but also original screenplays that he wrote for studios. Hammett's Continental Op detective in *Red Harvest* and *The Dain
Curse* marked a transition to the tough-guy detective culminating in Sam
Spade (*The Maltese Falcon* [Huston 1941]), who was the toughest of his
heroes. Chandler's detective-hero Marlowe, in comparison to other hardboiled protagonists, was "a romantic in an age when romanticism has died,
a chivalrous knight in a time when nobody knew what chivalry meant"
(Waugh 112). The streets of urban America were regarded as mean and the
hardboiled detective had to be tough to survive them, yet Chandler's hero
managed to retain an idealism absent in other hardboiled detectives.
Mickey Spillane's detective Mike Hammer was the hardest of the hardboiled detectives, a "one-man gang," and Spillane's fellow writers felt great
antipathy toward him because the hero was really more a villain. As Hillary
Waugh states, Marlowe may have walked the mean streets but he was not
mean, whereas Hammer was very much so (115).

Despite the critical popularity of the *noir*-detective film of the 1940s
and 1950s, the transitional detective did precede, coexist with, and, in some

FIGURE 5. Glenda Farrell in *Smart Blonde*. Detecting women: The 1930s and 1940s saw many successful female detectives, including Torchy Blane, played by Glenda Farrell in *Smart Blonde* (1936) and six other films. Photo from author's collection.

cases, succeed the hardboiled *noir*-hero. Within the seventeen-year period of *film noir* and preceding it, the detective that was most prevalent on the big screen in the 1930s and 1940s was, in fact, the transitional detective. As John Paul Athanasourelis notes in regard to the adaptations of Chandler's hardboiled stories to the screen, unlike the source texts,

> These films present a simplistic world in which the hero and heroine embrace at the end; where good, personified by these characters, triumphs over clearly-recognizable evil; where police are, at worst, absent, and never depicted as corrupt. They are consciously constructed so as to depict a black-and-white moral universe and to placate civic and religious groups who dictated this sanitized and simplified world-view to studio owners. (327)

The heroes of the Classical Hollywood detective film were the protagonists of the American hardboiled stories, but they were not presented as hardboiled as they were later in *film noir* of the 1940s and 1950s. Instead they were most often portrayed as suave, sophisticated, and erudite gentlemen: Americans made somewhat Anglicized; British sleuths made somewhat streetwise. The classical detective was defined by his superior intellectual capabilities and a desire to restore order to a world temporarily disrupted by murder; the transitional detective, on the other hand, was presented as a more average person, allowing the audience a greater sense of identification with the protagonist. No longer was the detective an unknowable figure of superior intellect, to whom access was only allowed through the Watson-figure who accompanied the sleuth, but was instead more like the Watson-figure himself. But, like the British sleuth, the transitional detective offered the reassurance that the evil in his society is manageable and stoppable by the individual.

S. S. Van Dine's detective-hero Philo Vance was brought to the screen with actor William Powell in twenty-seven films made between 1926 and 1936; one film was remade in 1940, and then three others followed in 1947.[6] Bulldog Drummond, the hero of Herman Cyril McNeile's detective stories, first appeared on screen in 1922 and continued sporadically into the early 1950s, with the majority of his films being made in the late 1930s. Most of Hollywood's studios had at least one successful "B"-detective throughout the 1930s and often into the 1940s: Bulldog Drummond at Paramount, The Saint at RKO, and The Lone Wolf at Columbia. The Saint, created by

Leslie Charteris, was the hero of several films from 1938 to 1941, and The Falcon, created by Michael Arlen, from 1941 to 1946. Detective series in the 1940s also included those starring The Crime Doctor, Michael Shayne, Dick Tracy, and Boston Blackie. Perry Mason arrived on the big screen in the mid-1930s and later on the small screen with the CBS television series that ran from 1957 to 1966, with 271 episodes.[7] Female amateur sleuths like Hildegarde Withers, Torchy Blane, and Nancy Drew appeared in film series in the 1930s, and the Asian detective was also popular in this period: Earl Derr Biggers's detective Charlie Chan appeared in forty-seven films from 1925 to 1949; John Marquand's Mr. Moto, in eight films from 1937 to 1939; and Mr. Wong, in six films from 1939 to 1940. The "B"-movie detective series that proved so popular in the 1930s and 1940s all but disappeared in the 1950s as television came to demand more of audience time (Cocchi, *II* 46). Nevertheless, some of the transitional detectives including The Saint, Michael Shayne, Ellery Queen, Boston Blackie, Perry Mason, and Charlie Chan left the big screen to become the stars of television series in the 1950s and 1960s.

These transitional detectives appeared not only in the film of the time but also on broadcast radio throughout the 1930s and 1940s.[8] The success of the detectives in the cinema was supported and sustained by audience familiarity with the characters due to the broadcast of detective serials on the radio. The first radio detective series followed the exploits of the villainous Fu Manchu and his detective nemesis, Nayland Smith, in 1929 (Harmon 169); however, the first successful and popular detective series was the *Sherlock Holmes* program that began in 1930 (Morrow 333). The first popular programs were based on the characters of well-known detective novels, but radio also created its own detective-heroes, including Richard Diamond. In the 1930s and 1940s many radio serials appeared that followed the exploits and adventures of detectives who simultaneously were appearing in the cinema, including Dick Tracy, Charlie Chan, Nero Wolfe, Philip Marlowe, Sam Spade, The Thin Man, Boston Blackie, Bulldog Drummond, The Saint, The Falcon, and Perry Mason, to name a few.[9] The overlap between the films and the radio programs included some of the actors who portrayed the detectives on screen reprising their roles for the radio—for example, Basil Rathbone and Nigel Bruce as Sherlock Holmes and Dr. Watson. In other cases, actors who were associated with detective-type roles on screen also portrayed detectives in radio series, including Tom Conway—who had played the Falcon's brother in film—as The Saint, and Dick Powell—who had played Philip Marlowe on screen—as Richard Diamond (ibid. 333).

The success of the ongoing radio series ensured an audience for further installments of the detective films by maintaining their level of popularity, and it established the detective as a staple of American popular culture throughout the 1930s and 1940s.

James Parish and Michael Pitts argue that more often than not the "B"-detective film series that began in the 1930s and continued into the 1940s catered to individual stars (xi). Yvonne Tasker differentiates among three types of on-screen presence: the performer, the actor, and the star (74). The performer simply plays his role, is not seen as a serious actor, and lacks extra-filmic exposure; the actor is seen as possessing talent and artistry and is taken seriously by audiences; the star may or may not be seen as a serious actor but possesses an extra-filmic dimension whereby audiences know of him beyond his roles. According to Richard Dyer, a star's image is not just generated by his films but by the promotion of those films and the star through pin-ups, public appearances, interviews, studio handouts, biographies, and coverage of the star's private life in the press (*Heavenly* 2–3). Dyer argues that stars play characters—"constructed representations of persons"—but also that his/her image as a star is also a constructed personage (*Stars* 99 and 109). A star, according to Dyer, tends to embody a specific social type and then plays characters that also personify specific social types, leading to various "fits" with the star in relation to the character: selective use, perfect fit, and problematic fit (ibid. 142–46). The selective use of a star occurs when a film exploits certain characteristics of the star's image but ignores others; the perfect fit occurs when the character's traits match those of the star's; and the problematic fit occurs when the star's image conflicts with the construction of the character's.

The construction of masculinity on screen is dependent upon the influence of external forces such as star persona and society's conception of masculinity at that moment of time. It is also dependent upon internal forces, as a film's representation of a character will be determined by preestablished generic codes of heroism and villainy regardless of star persona and social opinion. Which exerts the most influence—external or internal forces—is very much in debate among star studies critics. Andrew Britton disagrees with Dyer for seeing the star vehicle as a genre and argues that the existence of the genre is a prior condition to the star vehicle— it precedes the star (198). Therefore, in the detective genre, Britton would argue that the role of the detective precedes and dictates to the star rather than the role being structured around the star's persona. Whether stars precede the genre or the genre precedes the star, it is rare for a star to be cast in a role that contradicts the characteristics associated with his persona, and he will often be cast in a film because his persona is a "good fit" for the role. The role of the detective, however, has proved somewhat flexible, offering a tougher masculinity for a tough star persona, such as Humphrey Bogart, or a more gentlemanly type of hero, like William Powell.

The detective film—by definition—focuses on the protagonist, his success in defeating the criminals, and his alignment with good over evil. The genre, therefore, offers a positive, if not heroic, role for a star, which in the 1930s and 1940s easily led to serialization since the detective could be given more crimes to solve. The economic advantage of the "B"-detective film for Hollywood at the time was this possibility of capitalizing again and again on a star's popularity, as well as that of the character's, through serialization. As Parish and Pitts note, the detective series of the 1930s and 1940s were inexpensive vehicles for the cinematic personalities of their stars: Basil Rathbone *was* Sherlock Holmes; Tom Conway *was* the Falcon; Warner Baxter *was* the Crime Doctor; and Warren William *was* The Lone Wolf (xi). The films catered to the star's personas and his public image and, in the "B"-detective film, those stars tended to embody a general type: the transitional detectives tended to be portrayed by British actors or British-type actors (actors who looked and could sound British), including George Sanders, who played The Falcon and then The Saint, and William Powell, who played detectives Philo Vance and Nick Charles. This association with Britishness allowed this transitional-type of detective to embody conflicting notions of heroism that a specifically "American" hero might not be able to. This was because of the established association or Britishness with villainy: before being cast as detective-heroes, both Sanders and Powell found themselves playing villains.

George Sanders was British and brought with him a sense of polished sophistication to the screen. As Richard Griffith notes, actors whose chief characteristics are polish and suavity tend to be condemned to secondary roles in American films, whereas in British film actors like Rathbone and Sanders would have been the stars and not the villains (35). With Sanders's success in *Lloyds of London* (King 1936), his role as the movie villain was born, but a shift came the following year with his double role in *Lancer Spy* (Ratoff 1937) in which he played the two look-alike leads—a German officer and the British officer who impersonates him to infiltrate enemy circles. This shift to playing a hero while retaining his villainous associations set Sanders up for his role as the gentleman adventurer, questionable criminal, and detective-hero: The Saint for RKO Pictures. In his third outing as

The Saint, *The Saint's Double Trouble* (Hively 1940), Sanders again played
the dual leads of hero (The Saint) and villain (The Dutchman). The Saint
was suave and elegant but also a wisecracker, reacting "with the proverbial
grace under pressure" (Langman and Finn, *Thirties* 225–26). Sanders
played The Saint in five films between 1939 and 1941. But Leslie Charteris, who wrote the Saint novels, was dissatisfied with the character's on-
screen exploits in plots only remotely related to the author's storylines,
causing RKO to create a new detective role for Sanders to play: The Falcon
(VanDerBeets 41). The Falcon was based on a short story by Michael
Arlen, but the suave, sophisticated, man-about-town bore little resem-
blance to Arlen's tough hardboiled character in the story. In fact, the differences between the two on-screen detectives, The Saint and The Falcon,
as embodied by Sanders were minimal—except the name. RKO went so far
as to use The Saint's costar Wendy Barrie for the first two Falcon films as
well, and the similarities between the two series were not lost on Charteris:
he sued RKO (ibid. 41). When Sanders expressed the desire to stop playing The Falcon, the studio brought in his brother, Tom Conway, to take
over for the remaining nine Falcon films and play, as the title of his first
Falcon film suggests, *The Falcon's Brother* (Logan 1942).

William Powell's career followed a trajectory similar to Sanders's, from
playing cads and villains to playing suave and debonair detectives. In silent
film, Powell had played gigolos and petty thieves and his persona was firmly
associated with the cad or the villain: his first venture into detective films was
as the villain to John Barrymore's sleuth in Parker's 1922 film version of *Sherlock Holmes*. In 1929 he was cast as S. S. Van Dine's detective-hero, Philo
Vance, in *The Canary Murder Case* (St. Clair and Tuttle 1929) and played the
detective-hero four times until 1933. In 1934 he took up the role as Dashiell
Hammett's Nick Charles in *The Thin Man* (Van Dyke 1934) and played the
detective for almost a decade in five films until 1945. In 1936, Graham
Greene commented on Powell's "Britishness" as Nick Charles:

> Mr. Powell is a little too immaculate, his wit too well-turned just
> as his clothes are too well-made, he drinks hard but only at the best
> bars; he is rather like an advertisement of a man-about-town in
> Esquire, he shares some of the irritating day-dream quality of Lord
> Peter Wimsey. (qtd. in Shipman 449)

Greene compares Powell to Dorothy L. Sayers's quintessentially British
sleuth, Lord Peter Wimsey, and, despite the fact that Powell was American,

FIGURE 6. William Powell. From cad to softboiled "dick": Because of the star's associations with Britishness, William Powell tended to play suave and sophisticated detectives like *The Thin Man*'s (1934) Nick Charles. Photo from author's collection.

he was associated with Britishness because of his tendency to play cads and then sleuths as well because of his rather dapper and gentleman-like appearance. As the career paths of Sanders and Powell both demonstrate, there was an association in Classical Hollywood film between Britishness and villainy. But those associations could then be employed in the figure of the detective to explore notions of heroism other than the traditional tough American hero that originated with the frontier narrative. The Anglicized detective could—as James Bond still does for contemporary audiences—allow an indulgence in, and identification with, a type of masculinity that embodied suavity and culture, lived a lavish lifestyle, and bent the law without "tarnishing" American values or conceptions of heroic masculinity.

Pitts asserts that the Falcon series with Tom Conway and others like it "show us a different world, where villains were villains and good was good—no coloring, no excuses, and, most simply, no attempt to do anything other than amuse" (139). In opposition to this world it would seem that the world of the *noir*-detective film was pervaded by evil, and that heroism and villainy were not so clearly distinct. However, there was not such a dramatic shift from the transitional detective films to *noir* as Pitts's comment might suggest. The boundary between good and evil was already very gray even in the very earliest of detective films, and by 1905 some films suggested that policemen could be corrupt (Langman and Finn, *Silent* xiii). As well, the romantic ex-thief, such as The Lone Wolf and Boston Blackie, was a popular detective-figure. Bert Lytell played both characters in the 1910s and 1920s, suggesting that star persona and audience associations with that persona came into play fairly early on in the history of the detective film. The Saint also hovered on the thin line between law and order as a Robin Hood figure that assisted the police and was successful where they failed because he could carry out the violence and subterfuge they could not because of their adherence to the law. In *The Saint's Double Trouble*, a professor from the Saint's university days explains to his daughter that the Saint is not a crook or a criminal—or at least he has never been *convicted* as one. In *The Saint Strikes Back* (Farrow 1939) the "gangrene" that plagues society originates from within—a criminologist working within the police department; and in *The Saint in New York* (Holmes 1938), it is the head of the Citizen's Committee for Crime Prevention who is "The Big Fellow" running organized crime in the city. The pre-*noir* detective film did examine issues of police corruption and had a detective-hero with ties to criminals either because he used to be one or because he employs methods similar to them. But he did tend to comfort the viewer by promising that even if the police could not combat the crime of urban America, the classical Hollywood detective could.

That which marked the major difference between the hardboiled detective, in fiction or film, and the transitional detective was the element of comedy. The majority of the transitional detective series of the 1930s and 1940s had a dual focus on detection and comedy, with comic or romantic subplots and witty dialogue.[10] Perhaps the best-known example of this is *The Thin Man*, with its fast-paced repartee between William Powell's Nick and Myrna Loy's Nora—a married couple who, very charmingly, drink and argue their way through a mystery. These films, like those featuring the classical sleuth, guaranteed a happy ending whereby the detective solved the mystery, the villains were apprehended, and young lovers were often united. This optimistic view of society would be challenged by the dark and critical image of America painted by 1940s and 1950s *film noir*. But in the 1930s, this image of a stable and happy society was popular, and detective series were produced for a variety of different audience interests, from the female detective like Hildegarde Withers, to the child detective like Nancy Drew, to the Asian detective like Charlie Chan.

The Asian Detective

The Anglicized detective was able to evoke many of the qualities associated with Britishness, including those associated with the cad or villain, and offered a kind of heroism opposite to that of the *noir*-detective, which was identified as distinctly American. The association between nationality (or ethnicity) and heroism in American film was also evident in the proliferation of Asian detective films in the 1930s and 1940s. According to William Everson, the Asian detective was virtually absent from silent cinema because the "Yellow Peril" concern was at its height in the 1910s and 1920s (*Detective* 72)[11]; however, Asian sleuths—including Charlie Chan, Mr. Wong, and Mr. Moto—proved to be some of the earliest and most popular detectives on the screen in the 1930s and 1940s. In fact, Charlie Chan is second only to Sherlock Holmes in the number of films made with the detective-hero—more than fifty, as well as a radio series, a television series, a comic strip, a short-lived mystery magazine in the 1970s, and an animated television series for children (Karnick).

These detectives were consciously differentiated as "other" and constructed as nonwhite and non-American both in appearance and in their miscomprehension or incorrect use of the English language. The Asian detective was established as "other," however, not with villainous connotations. These sleuths were intelligent, generous, and skilled, offering their expertise to pursue and capture the villains of American society, and their "otherness" as a foreigner functioned to explain (and to disguise) their superior intellectual capabilities and deductive skills. The suggestion was that the Asian detective had acquired his wisdom from his culture and that the American viewer could, therefore, possess no knowledge of it. Thus, the Asian detective was aligned with detective-figures like Sherlock Holmes: just as the superior deductive abilities of Holmes's mind were kept hidden from the viewer through the mediating consciousness of Watson, so too were the Asian detective's intellectual capabilities concealed by cultural differences. By manufacturing distance between the detective and the viewer, the key clues and information were withheld from the viewer, and the detective's solution of the crime at the end of the narrative remained a surprise.

This distance functioned to mediate the viewer's access to the processes of the detective's mind, but it also functioned to prevent an overidentification with the "other"—something that Hollywood producers deemed necessary at the time. There seems to have been a reluctance on the part of Hollywood producers to sanction an identification between the white mainstream viewer and the "othered" Asian detective. Hollywood's representation of the racial "other" across all film in the Classical Hollywood period was mediated, whether by granting only minor roles to nonwhite characters or—as in the case of the Asian detective where a nonwhite character did fulfil the role of protagonist—the character was portrayed by a white actor, especially in sound films, in "yellow-face." As Ruth Vasey explains, Hollywood was not necessarily concerned with realism in its depictions of foreigners and, instead, opted for "colourful stereotypes":

> This came about not through ignorance, carelessness, or prejudice on the part of particular production personnel, but through the deliberate packaging of saleable elements. The picturesque, the exotic, and the quaint were all staple ingredients of Hollywood production; like spectacle, romance, and heroism, they formed part of the admixture of motion picture ingredients that the industry delivered for the price of a cinema ticket (227).

Charlie Chan made his screen debut a year after the first novel by Earl Derr Biggers was published, and proved to become one of the most popular and prolific screen detectives. Biggers was surprised by the popularity of Chan because he had been concerned about American audiences' response to the benign portrait of a Chinese character (Rimoldi, *I* 170). Chan was presented as a professional man who possessed superior intelligence; preceding him, the representation of Chinese and other Asian characters in American cinema was of two types: the image of evil as a result of "Yellow Peril" syndrome, and the servant who spoke broken English. If Hollywood assumed that mainstream audiences would resist such a depiction of an Asian character, why did Fox produce the Chan films? It was because the representation of the Chinese detective was made "nonthreatening." As Oscar Rimoldi states: "He had erudition without arrogance, impeccable manners, perfectly tailored suits and a progeny of Asian Americans totally in tune with the American way of life" (ibid. 170). More importantly, Rimoldi argues that Chan left confrontation and violence to the American police officers, thus never "subjecting" audiences to the image of an Asian overpowering a Caucasian. He was characterized as Chinese through his quiet and controlled manner and with his tendency to offer pearls of Confucian wisdom during his investigations. For example, in *Charlie Chan at the Circus* (Lachman 1936), Chan (Warner Oland) allays the police detective's fear that the criminal might strike again soon. He says, "No cause for hurry now. Enemy who misses mark, like serpent, must coil to strike again." He applies his Confucian proverbs to human nature, but also to his work as a detective. "Facts like photographic film," he explains to his Number One Son (Keye Luke), "must be exposed before developing."

When Chan was first introduced in the silent film *The House without a Key* (Bennet 1926), he was portrayed by a Japanese actor, George Kuwa, and then by another Japanese actor, Kamijama Sojin. But with the shift to sound in the late 1920s, the role of Chan was taken over by an English actor—E. L. Clark—and, from that point on, Chan was played by European actors, most memorably by Swedish actor Warner Oland and later Sidney Toler. Before he took over the role as the Chinese detective, Oland had established himself as Hollywood's premier "Asian" actor, playing the sinister Japanese villain Baron Huroki in the serial *Patria* (1919), Wu Fang in *The Lightning Raider* (Seitz 1919), and then, the most famous Asian villain of all, Dr. Fu Manchu in four films for Paramount from 1929 to 1931 (Wong 55 and 58). Just as the British or British-type actors were primarily associated with villainy before playing detectives in the 1930s and 1940s, so too were some of the actors who portrayed the Asian detective, most likely because the "othered" detective-hero can embody more complex and contradictory associations than the American detective.

The popularity and success of Charlie Chan opened the door for other Asian detective-heroes, including Mr. Wong, a character created by Hugh Wiley for stories in *Collier's* magazine, and Mr. Moto, from the novels of John P. Marquand. The Mr. Wong film series produced by Monogram was a low-budget affair that did not attempt to compete with Fox's successful Chan series but instead hoped to cash in on its popularity (Rimoldi, *I* 173). The success of Mr. Wong was most likely due to the star who portrayed him: Boris Karloff. The Japanese sleuth, Mr. Moto, made his film debut in *Think Fast, Mr. Moto* (Forster 1937) and was played by the Hungarian-born actor Peter Lorre, who was made to look stereotypically "Asian" with steel-rimmed spectacles, false buckteeth, and slicked-down hair.[12] Mr. Wong wore elegant Western clothes, including his trademark white carnation in his lapel, and tended to remain on the sidelines solving crimes through Holmes-like deduction. He concentrated on his own scientific methods of deduction while the dim-witted police rounded up the suspects, allowing Mr. Wong to step in at the final moment to identify the killer. Similarly, Lorre portrayed Moto as a quiet, calculating, intelligent detective who was able to overcome his aggressors with a physical stamina that he concealed beneath the guise of his small stature. Moto may have been a cerebral detective, but he was also an expert at *ju-jitsu*, which meant that, with the help of a stunt double, Lorre's Moto engaged in many lively and extremely physical fights. As Mr. Moto explains to his class of budding criminologists in *Mr. Moto's Gamble* (Tinling 1938): "Will you please remember, there's no situation that science and skill cannot master." Lieutenant Riggs, one of his students, challenges Mr. Moto, asking what good are science and skill if one is confronted with an armed suspect. Mr. Moto demonstrates: he grabs Riggs and flips him to the ground. The Asian detective was identified as possessing superior intellectual capabilities that were associated with his being "other," but he volunteered his energy for the benefit of American society with the apprehension of that society's villains.

The specificity of these detectives' nationalities was not stressed in these films, and each was presented as being "Oriental" rather than Chinese or Japanese—a result of Hollywood's approach to representing race. As Vasey states: "If a single factor distinguished Hollywood's amorphously drawn cinematic foreigners from each other in the 1930s, it was

FIGURE 7. Boris Karloff in *Mr. Wong in Chinatown*. A touch of class: Mr. Wong (played in "yellow face" by Boris Karloff) was Oxford-educated, spoke "proper" English, and wore elegant suits; however, like Mr. Moto and Charlie Chan, his deductive skills were aligned with his "otherness." Photo from author's collection.

less nationality or ethnicity than class" (217). Foreignness was portrayed in Classical Hollywood film as belonging either to the peasantry or to the aristocracy, whereas Americanness was presented as firmly a middle-class phenomenon. Mr. Wong, Mr. Moto, and Charlie Chan, as well as the British or British-type transitional detectives, were all assigned to the upper class, as evidenced by their dapper clothes, upright bearing, and the fact that they indulge in detective work for personal pleasure and intellectual stimulation rather than as a job or for the pecuniary reward (as opposed to the police). Thus, class defined but also contained the characterization of the Asian detective. As I shall explore in a later chapter, class and race become significant strategies of representation with the working-class cop-heroes of the 1980s and the African-American detective of the 1990s.

THE HARDBOILED DETECTIVE

The hardboiled detective novel, with its greater emphasis on realism, arose in a rebellion against the stylization of the classical detective novel; similarly, *film noir*, which the hardboiled novels inspired, arose in a rebellion against the Classical Hollywood mode of filmmaking. *Noir*-detective films attempted to be more realistic and gritty, but they were just as stylized in that they were shot in an expressionistic style—influenced by the German Expressionist and French Poetic Realist films of the 1920s and 1930s—with low-key lighting and action often taking place on rainy streets and at night. Hollywood had largely avoided hardboiled fiction in the 1930s because of its vicarious treatment of sex and violence, which challenged the restrictions of the Production Code, and instead focused on the exploits of the transitional detective, eliminating the implications of sexual relations, toning down the level of violence, and often introducing a comic overtone. But in the 1940s there were a great number of adaptations of hardboiled stories and thrillers made in the hardboiled mode. Frank Krutnik believes this shift in Hollywood's appropriation of the hardboiled tradition is related to the proliferation of Freudian psychoanalysis in American culture and film. No longer was crime seen so much as a social problem or necessarily even organized; instead it was attributed to individual criminals based on personal psychological problems, and this fascination with internal and subjective criminal impulses has been widely recognized as a crucial characteristic of 1940s *film noir*. According to Krutnik, this psychoanalytic framework was used to circumvent some of the institutional restrictions of the Production Code's form of censorship by "enabling a more elliptical and displaced mode of representation which could be 'decoded' by audiences familiar with the popularised psychoanalysis" (xii).[13]

The gangster film of the 1930s had arisen in reaction to the Great Depression, Prohibition, and widespread unemployment, offering a critique of the American Dream that had gone wrong. Similarly, *film noir* offered a critique of 1940s and 1950s society, even though this era was a time of peace and a booming economy. The desire for social criticism in 1940s cinema engaged with the anxieties of postwar masculinity—namely, veterans returning to a society different from that they had left to fight for. As Andrew Clay argues, crime films in the postwar period were not so much about crime itself but rather used crime as a means to express men's contradictory reactions to their experiences with power: within patriarchal society, masculinity may appear to be hegemonic, but the male individual can easily feel a sense of powerlessness, a contradiction that was particularly acute in the two decades after the war (51). According to Krutnik, the hero of *film noir* can be understood in terms of the conflict that a man encounters in the face of patriarchy's demand that he should know and accept his place under the law or face devastating consequences (75–76). The myths of rugged individualism and the American Dream that grew out of the frontier era promised that if a man worked hard and lived a moral life he would be successful. But returning ex-servicemen faced a myriad of problems: unemployment, alienation, degradation, disablement, and changed gender roles. For many of the veterans unemployment was less of an issue than the degradation they faced leaving the service and returning to their civilian lives. Fifteen million veterans returned home physically or mentally wounded: almost 15,000 soldiers returned minus one or more limbs (Goulden 3–4). The total number of outpatients in 1945 for VA hospitals was more than one million people, and the total number of cases for counseling by social workers was more than 140,000 individuals (Blum 335).

The American home had been one of the main ideals that the war had been fought to protect; instead, many men returned to the reality of broken homes. The United States had the highest divorce rate in the world in 1945, with thirty-one divorces for every 100 marriages—double what the divorce rate had been before the war (Kane 41). Returning veterans also faced the problems of reentering the workforce and unemployment. With many men away fighting, women had gone to work in support of the war effort. Many women did leave the workforce—some voluntarily, others forced—when the men returned from service, but there was still widespread unemployment among veterans. Men who had left to fight for their country returned to find it changed, and they struggled to readjust to a postwar society with new and different gender roles, including independent and working women. Men were expected to forget the war and focus on work, particularly in the role of breadwinner for the nuclear family; but that did not mean that that domesticity was embraced. As Barbara Ehrenreich notes, the war had produced a generation of men "whose memories of masculine adventure made them chafe at post-war civilian 'conformity'" (105).

This expectation to conform—to embrace the role of the "gray flannel suit," working for someone else rather than being one's own man—ran counter to the American ideal of "rugged individualism." This contradiction found itself expressed in all aspects of American culture, including its cinema, with *noir* exploring men's experiences of cultural myth and social reality through the divided masculinity of its heroes. Kaja Silverman notes that a handful of mainstream films from the 1940s, including the *noir* films *Spellbound* (Hitchcock 1945) and *Gilda* (Vidor 1946) and the social problem film *The Best Years of Our Lives* (Wyler 1946), examine male castration and speak in some way to the failure of the paternal function. The castration of the male heroes of the films forces the narrative agency to be thrust upon a female character, thereby further undermining the masculinity of the protagonists (Silverman 52). This castration of the male protagonist is not only a common theme in *film noir* but is also one of its defining characteristics; other detective films do indulge in either the castration of the male hero or the threat of his castration but often recover his damaged masculinity by reinscribing it to the side of the law. According to Silverman, the Law of psychoanalytic terms—the "Name of the Father"—in relation to which the psychic self is formed is often translated in *film noir* into the law—the police or justice system. By his reinstatement to the side of the law, the male hero is seen as embracing the Law of patriarchy and recovered to his socially prescribed role. The divided masculinity at the core of the *noir* narrative differentiated it from the other types of detective narratives that existed before, during, and after this period. Although the *noir* narrative introduced a mystery to initiate the narrative, the *noir*-detective was not so much investigating the mystery as he was investigating his own masculinity.

The hardboiled detective of *film noir* carried on the tradition of a tough, street-wise, violent American hero that pervaded frontier narratives;

but he was not the only type of *noir* protagonist. Krutnik divides *noir* narratives into three types: the investigative thriller with a detective protagonist who worked against the criminals in the story; the male suspense thriller that was the inverse of the first type, with a protagonist in a position of inferiority to the criminals; and the criminal-adventure thriller with a protagonist who, whether willfully or accidentally, engaged in an act of transgression of the law (86).[14] Thus, the protagonists of the *noir* film represented three very different types and offered their audiences different kinds of pleasure. Slotkin states that the essence of the hardboiled detective and the secret of his appeal lay in the fact that he offered pleasure in both his alignment with the law and his transgression of it:

> We are in love with authority, we know that on the one hand we need authority and hard lines of value, and on the other hand that authority is often corrupt and misdirected and that those hard lines of value are often blurry. The detective allows us to enjoy both of those features simultaneously, to play imaginatively at being both policeman and outlaw. (99–100)

In terms of identification with the transgression of the law, the *noir*'s detective-hero offered the least pleasure of transgression, the victim-hero more, and the criminal-hero the most. The *noir* detective-hero may have offered the double pleasure of the transgression of and punishment by the law; nevertheless, he was still more firmly aligned with the law as he brought the criminals to justice. But he was an image of masculinity in crisis—a victim of a male paternalist power as well as of independent and predatory women, and he was trapped in the urban environment and the seedy underbelly of American society in the 1940s and 1950s.

While the classical detective narrative aimed to return order to the society disrupted by the initial crime, the *noir* thriller sought to reorder the disruptions to masculine identity (Krutnik 93). Thus, whereas the puzzle surrounding the crime was foregrounded in the classical detective narrative, it was pushed to the background in *noir* and was often deemed irrelevant through the course of the narrative despite its seeming importance at the beginning.[15] Instead, the masculinity of the detective-hero became the main focus of the *noir* text; it was not unified or unproblematic and had to be proved and tested through not only the investigation, but also through the hero's interactions with the characters he encounters in his pursuit of that investigation. Often this test was performed through the hero's encounters with women: would he fall for the charms of the *femme fatale* or resist her and embrace the more natural, dependent, and nurturing woman? This constant testing and proving of the hero was tied to the attempt to reorder the disrupted masculine identity of the hero.

Peter Messent argues that the detective was the searcher who aimed to rebuild synchronic and diachronic continuity, filling in spatial or temporal gaps in the narrative, to restore a sense of coherence to the community or family history disrupted by the crime (5–6). In other words, the detective restored order to the chaos introduced into a society through murder. This is true of the classical sleuth who attempted to heal the disruption to the community or family by reconstructing the story of the crime: through the analysis of physical clues and the observation of human nature, the criminal could be identified, apprehended, and the community restored to a state of equilibrium. But the hardboiled detective could not restore equilibrium to the urban society to which he belonged because there was no initial equilibrium before the crime was committed: his world was disrupted before the crime and would remain so after it was solved. The equilibrium that the *noir*-detective sought was the unification of his masculine identity. As Jon Tuska states, the detective was a truth-seeker, but his acquisition of knowledge most often brought him loneliness (xix). In his search for the truth and the reconstruction of the crime narrative, the detective gained the knowledge of the evil that he pursued, and that knowledge tainted him while simultaneously empowering him. The detective's knowledge enabled him to pursue and catch the criminals that the police were unable to because, while the police may have possessed the power of authority, they lacked the knowledge of the underworld to which the criminals—and the detective—belonged. Therefore, the detective could, throughout the course of the story, gain the knowledge to identify the criminals and stop them; but the price for that knowledge was to be alone. The price for the ability to think like a criminal and to commit violence like a criminal is, like a criminal, to be distanced from "good" society and the benefits of that society, including community, marriage, and family: he remained—like the frontiersman—a lone hero.

A shift in the representation of the detective-hero occurred with the emergence of *film noir* and the Americanization of the hero in the 1940s. As Marc Vernet notes, this process of Americanization occurred in the hardboiled detective fiction of the 1920s and 1930s, but it did not occur in film until the 1940s, with a shift from British or British-type actors playing on-screen detectives to actors who encapsulated American values (23).

Actors like Basil Rathbone, William Powell, Tom Conway, and George Sanders who had too "English" a look that was associated with the classical sleuth were succeeded in *noir*-detective films by American-looking actors like Robert Montgomery, Dick Powell, Edward G. Robinson, and Humphrey Bogart who had played gangsters or "heavies" in the 1930s.

Today, Bogart is still regarded as an icon of American masculinity. Edward G. Robinson was up for the lead in the film *Black Legion* (Mayo 1937), but the film's producer, Robert Lord, thought there was a problem with casting him. As Lord wrote, "[T]he great trouble would be that he is decidedly not American looking. [. . .] My opinion is that we must have a distinctly American looking actor to play this part" (qtd. in Sklar 65). Although both Robinson and Bogart carried with them associations of toughness from playing gangsters and heavies in the 1930s, it was Bogart's evident "Americanness" that won him the part of the hero. The association of Bogart with toughness from his earlier roles as gangsters played a significant part in establishing the dominant characteristics of the *noir*-hero through his portrayal of two of the most famous *noir*-heroes: Sam Spade in *The Maltese Falcon* (Huston 1941) and Philip Marlowe in *The Big Sleep* (Hawks 1946). Bogart's tough image made his Sam Spade a very ambiguous character and, although Philip Marlowe was Chandler's romantic-knight and idealistic detective, Bogart's image brought to Marlowe a sense of world-weariness and street savvy. The toughness that Bogart and other actors brought to their *noir* roles from previous films made the *noir* detective-figure a much more ambiguous one than the classical or transitional detective.

Although *film noir* engaged in the representation of a problematic masculine identity, it did not fully embrace or sanction a "subversive" masculinity (Krutnik xiii). *Film noir* may have offered a resistance to paternal authority and the myth of hegemonic masculine dominance, but few *noir* films offered an outright rejection of dominant values since no *noir*-detective seemed to rise out of his position in defiance of the law or social order or to define himself as a type of masculinity that was both positive and deviant. Thus, despite its critique of 1940s and 1950s society, *noir* arguably remained rather conservative in its representation of a problematic society through troubled masculinity. The anti-hero who transgressed the law, like the gangster, was punished rather than being allowed to get away with his crime against society. The *noir*-detective was a conservative figure compared to the *noir* victim-hero, as the detective was aligned with the law and the preservation of the society that *noir* attempted to critique. No matter how corrupt society seemed to be, the *noir*-detective strove to protect and support

FIGURE 8. Humphrey Bogart in *The Maltese Falcon*. In the company of "men": Sam Spade (Humphrey Bogart) is contrasted with a variety of different kinds of evil in *The Maltese Falcon* (1946)—from effeminate men to the *femme fatale*. Photo from author's collection.

it; conversely, the very fact that *noir* offered masculinity in crisis and a critique of American society differentiated it from Classical Hollywood film. While many Classical Hollywood films offered an escape from the problems of society, *noir* did address an expression or critique of those problems. Like the gangster or the *femme fatale* whose transgressions were not necessarily contained through their death but could live on in the audience's memory, so too did *noir*'s critique of American society, through the divided hero, offer the audience a vicarious pleasure and thrill that was not contained by narrative closure.

THE POLICE DETECTIVE

The United States in the 1920s and 1930s saw the advent of organized crime, and law-enforcement restructured and expanded on a larger and more organized scale to combat the new crime wave. The police procedural as a subgenre arose in the detective fiction of the 1940s as a reflection of this professionalization of real-life crime detection. But, as Mandel indicates, the rise of the police officer as hero was not only a result of the changing nature of crime but, more importantly, was a result of a change in bourgeois values (53). The classical detective was an amateur and the hardboiled detective a private eye: they were not police officers because the police were seen as not doing their job; therefore, an outsider had to be introduced to bring the criminal to justice. Society perceived the police as being ineffectual at their job, unsuccessful at stopping crime, and sometimes corrupt in their morals. In the classical detective story, and even in many of the transitional detective narratives, police were portrayed as being working class and the classical detectives as upper class. According to Mandel, with the intensification of class struggle in the years following World War I, there was a change in the attitude of the upper and middle classes toward the police as an apparatus of the state. The police were no longer considered a necessary evil and came to be regarded by the bourgeoisie as the embodiment of social good, and the rise of the police officer as the star in detective stories represented the need to legitimize the police in the eyes of the public (Mandel 53–54). The procedural ignored the disillusionment and paranoia of the Cold War period and instead offered a hero that was effective and committed to eradicating crime; but he was also a rather sterile and conservative representation of masculinity.

The intention of the hardboiled detective story was to bring greater realism to the detective genre. But with its terse style, colloquial dialogue, and tough heroes, in many ways it was just as stylized and romanticized as the classical detective story. It was the police procedural that brought realism to the detective story with a focus on the rules of policing, the restraints of the law on detection, and on the actual methods used by the police encompassing the advances in police technology that had occurred—even if they were boring to watch. Real-life investigations were not as exciting or action-packed as the classical and hardboiled detective stories had led readers to believe, and the police procedural aimed to correct this misconception even if it meant concentrating on the more tedious aspects of police work. The procedural was distinguished from other types of detective stories in terms of the emphasis on the methods of police investigation: tracking and tailing, fingerprints and Photostats, surveillance and forensics were described in great detail. In the classical and the hardboiled detective story, the narrative stressed the "who," "how," and "why" of the crime that had been committed so that the mystery was foregrounded. But in the procedural, the emphasis on answering these questions was replaced with the process by which the mystery was solved. The process was foregrounded (Cawelti 126).

R. Austin Freeman, with the publication of *The Singing Bone* in 1912, was an early pioneer of the "inverted story" in which the crime was revealed first and the investigation of the detective followed, rather than the classical narrative where the detective's investigation led to the reconstruction of the crime. The procedural did not go so far as to invert the narrative, but the emphasis was on the process of detection rather than on a mystery. Lawrence Treat has been acknowledged as the first mystery writer to have, as the focus of his story, a professional policeman working in his own habitat and solving crime using authentic police methods, publishing his first procedural *V is for Victim* in 1945 (Waugh 118). In Britain, the procedural was developed in the work of Maurice Procter and, in the States, by Lawrence Treat, Hillary Waugh, and the radio and television series *Dragnet* (DeAndrea 403). *Dragnet* was a hit on radio from 1949 to 1956; it was also a phenomenon on television from 1951 to 1959, with a brief reprise in the 1960s. The show was highly influential, with its emphasis on police methods of crime detection and law enforcement and the terse, deadpan quality of its dialogue and voice-over narration. Although the policeman had appeared as detective-hero prior to the procedural—for example,

Wilkie Collins's Sergeant Cuff, Agatha Christie's Inspector Battle, and George Simenon's Inspector Maigret—these detectives worked alone and belong to what George Dove calls the "Great Policeman" tradition of the classical school (3). What distinguished the police detective of the procedural was the emphasis on teamwork, professionalism, and investigative technology. The police detective did not need the superior intellect of the sleuth or the street smarts of the hardboiled private eye, relying instead on the procedures of the organized police force and his own wealth of experience from years on the force. He represented an idealized image of masculinity as organized, methodical, and driven by duty.

In film, the procedural was exemplified by films like *The House on 92nd Street* (Hathaway 1945), *Call Northside 777* (Hathaway 1948), and *The Naked City* (Dassin 1948). The cinematic style of the procedural was distinct from the stylization of the hardboiled detective film as the films were shot in a semi-documentary style—on-location shooting, voice-over narration, and often with nonprofessional actors—in an attempt to offer a more realistic feel. According to Martin Rubin, several factors created a receptive climate for the factual story and authentic setting, including Hollywood filmmakers' participation in making wartime documentaries, audiences' growing familiarity with such documentaries and fact-based war movies, technical advances in lightweight camera equipment and faster film stocks, spiraling production costs and labor disputes in Hollywood, and the influence of the Italian Neo-Realist film movement with its use of location shooting and everyday-life subject matter (*Thrillers* 96–97). The police procedural tried to appear as less of a fictional narrative of crime and justice and more of a documentary of police investigation. Much of the narrative followed the investigative techniques of the police, including forensics, identification line-ups, interrogations, stakeouts, surveillance, and tailing and tracking.

Many detective films of the 1930s, however, anticipated the police procedural, offering audiences glimpses of the advances in crime-fighting technology and science. As Langman and Finn note, films like *From Headquarters* (Dieterle 1933), *Crash Donovan* (Nigh 1936), and *Persons in Hiding* (King 1939) showed the tools and processes of police procedure like the police radio and Teletype, as well as the high-tech laboratory tests for analyzing evidence like hair, prints, and bullets (*Thirties* xvi). These films tended to have scenes that marvel at the technology available to police. For example, in *Mr. Wong, Detective* (Nigh 1938) there is a sequence in which poison gases and their deadly effects are discussed by a science expert and the detective (and thus explained for the audience), and in *Charlie Chan at the Opera* (Humberstone 1937) there is an extended sequence in which Chan requests a photograph of a suspect in the case. While a Teletype message is sent to a newspaper in L.A., and then a photograph is sent as a Photostat back to Chicago, the film offers a running commentary about the processes of the new technology. Whereas such scenes of policing technology were infrequent in the detective film of the 1930s, they were the focus of the procedural. The police detective might be an ordinary person, but he had the support of an organized police force and access to new technology, which allowed him to become as effective a crime fighter as the sleuth with his superior mental processes or the hardboiled private eye with his violent capabilities.

Although the procedural was short-lived, its somewhat inverted story still has relevance for contemporary audiences, as evidenced by the continued success of the television series *Columbo* (1967 to the present). *Columbo* breaks all the rules of the detective show: there are no guns; there is no action or sex—in fact, there is not even a mystery as the identity of the killer is revealed early on in each episode. The procedural brought about two important shifts that affect the detective genre today. First, the procedural established the policeman as the detective-hero of the genre, and the majority of contemporary detective-heroes are police detectives rather than amateurs or private eyes. The police detective does not possess the mysterious powers of deduction and observation of the classical sleuth, nor the street smarts of, and a free hand to commit violence like, the hardboiled detective. Instead, the police detective is an ordinary person—the everyman—just doing his duty. Second, the procedural brought the science of crime to the foreground. Unlike the pedantic scenes of Photostats and surveillance that dominated the procedural, the technology of investigation in today's criminalist narrative has become a spectacle in itself, from the exposed internal body of autopsies to the ultraviolet exposure of blood at crime scenes, but the procedural did introduce this emphasis on police investigative techniques.

In terms of masculinity, the 1950s was the decade of containment. According to Wendy Chapman Peek, the media of the 1950s stressed that perils befell society's men at every turn, situation that was brought about by a number of factors after World War II: a precipitate rise in divorce rates; public debates of male sexuality, especially homosexuality; the rise of interest in psychoanalysis; and the recognition of the physical, emotional, and psychological burdens that came to rest on men who attempted to fulfill traditional male roles (74). The 1950s was dominated by the conflicting dialogues about masculinity: individualism versus conformity. The former was in keeping with traditional notions of masculinity while the latter was more closely associated with femininity. Yet, somehow, men in the 1950s were expected to embody both. In 1958 *Look* magazine ran a series on the "American Male," describing him as dominated by women, "afraid to be different," "fragile," and "impotent" (ibid. 76). This image of men in the 1950s—as attempting to fulfill their prescribed social roles while simultaneously attempting to avoid the feminization of that role—was echoed in the films of the decade, especially through those starring Jimmy Stewart.

In the 1950s Stewart portrayed the onscreen detective—whether an amateur in *Rear Window* (Hitchcock 1954), a police officer in *Vertigo* (Hitchcock 1958), or a lawyer in *Anatomy of a Murder* (Preminger 1959)—and the type of masculinity he embodied tended to be vulnerable, disillusioned, or cynical. Amy Lawrence argues that Stewart's star persona was one of the most sympathetic, troubled, and disturbing in Hollywood at this time (42); yet it was also evocative of contemporary social anxieties. As Britton states: "The meaning of the Stewart persona might be said to be—'if you are the perfect, middle-class, heterosexual American male you go mad'" (qtd. in Lawrence 46). Jimmy Stewart represented the more widespread deterioration of masculinity due to the changes in 1950s America, a masculinity that was less heroic and often feminized and victimized. These contradictions saw a conflation of the procedural and *film noir* as the detective genre came to be dominated by morally ambiguous anti-heroic—and sometimes downright criminal—cops.

Film noir had appeared with the entry of the United States into World War II and thrived in the war's aftermath, but it also continued into the 1950s during the Cold War. Across the two decades came a shift in the *noir*-hero from idealistic in the early and mid-1940s to a more disillusioned, violent, and, finally, corrupt hero in the late 1950s. Just as *noir* of the 1940s challenged the confident image of masculinity that the transitional detective film offered, so too did *noir* of the 1950s challenge the conservative and stable image of masculinity that the police procedural had offered in the late 1940s. The corrupt and violent detective became more common in the 1950s: Jim McCleod (Kirk Douglas) in *Detective Story* (Wyler 1951), Mike Hammer (Ralph Meeker) in *Kiss Me Deadly* (Aldrich

1955), and Hank Quinlan (Orson Welles) in *Touch of Evil* (Welles 1958). In *Detective Story*, the divided *noir* masculinity of the 1940s is superseded by a neurotic one and the film, rather than focusing on the story of a crime, attempts to reconstruct the story of the detective. Lieutenant McCleod is a strong-armed cop, and the film traces his methods back to his childhood with a brutal father who drove his mother to insanity. The cop as neurotic in the early 1950s was a precursor to the cop as criminal. In *Touch of Evil*, Vargas (Charlton Heston), the good detective, is successful but is over-shadowed by the grotesque and crooked cop Quinlan. The film suggests that after years of battling criminals, it is difficult not to become like them and, although Vargas may still be young and idealistic about law and order, he may one day end up like Quinlan. Mike Hammer in *Kiss Me Deadly* is a hardboiled detective who differs greatly from Marlowe, the chivalrous knight, and Spade, a man with a code of honor, as a "sadistic, crude, groin kicking, shoot-first-ask-questions-later private eye" (Rimoldi, *III* 312). The film appears late in the genre of *noir* and is concerned less with the issues that informed early *noir*—World War II, independent women, re-turning soldiers—and more with the McCarthy era, the Cold War, and a materialistic society in which the end justifies the means.

THE LEGACY OF THE
CLASSICAL HOLLYWOOD DETECTIVE FILM

The legacy of *film noir* has been a shift in focus from the investigation of a crime to the investigation of the hero's masculinity through his investigation of the crime. Whereas the classical detective story presented a society that was predominantly good, infiltrated by only occasional instances of crime that were detectable and stoppable by its detective-heroes, *noir* presented a society that was pervaded by evil, and any of its citizens, including the detective-hero, could be capable of evil. Thus, the classical detective narrative did not challenge the masculinity of its hero but rather presented him as almost in-fallible and as one who possessed the knowledge of evil but did not act upon it; on the other hand, the narrative of the *noir* film functioned as a test of the masculinity of the detective as well as of his morality. The investigation of the crime, which was foregrounded in importance as a puzzle in the classical de-tective story, became a vehicle for an investigation of the male hero in *noir*. The heroes of the classical, hardboiled, and procedural detective narratives defined the three major trends of the Classical Hollywood detective film, and it is variations of these three types and their relation to the law and myths of heroism that continue to influence the genre today. Associated with the sleuth is a reassuring image of a successful and infallible detective that relies on brainpower to track down the criminal; with the *noir*-detective, it is masculinity that is divided and alienated, with a hero who is a loner and who uses violence to defeat the evil of society; and with the policeman, it is the everyman hero who is torn between duty and his private life, who has a law-enforcement and forensic team to assist in his investigations. The corresponding emphasis on brains, brawn, and forensics is also reinscribed to evoke contemporary attitudes toward crime and crime-fighting, although it is not necessarily linked to their initial heroes. Since then, there has occurred a blurring of categories and a new pairing of characteristics and themes: in the 1980s, the cop employed tough action and, in the 1990s, the sleuth relied on procedure. These evolutions of the genre—and how they tie into cultural conversations about heroism and national identity—will be explored in the following chapters.

CHAPTER FOUR

Investigating Crisis:
Neo-Noir *Heroes and* Femmes Fatales

NEW WARS, NEW NOIR

Hollywood film has a history of negotiating masculinity through the denial of cinematic voice and space to women. As Susan Faludi notes, in the 1950s Hollywood film offered fewer emancipated women than they had in the 1930s and 1940s, and fewer films concerned with women in general (*Backlash* 143–44). With men off fighting in World War II, the majority of film viewers at the time were women, and Hollywood catered to the needs and desires of its wartime majority audience with film narratives that centered on female characters and desires. Jack Boozer argues that it is no coincidence that the emergence of Hollywood's lethal siren, the *femme fatale*, occurred simultaneously with postwar readjustment, and she—and the sexualized greed she represented—showed signs of weakening in the 1950s as the American economy boomed and the Cold War and nuclear paranoia pervaded social concerns (23). Classic *film noir* is generally seen to conclude with Orson Welles's *Touch of Evil* in 1958, and its concern with masculinity as conflicted and/or neurotic was somewhat absorbed into the mainstream—albeit in more conservative and contained ways—and the external projection of internal psychology in lighting, sets, and cinematographic techniques was no longer seen as remarkable or, perhaps, necessary. The *femme fatale*—the strong, independent woman that embodied all that ailed masculinity—accompanied *noir*'s departure from the screen; *noir*'s return in the 1980s also saw the return of the lethal siren as a projection of masculine crisis and anxiety. But in the 1970s, *noir* seemed less concerned with independent and predatory women and more so with political corruption and social malaise.

The 1970s—The Vietnam War

Classic *noir* appeared in reaction to World War II and its aftermath. Its return (or reintensification, if you regard the genre as continuous) in the 1970s, in a new self-conscious form, appeared in reaction to the aftermath of a new war—the American failure in Vietnam—as well as the Watergate scandal, the Penn State massacre, the women's movement, the civil rights movement, and other instances of social unrest and political scandal. Internal disturbances, social unrest, and the loss of confidence in the government as well as law enforcement institutions undermined traditional images of masculinity—including those portrayed in the cinema. As Linda Dittmar and Gene Michaud note, "What is important about this particular historic moment is that it deeply divided the country's population and brought about a profound crisis in the American imagination" (6). Rather than the *chiaroscuro* contrast of light and dark in black and white, the new *noir* films brought the problems, anxieties, and conflict of masculinity into broad daylight. Shot in color, but still set in Los Angeles whether past or present, films like *The Long Goodbye* (Altman 1973), *Chinatown* (Polanski 1974), *Farewell, My Lovely* (Richards 1975), and *The Big Sleep* (Winner 1978) exposed not only masculine malaise but also widespread corruption in American society. *Chinatown* is set back in the time of classic *noir* and exposes the impotence of the hero Jake Gittes (Jack Nicholson) in the face of political corruption, as water officials are involved in a scheme to make millions, and paternal corruption, as the nuclear family is contaminated by incest and murder. The other three films resurrected Raymond Chandler's hardboiled detective, Philip Marlowe, and offered remakes—or revisionings—of the previous films from the 1940s or transplanted Marlowe to a new seedy L.A. of the mid-1970s. Films other than the detective film, like *Taxi Driver* (Scorsese 1976), took up *noir*'s social critique, masculine crisis, and social underbelly—this time in another of America's big cities: New York. This transplantation of *noir* to the contemporary landscape offered a

FIGURE 9. Jack Nicholson in *Chinatown*. Sticking his nose where it doesn't belong: Jake Gittes (Jack Nicholson) is jaded by his experiences as a private "dick," and the effectiveness of the hardboiled hero is called into question in the 1970s in films like *Chinatown*. Photo from author's collection.

resurrection of *noir* themes but in a reaction to the specific social crisis of the aftermath of a different war.

Classic *noir* had identified women as the source of men's problems. But the neo-*noir* films of the 1970s seemed less concerned with *femmes fatales* and more so with an ineffective hero worn out by his attempt to fight the injustices and corruption of society (Jake Gittes in *Chinatown*), or misguided in his desire to clean up the streets (Travis Bickle in *Taxi Driver*), or jaded and unsurprised to discover his friend had betrayed him (Philip Marlowe in *The Long Goodbye*). In *The Big Sleep* (Hawks 1946), Marlowe (Humphrey Bogart) had a way with the ladies and pursued them with zest; but in *The Long Goodbye*, Marlowe (Elliot Gould) is not interested in his friendly neighbors—a group of often-naked young women—nor his attractive client with whom he does not pursue sexual relations. Women, in the neo-*noir* films of the 1970s, function less as the *femmes fatales* in their most destructive form and, instead, serve mainly as inspiration for the hero's quest: Gittes' involvement in the case in *Chinatown* is spurred on by his interest in Evelyn Mulwray (Faye Dunaway), the daughter of the water scheme's mastermind, Noah Cross (John Huston), and Bickle's in *Taxi Driver* by his desire to help Iris (Jodie Foster), a teenaged prostitute. But women also represent the betrayers of men in these neo-*noirs*: Eileen Wade (Nina Van Pallandt) in *The Long Goodbye* uses Marlowe to escape her husband and run off to Mexico with Marlowe's friend; Betsy (Cybill Shepherd), the woman that Bickle desires, rejects him; and Evelyn Mulwray has been sexually abused by her father, and her so-called sister proves to be her daughter. Films like *Chinatown*, *The Long Goodbye*, and *Taxi Driver* saw an updating of *noir* themes to address a moment of widespread disillusionment in American society that was the result of political scandal and social upheaval. Thus, the return of *noir* came about as a result of cultural associations with the genre as linked specifically to social critique and masculine crisis. In in the 1980s, however, *film noir* continued in a much more self-conscious way and the conventions of the genre were employed less to facilitate social critique than to evoke *noir*'s associations with women as dangerous and manipulating *femmes fatales*.

The 1980s—A Gender War

Noir's *chiaroscuro* lighting, rainy streets at night, guns and cigarette smoke, tough-guy criminals, *femmes fatales*, and hardboiled heroes appeared on the screen in the 1980s: these films used *noir* characters and themes in a self-conscious way to explore contemporary concerns incited by a gender war. The original movement of *film noir* occurred without premeditation—without filmmakers consciously setting out to produce a *noir* film. Instead, they produced a melodrama or a detective film with dark and ominous overtones, themes, and visual style. It was not until the 1950s that French critics, reviewing these Hollywood films of the 1940s, identified similarities among them and labeled them a genre.[1] In contrast, neo-*noir* films were, and still are, produced with the intention of evoking the classic *noir* tradition through specific elements of cinematography, setting, characters, and themes. Postclassical films that are presented to audiences as *noir* fall into one of two categories: retro-*noir* and neo-*noir* (although neo-*noir* is often used as a blanket term for both categories). Retro-*noir* films are considered the more "authentic" of the two—films like *Chinatown*, *The Postman Always Rings Twice* (Rafelson 1981), *Angel Heart* (Parker 1987), *Devil in a Blue Dress* (Franklin 1995), and *L.A. Confidential* (Hanson 1997). The retro-*noir* is set back in time to the period of classic *noir*, the 1940s or 1950s, in an attempt to invoke the same tone and atmosphere as the original films as well as their character-types and themes. On the other hand, a neo-*noir* film constructs the tone and atmosphere of *noir* through the use of similar themes, character-types, and visual style but in contemporary, and sometimes future, settings that evoke *noir* but do not try to replicate it—for example, *Body Heat* (Kasdan 1981), *Blade Runner* (Scott 1982), *Basic Instinct* (Verhoeven 1992), and *Seven* (Fincher 1995).

Although the retro-*noir* film may be hailed as the more authentic *noir*-like film, it does not address the issues and themes of classic *noir* because, ultimately, the opinions the film asserts are those of the society by which it is produced and consumed. What the pretence of *noir* allows is a complex negotiation of escape from, or the expression of, contemporary social issues. The testing of the detective as the central focus of the detective genre is one of the enduring influences of classic *noir*, and the return of *noir* was still predominantly male-oriented. The close association of *noir* with masculinity in crisis was the reason for its invocation in the wake of the feminist movement. Even today, when a film explores masculinity in negotiation or crisis, *noir* elements are often injected into films—whether in isolated moments or wholesale—because they offer an arena for the expression, exploration, and attempted resolution of male anxieties. As Alain Silver and Elizabeth Ward explain, the one aspect of *noir* that the films of the 1980s chose to highlight is its forlorn romanticism and "the need to find love and honor in a new society that tenders only to sex and money"

(370). Rather than a critique of changing social structures, globalization, the empowerment of sexual and ethnic minorities, or the information technology revolution—all of which threatened established social and gender roles—neo-*noir* films of the 1980s tended to center on sex and greed and corresponding gender roles—women as villainous and men as their victims.

The empowerment of women initiated by second-wave feminism and the changes in social structures affected by that empowerment are often identified as the main causes of the perceived crisis experienced by men in American society.[2] The women's movement that began in the 1960s enacted social change over the succeeding decades, with a movement of women out of the home and into the workplace—a sphere that had been seen as predominantly the domain of men. By the 1980s, not only had women moved into the workplace, they had also acquired higher-paying, professional and corporate positions, and these gains accomplished by the women's movement were seen as a challenge to masculine dominance. Faludi argues that in the 1980s there was "a powerful counterassault on women's rights, a backlash, an attempt to retract the handful of small and hard-won victories that the feminist movement did manage to win for women" (*Backlash* 12). Thus, the feminist movement that occurred in mainstream society and in the media (as opposed to the critical movement within academia) is seen by critics of masculinity as responsible for the jettisoning of masculinity into crisis in the 1980s. The empowerment of women resulted in a perceived decrease in the power of men, especially as women entered more and more into professional and corporate spheres. Feminist gains also saw the redefinition of what was considered admirable or ideal masculinity. According to John MacInnes,

> What were once claimed to be manly virtues (heroism, independence, courage, strength, rationality, will, backbone, virility) have become masculine vices (abuse, destructive aggression, coldness, emotional inarticulacy, detachment, isolation, an inability to be flexible, to communicate, to empathize, to be soft, supportive or life affirming). (47)

Traditional notions of masculinity such as aggression and independence came to be seen as outdated, and those previously regarded as effeminate came to be seen as more positive, such as romantic and emotional masculinity. These conflicting ideas of masculinity, shifting social structures, and changing experience of power are regarded as inciting a crisis of mas-

culinity for men in the 1980s, and Hollywood film attempted to process
and negotiate these anxieties through its images of masculinity—but also of
femininity.

The 1980s saw two types of response to the empowerment of women
and its impact on social conceptions of masculinity: the demonizing of
women or the exclusion of them. These two trends were evident in the detective genre in the 1980s, the former in neo-*noir* films and the latter in
cop-action films (which will be addressed in the following chapter). This
backlash against feminism was presented through troubled masculinities
masquerading as untroubled. While the *noir*-hero began the film as the
victim of the *femme fatale*, at the end he successfully extricated himself from
her web, and the cop-action hero triumphed over the enemies that threatened American society and the damsel in distress. The former dealt with
the female threat by offering women cinematic space only to present them
as evil, and the latter by excluding them from the center of the narrative
altogether and presenting those on the margins as needing to be saved by
the hero. Although the two trends offered differing responses to the perceived masculine crisis incited by women, both relied on the highlighting of
sexual difference.

While there is a growing social acceptance of the idea that gender is
at least in part a social construction as biologically determined by sex, there
is still a conflict between the notion of a socially constructed character and
that of an "authentic," "natural" one. As MacInnes argues,

> Men and women in contemporary society appear to treat each other
> increasingly as *equals* [. . .] while becoming increasingly preoccupied
> with discovering and expressing ("authentically") the symbolic mean-
> ing and social significance of their difference, through their sexed
> bodies. Changes in social relations and developments in technology
> mean that possession of a male or female body, or for that matter a
> strong or weak, short or tall body (regardless of its sex), while still sig-
> nificant, almost certainly has much less direct effect on our life expe-
> rience now than at any other time in human history (Dunning 1986).
> Yet we seem captivated by images of real or true men and women or
> "authentic" masculinity or "essential" feminism. (38–39)[3]

In American society in the 1980s, men and women were beginning to
treat each other as equals, yet the mainstream cinema of the time (and to a

large extent today) still perpetuated these myths of sexual difference—myths based in the outdated politics of patriarchy as a result of broader cinematic codes rather than social reality. As a culture, we are still captivated by the ideas of true, authentic, and essential masculinity and femininity and this is often played out in genre film[4]; furthermore, a "naturalized" difference between men and women also helps to simplify (or ignore) real-life concerns about gender roles. Film genres function for a culture by permitting viewers to consider and resolve, at least within the narrative of the film, contradictions that are not fully resolved in reality (Altman 26). The neo-*noir* films of the 1980s offered a critique of the more sensitive kind of masculinity demanded by feminism at a time when the neo-*noir* hero represented an inability to reconcile this new softer image of masculinity with what were seen as "real" men—the more traditional notions of heroic masculinity. Simultaneously, it critiqued the empowerment of women and their desire for independence from the home and equal opportunities in the professional world. The neo-*noir* film was a parable for the 1980s, warning men and women of the danger of transgressing established gender roles.

A RETURN TO THE PAST—THE EARLY 1980s

In the early 1980s, a handful of films were released that self-consciously and notably employed the conventions of *film noir*, including *Body Heat* and *Blade Runner*. *Body Heat* knowingly points to the *noir* classic *Double Indemnity* (Wilder 1944) as its precursor, and the film's hero Ned Racine (William Hurt), like Wilder's protagonist Walter Neff (Fred MacMurray), is an unsuspecting male that gets trapped in the web of a premeditating, calculating, and seductive *femme fatale*. While *Body Heat* is set in the present, *Blade Runner* is set in the future; nevertheless, both present their worlds with a 1940s look and feel. As with classic *film noir*, neo-*noir* protagonists could be victims, criminals, or detectives, and while *Body Heat* follows the exploits of a victim-hero drawn into the web of the *femme fatale*, *Blade Runner* offers a detective-hero.

Ridley Scott's *Blade Runner* is an innovative marrying of sci-fi and *film noir*, offering an image of the future as simultaneously nightmarish and beautiful—futuristic but retro. The city, almost always shown at night, is a spectacle when beheld from the air—full of twinkling lights and awesome architecture—but from the ground it is a dark, rainy, noisy, crowded place—a melange of images and a cacophony of sounds with billboards that move and talk overhead, blocking out the view. The exteriors offer an image of the future—the talking/moving billboards, towering buildings, and flying vehicles—while the interiors and costumes offer one of the past. The Tyrrell building, the police station, and even apartment rooms are dark and smoky—the only light that comes in from outside is cut into shafts by Venetian blinds and the smoky haze by slowly rotating ceiling fans. These images are straight out of classic *noir*. The lack of light in many of the scenes washes out the colors and makes them seem almost as if they were filmed in black and white. Similarly, the costumes are consciously designed to evoke 1940s and 1950s *noir*: the detective Deckard (Harrison Ford) sports a trenchcoat with turned-up collar, while the *femme fatale*, Rachel (Sean Young), wears broad-shouldered suit jackets, pencil skirts, high heels, red lipstick, and dark hair worn up with heavy, rolled bangs. The nightclub where Deckard finds Zhora, one of the replicants, is populated with women in hats and veils, smoking with long cigarette holders. This image of the future is one consciously based on the past to evoke the male crisis associated with it. In *Blade Runner*, the problems of the future are the same as those of the past—the 1980s *and* the 1940s.

Like the classic *noir*-hero, Deckard is a jaded man living in an urban nightmare: he lacks family and friends, a satisfying career, or prospects for the future. Deckard's job is to locate four remaining replicants that are on the run from the law and, through his encounters with the replicants, he discovers that the "truths" of his society may be false—that replicants are the enemy, that they are less than human, and that humanity is embodied only by humans. He finds himself in love with one replicant, Rachel, and in admiration of another, Roy Batty (Rutger Hauer). Although his boss, Bryant, calls him a "goddamn one-man slaughterhouse," Deckard has problems destroying the replicants and, when faced with Batty, a "combat model," he tries to run away. Rather than killing Deckard, Batty tells him how the memories of the things he has seen will be lost with his own death. In the film, it is memories that define humanity—that differentiate the humans from the replicants or that can be given to replicants to make them believe they are human. As Deckard watches Batty die, he recognizes that humanity is not so easily defined: he has seen the replicants react with more genuine emotion than many of the humans he encounters. What Deckard also finds in Batty is, in many ways, himself. The two are explicitly identified as doubles. Shots of Batty and Deckard individually preparing for their duel are intercut: for example, Batty feels his life failing and plunges a nail into his hand to evoke a response while Deckard cracks his broken fingers back into place in order to hold his gun. Through his experience with Batty, Deckard finds his sense of humanity or self; but their doubling also evokes a more sinister realization: that perhaps Deckard himself may be a replicant.

The replicant/human dialectic is a displaced racism in the film that is less obvious than the representation of Asians as the world's underclass. Humans are masters and replicants their slaves, and Deckard is a part of this system as the one who eliminates problem slaves. But he too is somewhat of a slave—a tool used to eliminate society's problems. Only at the end of the film does he choose to reject his prescribed social role: he rejects his mission by not "retiring" Rachel; he rejects racism by recognizing humanity in the "other"; and he rejects his society by choosing to leave it and head north. The ending of the "director's cut" of the film is ambiguous, giving no clear sense of whether the couple will escape, or be happy, or even live (if they are indeed both replicants). The film leaves open the question of whether or not Deckard himself is a replicant. His disillusionment with society is made complete with this recognition and the rejection of his social role, and he chooses to leave rather than remain a part of it. *Blade Runner* uses the social critique of classic *noir* and takes it to its nightmarish conclusion—namely, that there is no hope for the future of mankind and that society is unsalvageable. The neo-*noirs* of the early 1980s that featured victim-heroes, like *Body Heat*, do not offer such a cutting critique and, instead, focus much more on the seductive and dangerous power of female sexuality.

Body Heat opens with the credits rolling over shots of silk being drawn over the skin of various parts of a female body—a tantalizing collage forecasting that sex will be a driving force behind the narrative. The hero of the film is Ned Racine, a small-time and small-town lawyer. A heat wave is the backdrop of the narrative, and the heat, according to Ned's friend Oscar, the cop, can make people do extraordinary things:

> When it gets hot, people start trying to kill each other. We've got more of everything bad since the wave started. It's that crisis atmosphere, you know? People dress different, feel different; sweat more, wake up cranky, and never recover. [. . .] Everything is just a little askew. Pretty soon people think the old rules are not in effect. Start to break them, figuring it's okay because it's emergency time—time out.

But the heat that causes Ned to veer from the straight and narrow is not that of the weather, but that of the body of the seductive and desirable Matty Walker (Kathleen Turner). It is Ned's desire for her that leads him to agree to help Matty dispose of her husband and to cash in on his death: in other words, the desire for sex and money drives the narrative.

The film offers many tropes of classic *noir*, including the victim-hero and *femme fatale* caught in a love triangle with the paternal and controlling husband. Like *Double Indemnity*, this Oedipal narrative sees the symbolic mother encourage the son to kill his father in order to have her to himself. And, like classic *noir*, darkness comes to pervade the film as the terrible plot to commit murder begins to unfold. The film rarely shows Matty and Ned together during the day and instead offers many night scenes full of dark and shadow at seedy bars or in her seaside home. Similarly, the film offers the same kind of coded banter—full of sexual suggestiveness and *double entendre*—that defined the male-female relations of 1940s *noir*. Just as Walter Neff asks Phyllis Dietrichson in *Double Indemnity*, "How fast was I going?"[5] so too does Ned move fast when he first meets Matty. Their initial encounter occurs as Matty leaves a local concert by the ocean and Ned follows her to a railing by the beach. Here, on the border of floodlit civilization and nature shrouded in darkness, Ned makes his move.

NED: You can stand there with me if you want, but you'll have to agree not to talk about the heat.

MATTY: I'm a married woman.

NED: Meaning what?

MATTY: Meaning I'm not looking for company.

NED: Then you should have said, "I'm a happily married woman."

MATTY: That's my business.

NED: What?

MATTY: How happy I am.

NED: And how happy is that?

MATTY: You're not too smart, are you? I like that in a man.

NED: What else do you like? Lazy, ugly, horny . . . I got 'em all.

MATTY: You don't look lazy . . . [laughs]. Does chat like this work on some women?

NED: Only if they haven't been around much.

And, of course, Matty has been "around" and this is no chance encounter. Unsuspecting Ned does not realize that he is the one that has been hunted—not the other way around. As he discovers near the end of the film, Matty checked him out more than a year before, specifically in connection with the case where a will was declared void because of an error on his part—the exact same ploy Matty uses to get her husband's entire fortune. Matty is a cold and calculating woman who uses her attractiveness to men to get what she wants. But what does she want? According to her high school yearbook, "The Vamp's" ambition was "To be rich and live in an exotic land." At the end of the film, she has achieved her goal: the world thinks she is dead (she switched identities with her old high school friend whom she then killed) and sits on an island beach with a new victim in tow.

The femme fatale of the 1980s is not only independent, sexually aggressive, and dangerous like her classic *noir* predecessor, but she can do something that her predecessors never could: elude justice and survive the plot. Matty is evil—she has pursued an extramarital affair, plotted and executed the murder of her husband and best friend, and used the hero and abused the law to bring her plan about. According to the Production Code of classical era Hollywood, she should be killed off at the end of the film for these crimes; but the true danger of the neo-*noir* femme fatale is that she is not easily destroyed. As Ned says to Oscar at the end of *Body Heat*: "That was her one special gift—she was relentless." It is through sex that Matty lures the hero into her web to do her bidding, and it is sex that becomes the defining feature of 1980s neo-*noir*. The Production Code, in place during the time of classic *noir*, prohibited overt displays of sexuality in Hollywood film. In the precursors to these 1980s films, sex was notable by its suggestion but also its absence. A film with controversial scenes of violence and sex, which before would have been condemned under the Code, were allowed under the new ratings system (established in 1968) and, instead of being denied release, it merely received a higher (more restricted) rating. As the products of the post-1968 era, neo-*noir* finally brought the sexual relations implied in classic *film noir* to the surface. The act of adultery represented the transgression of one social law that often led to the that of another—murder. The attraction of the *femme fatale* to the victim-hero was ultimately based on sexual desire, and this would prove to be the central concern of neo-*noir* in the late 1980s and early 1990s, as neo-*noir* films mutated firmly into the genre of the erotic thriller with an emphasis on surprise and suspense rather than a dark vision of American society.

CONTEMPORARY CONCERNS—THE LATE 1980s

John Orr identifies an interesting development in the popular cinema of the 1980s and early 1990s: the emergence of the monstrous feminine as the evil that the hero has to defeat (190). Julianne Pidduck talks about a "fatal femme cycle" of films beginning with *Fatal Attraction* (Lyne 1987) and continuing with *Basic Instinct* (Verhoeven 1992), *The Hand that Rocks the Cradle* (Hanson 1992), *Final Analysis* (Joanou 1992), *Poison Ivy* (Shea 1992), *Body of Evidence* (Edel 1993), *The Crush* (Shapiro 1993), *The Temp* (Holland 1993), *Red Rock West* (Dahl 1992), and *The Last Seduction* (Dahl 1994), as well as some made-for-TV movies and spoof films (65). Celestino Deleyto, similarly, identifies a cycle of erotic thriller films, including *Fatal Attraction, Pacific Heights* (Schlesinger 1990), *Cape Fear* (Scorsese 1991), *Shattered* (Petersen 1991), *Basic Instinct, The Hand that Rocks the Cradle, Unlawful Entry* (Kaplan 1992), *Single White Female* (Schroeder 1992), *Final Analysis, Jennifer 8* (Robinson 1992), *Body of Evidence, Consenting Adults* (Pakula 1992), *Guilty as Sin* (Lumet 1993), *Falling Down* (Schumacher 1993), and *Disclosure* (Levinson 1994) (37 ff1). Barry Keith Grant sees some of these films as belonging to a subgenre he calls the "yuppie horror film," including *Fatal Attraction, Pacific Heights,* and *The Hand that Rocks the Cradle*—films that address contemporary economic fears rather than supernatural ones as does the classic horror film ("American" 26). Kate Stables, on the other hand, sees *Basic Instinct* as the beginning of a trend of erotic thrillers with potent *femme fatales* who get away with their crimes at the end of the film, a trend that continues with *The Last Seduction, Body of Evidence,* and *Jade* (Friedkin 1995) (165). What begins as a backlash against empowered women in the 1980s evolves into a celebration of the power of the independent woman by the mid-1990s.

These films tend to fall into two categories: those with a male protagonist as the victim of the *femme fatale* who then dies in the final act as her comeuppance, and those with a female protagonist who is the *femme fatale* but gets away with her crimes. I would disagree with Stables that *Basic Instinct* marks the beginning of this genre, as *Body Heat* also allows its *femme fatale* to get away with her crimes at the end of the film and sip cock-tails on a beach with her next victim. I would also argue that *Basic Instinct* offers elements of both the home wrecker/yuppie horror trend—with a victim protagonist—and also the erotic thriller/caper film—with a *femme fatale* protagonist who gets away at the end. Detective Nick Curran (Michael Douglas) is the protagonist of the film, but the *femme fatale* (played by Sharon Stone) is not killed by the hero at the end. Thus, *Body Heat* seems to have been a precursor to films like *Basic Instinct*, but films after *Basic Instinct*, such as *Bound* (Wachowski Bros. 1996), abandon the focus on the male victim-hero and instead celebrate their deadly *femme fatale* protagonists. *Basic Instinct* is also one of the few erotic thrillers of the 1980s and 1990s that is firmly aligned with the detective genre and features a detective who investigates the crime—a murder—and its suspected per-petrator—the *femme fatale*. But before I examine *Basic Instinct* as a detective film, I must first briefly consider the erotic thriller of the late 1980s and early 1990s as the precursor to the film and its use of *noir* conventions. The erotic thriller constructed the feminine as monstrous and identified the em-powered, independent, professional woman as either the cause of masculine crisis or, in some cases, as the manifestation of male paranoia regarding the female. This was a new twist, combining the two elements of genre film that were usually opposites: the evil the hero must defeat and the female that he desires. The *femme fatale* also represented a metaphor for AIDS at a time when the disease was becoming increasingly evident and a growing threat to heterosexual couples: the *femme fatale*, like AIDS, represented casual sex and sex outside the bounds of socially sanctioned marriage—sex that could kill.

For the late 1980s and early 1990s, Michael Douglas seemed to embody the central fears of the contemporary white, upwardly mobile, pro-fessional male. He battled the monstrous new independent women in *Fatal Attraction*, *Basic Instinct*, and *Disclosure* and then performed the ultimate masculinity-in-crisis in *Falling Down*, portraying unemployed defense worker William Foster/D-Fens, who cracks and retaliates against the soci-ety that he sees as flawed. According to Faludi, the year 1987 was the most prolific in terms of demonstrating the backlash against female indepen-dence in its top-earning films, such as *Fatal Attraction*, that focused on the danger that the independent woman posed for men (*Backlash* 145). Women in the backlash films of the late 1980s were separated into two categories: good women who were subservient and bland housewives but rewarded for their maintenance of their social role; and female villains, who failed to give

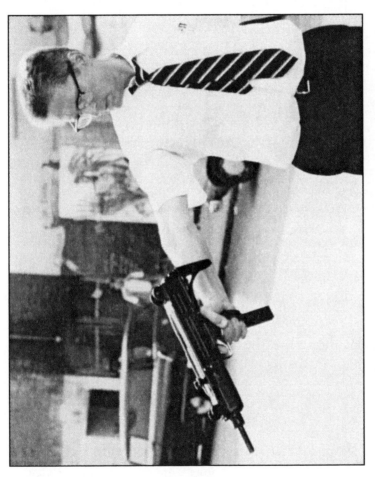

FIGURE 10. Michael Douglas in *Falling Down*. The ultimate defence: In *Falling Down* (1993), D-Fens (Michael Douglas) cracks under the pressure of contemporary demands on men and attempts to reclaim the "ground" that men felt they were losing to "others." Photo from author's collection.

up their independence and were punished for it. This division of the representation of women into two opposing categories is similar to that of women in classic *film noir*: women were portrayed either as nurturer or as *femme fatale*—the former driving the hero toward domesticity and the latter toward adultery and crime. But the *femme fatale* of the 1980s had more "phallic potency" than her *film noir* predecessor, being generally smarter and more sexually demonstrative (Boozer 26–27).

The films that I am particularly interested in are those that offer a hybridization of the detective film and the erotic thriller in which the male protagonist must play detective in order to survive the web the *femme fatale* weaves around him. The protagonist must investigate the enigma of the woman in order to demystify her—to discover if she is a psychopathic killer or an innocent victim. Although the hero may seem to be investigating the nature of the woman he pursues or is pursued by, ultimately he—like his *noir* predecessors—is, in fact, investigating his own masculinity. His relationship with the mysterious woman leads him to a personal crisis revolving around a choice between a nurturing woman, often his wife, and the seductive but dangerous fatal woman. Through his investigation the male not only demystifies the female "other," but he also identifies the source of his crisis: women's presence in the traditionally male social sphere. Women who remain in the domestic sphere are presented as good; those who transgress these socially prescribed boundaries are presented as evil. By choosing one of the two women, the hero chooses a related life path—one to the maintenance of marriage, family, and suburbia; the other to sex, excitement, and independent living. These oppositions are often manifested by objects in these films—the objects that identify and define the culture of consumerism of the late 1980s and early 1990s. The suburban home, countrified furniture, conservative clothing, and family car (most often a Volvo) differentiate the bland housewife from the exciting independent woman. This woman, on the other hand, lives in a downtown "bachelor" pad or works in a corporate office with stark contemporary design and furniture—for example, in *Fatal Attraction* and *Disclosure*—or is associated with upper-class wealth through opulent but cold mansions—for example, in *Basic Instinct* and *The Hand that Rocks the Cradle*.

Chris Straayer explains that classic *noir* offered a complication of assumed gender roles in the 1940s and 1950s (155). Femininity was differentiated as whore (the *femme fatale*) and virgin (the nurturer), and the coupling of the hero with a love interest was strictly heterosexual. But the *femme fatale* was also a masculinized image of femininity, with her assumption of traditional male traits—ambition, independence, sexual appetite—and her challenge of paternal authority coupled with a rejection of prescribed social roles. Similarly, the *noir*-hero was often feminized, especially the victim-hero, and presented as weak, vulnerable, impotent. Thus, *noir* "maintained difference-base while deconstructing gender-sex alignment and allowing for gender inversion, gender trading, and same-gender coupling" (Staayer 155). While the *noir*-hero could fall in love with the *femme fatale* as an equal partner—for example, Marlowe and Vivian in *The Big Sleep* or Johnny and Gilda in *Gilda* (Vidor 1946)—neo-*noir*, on the other hand, tends to offer a reaffirmation of the gender-sex alignment by demonizing the masculinized *femme fatale* and offering the feminine woman—the nurturing housewife—as the protagonist's only option. Women who transgressed traditional social and gender boundaries were marked as evil.

Women: Domestic vs. Independent

Fatal Attraction, released in 1987, was the first of a group of erotic thrillers that identified the cause of masculine crisis as the new woman of the 1980s—the independent, sexual, professional woman.[6] As Chris Holmlund notes, it was a box-office hit and seemed to strike a chord with the popular imagination as it was debated, vilified, and lauded by critics, audiences, newspapers, talk show hosts, and "fatal attraction" became a term in the national vocabulary ("Reading" 25). Alex Forrest (Glenn Close) and Dan Gallagher (Michael Douglas) meet through work, a meeting that leads to dinner and then a sexual encounter. Dan is a seemingly happily married man; however, he seems distressed by his wife's desire to live in the suburbs near her parents rather than in the city and also by the disruption of their sex life posed by their daughter, who shares their bed on occasion. With his wife away, Dan has a weekend affair with Alex. The suggestion is that sex with his wife Beth (Anne Archer) is not nearly as exciting. But, as Dan soon learns, that kind of sex comes with a price: Alex does not want the affair to end and she will do anything to keep him in her life.

In some ways, Alex is masculinized: she has a man's name, she initiates the relationship, she demands sex from Dan, and it is sex that is associated with male fantasies and the redefinition of domestic space as sexualized space—for example, the kitchen sink and the elevator. Dan enjoys the affair but wants no part of a relationship with Alex. He does everything to avoid her, but she demands his attention—calling and harassing him at work and then at home. He seems to think that a brief affair is a normal occurrence in a middle-class professional male's life. "Be reasonable," he says to her. "You knew the rules." It is his right as a man of the 1980s to be married but also to have an extramarital affair. Although Alex does exhibit pathological tendencies and eventually pours acid on his car, kidnaps his daughter, and boils the family's pet rabbit, Alex does have a point, especially as she is (or seems to be) pregnant by him. Dan tells her that she is "sick." Alex replies, "Why? Because I won't allow you to treat me like some slut you can just bang a couple of times and throw in the garbage? I'm gonna be the mother of your child. I want a little respect!" He does feel that he can "bang" her a couple of times and then throw her aside, and, if she is pregnant by him, then he is equally to blame. When she breaks the news to him, he is shocked to hear that she was not on "the pill"; he assumes the independent, sexually predatory female must sleep with many men and "protect" herself.

Dan is frustrated by Alex's blurring of the boundaries between his own idea of the independent woman and that of the nurturing wife-figure. Alex says she does not sleep around, that she is in love with him, that she is going to have his child—but this is not what he wants her to be. Of course, any sense of Alex as a sympathetic and complex character is immediately dismissed by the revelation that she is psychotic. But she does function as a warning to the middle-class professional male who contemplates transgressing the boundaries of socially sanctioned marriage. In an episode of *Biography* on Michael Douglas, the narrator explains, "In 1987 *Fatal Attraction* eerily captured the mood of the public as couples everywhere debated the hazards of indiscriminate sex. It became the year's highest grossing motion picture."[7] The film hit a nerve with audiences as a cautionary tale to men to be happy with domesticity and love their wives (even if the sex leaves something to be desired) because extramarital sex was suddenly dangerous in the late 1980s—not only because of independent, sexually aggressive women like Alex. AIDS meant sex could kill.

The two kinds of women of *Fatal Attraction*—the wife and the independent professional—occupy two distinct worlds. The opening credits show a cityscape, and, as the camera tracks to the right, an industrial skyline of factory towers gives way to the skyscrapers of Manhattan. Alex occupies the former and Beth the latter. Alex's apartment is down a seedy back alley; it is dark, dirty, and ends at the chrome door that marks her building. The interior of her apartment is, in contrast, starkly contemporary, sparsely furnished, and white—the walls, the furniture, even her clothes are almost always white—giving her world a contemporary and masculine feel. The

Gallaghers' downtown apartment is homey, not industrial or modern—
small but expensive, cluttered and lived in. Halfway through the film, the
family moves to a suburban home in the the countryside. It has an old-
fashioned feel and offers a sharp contrast to Alex's sparse and stark bachelor-
style apartment. At the end of the film, Alex's psychotic attack at their house
brings Dan and Beth together again. By having to fight to keep the family—
and the domesticity it represents—that he earlier took for granted, Dan recognizes how much he desires it. Alex is able to leave her world of the
back-alley apartment and penetrate idyllic bourgeois suburbia as a potentially destructive force. But by coming together, Dan and Beth are able to
destroy the evil force that is threatening their lives. Dan drowns Alex until
she appears dead, and when she rises up out of the water one last time to kill
Dan, it is Beth who shoots her dead. The final shot of the film is a photo in
the front hallway of the family: husband, wife, and child united.

But *Fatal Attraction* was not only a cautionary tale for errant husbands; it also offered a warning to women: nurturing wives were regarded
as good, and independent professional women as evil. Beth, by forgiving
her husband for his affair and supporting him through his ordeal with Alex,
is rewarded with a happy family and a home in the suburbs. The original
ending of the film mirrored that of Puccini's opera *Madame Butterfly* (for
which both Alex and Dan share a passion): Alex commits suicide out of despair. But test audiences reportedly did not think that suicide was a severe
enough punishment, and the ending was reshot with Beth and Dan killing
her together.[8] Dan's attempts to kill Alex in the bathroom of his suburban
home are—like his relationship with her—unsuccessful. Even when it
seems that she has drowned in the bathtub, she rises once again, this time
with her knife poised to kill Dan. The fact that it is Beth who must deal the
final blow—or in this case fire the deadly shot—offers a moment of empowerment for Beth but also represents the need for the "good" woman to
destroy the "evil" one.

Similarly, in *The Hand that Rocks the Cradle* (Hanson 1992), it is the
independent woman who is the potential home-wrecker and the wife who
must avenge the family by destroying her. However, unlike in *Fatal Attraction* where it is transgressive male desire that brings evil into the nuclear
family, in *The Hand that Rocks the Cradle*, it is the wife who does not take her
prescribed social role to heart. Claire (Annabella Sciorra) has a beautiful
home, a loving husband Michael (Matt McCoy), a daughter, and a newborn
baby. But rather than being grateful (as it is assumed she should be) for her
role as wife and, especially, mother, Claire feels restless. She volunteers at a

botanical garden and wants to build her own greenhouse in the backyard. In order to juggle all these responsibilities, she needs help and hires a nanny— Peyton (Rebecca De Mornay). But, as Claire's friend Marlene (Julianne Moore) explains, "The hand that rocks the cradle is the hand that rules the world." In this case the world is the middle-class suburban home and, although Claire should rule her own world, she allows a stranger to come into it and take over—with horrendous consequences—as Peyton tries to kill Claire and steal her infant son. Peyton holds Claire responsible for her own husband's suicide and her subsequent miscarriage; her revenge is to supplant Claire as wife and mother of her family. The final showdown of the film is between the two women—the victor will be the one who has "proven" her love for the family—while Claire's husband lies helpless in the basement with two broken legs inflicted upon him by Peyton. Throughout the film, whenever something stressful occurs, Claire is incapacitated by an asthma attack; her deception in the final duel is to fake an attack, lull Peyton into a false sense of security, and then push her out of the window where she falls to her death onto the family's white picket fence—a poetic, if not clichéd, retribution. Peyton—as the female monster—is the punishment for Claire's desire for independence. The independent woman poses the greatest threat to the middle-class family—whether the single professional woman or the wife and mother who desires release from her duties as such—and the film's message is clear: the woman's place is in the home.

Presumed Innocent (Pakula 1990) also sees a predatory woman sent as a punishment for the wife's attempt to be an independent woman. Barbara Sabich (Bonnie Bedelia) complains that her familial duties prevented her from having a career, and for ten years she has been trying to finish her graduate thesis while juggling a husband, home, and child. Her husband, Rusty (Harrison Ford), is accused of the murder of the *femme fatale* Caroline (Greta Scacchi), his colleague and fellow district attorney with whom he had an affair. The film begins with her brutal rape and murder and then follows Rusty's investigation of it in order to clear his own name when he is charged with the crime. The mystery has several twists and turns that eventually lead him to the truth: his wife killed Caroline in revenge for his affair and staged it as a murder perpetrated by Rusty knowing that he would be able to prove his innocence. With this revelation, Rusty is faced with a choice: turn in his own wife and mother of his children or live with the knowledge that she has committed murder. He feels partly responsible as it was his adultery that led his wife to commit murder. Their punishment is to remain together and live with the knowledge of each other's crimes, and, as Rusty's voice-over explains at the end of the film, "There is punishment." The film overturns the predatory female/nurturing woman dialectic and, instead, reveals that even the nurturing wife is capable of pathological behavior and violent murder.

Fighting One's Basic Instincts

The fear represented by the independent woman in the erotic thriller was that of the perceived threat of the empowerment of women and its "feminizing" effect on masculinity. The male heroes of these films suffer a crisis when torn between their love for the "good" women and their desire for the "bad" one. These films worked through the crisis of the 1980s male and resolved it by bringing about the destruction of the independent woman. But, the real fear that these films expressed is not that men in the late 1980s and early 1990s were afraid of the independent women penetrating the family sphere and seducing them away from their wives and children, but that women were penetrating the male sphere of work. By the mid- to late-1980s, women had successfully broken into professional and corporate spheres and often at higher levels than men; they had become breadwinners, supplanting men from their dominant role. Women had become, to some extent, masculinized, and the perceived threat was that, as a result, men would become feminized. While the empowerment of women may be seen as the cause of male crisis and the rise of the monstrous female in Hollywood film, predatory females are not the real cause of masculine crisis in many of these films; rather, the hero fears that his desire for the masculinized woman indicates a homosexual desire on his part.

Deleyto argues that, in the case of *Basic Instinct*, the film becomes a study in male paranoia and a pathological process of disavowal of the hero's latent homosexuality (28). According to Deleyto, the ice pick that the female murderer, who may be Catherine (Sharon Stone), uses to kill her victims can be seen as a symbol of *vagina dentata*, and thus deadly femininity, but it is really a projection of Nick's (Michael Douglas) paranoid perception of her. I would argue, though, that it also symbolizes a phallus with which the female killer can symbolically "fuck" her male victims to death. Male homosexuality is strenuously denied in the film while female homosexuality is ever-present and over-determined: every woman in the film is a lesbian or bisexual, and that sexual "deviance" is linked directly with criminality as each woman has a history, or is suspected, of murder. Although male homosexuality and the male heterosexual fear of it are suppressed in this film or redirected onto female hypersexuality, it is highlighted in other erotic thrillers. In *Fatal Attraction*, *Sea of Love* (Becker 1989), and *Disclosure* latent homosexuality in the heterosexual male is flagged up as part and parcel with masculine crisis in the erotic thriller.

Basic Instinct ends with a double fade out. Nick and Catherine are in bed and, as Catherine lies with her back to Nick, the shot fades out; however, it then fades back in to reveal an ice pick underneath the bed where Catherine can reach it, and then fades out again as she leaves it untouched. Deleyto describes the ending as a projection of Nick's paranoid point of view, the fear that Catherine is indeed the murderer after all (36). *Fatal Attraction* offers a similar moment of male paranoia, a moment that breaks through the realism of the text and makes obvious the skewed and subjective point of view of the hero with whom we are asked to identify. Dan has ended his affair with Alex, but she has become obsessed with him and is desperate to talk to him. As Dan drives home one evening to his new family home in the suburbs, he puts a cassette tape into his car stereo that he received earlier that day at the office. It is a message from Alex. She begins by chiding him for not acknowledging his responsibilities and then continues,

> You thought that you could just walk into my life and turn it upside down without a thought for anyone but yourself. You know what you are, Dan? You're a cock-sucking son of a bitch. I hate you. I bet you don't even like girls, do you? Huh! Yah, you flaming, fucking faggot . . .

The first part of the message plays as he leaves the toll bridge; the rest as he arrives in his driveway. With this final accusation of homosexuality, Dan is horrified and ejects the tape. Later that night, he retires to his study in the loft and plays the tape again—this time with his headphones on. Although there is no indication that Dan has rewound the tape, Alex's diatribe begins at the same spot as when he was driving on the toll bridge and the first half of the message is exactly the same—but the second half is not:

> You thought that you could just walk into my life and turn it upside down without a thought for anyone but yourself. You know what you are, Dan? You're a cock-sucking son of a bitch . . . You are. I bet you don't even like girls, do you? They probably scare you. Well, I know I do. So you're scared of me, aren't you? [. . .] You gutless, heartless, spineless, fucking son of a bitch, I hate you!

The monologue changes from the first listening to the second. Both times he *hears* her accuse him of being a "cock-sucking son of a bitch"; but the first time he also hears her accuse him of being a "flaming, fucking faggot" while the second time it is a "gutless, heartless, spineless, fucking son of a bitch." Why the discrepancy? Is it because her accusation of his being a "cock-sucking son of a bitch" that does not "even like girls" is a verbalization of his worst inner fears that he might harbor latent homosexual feelings? The first version of the tape, heard in the car, sounds clear and normal until Dan reaches his driveway and he hears the most damning part of the accusation—here the audio sounds quiet, tinny, and difficult to make out, unlike the rest of the tape. Just as the double fade-out at the end of *Basic Instinct* signifies the projection of the hero's subjective fears, so too is this double hearing—or initial mishearing—of the taped message a manifestation of Dan's paranoid fears of his own masculinity. She *says* he is scared of women; he *hears* that he is gay. Somehow heterosexual sex with the independent woman becomes linked with homosexuality because she is masculine in her drive, ambition, career, and desire for unconventional sex—sexual acts centered around male fantasies of public, dirty, or rough sex.

Fatal Attraction foregrounded fears of the time of indiscriminate sex; similarly, *Sea of Love* (Becker 1989) exploited fears related to the proliferation of personal ads as contemporary life in the big city seemed increasingly isolated and making connections with other people more difficult. Frank (Al Pacino) investigates a series of murders that are connected to a singles' column but falls for the most likely suspect—Helen (Ellen Barkin). He is torn between falling in love with her and suspecting her of the brutal murders of three men whom she dated through the column. During their first sexual encounter, she takes on a role associated with masculinity and authority. Earlier Frank had frisked her, looking for the gun he feared she was concealing; she in turn now frisks him. She pushes him up against the wall and presses up against him from behind while running her hands over his body and then concentrates on his genitalia. She discards her bathrobe and, naked, she begins to "hump" him as if their positions—and sexes—were reversed, or the same. Frank is aroused by her lovemaking and bends over and leans into her as she thrusts forward with her hips. This sex scene is overtly suggestive of a male homosexual act and establishes Helen as a masculinized woman as well as foreshadowing Frank's final confrontation with potential homosexuality.

In the end it is revealed that it is Helen's ex-husband, Terry (Michael Rooker), who stalks and kills the men that have tried to take his place in

FIGURE 11. Ellen Barkin in *Sea of Love*. Lady in red: In *Sea of Love* (1989), the detective (Al Pacino) is torn between suspecting the *femme fatale* (Ellen Barkin) of murder and falling for her seductive charms. Photo from author's collection.

her life, and the way that he kills them is a fusion of hyper-heterosexual and homosexual signifiers. He makes his victims lie on the bed naked, face down, and pretend that they are having sex with Helen. As they feverishly "fuck" the bed beneath them, Terry shoots them in the head. Two of the three killings are revealed to the audience and, as the camera glides across their naked legs, buttocks, and backs in action, it is at first not readily apparent that they are alone on the bed. Instead, the first impression is that they are having sex with a woman. Helen's latest love interest and, thus, Terry's next victim, is Frank. Terry forces his way into Frank's apartment shortly after Helen has left and thrusts Frank face down on the bed. Terry then sits astride Frank and, with a gun to his head, he "fucks" Frank's buttocks in order to make Frank "fuck" the bed beneath him. Frank is able to locate a weapon and get Terry off him, but not before he has felt fear and humiliation because of the simulated homosexual act.

Disclosure (Levinson 1994) comes as somewhat of an afterthought in the female monstrosity cycle as, by 1994, the erotic thriller had moved away from the male victim as protagonist to the *femme fatale* that gets away with her crimes—for example, *The Last Seduction*. *Disclosure* offers the most blatant association of the independent female professional with masculinity and, thus, its suggestion of emasculating the hero through male homosexuality. Once again, Michael Douglas plays the victim of a predatory female, Meredith (Demi Moore). At one time they were lovers who took part in weekend wine-tastings and sadomasochistic sexual practices; now Tom is married with two children and a house in the suburbs and Meredith is vice president of the company—a position to which Tom was hoping to be promoted. She gets him alone in her office and tries to seduce him, an event that leads to a sexual harassment suit brought by her against him, and then a counter-suit brought by him against her.

The film establishes that although Tom was not completely innocent in the encounter, torn between his desire for the seductive and persuasive Meredith and his love for his family, Meredith was definitely guilty of using her sexuality to play a power game with him. Tom does feel used and humiliated because "she did everything short of rape me," he explains, and rushes home to take a shower and go to bed as is the typical reaction to a rape. The next scene is odd: ominous music plays as Tom arrives for work. In the elevator he meets his boss Bob (Donald Sutherland), who comments on Tom's new suit. Bob, who is normally disapproving of Tom, is friendly and slips his arm around Tom's shoulder before moving in to kiss him. The kiss is exaggerated and the camera offers Tom's distorted point of view as

Bob's large mouth and tongue descend on Tom/the camera. Tom awakens with a start to realize that the scene was just a nightmare. The homosexual implications of the scene are then left unexplored in the film. But the scene brings to light the ineffable implication that Meredith is a man—metaphorically speaking. The independent, professional woman must suppress many of her traditionally feminine traits and display those that are viewed as male in order to make it in the "man's world." She must deny her emotions and softer characteristics, talk tough and play harder in order to compete with the men. As one of Tom's female colleagues says, "All I know is any woman has to be twice as good as a man, work twice as hard to get the same job for less pay." The film takes up the growing concern of sexual harassment in the workplace perpetrated against women and flips it so that it is the man who is the victim of harassment perpetrated by an empowered woman. By turning the issue of sexual harassment of women into a problem faced by men, *Disclosure* defuses the issue and marks women once again as the villains rather than as victims and exploits women as fodder for paranoid male-centered fantasies. As one of Tom's male colleagues states: "What do you expect? They're stronger, they're smarter, and they don't fight fair. It's the next step in human evolution. It's like the Amazons—keep a few of us around for sperm and kill off the rest."

The End of Noir?

The representation of the independent, professional woman as predator was prefigured in *Body Heat*, established with *Fatal Attraction*, peaked with *Basic Instinct*, but seemed to have lost its significance for audiences by *Disclosure* in 1994. Certainly, the trend in neo-*noir* since *Disclosure* has been to celebrate empowered female criminals in the face of weak and impotent patriarchal masculinity, as in *The Last Seduction* (Dahl 1994), *Diabolique* (Chechik 1996), *Wild Things* (McNaughton 1998), *Bound*, and *Femme Fatale* (De Palma 2002). An interesting case is *Unfaithful* (2002), directed by *Fatal Attraction*'s Adrian Lyne. The film offered a return to the erotic thrillers of the late 1980s and early 1990s as a parable of the danger of illicit affairs and their destructiveness in the face of the nuclear family. But *Unfaithful* shifts the focus to the wife, Constance Sumner (Diane Lane), who cheats on her husband Ed (Richard Gere) and suffers the opposing impulses of guilt and desire. She has a torrid affair with a young French book dealer, Paul (Oliver Martinez); her husband discovers the affair and kills the lover in a fit of jealous rage. Rather than the death of the lover, as in *Fatal Attrac-*

tion, or of the substitute mother, as in *The Hand that Rocks the Cradle,* offering a conclusion to the story and reuniting the family, in *Unfaithful* it is the starting point of the final chapter in which the family is haunted by Paul's death at Ed's hands. Constance and Ed have been brought back together with the conclusion of the affair, but the death of Paul hangs between them and prevents their happiness. The film concludes with the family sitting in their SUV (replacing the Volvo as the contemporary symbol of yuppie-hood) outside the police station where Ed wants to turn himself in. Constance tries to talk him out of it, telling him that they could sell up, move away, live on the beach in another country. But the tears flowing down her cheeks confirm that they will not run and that Ed will turn himself in. Rather than the death of the lover being the salvation of the family as it was in the heyday of the erotic thriller, here it is the family's downfall: adultery is a forgivable crime but murder is not. Unlike in *Presumed Innocent*, where punishment for the crime is living with the knowledge of it, in the 2000s this is not enough for contemporary sensibilities. The dark side of the human soul must be curbed and, if it commits a transgression, be punished. It is a much more conservative picture of illicit affairs than that of the 1980s and focuses on the crisis of the woman incited by vacuous suburban living rather than that of the man.

So *noir*'s engagement with masculine crisis incited by women seems to have run its course, just as it did in the 1950s. At some point by the late 1980s and early 1990s, *noir* became detached in many ways from its original signifiers. As Straayer argues, "Now the *femme fatale* is a metonym that travels among a variety of genres, summoning film noirness for atmospheric or hermeneutic effect" (152). Just like the *femme fatale*, the other signifiers of *noir*—cigarette smoking, hazy light cut by ceiling fans or Venetian blinds, contrast between light and dark, shadows, rainy streets at night, etc.—instantly evoke *noir*'s association with dark psychology, crime, and intrigue. As the product of postmodernity, the contemporary crime film picks-and-mixes different styles and uses *noir* conventions to evoke associations of villainous behavior and morally questionable characters rather than masculinity in crisis.[9] This seems to be the result of a revisioning of *film noir* by contemporary audiences and society in general.

Although contemporary film critics identify a crisis in the *noir*-hero, contemporary culture has chosen not to. Bogart, the definitive hero of classic *noir*, is now associated with being tough, smooth-talking, and cool—not internally divided and troubled. He is the man who always gets the job done, gets the woman (even if he does not keep her), and gets the villains, yet is unperturbed by any violence. Depicted with his trench-coat collar turned up, his gun in his pocket, and a cigarette hanging from his lip, "Bogie" is an icon of tough masculinity. In fact, in recent years Bogart's image has been used for two different advertising campaigns. The first is a print ad for the Longines Dolce Vita watch showing Bogart reclining in a tailored pinstripe suit with white shirt, dark tie, handkerchief in his breast pocket, and displaying a cufflink and ring. Accompanying this suave image of the star is the phrase "Elegance is an attitude." The second is a television ad for Thomasville's new line of furniture called *The Bogart Collection*. As the voice-over explains, "Thomasville presents *The Bogart Collection*. Piece by piece, room by room—all designed with the style and elegance of one of Hollywood's most romantic legends." The ad shows the unveiling of the new collection, along with a glamorous model in a silk dress and full-length gloves, to a gathering of 1940s photographers in trench coats and fedoras armed with flashbulb cameras. The final image is of Bogart and—like the Longines ad—presents him in a reclining pose, with a dark suit, white shirt, and a handkerchief in his breast pocket. For the contemporary audience, Bogart exemplifies 1940s elegance, style, and manliness—not necessarily the divided anti-hero he represented in his own time.

The contemporary heroes of neo-*noir* echo these associations with the *noir*-hero moreso than the original cast that was born out of the era of the Depression, Prohibition, and post-World War II disillusionment. This has occurred because of society's nostalgic desire for a stable past. As Harry Brod explains, "Most men today are nostalgic for a past they conceptualize as having contained a secure and stable male identity" ("Case" 48). Thus, audiences often take pleasure from readings different to those purported by critics, as can be seen here with an example of masculine instability recovered by a culture as a defining example of manly masculinity. But this rereading of the *noir*-hero seems also to be connected to a general revisioning of *noir* in the popular imagination. The signifiers of *noir* have become in many ways detached from their original meaning—social critique, gender, war, masculine crisis, postwar trauma—and have been attributed new significations that evoke some aspects of classic *noir* but also bring new associations specific to contemporary society. Tied to this reimagining of Bogart in the Longines and Thomasville ads, *noir* now evokes an image of 1940s America as elegant and exciting, populated by suave, manly heroes in fedoras and glamorous, seductive women between whom sexual attraction crackles.

The heyday of the erotic thriller came to a close as *noir* was reimagined by the turn of the new millennium. The *femme fatale* evolved from being deadly to being exciting; similarly, the male victim went from being the hero to being pathetic. Today audiences relish the empowered woman who is surrounded by weak men. As Tom's colleague in *Disclosure* states, the Amazon woman is the new stage in human—or at least cinematic—evolution. But the detective genre moved away from men in crisis who had to prove their masculinity—and often heterosexuality—in order to survive the case: the detective heroes of the 1990s tended to be stable and successful men. The *femme fatale* was replaced by a new adversary—the serial killer—who was most often male and preyed on women. Powerful women were once again removed from the picture quite literally as the male-female relationship of the *femme fatale* and victim-hero came to be replaced by the male-male relationship of the intelligent detective and the equally, if not more, intelligent adversary. Sex and greed were no longer the driving force of the narrative but, instead, the detective films of the 1990s returned to a focus on investigating murder. That said, the neo-*noir* hero was not the only kind of masculinity that popular film offered its audiences in the 1980s. The cop action film was a dominant trend in the same period, which, unlike the neo-*noir* film that explored masculine crisis, denied it with a masquerade of "musculinity."

CHAPTER FIVE

Investigating Crisis:
The Spectacle of "Masculinity"

CHANGING TIMES, CHANGING MEN

The 1980s witnessed the return to *noir* aesthetics and themes, but parallel to this trend was that of the action film, and its popularity affected the detective genre, with a proliferation of the cop action hero. The cop action film offered a hybridization of the detective and action film by having a detective as protagonist who investigates a crime, with an emphasis on spectacular action as the way to resolve the case and bring the criminals to justice. Epitomized by Bruce Willis in *Die Hard* (McTiernan 1988) and Mel Gibson in *Lethal Weapon* (Donner 1987), the cop action hero represented an idealized image of Americanized heroism and masculinity—violent, strong, independent, white, muscular, and victorious.

The Vigilante Hero

The origins of the 1980s cop action film are in the vigilante cop film of the late 1960s and early 1970s, and its appearance coincided with industrial and social shifts. As Martin Rubin explains,

> The late 1960s saw a marked increase in the consciousness of violence in America, spurred by such highly visible phenomena as war, urban

riots, assassinations, political demonstrations, and the suppression of those demonstrations. One manifestation of this consciousness was a quantum leap in the depiction of screen violence. ("Grayness" 54)

Changing social factors led to a loosening of Hollywood's observation of the Production Code since the 1950s, and this increase of consciousness regarding violence in the late 1960s led, in part, to the abolition of the Code by 1968 and its replacement with the ratings system. Thus, films like *Bullitt* (Yates 1968), *Coogan's Bluff* (Siegel 1968), *The French Connection* (Friedkin 1971), and *Dirty Harry* (Siegel 1971) appeared on the screen and introduced the tough and often angry hero who annihilated crime at any cost, even to the extent of ignoring or even breaking the law to get the job done. In a period when President Nixon's hard-line politics on crime and the widespread loss of confidence in law-enforcement were dominating the American psyche, the vigilante cop film presented masculinity that was tough, independent, violent, and successful in the war against crime.

The vigilante cop is associated most closely with Clint Eastwood's Inspector Harry Callahan—"Dirty" Harry.[1] Eastwood brought to the detective genre the associations of lawlessness, extreme violence, and toughness that his persona had embodied during his spaghetti Western days, and Harry was, in many ways, a Western hero transplanted onto the city streets. In the cop films of the late 1960s and 1970s, police procedure was shown as impotent in the face of violent and pervasive crime, and only the lone streetwise cop, who understood the nature of the criminal because he was very much like one, could deal with it effectively—most often by defying the rules and restraints of the law. Harry represented a law officer who thought and, more importantly, acted along the same lines as the villains he pursued. As he says in *Dirty Harry*, he is the man they call to do the "dirty jobs" when no one else can, and he ignores his superiors' orders and abandons the rules of the force to get the job done. In the final scene of *Dirty Harry*, after he has dispatched the psychotic serial killer, the hero throws away his badge and walks off alone rather than being recouped back into the force or society. Once before, he had brought the killer, Scorpio, in only to be told that the law could not punish him: the evidence they had against him had been seized without a warrant and was, thus, inadmissible in court. The killer, once loose, goes back to terrorizing society, this time taking a school bus of children hostage. Harry pursues the killer beyond the city boundaries to an abandoned quarry and there confronts and kills Scorpio. His version of justice is exacted outside the boundaries of the law and society but is seen as

FIGURE 12. Clint Eastwood in *Dirty Harry*. A man in action—in front and behind the camera: Clint Eastwood performs his own stunt for the scene where the hero jumps off the bridge onto a moving bus in *Dirty Harry* (1971). Photo from author's collection.

necessary when the law is made impotent by bureaucracy. The vigilante hero can be seen as a renovation of traditional models of masculinity to cope with the changing social and political landscape—as a response to social fears regarding crime out of control and a system of law enforcement that favored the criminal's rights over those of innocent civilians and police officers.

Similarly, the cop action hero can be regarded as a redefinition of heroic masculinity for the social and political landscape of the 1980s. Susan Jeffords argues that the 1980s saw an emphasis on what she defines as "hard bodies"—an idealization of American masculinity as heroic in light of the political and philosophical ideas underpinning Reagan's presidential administration. The hard body was understood to be in direct contrast to the soft body—"the errant body containing sexually transmitted disease, immorality, illegal chemicals, 'laziness,' and endangered fetuses"—that seemed to threaten the "health" of American society (*Hard* 24–25). Although Harry Callahan could be regarded in many ways as a hard-body hero, he represented a vigilante hero who stood outside the society that he protected—not unlike the hero of the Western—rather than being a part of it as would be the case in the 1980s. The 1980s hero was a more populist one—an average American—and, as such, could represent a national hero. As Jeffords argues, Reagan's philosophy as President of the United States in the 1980s involved an equating of individual actions with national actions, which was manifested in "a systematic interdependence between individual and nation as linked through the male body" in Reagan's own popular persona as well as the Hollywood action heroes of the time (ibid. 14). The cop action hero of the 1980s resurrected many of the same traits as the vigilante cop hero—the law was often seen as ineffectual and the hero had to break the rules or bend the law to successfully bring the villain to justice. The cop action hero, however, also had a more immediate predecessor, one that shared the fear of masculinity's loss of identity in the face of empowered women and minority men but was born out of a need to reclaim masculinity in the wake of the American failure in Vietnam: the male rampage hero.

The Male Rampage Hero

Film and men's studies critics alike have noted the potent and dramatic effect of war on masculinity in society: World War I offered a resolution of the turn-of-the-century crisis of masculinity as men had an occasion to prove their manliness through wartime fighting and patriotism; and, while masculinity had been humiliated and emasculated during the Depression years, World War II offered the opportunity once again for men to prove their masculinity through battle and bravery. But the possibilities for masculine action were then abruptly dissipated in the aftermath of each war, as men were expected to reject their roles as soldiers—and the associated sanctioned violence that that role demanded—and return to domesticated lives. This sudden contradiction in what society expected of its men led to discontentment, confusion, and resentment. These effects were even more acutely felt in the wake of the Vietnam War because, unlike the case of the two World Wars, the United States was not victorious and instead withdrew from the conflict. The action films of the 1980s offered a hero that symbolically refought—and often won—the war in Vietnam and, in doing so, regenerated American conceptions of masculinity or, as Jeffords describes it, offered a "remasculinization of America" (*Remasculinization* 168).

Rambo, played by Sylvester Stallone, offered an antidote to the seeming failure of masculinity in response to the American withdrawal from Vietnam.[2] In *Rambo: First Blood Part II* (Cosmatos 1985), Rambo returns to Vietnam to seek out Americans missing in action that may have been left behind after the war was over and are being held in prisoner-of-war camps. Rambo is presented as the ultimate hero—the strong, silent type who uses skilled and violent action. It is Colonel Trautman (Richard Crenna) who requests that Rambo be brought in for the top-secret mission. He describes Rambo as a "killing machine," a man who regards what other men call "hell" (the jungle) as "home." Rambo's preparations for his mission are intercut with the preparations of another war machine: the helicopter that will transport him to the heart of the jungle. As the helicopter's engine is fired and warms up, Rambo collects and preps his arsenal of weapons: crossbow arrows, explosives, guns, and his signature fourteen-inch, serrated blade hunting knife. The first shot of this sequence is an extreme close-up of his shoulder and then a tracking shot of his well-developed arm as he sharpens his knife in long, smooth strokes. His arm, with its bulging muscles and pulsing veins, suggests a phallus—the epitome of masculine potency and virility. As a one-man killing machine, Rambo offers a lone hero who can singlehandedly accomplish a mission that was deemed, by the legitimate authority of the U.S. government, too risky and politically controversial to pursue.

Early in the film, Rambo's racial background is highlighted—he is an American of German and Native American descent—and this identity offers a negotiation of the positive and negative implications of his vigilante and violent tendencies. Long hair beneath a headband, tanned arms bared, and carrying a crossbow, Rambo is the incarnation of an Indian brave from a Western film. Rather than "othering" him, his Native American background is used to negotiate his wild and violent ways with mainstream American masculinity. Just as Fenimore Cooper's hero, Natty Bumpo, was white but raised by Mohicans, an identity that differentiates him from the ineffectual British and the "savage" Indian, so too does Rambo's ethnicity "allow" the hero to be both American and violent as necessary. Despite this ethnic background, Rambo is still firmly identified as a white, masculine, American hero in the face of the feminizing and racially "other" enemy—the Vietnamese—and also the villainous Russians, the more contemporary American enemy, who are assisting the Vietnamese. Rambo symbolically refights—and this time wins—the Vietnam conflict for America, blowing away the enemy and saving his fellow Americans that the government had left behind.

The "New Man"

Like the male rampage hero, the hard-body hero of the cop action film in the second half of the 1980s presented a denial of the failure of masculinity incited by the conclusion of Vietnam, but he also represented a backlash against the "feminization" of society that became apparent with the empowerment of women and the appearance of more feminized conceptions of masculinity—including the "New Man." Jennifer Craik notes that the term "New Man" was introduced into fashion culture in the late 1980s (197). A new consumerism aimed at men arose in the 1980s, with the male body seen as the center of male identity and sexuality; the New Man was aware of his body, narcissistic, and a consumer of fashion. Feminist empowerment brought about changes in the type of masculinity that society deemed admirable: for example, macho and chauvinistic behavior became seen as negative qualities for a man to embody, and narcissistic and nurturing tendencies came to be considered positive. This incorporation of feminine characteristics into the conceptions of masculinity was, according to Tania Modleski, an attempt to diffuse feminism and that "male power is actually consolidated through cycles of crisis and resolution, whereby men ultimately deal with the threat of female power by incorporating it" (7). The New Man, thus, could be regarded as a positive shift in conceptions of masculinity as the gains of feminism had incited a change in gender roles. But he could equally be identified as the result of a masculine assimilation of feminist power.

As an image of masculinity that exhibited "feminine" traits and an ideal that society, influenced by female empowerment, hoped men would aspire to, many critics argue that the New Man seems to have existed more in magazine editorials than in reality. Tim Edwards argues that the New Man can be regarded as a product of the media, a response to the attack on men incited by the impact of feminism, and a crystallization of consequences in economics, marketing, political ideology, demography, and consumer society in the 1980s (39–40). The New Man, according to Jonathan Rutherford, was "an expression of the repressed body in masculinity [. . .] a fraught and uneven attempt to express masculine emotional and sexual life" ("Who's" 32). Just as fashion became a status symbol for men because of its ties to the consumer market, enabling men to purchase style and appearance, so too was the New Man a part of this culture as a fashionable, image-conscious, male consumer. But this desire to be fashionable also entailed putting the body on display, an act associated with femininity and passivity and in contradiction to the codes of the look—who possesses it and who is the object of it. Therefore, the New Man was a contradiction because, as fashionable, he was put on display, but, as masculine, he should have denied the look and been the possessor of it. The New Man, however, was not the only response to the changes in gender roles at the time and, while he may have dominated fashion magazine editorials of the 1980s, he—and the concession to female empowerment he represented—was overshadowed in popular film by his opposite: the Retributive Man.

The Retributive Man

The Retributive Man represented a struggle to reassert a traditional image of masculinity that was tough and independent as a toned-down version of the male rampage hero. He represented a destructive machismo as the solution for men's problems and confronted "a world gone soft, pacified by traitors and cowards, dishonourable feminized men" (Rutherford, "Who's" 28). Just as the men at the turn of the last century responded to the "new woman" with a focus on sport, action, male homosocial bonding, and the exclusion of women, so too did the men of 1980s popular culture respond to the "threat" of women with action, violence, male bonding under extreme duress—and the absence of women. With the emphasis on producing another generation of "real" men, the anxieties of men in the 1980s also trickled down to their children with the spectacle of a violent kind of masculinity represented by Sylvester Stallone and Arnold Schwarzenegger echoed in toys and television programs like *He-Man*, *Transformers*, and *G.I. Joe*. The muscular action hero played by stars like Stallone and Schwarzenegger were the antithesis of the New Man, and the success of action films and their stars could be seen as a backlash against feminism and as indicative of a new political conservatism. Jeffords states that the action films of the 1980s were "part of a widespread cultural effort to respond to perceived deterioration in masculine forms of power" ("Terminated?" 246).

Feminism attempted to lessen the differences between men and women, and images of new masculinities—such as the New Man—had begun to appear in the media as a redefinition of masculinity embodying "feminized" traits of sensitivity, nurturing, and vanity. In response to this eradication of difference, images like the Retributive Man presented an excess of manliness and an increase in differentiation between masculinity and femininity through the embodiment of hypermasculinity. Thus, the hard-body action man of the 1980s restored a fictive traditional masculinity to the forefront in 1980s films performing violent—presented as heroic—action. As Douglas Kellner argues,

> The Rocky-Rambo syndrome puts on display the raw *masculism* which is at the bottom of conservative socialization and ideology. The only way that the Rockys and Rambos of the world can gain recognition and self-affirmation is through violent and aggressive self-display. (7)[3]

Specifically, the 1980s cop action hero—like "Dirty" Harry in the 1970s—presented a solution to the problem of law and order made impotent by bureaucracy. For example, in *Cobra* (Cosmatos 1986), the villain, not unlike Scorpio in *Dirty Harry*, taunts the hero, Lieutenant Cobretti (Sylvester Stallone), "Even I have rights . . . don't I, pig? Take me in. They'll say I'm insane, won't they? The court is civilized. Isn't it, pig?" Cobretti replies, "But I'm not. This is where the law stops and I start." Like Harry, Cobretti sees himself as the embodiment of justice when the system's hands are tied by bureaucracy and the Miranda rights. As the tagline for the film states: "Crime is a disease. Meet the cure."

THE COP ACTION FILM

According to Susan Jeffords, despite the many types of masculinity that popular film offered in the 1980s, audiences chose to watch films concerned with portrayals of white, working-class, male, action heroes (*Hard* 12).[4] In the Hollywood action film of the 1980s, the heroic male body was presented as stripped and on display, offering a spectacle of hypermasculinity through which masculine crisis could be performed and resolved. Mark Gallagher argues that capitalist society severely limited and codified the bourgeois male's ability to establish identity through physical activity; the action film provided him with fantasies of heroic omnipotence and escape from cultural pressures (199). The action film can be regarded as a response to this challenge to masculine dominance, offering a space for the expression and fictional resolution of the problems of race, class, and gender that overwhelmed American masculinity at a time when dominant masculinity appeared to be "losing ground." The action heroes of the 1980s were defined as hypermasculine, to differentiate them from the empowered female, but they were also working-class, to differentiate them from the seemingly impotent middle-class male. Middle-class men, like the New Man, had become "feminized" by changing social structures, especially by changing gender roles. Just as women were perceived as a threat to dominant masculinity in the 1980s and the hero was presented as hypermasculine in response, so too was he presented as white in a reaction to the gains made by African Americans in the wake of the civil rights movement.

The heroes of *noir*—classic and neo—were never on display to the same degree as were the heroes of the cop action film. Their bodies were rarely revealed and, instead, the body of the *femme fatale* was the spectacular one of the film. Her body as an erotic object was displayed for the male hero, and the male audience, whether in passivity or in performance, whether literally throwing herself at the hero, as Carmen Sternwood does in *The Big Sleep* (Hawks 1946) as she attempts to sit in Marlowe's lap while he is standing up, or on stage as Gilda in *Gilda* (Vidor 1946) performs the song "Put the Blame on Mame" in a strapless gown and full-length gloves. In the cop action film, it is the body of the hero that becomes the spectacle of the film, often stripped and performing violence. The white male body became the hero's most effective weapon in the fight against crime, but more importantly it was also the site of racial, class, and sexual difference and a space for the expression and negotiation of personal, as well as national, crisis.

Gwendolyn Audrey Foster notes that, according to contemporary race studies critics, whiteness should not be described as a group or race but a term that makes the logic of race thinking possible: "whiteness" does not exist at the biological level but is a cultural construct that is performed (*Performing* 1–2). This is not unlike the term "Orientalism"—a construct of Western society to "other" the people and cultures of the East—which has been demystified by critics like Edward Said. Thus, just as gender can be seen as something that is performed by social subjects in keeping with cultural ideology, so too is whiteness. Foster introduces the concept of "whiteface"—a term that alludes to "blackface" in order to expose the constructedness of whiteness—and connects it to "white space"—on-screen space where identity is "negotiated, mutable, and transitory" (ibid. 3). The cop action film opens up "white space" with the contrast of the white hero—made obvious by the display of his white body—to the villains and often the hero's buddy, who are most often marked as racially "other," or non-white. Whiteness then becomes aligned with the other markers of the hero—masculinity, heroism, and Americanness—and the hero thus performs his whiteness just as he performs masculinity through violent and triumphant action. Daniel Bernardi argues that whiteness in film may aspire to be invisible, but

> This form of whiteness is nonetheless visible as white, replete with its own body of visual and narratological evidence. Ranging from white characters to white lighting techniques to stories of white superiority, this evidence is the stuff of texts and tales. (xvi)

Whiteness, as Bernardi suggests, may be visible because of its dominance to critics of race studies but, as Richard Dyer argues, mainstream cinema is predominantly an articulation of white experience that "secures its dominance by seeming to be nothing in particular" ("White" 44). I would argue that, while this may be true in general, the mid- to late-1980s was a period in Hollywood film when the male body was not "invisible" but was instead put on display as white, male, and working-class in opposition to the female or racially "othered" body.

The cop action film of the 1980s drew attention to the masculinity and whiteness of the hero's body in moments of exaggerated and sustained display and spectacle. The male body was specularized, overdetermined, and hypervisible through being stripped, beaten, tortured, and put into action in order to further the themes of the film—namely, the white male body as triumphant in the face of the threats to masculinity. In *Die Hard*, the class, race, and masculinity of the hero John McClane (Bruce Willis) are emphasized in light of personal crisis—the imminent loss of wife and family—and national threats—Japanese corporations and German terrorists. In *Lethal Weapon*, the white male hero Martin Riggs (Mel Gibson) is established in opposition not only to his buddy—a middle-class, domesticated, African-American male—but also to his *doppelganger*—the villainous, hyper-white (described as albino) Mr. Joshua. Heroism in the cop action film of the 1980s was defined by a specularized and explicitly white, working-class, hypermasculine male body upon which crisis and triumph were inscribed. Jeffords argues that the impact of American failure in Vietnam was worked through in war films of the 1980s through a discourse of gender—heroism was equated with masculinity and weakness with femininity (*Remasculinization* 1). Similarly, the white male body in the 1980s cop action film offered a site upon which masculine crisis—personal and often national—could be expressed and resolved through action, beatings, and eventual defeat of the enemy, whether international terrorists, African Americans, or women.

A Class of Action

Social change, the gains of women, and the evolving workplace were seen as eroding the dominance of white middle-class men. Films like *Fatal Attraction* (Lyne 1987), *Basic Instinct* (Verhoeven 1992), *Falling Down* (Schumacher 1993), and *Disclosure* (Levinson 1994) saw Michael Douglas, as the paragon of middle-class, professional, white masculinity, suffering the impact of the "feminization" of society as his workplace, his home, and often his very sanity were altered and challenged by independent women. The cop action hero was defined as working-class in order to differentiate him from the seemingly impotent and emasculated middle-class man who was seen as the victim of this social change. Chuck Kleinhans argues that the reason for the cop's popularity as hero even today is because he is a worker and, even if he is not necessarily always working-class (like the heroes of television's *Miami Vice*, 1984–89), he is always in a working-class environment rather than a professional one (260). The working-class hero represented a more traditional masculinity, unaffected by female empowerment, because his job involved hard physical labor and required a hypermasculine physique to perform, neither of which a woman could necessarily perform or attain. Women may have become a significant presence in the professional sphere by the 1980s, but they could not so readily invade the space of the working-class male. According to Neal King, film cops are working-class "community protectors" who "blow through the racial guilt, sexual hostility, and class resentment with a wise-cracking defiance and a lot of fire-power" (2).

The identity of the cop action hero as a working-class male is presented through the body—through costume, muscle, and action. The cop action hero does not wear the suit of the police detective: Axel Foley (Eddie Murphy) sports jeans and a baseball jacket in *Beverly Hills Cop* (Brest 1984) while his L.A. colleagues wear three-piece suits, and John McClane in *Die Hard* wears a tank top, khakis, and bare feet in comparison to the designer suit worn by the villain. Similarly, the hero's body is associated through work as the tool and product of labor: bulging muscles are readily displayed as the hero strips off in the course of action. In *Die Hard*, McClane is initially uncomfortable with and intimidated by his wife's corporate surroundings at her new job, but when the Nakatomi Corporation's building and employees are taken hostage by German terrorists, it is Holly's middle-class, professional, and emasculated coworker who is killed by the villains and her working-class husband, McClane, who defeats them single-handedly. Similarly, in *Lethal Weapon*, Murtaugh (Danny Glover) is introduced as the middle-class male who has become impotent through domesticity—represented by his suburban home, his car and boat in the driveway, and his large family. It is his partner Riggs (Mel Gibson), the working-class male, who is potent and responsible for, as the title of Christopher Ames's 1992 article suggests, "restoring the black man's lethal weapon" by encouraging Murtaugh to get in touch once again with his more masculine instincts, including violence.

Buddies and Race

Increasing opportunities for African Americans after the civil rights movement posed a seeming threat to the dominance of white masculinity. The cop action film denied this reality by presenting heroism as the territory of white men. According to Neal King, in the 193 cop films he examined, 80% of cop heroes were white males and the majority of the other 20% were black males, with a few women and Latino or Jewish men (13). The biracial buddy film of the 1980s was a popular subgroup of the cop action film, teaming a central white hero with a black sidekick. The biracial buddy narrative offered the representation of African Americans but negated the threat of their civil rights gains with the black buddy being placed in a subordinate role to the white cop-hero. The black sidekick offered his skills to fight the crime that threatened white America, as in *48 Hrs* (1982) starring Nick Nolte and Eddie Murphy and the *Lethal Weapon* films starring Mel Gibson and Danny Glover (Donner 1987, 1989, 1992, and 1998). Although Eddie Murphy played a black working-class cop as the central hero in the *Beverly Hills Cop* films (Brest 1984, Scott 1987, and Landis 1994), he was still assisted in his investigation by two white sidekicks, and his fight against crime occurs in very rich—and very white—Beverly Hills. As a buddy narrative, these films focused on the relationship between the two men and the contrast of their often-opposing types of masculinity. Films like *Tango & Cash* (Konchalovsky and Magnoli 1989) offered buddies from clashing backgrounds, whereas films like *Beverly Hills Cop* explored the juxtaposition of class and race. The films stress the overcoming of these differences in order for masculinity to successfully defeat the common enemy and preserve mainstream (read "white") American society. Issues of class and race were explored in these films through the clash and resolution of the heroes' differences. But these films tended to simplify important issues—especially race—and reduce them to narrative tropes to create dramatic effect rather than truly addressing them as important issues in American society.

The biracial buddy film performed two functions: first, to place black masculinity in a subservient role to white masculinity, and, second, to exclude women from the center of the narrative. The history of the biracial buddy narrative is much longer than Hollywood's representation of it: Leslie Fiedler traces this history through American literature from Fenimore Cooper's *Leatherstocking Tales* to Twain's *Huckleberry Finn* and Melville's *Moby Dick* and the persistence of the archetypal relationship "between a white refugee from 'civilization' and a dark-skinned 'savage', both [. . .] male" (15). Ames remarks that this archetypal relationship is most prominent in the biracial buddy film and that the most successful of these films have been the ones that reverse the conventional polarity of civilization and savagery, with the black man as the civilized one who has lost touch with his savage masculinity and the white man as the one equipped for survival in the metaphoric wilderness of the urban landscape (52–53). In *Lethal Weapon*, it is Murtaugh, the black detective, who is the civilized (in other words, domesticated) man, whereas Riggs, the white man, is the savage. He may be suicidal and dangerous but he also possesses the necessary violence to defeat the villains.

Although Murtaugh as the black buddy performs feats of spectacular action alongside the white hero and is also stripped off, it is the white hero's

FIGURE 13. Danny Glover and Mel Gibson in *Lethal Weapon*. "Restoring the black man's lethal weapon": It is only through his white partner Riggs (Mel Gibson) that Murtaugh (Danny Glover) is able to get in touch with his masculinity. Photo from author's collection.

body that is the focus of the film and the lethal weapon of the film's title. As Jeffords explains, in the ideological system of Reaganite policy and philosophy, bodies are raced and gendered: the "soft body" is associated with women or people of color while the "hard body," like Reagan's, is male and white (*Hard* 25). At one point in the film, the two heroes are captured by the villains and are tortured for information. Murtaugh is tied up, stripped to a vest, and beaten. To encourage him to talk, the villains rub salt into a gaping wound on his shoulder and then threaten to harm his daughter. Throughout the film (and the sequels that follow), much is made of Murtaugh's age and his body as that of a middle-aged man—for example, when his family burst in on him in the bathtub on his fiftieth birthday and make comments about the grey in his beard. On the other hand, Riggs's body is constantly displayed as the ideal—the film introduces his character with a shot of him in the nude, and later Murtaugh's daughter flirts with him. Murtaugh is stripped off and beaten in the scene. But his bleeding and battered body is not so much heroic as defeated. Juxtaposed to this is Riggs's body: his torso is naked and he is strung up by his hands on a hook as the Asian villain Endo shocks him with electric current. Riggs is presented as a Christ-like figure, with his torture presented as a contemporary crucifixion; his torturer comments on his ability to sustain more abuse than he has ever witnessed. When Riggs appears unconscious, the torturer lets down his guard and Riggs uses his legs to break the man's neck. He then rushes to the rescue of his black buddy and his daughter. As Justin Wyatt notes in his examination of films that co-opt gay male friendship in supposedly straight films, critics have explored the homoeroticism that is generated and simultaneously denied in the buddy cop action film (53). Films like *Lethal Weapon* maintain a tension between the moments of action that facilitate physical and emotional intimacy between the two heroes and the attempts to heterosexualize the homosocial protagonists through homophobic jokes and marginal love interests.

Damsels in Distress

This buddy relationship at once expressed and denied black experience while highlighting the centrality and superiority of the white male, but it also functioned to push women, quite literally, out of the picture. The cop action film, in general, offered an antidote to the perceived female threat with an emphasis on the hero's body as muscular, manly, and spectacular. The male body as the hero's most effective weapon in the fight against crime and injustice compounded issues of sexual difference. Cop action films revelled in scenes of action and violence with the male body at the center engaging in fistfights, kickboxing, car chases, and gunplay. Women were either absent from the film because the buddy relationship is the one central to the development of the narrative, or they were pushed to the edges of the screen as girlfriends to prove the hero's heterosexuality or as victims to be saved. In *Lethal Weapon*, women serve to inspire the heroes to act: the death of his wife pushes Riggs to the edge of sanity and makes him more volatile and effective because he does not care if he lives or dies. Similarly, it is only through the capture of Murtaugh's daughter that the heroes are finally placed in a position of vulnerability, enabling their capture and torture. But although the threat of violence against Murtaugh's daughter may initially make the heroes vulnerable, it also inspires them to act.

In *Die Hard*, McClane only becomes involved in the situation because his estranged wife, with whom he is trying to reconcile, is being held hostage by terrorists. The impulse to rescue Holly is what drives McClane to take on the German terrorists. The film also places blame on the independent woman; if Holly had not left her husband in New York and moved out to California with their children to pursue a career, neither she nor McClane would have been in this danger. Holly's abandonment of their marriage is indicated by her return to her maiden name. She explains to McClane that it is easier to declare herself single for her job than to deal with the implications of having an absent husband. After McClane defeats the enemy, saves the hostages, and wins back his wife, Holly introduces herself as "Holly McClane" instead of "Holly Gennaro." The lone hero like McClane and the hero with a buddy like Riggs occupy the center of the film, with little room for romantic entanglements, which, if they occur, must be tacked on at the end of the film. Women are pushed to the side or are absent from the screen because they are not necessary to the action film either to drive the narrative or as eye candy: the villains provide the disruption necessary to engage the hero and forward the plot, and the hero's male body is the spectacular in the film.

The Hard Body as Lethal Weapon

In *Lethal Weapon*, the identity of the hero Riggs is not made clear at the beginning of the film. He is not clearly presented as a police detective; he is dishevelled and unkempt, living in a run-down trailer and waking up in the morning with a cigarette in his mouth, a gun next to him in bed, and a beer as his breakfast. In the next scene, he buys drugs from dealers in a Christmas tree lot, but the audience is not sure if this is a personal call or an undercover sting. When the dealers tell him they want "a hundred" for the drugs (meaning $100,000), Riggs offers them $100 and a fight ensues, culminating in a shoot-out between the dealers, their gunmen, and the police. As the cops surround the tree lot, the remaining dealer holds Riggs hostage with a gun to his temple. But Riggs demands that his fellow officers shoot the dealer, unperturbed by the threat to his own safety. Riggs's demands escalate to near hysteria and he finally loses control, grabs the weapon from the dealer, and head-butts him into submission. As the other officers seize the dealer, Riggs is shown wild-eyed and struggling to bring himself under control. Riggs is thus established as a borderline psychotic and an unstable masculinity.

Riggs's demonstration of the violent and heroic side of his masculinity is immediately contrasted in the next scene with the revelation of his emotional and traumatized side. Alone in his trailer, nursing a drink in one hand and contemplating his wedding photos in another, Riggs breaks down. He examines a bullet (later explained to be a special hollow-tipped one that he has purchased for his own suicide), loads it into his gun, and then studies the loaded weapon. Suddenly, he raises the gun to his forehead and struggles to pull the trigger; frustrated by his inability to pull the trigger, he places the gun in his mouth and tries again to end his life. Tears of frustration and disappointment fill his eyes and he returns to the photo of his bride. "I miss you," he says to the photo. "It's silly, isn't it? . . . I'll see you later. I'll see you much later." As is later revealed by the police department's psychologist, Riggs has recently lost his wife of eleven years in a car accident, and his grief has pushed him to the edge: he is pulling dangerous stunts in the line of duty and is psychotic, suicidal, and, as his partner Murtaugh jokes, a "lethal weapon."

This juxtaposition of excessive violence and then excessive emotion marks Riggs as an exploration of divided and traumatized masculinity. His internalized grief stemming from his wife's death is, thus, transferred into externalized physical action, and his body becomes the site of the film's deliberation of masculinity. A masquerade of hypermasculinity overrides the feminizing connotations of his emotionality and offers an internally troubled masculinity disguised as an externally untroubled one. But his idealized body becomes "despecularized" as it incurs bruises and wounds and becomes marred with blood, sweat, and dirt. Mary Ann Doane argues that the female body in "the woman's film" becomes despecularized due to mental illness and her inattention to her looks makes her unattractive to the erotic male gaze (43). The female body then is not on display as spectacle, but as a manuscript to be read for symptoms, which will betray her identity. In the same way, Gibson/Riggs's body is a hysterical one—its surface is punctured by wounds and smeared with dirt and blood as the trauma he represses forces its way to expression. The woman must be *re*specularized by the end of the narrative in order to attract a man who will marry her and, thus, allow her to fulfill her socially prescribed role. But the action hero need not be respecularized in the same way. The male body is made spectacular through its *de*specularization, unlike the woman's body that becomes unspectacular. By making the man's appearance dishevelled and his body damaged, one only draws attention to it—the clothes rip and tear to reveal skin and bulging muscle, and wounds draw attention to the permeability of the surface of the body. The hero, thus, becomes specularized through despecularization, and it is in these moments of mutilation that the race, class, and gender of the male hero are highlighted.

The physical action that Gibson/Riggs's body performs and the injuries that are incurred through that performance of violence are an externalization of the internal battle Riggs fights between his emotional vulnerability and his tough manliness. The climax of this internal battle is symbolized in his final fight with the villainous Mr. Joshua (Gary Busey). Riggs has him in custody and could simply arrest, cuff, and take him away. But Riggs must *perform* his manliness and challenges Joshua to hand-to-hand combat in a modern-day showdown. Rather than a racially "other" villain, like the Vietnamese or Russians in *Rambo*, Joshua is a white American. According to Neal King, the villains of films like *Lethal Weapon*, *Die Hard*, *Die Harder* (Harlin 1990), and *Passenger 57* (Hooks 1992) are made white in order to offer an image of villainy that is not offensive to a particular racial or ethnic group (69–70). But although the villains may be white they are most often still presented as of foreign extraction, often German (see the discussion of *Die Hard* below), and thus are, linked with ideas of America's past enemies and the opposite of the American hero. Joshua, however, is not identified as being foreign and, instead, is identified as Riggs's *doppelganger*: they both served in Special Forces units in Vietnam, and they both found employment after the war in which they use the skills they honed in Vietnam. The only difference between them is which side of the law they fight on. Joshua represents what Riggs could become if he does not harness his violent and insane impulses and employ them for the good of society. Joshua and the rest of General McAllister's gang represent an internal threat as drug dealers in American society. Through his defeat of Joshua, Riggs asserts his difference from the enemy, confirms his ability to be a good cop, and proves his masculinity to himself and the audience, thus bringing a conclusion to his crisis. Riggs confirms the end of his internal struggle by offering Murtaugh his "special" bullet as a Christmas present. And—unlike the lone Western-hero who rides off into the sunset or the *noir*-hero who returns to the mean streets—Riggs is embraced into the society from which he has purged evil with Murtaugh's invitation to celebrate Christmas with his family and in his home; he is thus simultaneously stabilized and made ineffective (according to the rules of genre film). It is, therefore, ironic that he should return for the sequel *Lethal Weapon 2* (Donner 1989). But the film justifies his return to borderline psychosis with the death of his new love interest.

The Die-Hard Hero

In *Die Hard*, McClane attempts to resolve his estrangement from his wife and children, but the resolution of this personal issue is interrupted by, and becomes entangled with, the more immediate threat of the German terrorists, led by Hans Gruber (Alan Rickman), who hold Holly and her coworkers hostage. To win back Holly's love, McClane must first prove his masculinity and heroism by defeating the villains that threaten Holly. McClane's body is the site upon which his crisis is expressed through the exposure of his naked, well-muscled physique and then its incurrence of cuts, scars, and injuries as he battles the villains. Nevertheless, the crisis worked through on his body is not just his own personal crisis but also a national one. As Jeffords argues, the wounds incurred by the hero offer a theme of national survival: the hard body may be vulnerable but it can carry on fighting despite its wounds and, thus, offers a reassuring image of the hard body as a national one that will continue to fight and ultimately defeat its enemies (*Hard* 51).

The Nakatomi Corporation that employs Holly represents the globalization and infiltration of Japanese big business into America, and Gruber and his associates represent the threat of terrorism and takeover by the Germans—both former enemies of the United States. McClane's success or defeat as the action hero must bear the weight of U.S. international interests, and he must be distinguished as an American hero in the face of the foreign enemy. The film thus aligns McClane with traditional figures of American heroism. Gruber accuses McClane of having watched too many movies, as he seems to think of himself as John Wayne or Rambo. Mc-Clane, not wishing to reveal his name over the radio to the L.A.P.D. in case the enemy hears it, identifies himself as "Roy Rogers," so Gruber calls him "Mr. Cowboy." McClane's identity is established through this series of associations with traditional American heroes: Rambo evokes associations of the male rampage hero and John Wayne and Roy Rogers the Western hero. Both Rambo and the Western hero are lone heroes: men who are violent, tough, and operate outside the bounds of the society that they help. As a cop from New York, McClane is out of his jurisdiction and is fighting someone else's battle without official authority and without assistance. He is the lone hero who must fight the enemy following his own code of violence and heroism as those of the official law enforcement are no match for the lawless terrorists. The appeal of the cop action hero and the pleasure that he affords audiences is his dual role as law enforcer and outlaw: his alignment with the law as a cop and his simultaneous transgression of it as one operating outside of the rules. The cop action hero does not do things by the book, thus evoking the traditional myth of American masculinity and heroism whereby the hero is triumphant through violence and successful at any cost. This image is especially potent and meaningful at a moment when society was seen as overly feminized and men as increasingly domesticated. Not only is McClane constructed as the lone cowboy and the action hero, but he—like Riggs—is also identified as a savior. In one scene he walks into the room limping, wounded, half-naked, carrying a machine gun, and silhouetted against a backdrop of light; Holly identifies him. Only one word escapes her lips at the sight of him: "Jesus."

Despite the alignment of the cop action hero with very manly and traditional figures of American heroism, McClane also exhibits child-like qualities. As Yvonne Tasker notes: "A perpetual adolescent, even if a knowing one, there is a sense in which he seems to be playing games (cops and robbers, cowboys and Indians)" (88). Rather than performing the role of the dutiful police officer, McClane treats his pursuit of the villains as a kind of game. For example, after dispatching one of Gruber's minions, McClane sends the body to Gruber in the elevator, wearing a Santa's hat and with the message "Now I have a machine gun—Ho-Ho-Ho" written in blood on the victim's shirt. The pleasure for McClane is the pursuit of enemies, not killing them, which appears to be somewhat distasteful to him; similarly, the pleasure for the audience is the game McClane plays and the witty commentary and wisecracks directed at the enemy that accompany it. The construction of McClane as a wise-cracking hero is due partly to Hollywood's tradition of the action hero always having a comeback line—such as "Dirty" Harry's "Make My Day!" or "Do you feel lucky?"—but is also due to the associations with Willis's star persona. *Die Hard* capitalizes on Willis's persona established in the hit television series *Moonlighting* (1985–89), in which he was more a wise-guy than a tough-guy. But although McClane may play the adolescent in terms of his behavior, his body is hypermasculine. The employment of a masquerade of manliness—for example, his ability to wisecrack in the face of death and his physique being a masculine ideal—means that the crisis of masculinity McClane faces—the loss of his wife and children through a failed marriage—is effectively disguised. Internalized emotion is displaced onto the exposed body of McClane in his performance of violence and heroism.

Riggs's and McClane's bodies thus become the canvas upon which their masculine trauma is inscribed. Rather than expressing his emotions, which would be interpreted as a sign of weakness, the action hero channels his emotionality into violent retaliation. This working out of masculine crisis at the level of spectacle means that the male body of the action hero can be regarded as the triumphant assertion of male power or as the articulation of anxieties about the masculine identity they seem to embody (Tasker 9). The body, however, is not merely the site of masculine identity; it is also that of national identity. While Riggs relives Vietnam in his battle with Mr. Joshua and the other ex-servicemen, McClane fights America's battle against foreign corporate globalization and terrorism. America's politics are transferred from the public level to the private, and it is the lone action hero who defeats the threat to American society. Thus, the 1980s cop action film, with its meditation on masculinity and nationalism, transfers internal conflict into external expression on the body of its action hero.

CHANGING TIMES—THE 1990s

The Family Man

A shift occurred at the beginning of the 1990s from the representation of a muscular masculinity to a more internalized one, with more emphasis on the ethical dilemmas, emotional traumas, and psychological goals of the heroes rather than on their skill with weapons and their ability to defeat the villains (Jeffords, "Terminated?" 245). Fred Pfeil describes 1991 as "the year of living sensitively" for Hollywood film, with the release of films concerned with sensitive masculinity like *City Slickers* (Underwood 1991), *Regarding Henry* (Nichols 1991), *The Doctor* (Haines 1991), and *The Fisher King* (Gilliam 1991) (37). Jeffords adds *Field of Dreams* (Robinson 1989), *Robin Hood: Prince of Thieves* (Reynolds 1991), Disney's *Beauty and the Beast* (Thousdale and Wise 1991), and *Boyz N the Hood* (Singleton 1991) to the list of films at the turn of the decade that replace the spectacle of male muscularity and violence with that of a self-effacing man who gets in touch with his feelings ("Terminated?" 245). The protagonists of these films represent a shift from male violence and muscularity to physical and emotional vulnerability by undergoing a conversion to sensitivity through the course of the film. But they also represent a shift in class from the working-class hero of the action film to a middle- and professional-class protagonist of the "sensitive man" film. The "sensitive man" films offer an image of masculinity that is the obverse of—yet complement to—the male rampage hero (Pfeil 38). Jeffords argues that Schwarzenegger's shift from playing a retributive man to playing a sensitive one in *Kindergarten Cop* (Reitman 1990) offers a retrospective apology for the violent and often vigilante men of 1980s action films ("Big" 200). The clear message of *Kindergarten Cop* is that the hardbody hero of the 1980s was not retributive by choice but was merely attempting to fulfill his social role as defined by our social-climbing, crime-conscious, techno-consumer society (ibid. 200). But this is a revisionist message, retroactively giving the men of the 1980s feelings that were presumably disguised beneath the tough exterior of their hard bodies. This was not the message offered by the films of the 1980s that embraced the hardbody heroes and glorified their violence. The two kinds of film offer two different kinds of response to the empowerment of women: the muscular hero as the disavowal of it, and the sensitive hero as the assumption of it.

The movement to the sensitive hero can be regarded not so much as a concession to female power as an attempt to deny it by incorporating it into masculinity itself. But the shift to a more vulnerable hero can also be regarded as positive by offering audiences models of masculinity alternative to that embodied by the retributive hero. It is unlikely that audiences necessarily regarded the presence of sensitive men on the big screen as a method by which to exclude women from the screen and incorporate female power, as many of these films revel in the emasculation of the male hero and promote empowered women. For example, *Regarding Henry* is a film that reduces its powerful and unpleasant protagonist (Harrison Ford) to a good-natured, child-like man after he is shot in the head but survives;

his loss of power, as breadwinner and head of the household, motivates his society wife (Annette Bening) to take control of her life and the family. These films offer an apology for the Retributive Man of the 1980s with the presence of new sensitive male heroes, but they also suggest that female empowerment and desire *have* had an impact on society's expectations of men.

In the action film of the 1990s, the appreciation of muscle came to be reconciled with that of brains and emotionality. Not only did the great musclemen of the 1980s—Arnold Schwarzenegger and Sylvester Stallone—play roles opposite to those they had played throughout the 1980s—for example, in *Junior* (Reitman 1994) and *Cop Land* (Mangold 1997), respectively—but also the macho masculinity that their characters represented was often killed off, quite literally, in favor of a new, smarter and more sensitive kind of masculinity. For example, in *Armageddon* (Bay 1998) the brawny hero who thinks with his fists (Bruce Willis) dies so that the brighter and more sensitive young hero (Ben Affleck) can save the day and marry the love interest. Similarly, in *Executive Decision* (Baird 1996) the muscle man and expected hero of the film (Steven Seagal) is killed off early on and the smarter, less physical man (Kurt Russell) takes over the role as hero. Many films of the early 1990s, such as *Cliffhanger* (Harlin 1993) with Stallone and *Last Action Hero* (McTiernan 1993) with Schwarzenegger, still drew upon "torso politics" in their representation of heroes (Branston 37). But as Frank Grady indicates, these films shift into self-consciousness and parody of the action star's status as such, and movies like *Unforgiven* (Eastwood 1993) starring Eastwood and *Demolition Man* (Brambilla 1993) starring Stallone offer "reflections on, or cannibalizations of, their stars' box-office biographies" (52–53). In these films and those that followed, the heroes became smaller, slimmer, less muscular men and sometimes were not men at all, but rather boys or women (which will be discussed in a subsequent chapter).

Although new and more "feminized" versions of masculinity appeared on the screen in the 1990s—men who are loving, nurturing, openly emotional, and vulnerable—many of the staple stereotypes of masculinity—men who are aggressive, violent, powerful, and independent—did continue, most notably in the sequels to 1980s muscular action films like *Die Hard*, *Lethal Weapon*, and *Terminator* and in other films with 1980s action-hero stars, including Stallone and Schwarzenegger.[5] But the action heroes that Stallone, Schwarzenegger, Willis, and Jean-Claude Van

FIGURE 14. Arnold Schwarzenegger. A parody of masculinity: Arnold Schwarzenegger in the 1980s presented himself as big and tough. By the mid-1990s, he performed send ups of his own persona in films like *Last Action Hero* (1993) and *Junior* (1994). Photo from author's collection.

Damme played in the 1990s were differentiated from their 1980s counterparts: they were more restrained in their reliance on and use of firepower; their bodies were slimmer and toned rather than massive and muscled; and their mission, rather than save American society from an invasive threat, was ultimately to preserve or complete a nuclear family.

More recently, Schwarzenegger returned to the screen as the Terminator almost twenty years after his first venture as the action hero (then a villain) in *Terminator 3: The Rise of the Machines* (Mostow 2003). The film's release was accompanied by a great deal of media attention centered mainly on Schwarzenegger's body and the fact that he had been able to get it back into the same shape it had been for *Terminator 2* more than a decade before. As he said in an interview, "As long as I keep my same weight and do my cardiovascular and stretching exercises and weight training, then I'm fine" (Dittman 21). What is interesting is that by the time *Terminator 2* was made, Schwarzenegger had dropped a lot of weight and muscle and appeared significantly smaller and slimmer that he had been in the first film. Rather than revealing bulging muscles in scant outfits as he had done in 1984, in the second and third films Schwarzenegger—other than a single nude shot at the beginning of each film as he arrives from the future—was covered up in black leather trousers and a jacket.

The action heroes of the 1990s did not represent an inversion of character type from those of the 1980s but more of a softening or sensitizing of them. They were less violent, less vigilante, and always out to heal the nuclear family. They were also less traumatized: rather than suffering from a crisis that has a major impact on their lives, such as McClane's failed marriage or Riggs's death wish, the action hero of the last decade merely faces another job that needs to be done. No longer does the hero represent masculinity in crisis—employing a masquerade of comic-book masculinity to disguise it—but instead embodies a more realistic kind of hero. And rather than walk into the sunset alone at the end of the film like the Western hero (*Dirty Harry*), or temporarily join the nuclear family of his buddy (*Lethal Weapon*), or patch things up temporarily with his ex-wife (*Die Hard*), the hero of the 1990s tended to settle down at the end of the film. He often got the girl (*Cliffhanger, Universal Soldier, Eraser,* and *Demolition Man*), or got the girl and her kid/s (*Kindergarten Cop* and *Nowhere to Run*), or kept his family safe (*True Lies, Sudden Death,* and *The 6th Day*). Whereas in the 1980s Martin Riggs's love interests were killed off—his wife in *Lethal Weapon* and his girlfriend in *Lethal Weapon 2*—in the 1990s, his love interest from *Lethal Weapon 3* (Donner 1992), Lorna (Rene Russo), has stuck around for *Lethal Weapon 4* (Donner 1998) and does not function as a damsel in distress but as an equal partner and an investigator as well. In *Lethal Weapon 4*, Riggs admits that he too is getting too old for the job and looks forward to settling down with Lorna and their newborn baby.

In his interview with Schwarzenegger about the release of *Terminator 3*, Earl Dittman asked, "Do you think we've come to judge manliness by the standards you've set in your movies?" Schwarzenegger replied,

> I hope not, because they are just characters. And they are larger-than-life characters. You're not necessarily a real man because you can beat up an alien or a bad guy. I'd like to think that I have contributed to the re-emergence of the hero or the heroic character. But it takes more than just being overly masculine. A real man is someone who cares for his family and provides for them, shows love for his wife and kids and someone who tries to make this world a better place to live. [. . .] I used to want to be like John Wayne or Gary Cooper when I was a kid. But as I grew older, my idol, or the biggest influence in my life, was my father. I think people are smart enough to know the difference between movie characters and real men. At least, I hope so. (22)

As Jeffords would say, this is a revisionist message from the present, and I doubt that Schwarzenegger would have defined heroism as such two decades ago when he made the first *Terminator* film and maybe not even when he made the second. But this is the new definition of the American hero. Thus, the cop action film has seen a shift from the 1980s to the 1990s as hard bodies gave way to soft hearts, and as defeating foreign villains gave way to saving the nuclear family. As Hollywood film witnessed the proliferation of black stars and female action-heroes, the cop action film and its emphasis on masculine crisis was perhaps no longer necessary: the white male body as the site for the expression and resolution of issues of race, class, and gender was no longer relevant for film-going audiences.

A SHIFT IN PERSONA: BRUCE WILLIS AS A CASE STUDY

Some big action stars of the 1980s continued making action films in the 1990s with varying degrees of success, and even some of Schwarzenegger's films have been box-office flops, like *Collateral Damage* (Davis 2002) and *The 6th Day* (Spottiswoode 2000).[6] The big budget and box-office successes of the last decade have tended to fall into one of the two dominant trends: the spy film or the action-adventure film with younger heroes (*Titanic* [Cameron 1997] and *The Bourne Identity* [Liman 2002])—or centered on the family (*Jurassic Park* [Spielberg 1993] and *The Mummy Returns* [Sommers 2001]); or the cop-action comedy like the *Bad Boys* series (Bay 1995 and 2003) and the *Rush Hour* series (Ratner 1998 and 2001). The cop action film was one of the dominant trends of the detective film in the 1980s, as the career trajectory of Bruce Willis illustrates, the detective-hero was redefined in the decade that followed.

In the 1980s Bruce Willis epitomized the figure of the cop action hero. In the 1990s Willis continued to play detective-heroes, but he has since portrayed ones less reliant on their muscle than on their intelligence, as in *Mercury Rising* (Becker 1998) and *The Sixth Sense* (Shyamalan 1999). In *Mercury Rising*, Willis plays Art Jeffries, an FBI agent who tries to protect a boy with autism, Simon (Miko Hughes), from the villains whose secret code he has cracked. The first scene of the film knowingly plays off Willis's persona as he is presented as a country redneck, unshaven, and dressed in fatigues. This is not the image associated with Willis and his role as the physical working-class action hero. But the scene soon reveals that he is, in fact, an agent undercover. Art is a tough-looking hero, but unlike Willis's former roles he does not repeatedly reveal his muscularity or leap into action through a hail of bullets. His ability to solve the case is accomplished through mental exertion rather than physical, and it is his experience on the job that helps him unravel the villains' plot. He is also presented as a sensitive man who is haunted by guilt over the death of a youth that occurred during one of his undercover missions. He grows very fond of Simon, the boy he is trying to protect, and tries to be a substitute father for him. In the final scene of the film, Art visits Simon in foster care and is teary-eyed as he hugs the boy goodbye. Such displays of emotionality, sensitivity, and affection were absent from the majority of Willis's previous roles (his children in the *Die Hard* films are present only in a photograph), especially his action ones, but have come to define his more recent thinking-detective roles.

In *The Sixth Sense*, Willis plays child psychologist Malcolm, who, after being shot by a former patient, attempts to rebuild his career and marriage. He does so through helping a young boy, Cole (Haley Joel Osment), who claims that he sees dead people. Malcolm possesses a very quiet and sensitive masculinity, deeply concerned for the mental well-being of Cole, as well as desperate to save his failed marriage. He offers no overt heroics or displays of action and, instead, uses his intellectual capacities to solve the mystery of Cole's encounters with the dead. Although the film centers on the mystery of Cole's interaction with dead people, it concludes with a twist: Malcolm is one of the dead. Thus, the solution to the mystery of Cole's experiences is also the solution to Malcolm's investigation into his own failings as a man. He cannot save his marriage because he is dead, but he can let his wife move on to a new life without him.

In late 2001, Willis announced he was through with making "blow-'em-up movies," and, as Sean Daly of the *Toronto Star* reported in 2003, Willis credited much of his "kinder, gentler attitude" to the tight bond he shares with his daughters (E1+). Even though he returned to action in the war movie *Tears of the Sun* (Fuqua 2003), in the film Willis plays a sensitive hero who does not blow anyone up himself. The film posits that the most effective weapon available to today's hero is technology, not a hard body. Lieutenant Waters (Bruce Willis) begins his mission obeying orders to get Dr. Kendricks (Monica Belluci) out of danger. When Waters chooses to ignore the orders and goes back to save a group of innocent civilians, his superior (Tom Skerritt) accuses him of failing his mission. But Dr. Kendricks praises Waters for his moral conviction: "You did a good thing today," she says. Waters, somewhat jaded from his years in the military, replies: "I don't know if it was a good thing or not. It's been so long since I did a good thing . . . the right thing." The film offers a retrospective apology for 1980s war films in which American men were shown to commit atrocities in the fulfillment of their orders and presents a new kind of war hero—one who makes the moral choice over the political.

These roles demonstrate a departure for Willis from the kinds of heroes he had played in the past, most obviously John McClane in the *Die Hard* films. Rather than offering moments of action to showcase Willis's muscular physique, these films allow Willis the opportunity to portray intelligent and sensitive men and to showcase his acting abilities. Willis has repeatedly chosen two types of roles over the past few years: comedic and sensitive. This departure from the action film is most likely the result of two things: first, "torso politics" has found itself somewhat out of fashion; and second, Willis is getting older. Like other aging actors, including former cop action star Clint Eastwood, Willis seems to be looking for roles that are less reliant on a hard-body physique. Willis's move from playing a wise-cracking detective in the 1980s to the thinking detective of contemporary film echoes the shift in the representation of the detective-hero in the last decade. With the emphasis on intelligence and cerebral abilities, the actors who fulfill the role of detective no longer have to fit the white, muscled, action-man stereotype—they can be older men, black men, and, sometimes, not men at all.

PART III

*Investigating
The Crime Scene*

The 1990s and 2000s

CHAPTER SIX

Investigating the Hero:
The Criminalist

Solving a crime is very much like making a medical diagnosis. You look
for evidence, of course, and you try to put all the clues together and then
you go through the process of or sorting out the things that don't seem
to fit. And if you're lucky, you've got yourself a disease . . . or a murder.

—Dr. Mark Sloan, "The Mouth that Roared," *Diagnosis Murder*

FROM BRAWN TO BRAINS

The 1980s were dominated by a processing of masculine crisis and a backlash
against feminist empowerment in films like the neo-*noir* and the cop action
film. But the early 1990s experienced a shift to "sensitive men," which was
mirrored in the detective film by the appearance of protagonists who were defined by brains instead of brawn. This shift occurred in a negotiation of
broader social change and the appreciation of a thinking, feeling, and more
sensitive masculinity over the muscle-bound, violent masculinity that was on
the rampage in the 1980s. Because detective-heroes no longer had to be action
men like John McClane or Martin Riggs and could be a more realistic size,

shape, and age, the detective film explored types of detectives other than the gun-wielding law enforcement type. Heroism was no longer necessarily defined as white, muscular, working-class, and male, and, instead, a new ideal of masculinity was presented on screen: the detective-hero who did not need to be tough so much as smart to bring the new highly intelligent criminals of the 1990s to justice.

The shift from the 1980s to the 1990s saw the return of several earlier elements of the detective film: a sleuth-like detective, but with a focus on police procedure—namely, crime scene investigation and forensic analysis—as the key to catching the criminal rather than a reliance on the sleuth's intelligence. This was accompanied by a new relationship as the focus of the narrative—not the one that develops between the hero and a *femme fatale* as in *noir*, nor between the hero and a buddy as in the cop action film, but between the detective and his adversary. This exploration of the bond that forms between the hero and that which he seeks echoes the classical detective story in which the sleuth was often pitted against a criminal who was his equal—the same kind of person but from the other side of the coin—for example, Sherlock Holmes and his nemesis Professor Moriarty. The new thinking detective represented a relocation to the middle class as an educated and professional hero: he/she is the criminalist: a specialist in forensics and the science of detection who relies on his/her deductive skills to bring the killer to justice. And accompanying the criminalist was a concern with a specific kind of crime: murder. The cop action hero often chased criminals involved in drug deals, heists, terrorism, or political corruption that may have resulted in a number of deaths; on the other hand, the criminalist narrative is concerned with mysteries surrounding often seemingly random, unmotivated, and serial homicide.[1] The criminalist may be a cerebral detective but he/she can be physical when necessary, thus offering not only a hybridization of the sleuth and the police detective but also the American working-class detective whether *noir*'s private eye or the action cop—and as such is an embodiment of contemporary ideals of masculinity and heroism.

Despite the shift to the cerebral, the American hero, nonetheless, must be a man or woman of action, and the new smarter and more sensitive detective must always learn how to be somewhat physical and violent before he can successfully defeat the villain. For example, even the quadriplegic detective Lincoln Rhyme (Denzel Washington) in *The Bone Collector* (Noyce 1999) becomes an action hero. In a duel of wits, Rhyme manages to prevent the psychopathic killer from slashing him open with a scalpel by biting through the killer's jugular vein. The representation of the detective-hero as intelligent is carefully negotiated as he/she is presented as *intelligent* in terms of his or her profession—usually scientific, forensic, medical, or historical knowledge—not as *intellectual* like the villains. A protagonist with a higher education and a knowledge of the literary classics no longer is necessarily regarded as an ineffectual intellectual or a sinister villain; he can now be a hero—a forensic scientist and a contemporary criminalist—the descendent of the classical sleuth. The arrival of the thinking detective in the place of tough-guys and action heroes echoes shifting social conceptions of masculinity. But the thinking detective can also be seen as a response to the arrival of the more intelligent criminal: the serial killer.

"MR. NOBODY": THE 1990s SERIAL KILLER

Hollywood has been obsessed with murder for the last decade, and even moreso with serial murder. Films like *The Silence of the Lambs* (Demme 1991), *Copycat* (Amiel 1995), *Citizen X* (Gerolmo 1995), *Seven* (Fincher 1995), *Just Cause* (Glimcher 1995), *Serial Killer* (David 1995), *Kiss the Girls* (Fleder 1997), *The Bone Collector* (Noyce 1999), *American Psycho* (Harron 2000), *Along Came a Spider* (Tamahori 2001), *Blood Work* (Eastwood 2002), *Insomnia* (Nolan 2002), *Red Dragon* (Ratner 2002), *Murder by Numbers* (Schroeder 2002), and *Taking Lives* (Caruso 2004) focus on a detective's investigation of serial murders. Although the fictional serial killer has become a popular trend in mainstream film since 1995, America's obsession with serial killings has been longer than its dominance in mainstream film would suggest. The 1980s saw the proliferation of the serial killer narrative in fiction, most notably in the novels of Thomas Harris, at the same time as American society began to note the burgeoning of real serial killers. A fascination with real killers led to a barrage of TV movies beginning in the 1970s and snowballing in the 1980s as real-life incidents became fodder for the mass audience. These TV movies included *The Deadly Tower* (Jameson 1975), about Charles Whitman; *Helter Skelter* (Gries 1976), about the Manson Family; *Guyana Tragedy: The Story of Jim Jones* (Graham 1980), about Jim Jones; *The Executioner's Song* (Shiller 1982), about Gary Gilmore; *Out of the Darkness* (Taylor 1985), about "The Son of Sam" killer David Berkowitz; *The Deliberate Stranger* (Chomsky 1986), about Ted Bundy; *The Case of the Hillside Stranglers* (Gethers 1988), about Kenneth Bianchi and Angelo Buono; *Manhunt: Search for the Night Stalker* (Green 1989), about Richard Ramirez; *To Catch a Killer* (Till 1992), about John

Wayne Gacy; *Murder in the Heartland* (Markowitz 1993), about Charles Starkweather and Caril Fugate (the couple who inspired Terence Malick's 1973 film *Badlands*); and *Citizen X* (Gerolmo 1995), about Russian killer Andrei Chikatilo.[2] What distinguishes the big screen version of serial killing since the early 1990s is that the majority of the serial killers on screen are fictional and the violence they commit exponentially increased. The TV movies of the 1980s, whether dramatized accounts of the real-life killers or documentaries, offered the stories of brutal murder—but not the image or violence of it—because they were aimed at prime-time audiences.

The serial killer has captured the popular imagination because he is the most violent, most gruesome, and most elusive of criminal types.[3] He does not kill for the traditional motives of jealousy, greed, and power but because he is psychopathic and cannot refrain from killing until he is stopped by the law. As Dr. Hudson (Sigourney Weaver) explains in her lecture at the beginning of the film *Copycat*, the serial killer is not an invention of the twentieth century, contemporary society does seem to be spawning them in even greater numbers. She goes on to explain that 90% of serial killers are white males aged twenty to thirty-five and are, in general, normal, nice, and unassuming. According to author Patricia Cornwell, the psychiatric community defines psychopathy as "an antisocial behavioural disorder, more dominant in males than females" (26). As Christian Fuchs notes, the FBI assumes that less than 5% of all serial killers are women, and those that are mainly kill direct relatives. Aileen Wuornos is "the great exception" (188). Similarly, the cinematic serial killer is almost always male and there are only a few exceptions, including *Eye of the Beholder* (Elliott 2002), starring Ashley Judd as a fictional serial killer, and *Monster* (Jenkins 2003), starring Charlize Theron as real-life killer Wuornos. In the documentary *Science of Crime*, experts explain that the psychopath is born, not made, and "he kisses or kills without a thought" because he experiences emotions differently from normal people ("Psychopaths"). Not all psychopaths are serial killers, but they tend to be versatile in their crimes, exhibiting the entire range of criminal behavior. They are not prolific in numbers—about 0.5 percent of the general population in Britain and 1 percent in the United States—but they are considered public enemy number one because of the amount of damage they cause: 50 percent of violent crime in society is committed by psychopaths. Hollywood is obsessed with the serial killer as the perpetrator of contemporary crime, but this is a misrepresentation of the reality of criminal behavior, as serial killers account for only a fraction of the national murder rate (Fleck 36). The 1990s were marked by an increase in public interest in crime. But the kind of crime on which the media and popular culture have chosen to focus is not necessarily an accurate reflection of real crime. As Jay Livingstone indicates, murder accounts for only 0.27 percent of felonies in the FBI's *Index of Serious Crime* and only 1.27 percent of violent incidents (40). The popularity of the serial killer narrative may be explained as a result of society's fascination with and fear of this elusive but terrifying criminal.

The screen serial killer of the last decade, unlike previous villains, is not defined by the obvious external markings of "otherness," whether femininity, homosexuality, or foreignness: he is invisible. He can remain undiscovered because he does not look like a killer—a strong and violent man—and instead *appears* weak and/or effeminate. He is not, in fact, weak, as he does physically dominate and kill his victims, but he often disguises his power behind the masquerade of insubstantial masculinity or projects a mask of normalcy in his everyday life. Although the serial killer can be the handsome "boy next-door"—as is the case with Casanova in *Kiss the Girls* (novel and film) and Gary Murphy in *Along Came a Spider* (novel)—he is most often small, innocuous, and seemingly feeble like John Doe in *Seven*, Richard Thompson in *The Bone Collector* (film), and Roy McCorkle and Steven Spurrier, the killers of Patricia Cornwell's novels *Postmortem* and *All that Remains*, respectively. As Cornwell writes in *Postmortem*, "He could be anybody and he was nobody. Mr. Nobody. The kind of guy you don't remember after riding up twenty floors alone with him inside an elevator" (2). The serial killer is most often "Mr. Nobody"—physically unremarkable and remaining hidden in the crowd until the examination of the evidence of his killings identifies him. He employs the masquerade, offering one face of normalcy to the world that is pleasant and nonthreatening and another of evil to his victims to instill terror in them (Simpson, *Psycho* 4). He can appear normal, seeming an ineffectual and effeminate masculinity, but beneath this mask is a violent, often hypersexualized, masculinity.

Real-life serial killers are often described as "abnormally normal" (Seltzer 10). In other words, they appear normal but obviously are abnormal in their need to commit multiple murders. According to Cornwell, "the most distinctive and profound characteristics of *all* psychopaths is that they do not feel remorse. They have no concept of guilt. They do not have a conscience" (*Portrait* 27).[4] Research into criminal behavior is beginning to suggest that the brain of the psychopath is "not necessarily normal"; scientific studies show that there is noticeably less neural activity in a psychopath's frontal lobe than in a "normal" person's, and the frontal lobe is "the master control for civilized human behavior" (ibid. 28–29). Its malfunction means that the psychopath's brain does not register the same kind of reaction to violent impulses as does that of the normal person—namely, a reaction that prevents us from acting out those violent impulses. As a society, we label serial killers as pathological, insane, and abnormal in order to differentiate them from us and our supposed normalcy. The detection of the serial killer in the contemporary detective narrative thus functions to identify the abnormal that masquerades as normal so that it can be extracted from society and, presumably, contemporary crime with it. And, as such, the serial killer film is Hollywood's response to the national conversation about crime: the conservative discourse about crime in American society points to a degeneration of morals as the cause of this kind of crime (Fleck 35). As Woody Haut argues, contemporary crime fiction turns "the fear of violent death into a narrative subtext while investigating the society from which that fear derives" and identifies that fear as an end-of-the-millennium obsession with personality disorders, sexual deviancy, and AIDS (207 and 209). Similarly, contemporary crime films, many of which are based on contemporary crime novels, explore these social fears regarding alienation and disease. The serial killer—especially with the tendency for serial murder to be preceded by sexual assault or the result of sexual impotence—is a social disease and a metaphor for AIDS.

But it is also our increasing reliance on technology and the isolation of contemporary urban living that makes us vulnerable to the anonymous killer. As Suzanne Hatty explains, films centered on serial killers can be regarded as a cinematic response to the contemporary fear and anxiety about victimization and public safety that has been evident since the 1980s (83). And as Gerard Collins discusses in relation to Cornwell's novels, serial killers are "the embodiment of a disease that permeates modern western society: isolation" (159). Our growing cities produce increasing proportions of crime and at the same time individuals are more isolated despite electronic technology—technology that improves global communications but deters face-to-face interactions with our reliance on voicemail, e-mail, cell phones, and text messaging. The serial killer plays on this fear of alienation by suggesting that the greatest threat to the individual is the anonymous "other" who can be a neighbor or a stranger but who is imperceptible to us. But the contemporary detective film assures us that while science and technology may be responsible for our vulnerability to the serial killer, the detective-hero has mastered the science and technology to track, identify, and stop the killer. From crime labs to computer databases to recreating crime events, the criminalist is trained in a variety of different disciplines to use scientific and information technologies to hunt criminals; in other words, what *CSI*'s Warrick Brown (Gary Dourdan) calls a "copologist." Although the serial killer may not be the cause of the majority of crime in society, he does represent the most violent kind of criminal to affect the middle-class society of mainstream film audiences and readers of fiction. Thus, the proliferation of the serial killer in film can be seen as emerging from a desire to entertain audiences rather than to portray crime accurately.

There is something almost admirable about the contemporary villain because of his violence and the freedom from society that he represents, not unlike the film gangster of the early 1930s. As Wayne Douglas explains, the gangster was admirable because he possessed the qualities to adapt to the urban environment of the 1930s; similarly, the psychopath is equally admirable for adapting to the even more complex, bureaucratized, urban environment (32). He is D-Fens, the "hero" of *Falling Down* (Schumacher 1993), taken to the next level, and his violence is a backlash against the loss of power experienced by dominant males. And several villains of the last decade have become cult heroes: Keyser Soze of *The Usual Suspects* (Singer 1995), John Doe of *Seven* (Fincher 1995), and Hannibal Lecter of *The Silence of the Lambs* (Demme 1991), *Hannibal* (Scott 2001), and *Red Dragon* (Ratner 2002). Many film and pop culture critics see the serial killer as the ultimate hero of American culture. Christopher Sharrett argues it is because he is "the most genuine representative of American life" through his embodiment of violence ("Introduction" 13); Jane Caputi, because he enacts traditionally masculine traits of violence and independence and enforces male dominance through killing women or feminized males (150); and Fuchs, because he offers a contemporary evocation of the frontier hero (244). Linnie Blake argues that

> we can perceive peculiarly heroic villains emerging: characters who are simultaneously monsters that threaten the social cohesiveness and stability of everyday American life through their violent acts and outrageous fantasies and heroic outlaws who give voice to the quintessentially American notion of individual freedom beyond the rule of the law or injunctions of the state. Whoever fights monsters, it seems, must be willing to discover that the serial killer is nothing less than the last American hero. (208)

But only a very few of these onscreen criminals are presented as a kind of hero, and they are not the "Mr. Nobody" serial killers—weak, emasculated males who want revenge—but villains like Doe, Soze, and Hannibal who are intelligent and intriguing (they will be discussed in a later chapter). And despite the potentially admirable and heroic qualities that the serial killer may possess, the contemporary serial killer narrative offers little opportunity for identification or alignment with the criminal. While the serial killer may embody an idealized, if perverted, image of traditional masculinity and heroism, the serial killer is *not* the center of these narratives—the detective is. As Philip Simpson explains,

> While sensational depictions of violence can radically subvert cultural ideology, the latest serial killer films typically construct their sensationalism from a conservative political stance that allows for commercial success. Thus, while the films radically appear to transgress taboo, especially in their depiction of violence, they actually serve to uphold a patriarchal, law-and-order status quo derived in large measure from a repressively patriarchal heritage. ("Politics" 119)

These films rarely offer the "pleasure" of alignment with the killer in his perpetration of violence and, instead, focus on the postmortem examination of the killer's violence and align audiences with the detective-hero and the pleasure of detection.

A NEW KIND OF DETECTIVE: THE CRIMINALIST

The serial killer is both incredibly intelligent and brutally violent, and what is required to stop him is a very special kind of detective-hero: "the 'profiler,' the genius-like investigator able, on the basis of clues at the scene of the crime, to narrow down the social and geographical location of the killer as well as his psychological make-up" (Dyer, "Kill" 17). In other words, what is needed to stop the extraordinary "superpsycho" is an extraordinary law enforcer—the "supercop." The two become "two sides of the same coin" (Rubin, "Grayness" 59). Whether a forensic scientist, psychologist, medical examiner, or homicide detective, the hero of the contemporary detective film is the criminalist. The California Association of Criminalists explains that its members come from a variety of forensic science specialities: criminalists, document examiners, serologists, toxicologists, chemists, molecular biologists, firearm and toolmark examiners, and educators (www.cacnews.org). Similarly, an advertisement on NYC.gov for a position in the New York Police Department defines the responsibilities for a criminalist, including

> performing and/or overseeing or supervising professional work in the chemical and/or physical analyses of evidentiary materials such as hairs, fibers, body fluids, fingerprints, gunshot residue, fire accelerants, questioned documents, controlled substances, soil, metals, polymers, toolmarks, paints, glass, and other types of forensic trace evidence required in scientific criminal investigations.(www.ci.nyc.ny.us)

The real-life criminalist thus must possess a diverse range of skills and specialized knowledge.

While the fictional criminalist may be an expert in analyzing "trace" evidence, more importantly, he/she is an expert in human behavior, which is how he/she tracks down the killer: he/she is—as the title of Michael Mann's 1986 film suggests—a "manhunter." Although the emphasis on intelligence and knowledge as the most effective weapons in the fight against crime might evoke images of the classical sleuth, the contemporary criminalist is a sleuth, but something more besides: he/she borrows some of his/her traits from the detective of the police procedural. From the sleuth came the notion that the detective must possess a sophisticated understanding of human and criminal behavior; Miss Marple and Jessica Fletcher may not be from the big city, but they know human nature from observing neighbors and strangers in their respective small towns. But while Sherlock Holmes was able to distinguish between a great number of kinds of tobacco and tires, he was not a specialist in scientific tests like fingerprint identification and ballistics. The criminalist marries the observation and deductive skills of the sleuth with the science and technology from the procedural to offer a detective-hero who mirrors contemporary attitudes to heroic masculinity and, sometimes, femininity.

The appeal of the criminalist is his/her knowledge and use of science and technology in an era defined by information technology, and there has been a proliferation of criminalists in all forms of the detective genre: in the fiction of authors like Thomas Harris, Patricia Cornwell, James Patterson, and Jeffrey Deaver; in films like *Kiss the Girls* and *Blood Work*; and on television with series like *McCallum* (1995–98), *Silent Witness* (1996–), and *Prime Suspect* (1990–96) in Britain, *Da Vinci's Inquest* (1998–) and *Cold*

Squad (1998–) in Canada, and *CSI: Crime Scene Investigation* (2000–), *Crossing Jordan* (2001–), and *Law & Order: Criminal Intent* (2001–) in the United States. Several documentary series have also cashed in on the popularity of the serial killer and forensic investigations, including *IR: Cold Case Files* (part of the *Investigative Reports* series [1991–]), *American Justice* (1992–), *Medical Detectives* (1998–), and *City Confidential* (1998–). Unlike the criminalist narrative in fiction and in film, the ones on television rarely present investigations of serial killers and instead bring the contemporary fascination with forensics to the traditional cop show. Also, the television detective dramas tend to focus on a team of heroes (an ensemble cast) rather than one person, as the hardboiled influenced shows of the 1980s did. As Susanna Lee notes, television crime and detective dramas have "substituted the institution for the individual, the team for the loner, the establishment for the renegade" and tend to focus on procedure, rules and regulations, and the resolution of problems related to law enforcement within the constraints of the institutions (52).

Forensics seems to hold many attractions for the present-day audience: it allows an indulgence in a spectacle that is gross in nature—gory murder scenes and cadavers—similar to the visual pleasure and excitement offered to audiences in hospital dramas like America's *ER* (1994–), without the guilt of association with the doer of the crimes, as is the case of the horror film. The violence becomes sanitized because it is associated purely with the process of investigation and with the law—the detective—who is trying to stop the villain from committing similar crimes. In most cases the acts of violence are not necessarily shown and only the aftermath—the postmortem horror—is revealed to the viewer. This allows an indulgence in the spectacle of murder yet distances the viewer from associating him/herself with the perpetrator of the crime and aligns him/her with the law instead. With the emergence of the criminalist as detective, the process of detection is transferred from the muscle and violence of the 1980s cop action hero, the unascertainable workings of the sleuth's ratiocination, and the trial-and-error of the amateur, and is firmly aligned in the comprehensible field of science. No longer is the process of detection a game of chance, brute force, or solving a puzzle, but is finally an exact science. The serial killer is not easily recognizable. It takes the trained eye of the detective to identify him; as Steffen Hantke notes, the killer's evil is not written on his body (36). Instead it is the body of the victim that becomes the abject one, written upon by the killer and thus becomes a text to be read by the detective—and a spectacle to be beheld by the audience.

The Spectacle of the Gross

In her discussion of the "body genres" of porn and horror films, Linda Williams argues that there is a "system of excess" with a "gross display of the human body" (3). Similarly, the serial killer film (as an offshoot of the horror genre) offers a visceral pleasure for the audience and something that the serial killer narrative in fiction can only achieve to a degree: a spectacle of the gross in relation to the representation of the human body. "Gorenography" is a term that has appeared in the popular media to describe films and other visual texts that offer sensationalized and eroticized depictions of violence (Caputi and Russell 18). While the violence is not necessarily eroticized in the criminalist film and television series, it is sensationalized and can often feel like an onslaught on the senses, not unlike the violence that dominated the opening sequence of *Saving Private Ryan* (Spielberg 1998). Mark Seltzer identifies this impulse as a product of our contemporary "wound" culture, "a culture centered on trauma (Greek for wound): a culture of the atrocity, exhibition, in which people wear their damage like badges of identity, or fashion accessories" (2). Wound culture is evident in Western culture's obsession with the violence of death perpetrated on the human body—with the penetration of the body and making visible the inside of the body through wounds, violence, and autopsies. This obsession with bodily trauma is evident as passersby rubberneck at car crashes and as people patronize controversial art exhibitions, such as the "Sensation" exhibit at the Brooklyn Museum in 1999, which included Damien Hirst's collection of dissected and preserved livestock displayed in glass cases. Even the public autopsy has made a reappearance: in London in 2002 Professor Gunther von Hagens of Germany invited 500 spectators to view the first public autopsy in Britain in 170 years (Wardell A16). The emphasis during the autopsy was less on the scientific or the medical and more on the performative as Professor von Hagens wore a black fedora and blue surgical gown; the autopsy was shown on giant screens inside the gallery; a television network said they would broadcast edited footage; and the organs of the deceased were passed amongst the spectators in trays. Similarly, in film, violence is no longer merely shown exacted and somebody killed, but is lingered over in close-up as bodies are dissected and innards exposed in autopsies.

Our desire for trauma is manifested in our cultural texts through the spectacle of the gross. The visualization of death and mutilation has escalated in frequency and detail in the last decade or so in popular culture as our alignment—as spectators and consumers—has shifted from the perpetration of trauma to its investigation. The committing of the violence tends to be withheld, leaving such horrors up to the imagination of the viewer—for example, the atrocities committed by Hannibal Lecter in *The Silence of the Lambs* are not revealed; instead, the mutilated corpse and its relevance to the investigation of a crime have become the focus of cultural narrative. At the time when Seltzer was writing *Serial Killers* (1998), *ER* was the most popular series on television and the prime example of what Seltzer describes as "pure wound culture." *ER* offers its audiences "an endless series of torn and opened bodies and an endless series of emotionally torn and exposed biotechnicians"—the spectacles that make up wound culture (Seltzer 22). The most popular show in 2003 was *CSI*,[5] and it too is representative of the same impulse to indulge in the gross. Seltzer argues that the appeal of wound culture seems to be its spectacle where private desire and public fantasy intersect; because it offers a private motivation for public violence—for example, childhood abuse—wound culture gives comfort to viewers that there is a reason for violent trauma (257–58).

Similarly, Ken Morrison notes a shift in the attitudes toward the body in Hollywood films about murder, which is evident in patterns of destruction, wound style, and homicide technique; the representation of death has altered from the body being closed and concealed to "cadaverous death," whereby the living body and dead body are presented simultaneously (301). For example, while *Psycho* (Hitchcock 1960) presented the woundless murder of Marion in the shower—the knife is never shown to pierce the flesh of her body—Zapruder's film of John F. Kennedy's assassination revealed the President's death frame-by-frame as his body jerked with the impact of the fatal bullet to the head and indicated the moment of transition between life and death—the body at once cadaver and living (310–12). Similarly, television shows like *ER* focus on the wounded body and the instant when the body shifts from life to death, and many episodes feature bodies that are shocked back to life. The criminalist narrative (including the serial killer film and shows like *CSI*) also offers cadavers as spectacular bodies with gaping wounds that repulse and attract simultaneously.

The cadaver is read as a text to determine what caused the body to pass from life into death and, on *CSI*, this reading leads to an oral—accompanied by a visualized—reconstruction of the crime in which the cadaver is seen alive and then killed again. These sequences are done with digital and/or computer-generated effects; for example, the camera/viewer follows the passage of a bullet through a wall and into the head of a sleeping child or witnesses the impact of an axe into a skull from beneath the blade. In the serial killer film of the last decade, the horrors perpetrated by the killer that were hidden in films like *The Silence of the Lambs* are not only exposed but indulged in as cameras offer these extended and hypergraphic scenes of mutilation. In *Murder by Numbers*, the young killers in eerie, astronaut-like suits choke the life out of a panicked victim and blow the brains out of another; in *Twisted*, a victim's face is so viciously battered that the detective only recognizes the corpse by a tattoo on his hand; and in *Taking Lives*, the disfigured faces of the victims, their hands sawn off at the wrists, and the photos of the crime scenes are given lingering and detailed close-ups. As Murray Pomerance suggests, there has been a dramatic increase in the illustration of violence over the past few decades; audiences are now brought "face to face with a vision of conflict and decay that had heretofore been scarcely imaginable in such detail, suggested and implied rather than directly shown" ("Bad" 3). In *The Bone Collector*, the foregrounding of the investigation, according to Amy Taubin, "allows director Phillip Noyce to display hideously mutilated corpses and to fetishize the details—skin carved, burnt, or bitten down to the bone—in giant digitized close-up. We've come a long way—technologically speaking—since *Blow-Up*" ("Death" 136). This embodies a kind of pornography of violence, a fetishization of the body in death rather than sex. Just as the serial killer is almost always male, so too is his "work" almost always performed through the female body. Rather than necessarily being offered as an erotic object, the female body becomes a text to be objectified, analyzed, and probed in order to identify the real enigma of the narrative—the male serial killer.

The diegetic world of the film is one that is saturated with signs, and, from a self-awareness of the text, it follows that those signs are loaded with meaning and should be read as such. As Walter Burket argues, human beings "create perceptible signs which act to stabilize the common world as it has been formed by language and cultural tradition," and one such system of signs to reveal meaning on the surface, at a visual level, is the marking of territory and the body (165). The main spectacle of the serial killer film is the "work" of the killer—a code or language—that, if analyzed and interpreted correctly, gives clues to the killer's identity and his moral project as exhibited through the body of his victim (Fleck 39). The detective's reading of the text, or profiling, is "an attempt to appropriate the text's language in order to identify the author" (Simpson, *Psycho* 80). In reading the text, the detective—like a semiotician—tries to discern the patterns of the author's "writing" and, through unraveling and recognizing those patterns, discern the identity of the killer.

A "literacy" between the serial killer and the detective is established whereby the killer produces a system of symbols through his victims that the detective must decipher in order to stop and capture the killer (ibid. 35). The female body thus becomes a mode of communication for the two men—one as author (the killer) and the other as reader (the detective).

Fans of the criminalist narrative are rewarded for their devotion to the genre as they are invited by the text to read the signs alongside the detective and to try to solve the mystery before he/she does. But the genre has also reached a new level of self-consciousness due to audience familiarity with the conventions/signs of the genre as well as its increasing popularity in fiction, film, and television. The language, rules, and ritual of investigation in the criminalist film or show include the crime scene kit, the "Luminol" and ultraviolet light that exposes blood, the "cracked" chest and weighing of organs in the autopsy, the lifting of "partials" (fingerprints), the magnification of fibers and hair "tags" (skin on the end of the follicle), the killer's "MO," and "unsubs" (unknown subjects) at the scene. The ritual is so familiar that more recent films like *Murder by Numbers* engage in a postmodern play with the audience who knows the language of the criminalist narrative. Where once the killer unintentionally left behind clues to his identity through his killings, now he often stages his "work" in order for it to be read in a specific way with its audience—the detective-hero—in mind.

The crimes of the serial killer strike fear in the popular imagination because they appear motiveless; he does not necessarily choose people he knows as his victims, but rather strangers—anyone can be his victim. The detective's investigation of the killer's crimes functions to demystify the seemingly motiveless and random killings by attributing to them a pattern—whether to capture intelligent, talented women as in *Kiss the Girls* or to punish sinners as in *Seven*—and, thus, a motive. The motivation for the killings is often attributed to an abusive childhood or major trauma that then has been repressed and resurfaces in the need to kill. The pattern of the killings and the psychology of the killer produce a motive so that the audience feels reassured that even "motiveless" crimes can be understood and resolved—effectively given some kind of motive. As noted previously, motive became one of the key ingredients (along with the rule of fair play) for the classical detective story. The killer's pattern or MO (*modus operandi*) functions as a "signature" that can identify the seemingly invisible and elusive killer and, as Richard Dyer argues, the appeal of the serial killer for film audiences is the attempt to discern this pattern ("Kill" 16). However, the serial killer narrative is merely the formalization and simplification of a pattern established in classical detective fiction by authors like Agatha Christie: the killer only means to dispose of one victim but then is forced to kill others who stumble onto the truth of the crime and threaten to reveal the killer's identity. While there was a need to manufacture the potential threat of more murders in order to maintain urgency and suspense in the classical detective narrative, the serial killer narrative circumvents any plot contrivances to increase the story's body count because multiple murders are the defining feature of the criminal's MO. The pleasure for the viewer of the serial killer film is, thus, to identify the pattern and, therefore, the killer before the detective does. The detective narrative, however, also offers reassurance to its audience: the pattern of the killings, in a reflection of the killer's psychological state of mind, produces a motive so that even seemingly "motiveless" crimes can be understood and resolved. No matter how chaotic and dangerous contemporary society seems to be, the contemporary detective film assures audiences that there is a hero who can restore order or normalcy to the society disrupted by the killer by identifying and removing that "abnormality" through death or incarceration.

FAILING TO DETECT: THE USUAL SUSPECTS

With the shift from brawn to brains in the 1990s, the contemporary detective film was quick to demonstrate what happens when an old-fashioned type of hero tries to employ brute force in the face of the intelligent criminal mind. *The Usual Suspects*, although not strictly speaking a detective film, is marked by the presence of a detective-hero. The film spends more screen time on the exploits of the criminals than on the investigation conducted by the detective; nevertheless, the criminals' activities are shown only as they are related to the detective's investigation. This is done in a flashback structure from the interrogation of the suspected criminal, similar to the classic *noir* film *Mildred Pierce* (Curtiz 1945). The flashback is the narrative told by Verbal Kint (Kevin Spacey) at the San Pedro police station to U.S. Customs Agent Kujan (Chazz Palminteri). It is Verbal's narrative that yields clues to the reconstruction of the story of the crime rather than the investigation of the detectives. Verbal knows the true story of the events and deliberately manufactures a false narrative to divert suspicion away from himself. The detective-hero, Kujan, is a tough guy who is not so much concerned with discovering the "truth" but in justifying his own theory that it was Keaton (Gabriel Byrne) who was behind the heist and who is the elusive criminal mastermind Keyser Soze. The film's surprise ending occurs because the reconstruction of the story of the crime, as presented by the detective Kujan, seems to be the truth as based on the facts given by Verbal.

Like the classical detective story, *The Usual Suspects* has a revelation scene in which the detective tells the events of the crime as he has deduced them from the clues that he has uncovered: a series of images drawn from Verbal's flashbacks are shown in rapid succession, images that support the theory Kujan puts forth—that Keaton was the mastermind behind the plot. Kujan accepts this theory as the truth, and it is seemingly corroborated by the facts presented by Verbal's narrative. But as Verbal leaves the station, Kujan sits on the desk in the office facing the same direction that Verbal faced during the interrogation. Now that he is able to share, quite literally, Verbal's point of view, Kujan can see the "truth" of Verbal's narrative. At the beginning of the film when Verbal was brought into the office, he scanned the "Wanted" posters and miscellaneous information posted on the notice board behind the desk. Now that Kujan sits in Verbal's place, he can see that the information given in Verbal's narrative was taken randomly from the notice board, objects in the room, and even from the bottom of Kujan's coffee mug (the name of Soze's right-hand man is the name of the company that made the mug—Kobayashi). Following Kujan's recognition of Verbal's deception, a second montage of images is revealed that matches the information in Verbal's narrative (heard in voice-over) to their origin from the notice board.

The audience is aligned with Kujan as his is a strong and intelligent masculinity, one that promises to uncover the truth, but the audience also sympathizes with Verbal as a seemingly weak masculinity, first at the mercy of the other criminals and now at that of the detectives.[6] The audience, like Kujan, believes Verbal's story because he gives a desirable and credible solution to the puzzle of the story. The expectations of the audience, founded on years of watching detective films, are aligned with those of Kujan and lead to the conclusion that Keaton is Soze. The audience is surprised, just as Kujan is, at the discovery that Verbal lied and is himself Soze. The film debunks viewer expectations by revealing Verbal's story to be a lie, by having the villain as the least likely suspect, and by letting him elude justice by walking away at the end of the film. The detective-hero, Kujan, is then not heroic because he has failed in his duty and also because it is his fault he has failed, enabling the villain to deceive him because of his reliance on his preconceptions. Kujan does not give the clever villain the respect he deserves; he should have recognized that a man intelligent enough to engineer the heist at the harbor is intelligent enough not to get caught. Instead Kujan despises Verbal for being small and weak. He says to Verbal: "I'm smarter than you and I'm gonna find out what I want to know . . . and I'm gonna get it from you whether you like it or not." Verbal does exactly that: he gives Kujan what he wants to know—namely, that Keaton is Soze. But he does not give Kujan the truth. *The Usual Suspects* celebrates the intelligence of the criminal and the failure of the tough-guy detective.

THE RETURN OF THE SLEUTH: *SEVEN*

In *Seven* (Fincher 1995) the two police detectives, Somerset (Morgan Freeman) and Mills (Brad Pitt), investigate together, but only Somerset is successful and survives their encounter with the criminal. Mills, the physical, anti-intellectual, masculinity—in other words, the action cop— fails where Somerset, the thinking, intellectual, and experienced masculinity—the sleuth—succeeds. *Seven* offers itself ambiguously as both retro-*noir* and neo-*noir*. The aesthetic of the film is taken from *film noir*, with the dark and foreboding atmosphere of the city and its wet and dirty streets. Most of the interior scenes are dark or are slated with shadow. There is an astonishing lack of color to the film: the city seems to contain only varying shades of brown, grey, and black. The film gives the impression of being black and white in tone without resorting to black and white photography. The only scene flooded with light and color is the final sequence on the outskirts of the city; the saturation of color and the intensity of the brightness are powerfully evocative after the film's predominant colorlessness. The costumes, cars, and settings are ambiguous in indicating the period of the setting of the story. The police department contains tropes of the 1940s, with old-fashioned typewriters and Somerset's name being removed from his glass door. Even the diner where Somerset meets with Mills's wife, Tracy (Gwyneth Paltrow), has a distinctly 1940s feel with its greasy-spoon atmosphere. But it is the clothes that most obviously evoke a retro-*noir* tone as the heroes wear old-fashioned suits, shirts and ties, braces, overcoats, and hats. The film's aesthetic is more reminiscent of 1940s *noir* or a retro-*noir* like *Devil in a Blue Dress* (Franklin 1995) than the neo-*noir* films like *The Usual Suspects*. There are a few moments in the film that alert the viewer to the film's setting being contemporary—for example, the pristine apartments of the Doe's wealthy victims, the model and the lawyer. But the story and characters of the film are never restricted to a specific city or time. The city is representational of any city; its time, of any time: the film transcends specificities.

The retro-*noir* feel of the film allows for the resurrection of two kinds of detective: the infallible sleuth and the idealistic young cop. The film is concerned with contrasting the two kinds of masculinity: Somerset, the older detective, is preparing to retire while Mills, the young cop, will take his place. The former is patient, methodical, and precise; the latter is outgoing, heedless, and impatient. They are forced to work together, despite their differences, to track down and stop the serial killer John Doe (Kevin Spacey). Unlike the action movie *Armageddon* (Bay 1998), which extols the virtues of the younger and more sensitive generation over those of the older, *Seven* praises experience acquired with time over the enthusiasm and good intentions of youth. It is Somerset who recognizes the significance of the scrapings of plastic that lead to the first real clue in the case: "gluttony" written on the wall in grease. And it is his knowledge of classic literature that leads him to Milton's *Paradise Lost* and the seven deadly sins, alerting him to the fact that two killings are only the beginning. Somerset is not an ordinary cop. The other detectives in the department despair of his analytical and mental gymnastics, and they insist that the case should be solvable through gut instinct and police know-how. "Always these questions with you?" one officer complains. "Don't start your big brain cooking on this," his superintendent implores Somerset. But it is Somerset's "big brain" that tracks down the killer, and not just because Somerset knows his Milton, but because he knows how to access FBI information of Doe's library card use. Somerset's skills as a detective are more than just education and an appreciation for literature; like the sleuth, he depends upon deductive reasoning and ratiocination to recognize the elusive importance of the clues that do not readily identify themselves as such and that offer insight into the workings of the criminal mind. And, thus, Somerset succeeds where Mills fails.

Mills represents another kind of detective-figure—the idealistic cop. He faces the problems of the young officer: not being taken seriously by his fellow officers and neglecting his young wife because of his job. As Royal Brown explains, Mills has moved to the big city in order to become "the lethal weapon/avenger type of cop" he knows from films and television (44). Mills has a bright future as a detective, having made detective so young— "Not even thirty years old," one officer remarks—and having been transferred to the big city from upstate. But his youth—his exuberant self-confidence, desire to prove himself to Somerset and his department, his lack of respect for the criminal mind, and his vulnerability in loving his wife—lead to his downfall. Doe is a highly intelligent adversary, but Mills refuses to acknowledge this fact. Mills fails because his vanity prevents him from heeding the advice of the wiser and more experienced Somerset, who warns Mills that he talks, but does not see. "Just because he has a library card doesn't make him Yoda," Mills proclaims. He insists that Doe must be insane, "running around in his grandma's underpants and rubbing himself with peanut butter," and cannot conceive that one who possesses evil can also possess brilliance. Nor can he foresee that Doe will include his adversaries in his evil machinations, the result of which is the death of Mills's wife and unborn child. Mills's youthful pride and his pursuit of personal desires over those of his duty—namely, his shooting of Doe instead of leaving justice to the legal system—seals the end of his career as a man of the law. The result is that Somerset cannot leave the force because he still believes the world is "worth fighting for" and realizes that the new generation of detectives still has much to learn. The film's retrospective atmosphere lends itself to a reading of its narrative as taking place in any city and in any time. Nevertheless, the final message of the film remains unambiguous and timeless: namely, that a detective must put his duty as a law enforcer before his personal desires in order to successfully defeat the evil of society.

THE SMART GUY TAKES OVER:
L.A. CONFIDENTIAL

L.A. Confidential (Hanson 1997) is a retro-*noir* and its title is meant to invoke the "confidential" films produced in the 1950s—like *Kansas City Confidential* (Karlson 1952), *The Phoenix City Confidential* (Karlson 1955), *New York Confidential* (Rouse 1955), and *Chicago Confidential* (Salkow 1957)—that purported to tell the inside stories of supposedly corrupt cities (Pratt 197). The film follows the investigations of three detective-heroes who represent different types of masculinity, and the one who survives and succeeds is not the tough-guy hero but the smart one who knows how to play the game of politics and bureaucracy in the police department.

The story is set in 1953 Los Angeles and the opening scene is a montage of images of a sunny paradise. This montage is accompanied by a voice-over that contradicts the images and dispels the myth they evoke. This echoes what the film attempts to do as a whole: to expose the dark side of the Los Angeles presented to 1950s America. The images in the sequence are taken from 1940s and 1950s films and footage of Hollywood life and show California as a paradise, the land of opportunity and the American dream, the home of the all-American family and of famous stars alike. The running commentary that accompanies the images is given by Sid Hudgens (Danny De Vito), a reporter.

> Come to Los Angeles! The sun shines bright. The beaches are wide and inviting and orange groves stretch as far as the eye can see. There are jobs aplenty and land is cheap. Every working man can have his own house, and in every house . . . a happy all-American family. You can have all this and, who knows, you could even be discovered, become a movie star or at least see one. Life is good in Los Angeles! It's paradise on Earth . . . Ha! Ha! That's what they tell you anyway because they're selling an image! They're selling it through the movies, radio, and television. In the hit show *Badge of Honor* the L.A. cops walk on water as they keep the city clean of crooks. Yup! You'd think this place was the Garden of Eden. But there is trouble in paradise . . .

Through the course of the film, this image of L.A. is shattered: the film stars are hookers surgically enhanced to look like famous stars; the politicians are corrupt and their influence easily bought; and the cops are taking over the organized crime racket from the criminals they catch. Yet the film ends on a happy note, with the cooperation of three good cops bringing an end to police corruption in L.A., at least in the interim.

The film explores the relationship formed between three different types of masculinity. Jack Vincennes (Kevin Spacey) is an older cop who has become disillusioned with the force. He takes pay-offs from Sid Hudgens for stories and set-ups for the scandal rag, *Hush–Hush* magazine, and seems to derive his only pleasure from his job as technical advisor on the cop television show *Badge of Honor*. Bud White (Russell Crowe) is a tough-guy cop with muscle, which makes everyone assume he is stupid, and he begins to believe them. He is brought in on jobs only to beat information and confessions out of suspects, never to actively investigate a case. Ed Exley (Guy Pearce) is the son of a well-respected cop. He is only thirty years old, college-educated, and highly ambitious. Using his intelligence and wiles to guide him up the departmental and political ladder as quickly as possible, he makes himself unpopular with the other men on the force. He is also intensely idealistic about justice. But his captain, Dudley Smith (James Cromwell), values deceit and places the interests of the force before

FIGURE 15. Guy Pearce, Russell Crowe, and Kevin Spacey in *L.A. Confidential*. Brains over brawn: *L.A. Confidential* (1997) offers three different kinds of hero (played by Guy Pearce, Russell Crowe, and Kevin Spacey) but only the one who uses his brains to solve the case (Exley) will have a successful career in law enforcement. Photo from author's collection.

those of justice. As Smith tells Ed at the beginning of the film, "You have the eye for human weakness, but not the stomach."

The characters of each cop are best encapsulated by their individual reasons for joining the police force: Bud did so because he saw his father beat his mother to death; Ed because his father was killed by a crook who was never caught and because he wanted "to help people"; and Jack cannot remember why. Even though these three men are very different and do not necessarily like one another, they work together to investigate the Night Owl Cafe murder case despite its having already been officially solved. The individual investigative talents of each man and the leads each follows result in the discovery of police corruption going right up to their captain. More importantly, through the course of the investigation, each man learns something about the others as well as about himself. Ed discovers that although the truth is valuable, justice requires a bending of the rules; Jack learns that pursuing the truth is a reward in itself; and Bud learns that he can use his brains as well as his brawn. Because Australian actors Pearce and Crowe were at this point in their careers unknown to American audiences, they brought with them no set associations to their characters. In fact, as the film's director Curtis Hanson indicates in the Regency Enterprises' *Media Release* for the film, this was the very reason the two actors were chosen to play the detectives:

> I wanted the audience to accept Bud and Exley at face value. Then, as the story goes along, they begin to wonder if their first impressions were accurate or not. Therefore, it's an advantage that Russell and Guy are somewhat new faces; the audience doesn't make assumptions on the basis of roles they've played before. (5)

The film is very sophisticated in evoking the tone and time of *film noir*, not merely for the sake of making the film *noir*-like, but in order to expose the truth behind the façade of Hollywood's promotion of the American Dream and the paradise of California. It explores issues like police corruption on a large scale, which was not necessarily acknowledged in the police procedural films of the 1940s and 1950s. Although the film is established as an exposé of 1950s society, it is fuelled by contemporary attitudes and social fears. Police corruption and organized drug rackets are social fears of present-day society, and rather than actually exposing crimes of the past, the film instead tries to allay our fears of the present. The film can address and resolve these issues by attributing them to a past when three men could uncover and disband such a crime ring, rather than attempting to acknowledge these issues head-on as a problem of contemporary society.

But the film does present contemporary notions of masculinity. Bud and Jack represent old-fashioned types of masculinity that may seem heroic by 1950s standards but seem outdated by contemporary ones. Jack is a corrupt cop himself (he is on the take) with little sense of compassion or duty. Bud is a tough-guy cop, brought in on a job when muscle is needed, and discovers that he may be more like his abusive father than he ever realized when he strikes his girlfriend. By the end of the film, the old-fashioned types are killed off—like Jack, the jaded cop—or sent away broken men—like Bud, the muscle cop. Only Ed, the new, smarter detective, survives and continues the fight against injustice. But Ed is no longer a wet-behind-the-ears innocent; he is a good detective but he has also learned to be a successful politician who can "play the game." Rather than sticking to his ideals about exposing political corruption, he agrees to help the cover-up of the incident in exchange for a promotion and a Medal of Honor. Thus, the film suggests that the old-fashioned types of tough-guy heroes cannot but fail in a world of corruption where only the new-thinking detective can succeed, but also that law enforcement is no place for high ideals.

L.A. Confidential picks up where *Touch of Evil* (Welles 1958) and *Chinatown* (Polanski 1974) left off in addressing the issue of corruption in the higher echelons of *noir* society, including that of law enforcement. *L.A. Confidential* rewrites the history of the society that the other two films explored and offers a darker image of the pervasiveness of evil in American society. Nevertheless, unlike the two earlier films, *L.A. Confidential* promises that there is a smart cop who can discover the truth and bring to justice some of the corrupt individuals. He is successful because he plays by the rules that previously tied the hands of the police officer—most notably in the vigilante film and the cop action film. The contemporary detective film, unlike the pessimistic *noir* film with its dark image of 1940s and 1950s America, offers an optimistic image of American society. Crime may be pervasive and violent, but society has a weapon with which to fight back—the thinking detective.

"OTHER" KINDS OF DETECTIVES

With knowledge as the key to the solution of crime rather than firepower and muscularity, and with the hero's body no longer required to work through masculine crisis, characters other than the white action hero have come to fulfill the role of the detective-hero, including women and black men who until recently were thrust to the margins of the detective film. The detective film of the golden age had a few female detectives, such as Nancy Drew, Hildegard Withers, and Kitty O'Day, but the female detective was distinctly absent from the detective genre from the 1950s to the 1980s. In the 1980s the female detective returned to television with Jessica Fletcher (*Murder, She Wrote* [1984–96]) and Jennifer Hart (*Hart to Hart* [1979–84]) and to the big screen in occasional appearances and then most often as a lawyer. But since Jodie Foster played Clarice Starling, an FBI agent-in-training, in *The Silence of the Lambs*, the female detective has become more prevalent; two of 2002's big releases starred women as detectives: Sandra Bullock in *Murder by Numbers* and Ashley Judd in *High Crimes* (Franklin 2002). The black detective found exposure in the late 1960s in *In the Heat of the Night* (Jewison 1967), in the 1970s with Blaxploitation heroes like John Shaft, and in the 1980s with Eddie Murphy's comedic Beverly Hills cop. In the 1990s, Wesley Snipes and Will Smith also played the action hero. But in recent years Samuel L. Jackson, Morgan Freeman, and Denzel Washington have come to portray the thinking detective with greater frequency (both the female and the black detective will be discussed in the subsequent chapters).

Just as the trend of the criminalist has opened up the detective's role to women and black men, so too has the emphasis on brains over brawn encouraged the appearance of the detective with a physical disability. Hollywood's representation of disability is not unlike its representation of race and homosexuality: it is getting better but leaves much to be desired.[7] In the detective genre, the association of disability with villainy is common, especially because mental illness is often identified as the cause of a killer's driving impulse. But in recent years, just as positive images of disability are more prevalent in mainstream culture in general, so too has disability come to the fore in the detective genre. In Thom Racina's novel *Secret Weekend* (1999), it is the wheelchair-bound Dean who comes to the rescue and wins the heart of the attractive and successful heroine. In the TV movie *Closer and Closer* (Gerber 1996), a woman (Kim Delaney), disabled by her last brush with a serial killer, becomes the target of another. Despite being wheelchair-bound she successfully confronts and defeats the killer, who is also wheelchair-bound. TV crime shows like *Second Sight* (1999–2000), *Sue Thomas: F.B.Eye* (2002–), *CSI: Crime Scene Investigation*, and *Blind Justice* (2005) also showcase disabled heroes. Ross Tanner (Clive Owen) of *Second Sight* is losing his sight and may go blind; Sue Thomas (Deanne Bray) is deaf; in one season Gil Grissom (William Petersen) of *CSI* was losing his hearing; and Jim Dunbar is, as the title *Blind Justice* suggests, blinded in the line of duty. Each show explores the impact of its hero's disability on his/her capabilities as a crime scene investigator. But *Sue Thomas* highlights the unique skill the hero's disability gives her as a surveillance expert who can read lips. There have been a few notable detectives with disabilities in the past, including Spencer Tracy as the one-armed sleuth in *Bad Day at Black Rock* (Sturges 1955) and Raymond Burr as the wheelchair-bound Robert Ironside in television's *Ironside* (1967–75).[8] But the contemporary trend in the detective film seems to be presenting them in greater numbers. On the big screen it is author Jeffrey Deaver's Lincoln Rhyme that has been the most notable exploration of disability in the detective genre, with Denzel Washington portraying the quadriplegic hero in *The Bone Collector*. It is, however, worth noting that in the case of *Sue Thomas* the protagonist is played by a deaf actor, whereas Washington is an able-bodied actor playing a disabled man. Actor Christopher Reeve, who became a quadriplegic after falling from a horse in the early 1990s, starred in a TV-movie remake of Hitchcock's *Rear Window* (Bleckner 1998), but he had only limited success returning to movies as a disabled actor. Because the criminalist narrative offers a specific kind of heroism defined by brains rather than physical ability, perhaps as the genre searches for new narratives and themes to remain fresh, more characters—and hopefully actors—with disabilities may appear.

Knowledge, experience, and wisdom are the weapons that the contemporary detective must possess in order to defeat the ingenious criminal, and this means that age can even be considered an asset where once it was seen as an impediment to the hero. On television, the stars who portray the detective, such as Angela Lansbury of *Murder, She Wrote*, David Jason of *A Touch of Frost* (1992–), and Dick Van Dyke of *Diagnosis Murder* (1993–2001), are senior citizens. In fact, *Diagnosis Murder* pits the action-cop son (Barry Van Dyke) against his on-screen and real-life father, the medical doctor and sleuth, who solves the case in every episode when the son fails to. And as Hollywood's prominent but aging actors begin to move past the stage of playing romantic leads and action heroes, more of them are turning to the role of the detective, including Bruce Willis, Morgan Freeman, and Clint Eastwood. Few Hollywood films deal with or explore the aging male body, but Eastwood's films not only portray him as the hero but also expose his aging body in order to play out fantasies of potency in old age.

FIGURE 16. Barry and Dick Van Dyke in *Diagnosis Murder*. Like father, like son?: In television's *Diagnosis Murder*, Dick Van Dyke, opposite his real-life son (Barry Van Dyke), plays the contemporary sleuth, Dr. Sloan, whose help his action-cop son invariably enlists to solve a case. Photo from author's collection.

FROM DIRTY JOBS TO BLOOD WORK:
CLINT EASTWOOD AS A CASE STUDY

Clint Eastwood is a Hollywood persona associated with tough American masculinity and heroism due to his starring roles in Westerns in the 1960s and 1970s. With the Sensitive Man replacing the Retributive Man by the early 1990s, it seemed that Eastwood would be out of a job. But just like Bruce Willis, Eastwood moved with the times and began to play smarter and less violent heroes and, like Schwarzenegger and Stallone, often played roles that sent up his own persona as tough vigilante. As Chris Holmlund notes, Eastwood's career has spanned several decades and has involved a shift in his persona from his days as the young vigilante (up to 1973) to middle-aged (up to 1985) to old age (1985 onwards); the last group of films present Eastwood as visibly old (*Impossible* 148). As a senior citizen, Eastwood, like Willis, has abandoned playing hard-body, action heroes and, instead, has tended to play more sensitive heroes. In the case of Eastwood, however, he has specifically chosen the role of thinking detective in several of his more recent films: *In the Line of Fire* (Petersen 1993), *Absolute Power* (Eastwood 1997), *True Crime* (Eastwood 1999), and *Blood Work* (Eastwood 2002). Eastwood had played the detective-hero before the 1990s as "Dirty" Harry from 1973 to 1988. His persona had been firmly aligned with vengeful, violent, tough, American heroes, but as he has aged audiences have accepted him as more mellow, re-strained, and fragile. This interconnecting set of conflicting associations allowed Eastwood to reinvent himself as a hero that could be flawed and vulnerable due to his age but also successful and, therefore, in keeping with more current conceptions of masculinity and heroism. Although some of Eastwood's earlier detective roles saw him in pursuit of a serial killer—including *Dirty Harry*—the focus of the narratives and the skills required for him to bring the killers to justice have changed.

In *Dirty Harry*, Harry is on the trail of a serial killer. He is not, however, a detective renowned for intellectual capabilities but rather for doing the dirty jobs that no one else will do. He has a reputation for being tough, and all his partners have been killed on the job with him. His newest partner is a young man fresh out of college with a degree in sociology. "Don't let your degree get you killed," Harry warns him. Harry does not have a degree; instead he knows his job from his years on the force. Although it takes knowledge of the criminal mind to track down the serial killer—a sniper who shoots innocent victims from rooftops—Harry knows that what is needed to stop him is a gun. Harry captures the sniper, Scorpio, but the killer is released when it is discovered that the evidence gathered by Harry to convict him was seized without a warrant. The bureaucracy of law enforcement is portrayed in the film as tying the hands of police when it comes to violent crime. When Harry asks Scorpio where the girl is that he has kidnapped and threatened to kill, Scorpio replies, "I have rights. I want a lawyer." If the police follow procedure, the killer would remain on the loose. But Harry stalks Scorpio on his own time (therefore not technically disobeying orders) and eventually kills him when he threatens the lives of a schoolbus full of children. His job is done, but he is disgusted with the justice system that he is a part of and tosses his badge away. Similarly, in *The Dead Pool* (VanHorn 1988), in the 1980s Harry blows away an impossible number of people with his big gun and the serial killer with a massive harpoon gun. This lone vigilante that exacts justice with a bullet from his .44 Magnum revolver is a different kind of manhunter from the criminalist detective of the 1990s.

In *In the Line of Fire* Eastwood plays Secret Service agent Frank Horrigan, who discovers that a killer has set his sights on assassinating the president of the United States. The killer (John Malkovich), who calls himself "Booth" after Abe Lincoln's assassin, identifies with Frank as both were trained to kill by their government: Frank as a Secret Service agent and Booth as a CIA "wet boy" (an assassin). As Booth says to Frank, "There's no cause left worth fighting for, Frank. All we have is the game. I'm on offence; you're on defence." Booth is presented as a monster who stalks and kills his prey with no remorse, but in some ways he is sympathetic—trained by the government to kill and then declared disposable when his usefulness is deemed as over. As he tells Frank during one of their many phone exchanges, "I don't even remember who I was before they sunk their claws into me." He may be a kind of killing machine but he is also incredibly clever, using disguises, aliases, and technology to avoid detection, and we are shown the intricate and involved planning it takes to get into a position where he can easily assassinate the president. But in Frank he has met his match, which is what he desires: an adversary worthy of him. This overidentification with Frank makes the game exciting and challenging for Booth, but it repulses Frank—he does not want to recognize the similarities between himself and the killer.

In *Absolute Power*, Eastwood plays a successful cat burglar who witnesses a crime and must bring the true killer to justice in order to save his own neck. In *True Crime*, Eastwood plays a reporter who investigates the case of an alleged murderer on death row and produces evidence at the eleventh hour to stop the man's execution. Both of these roles have East-wood playing detectives that need to unravel a mystery in order to see justice done. But in *Blood Work*, Eastwood plays Terry McCaleb, a former FBI profiler—a criminalist on the trail of a serial killer. Terry was forced to retire when he had a heart attack while chasing the "Code Killer," but when he discovers that the woman whose heart was used for his transplant was murdered, Terry comes out of retirement to track down her killer. What he discovers is that she, as well as another man, were killed because their blood type matched Terry's and their heart could be donated to him. The "Code Killer" wanted his adversary back in business, so he killed in order that Terry might live. More shocking than this is the revelation that Terry's neighbor and assistant, Buddy (Jeff Daniels), is the killer. Buddy tries to convince Terry of their connection: they are the battle of good and evil, Cain and Abel, or Kennedy and Oswald. "We were meant to be," he proclaims. In their final showdown, Buddy pleads with Terry that he needs him. Terry replies, "I don't need you at all."

Much is made of Eastwood's age in each of these films and the fact that he is no longer an action hero—Eastwood was seventy-two years old when *Blood Work* was released. When Frank asks for assignment to the president's detail in *In the Line of Fire*, he huffs and puffs, sweats, and struggles to keep up with the president's car. But while his age may be a deficiency in this aspect of his duty, it is an asset when it comes to identifying Booth and predicting his game plan because he has many years of experience on the job. Also, his age does not stop him from preventing the assassination and dispatching of the would-be assassin, nor from winning the affection of the attractive young female agent (played by Rene Russo). Similarly, in *Blood Work*, attention is continuously drawn to the frailty of Terry's body and the massive scar down the center of his chest from the heart transplant operation. But his health does not stop him from successfully cracking the case, shooting the killer, or from winning the heart of his heart donor's sister, the much younger Graciella (Wanda De Jesus).

Rather than a reliance on firepower to battle evil, Eastwood's heroes of the last decade have other skills to track and dispose of the bad guys. Detective Arrango (Paul Rodriguez) in *Blood Work* argues that a criminal with the "right ratio of balls to brains" will pull the trigger, and perhaps the vigilante cop heroes of the 1970s and the cop action heroes of the 1980s possessed this ratio. While "Dirty" Harry might be indistinguishable from the scum he seeks, the thinking detective of the last decade can then be seen as having the inverse ratio—with the emphasis on brains over balls. In

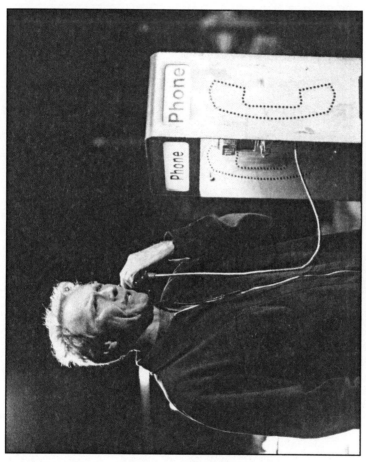

FIGURE 17. Clint Eastwood in *Blood Work*. Getting better with age: In *Blood Work* (2002), Terry (Clint Eastwood) uses his brain rather than a .44 Magnum to stop a serial killer. It is his body's new vulnerability as visibly older that has enabled Eastwood to make the shift from action hero to criminalist. Photo from author's collection.

Dirty Harry, Eastwood's hero is successful because of his .44 Magnum, his switchblade, and the fact that he's used to doing the dirty work; on the other hand, in *In the Line of Fire*, Frank is successful because he "knows things about people"—he's a profiler and understands human nature; in *True Crime*, it is Everett's "nose" that, when unimpeded by drink, will always lead him to the truth; and in *Blood Work*, it is Terry's being "connected" to the killer, the victim, and the scene that helps him solve the case. In these films, as well as his action-adventure role in *Space Cowboys* (Eastwood 2000), Eastwood offers fantasies of old age in which men are presented as initially flawed and failing but eventually valued, praised, and sexually attractive to younger women. Although Scott Feschuk of *The National Post* describes *Space Cowboys* as a film that targets the "Queen Mum's demographic" (B3), Eastwood's detective films offer a broader appeal. The detective film can star an aging hero because he "fits the profile"—smart, educated, and experienced—and the focus on the "whodunnit" mystery replaces the need for the hero to perform physical feats of heroism, although Eastwood invariably does prove his virility through some kind of physical showdown.

BACKLASH?

The 1980s were dominated by a masculine backlash in crime films, whether the erotic thriller with a male hero as the victim of the lethal *femme fatale* or the cop action film with the hero who had eyes only for his male buddy and pushed women to the margins as damsels to be distressed. The criminalist narrative represents a shift toward a positive, more realistic, secure male hero that need not fear women—only the mastermind criminal with whom he must match wits. But the representation of women in the criminalist narrative with a serial killer can be regarded as just another mutation of masculine backlash—only this time it is not the hero with whom the backlash is associated. The male criminalist-hero does not fear women; in fact, he most often takes one as a partner. But the serial killer almost always is male and his victims almost always female. Women appear in the genre frequently as the criminalist's assistant or sometimes as the central hero herself, but she is often presented as a previous or potential victim of male violence. The female criminalist is more prolific on television, but then again the serial killer is notably absent from TV and the criminalist tends to investigate isolated murders. In a two-part episode of *Crossing Jordan* in which Jordan (Jill Hennessey) helps hunt a serial killer, she becomes one of his victims, is buried alive, and is saved at the last minute. When the serial killer's victims are male, they are often gay—for example, in *Copycat*—or associated with homosexuality—for example, in *Sea of Love*. Thus, masculinity transfers its fears of failure onto the others who represent the opposite of the "ideal": women and gay men.

Michael Douglas embodied the downward spiral of the white, middle-class male "losing ground," playing a man who was the victim of a female predator in *Fatal Attraction* (Lyne 1987) and a man who is the predator in *Falling Down*. He thus foreshadowed the shift from male victims to serial killers and from women as empowered to women as victims of predatory men. Douglas should have portrayed the serial killer in the last decade as the male victims of *Fatal Attraction* and *Disclosure* (Levinson 1994) are the predecessors of Hannibal Lecter and Jasper 'Buddy' Noone. In the serial killer narrative, women—the major threat to dominant masculinity—are kidnapped, tortured, raped, mutilated, and killed in a spectacularly gruesome manner. Their deaths represent the extreme of violence—excessive, grotesque, and, in some ways, inconceivable. Why would anyone commit these atrocities? Because as society's seeming desertion of masculinity increases, so too does the reaction escalate. Whereas in the 1980s the *noir*-hero's retaliation against feminist empowerment was sanctioned, in the 1990s and 2000s that retaliation must be disguised, codified, and masked as it is now politically incorrect. The vengeful impulse was transposed from the hero to the villain, leaving heroism and villainy uncomplicated opposites. And with the violence against women aligned with villainy, it could increase in quantity—i.e., become serial—and in intensity—i.e., become more brutal and gruesome. Thus, while the contemporary criminalist narrative offers stable male heroes, it has simply—and most likely only temporarily—repressed the fears and anxieties of masculinity. So perhaps the greatest danger of overidentification with the serial killer for the criminalist is that the serial killer is actually carrying out the criminalist's own secret, and similar, desires.

CHAPTER SEVEN

Investigating the "Other": Race and the Detective

The first detective film with a black protagonist was R. W. Phillips's 1918 film *A Black Sherlock Holmes* (Langman and Finn, *Silent* xv). Although the black detective may have appeared early in the history of the detective genre, this single film is an anomaly, and the black detective as a prevalent character would not emerge for another fifty years, when Sidney Poitier played Mr. Tibbs in *In the Heat of the Night* (Jewison 1967), and it was not a regular occurrence until the 1990s. The detective film is concerned with the hero triumphing over injustice and evil, but like the majority of mainstream American film, it has been predominantly concerned with the triumph of a hero firmly distinguished as white. "Otherness" in the form of racial and ethnic difference did exist in the detective genre before the 1990s, but usually in the form of the villain or the white detective's sidekick and, until recently, was rarely given center stage.[1]

As discussed in relation to the cop action film of the 1980s, mainstream cinema is predominantly concerned with white experience; nevertheless, that experience is not identified as belonging to a specific race, class, or culture and instead masquerades as the norm—as American society as a whole. The "other"—the homosexual, the foreigner, and the nonwhite—is most often cast in the role of the villain in popular film to offer an opposition to the heroism and Americanness of the protagonist.

Nevertheless, as I have demonstrated in regard to the Asian and Anglicized detective, "otherness" can also be used to construct different notions of heroism—ones that combine traditional notions of American action and toughness with notions of foreign intellectualism and potential transgression. Similarly, the contemporary African-American detective is marked as "other" in the white mainstream society within the detective film, and his otherness can function like that of the Asian detective to allow him an objectivity in regard to the society from which he is excluded but which he attempts to help. The notion of the outsider stems once again from the frontier tradition and the film Western, in which the hero enters the social space at the beginning of the film to resolve a conflict and then leaves at the end, remaining an outsider to the community he has assisted. So too does the black detective enter a predominantly white social space in which a white perpetrator kills white victims. In fact, it is often his status as an outsider, his objectivity, and his specialized knowledge that give him an insight into the mystery of the identity of the killer.

Even though American culture would like to present itself as a melting pot of ethnic and racial difference, contemporary popular American film still gives little screen consideration to the nonwhite and/or the non-American experience and, even when it does, the representations are often problematic.[2] Manthia Diawara states that white people occupy the center in mainstream film and that blacks only exist in relation to whites: "Thus space is related to power and powerlessness, in so far as those who occupy the center of the screen are usually more powerful than those situated in the background or completely absent from the screen" ("American" 11). Nonwhite individuals, when absent from the screen, are then absent from the image of America constructed by Hollywood, and when present are less powerful and less "virtuous" than the white individuals occupying the center. Lola Young argues that in mainstream cinema race is used in a much more conscious way by Hollywood to construct an "otherness" to white in a set of binary oppositions. Black is then evil and alien; white is good, pure, and normal (39). Often positive images of racial "otherness" in mainstream cinema tend to be merely token representations as opposed to representations that truly address the specificity of the black experience. As David Molden states:

> African Americans are tired of the same types of films depicting us in a negative lifestyle. This is such a small picture of Black America.

The Black middle and upper classes—educated and employed—have grown by leaps and bounds. [. . .] Furthermore, all other ethnic groups would be likely to support our work if we stopped always presenting African Americans as inept, ghetto-ridden, down-trodden and oppressed, and instead began to present a more accurate picture of the total African-American community. (112)

Many commentators and even individuals from within Hollywood have criticized Hollywood for being racist in its representation of African Americans and other ethnic groups. Willis Edwards, president of the Beverly Hills/Hollywood branch of the NAACP—a chapter that monitors race relations in the film industry—and Stan Robertson, a consultant to Columbia Pictures, believe that Hollywood is racist. "It's all about racism," he says. "Most movies about Blacks are done by Whites. There are no Blacks in decision-making positions" (qtd. in Collier 41). Black stars in Hollywood are also discontented with the industry's treatment of African Americans. Morgan Freeman says that "Hollywood racism" has led to a

lack of opportunities for African Americans, even well-educated ones. Women as well as men don't receive opportunities to direct, write or produce films. I have been trying to put some pressure on the studios to hire more blacks and people of color. (qtd. in Breathwaite 38)

While there has been a lack of opportunity for African Americans to attain positions of influence and power in terms of the production of films, there has been a proliferation of African-American characters in mainstream film since the mid-1990s, and the Academy Awards of 2002 acknowledged the contribution of African-American stars to the industry with the award for Best Actress going to Halle Berry and Best Actor to Denzel Washington, as well as a lifetime achievement award to Sidney Poitier. The African-American detective has become a popular and prolific figure in contemporary film, beginning with Eddie Murphy in *Beverly Hills Cop* (Brest 1984) in the 1980s and continuing with Morgan Freeman in *Seven* (Fincher 1995), *Kiss the Girls* (Fleder 1997), and *Along Came a Spider* (Tamahori 2001); Denzel Washington in *The Pelican Brief* (Pakula 1993), *Devil in a Blue Dress* (Franklin 1995), and *The Bone Collector* (Noyce 1999); Wesley Snipes in *Passenger 57* (Hooks 1992) and *Murder at 1600* (Little 1997); Sidney Poitier in *The Jackal* (Caton-Jones 1997); and Samuel L. Jackson in *Die Hard with a Vengeance* (McTiernan 1993), *The Negotiator*

FIGURE 18. Morgan Freeman in *Seven*. Bringing evil to light: In *Seven* (1995), it is Detective Somerset (Morgan Freeman) who is the moral center of the film and who, using his intelligence, knowledge, and wits, solves the mystery and remains unaffected by the villain—unlike his white partner. Photo from author's collection.

(Gray 1998), and *Shaft* (Singleton 2000). Black characters and actors are appearing with increasing frequency in contemporary film, especially in the detective genre, and while this may be regarded as a positive step with the actual presence of African Americans on the screen, those images are offered only when they can be contained and regulated by specific cinematic codes of representation. In this chapter, I will explore how the criminalist narrative offers space for the expression and containment of black masculinity because of the very nature of the detective film and that this is most likely the reason for the proliferation of the Hollywood black detective in the last decade. The contemporary detective film, through its code of isolating the hero, can offer a representation of black experience that is "nonthreatening" (in Hollywood's terms) to mainstream (white) audiences with the presence of black stars on screen but without an address of race or ethnicity as a central issue.

REPRESENTING BLACK EXPERIENCE

The representation of the black experience in mainstream cinema has been problematic and widely criticized as racist and stereotypical.[3] Historically, Hollywood has tended to negatively portray ethnic and racial minorities as infantilized, presenting them as primitive and as children trapped in adult bodies; as animalized, as apes, savages, and associated with nature while white is associated with civilization; as sexualized, as lusty and libidinous; and as debased, being portrayed as immoral and evil (Kaplan, *Looking* 80). Often minorities have also been portrayed as desexualized—asexual and/or sexually passive. Stuart Hall argues that racism in dominant culture is constructed through a play between identity and difference, and this play is powered by the conception of blacks as of an inferior race, yet, at the same time, by an inexpressible envy: "Just as masculinity always constructs femininity as double—simultaneously Madonna and Whore—so racism constructs the black subject: noble savage and violent avenger" (167).

Hollywood seems to be comfortable offering black male protagonists only when their sexuality can be contained. As Aldore Collier of *Ebony Magazine* argues:

> For Black actors, though, romance has been, for the most part, an unrequited experience. [. . .] For decades, there was no intimacy or

passion for Black actors on screen. All emotion was implied or simply ignored. Screen legends such as Lena Horne, Dorothy Dandridge and Sidney Poitier either had no romantic partners or their on-screen relationships with the opposite sex were in most cases devoid of intimacy. (41)

Why must the sexuality of black characters, especially black masculinity, be contained in mainstream cinema, when other kinds of cinema—most notably the American black independent cinema—are able to express and explore the sexuality of the black individual? For Hollywood, black masculinity has traditionally represented a threat to mainstream, white, American culture with its potential to be hypersexual—namely, being attracted to and attractive to white women. Thus, despite the proliferation of interracial marriages and relationships within American culture, Hollywood cinema seems to regard it as necessary to *contain* the threat of black sexuality for fear of offending white mainstream audiences. As Ed Guerrero argues, mainstream cinema suppresses any threat that black masculinity might seem to imply by a variety of "strategies of containment"—including the denial of black romance and sexuality ("Black" 237–38).[4]

AN INTEGRATIONIST HERO—THE 1960s

The first black actor to rival white stars in terms of star status—popularity with white and black audiences on a mass scale—was Sidney Poitier. Poitier was the hero for 1960s America and its integrationist policy regarding blacks. As an actor and also as the characters he portrayed, Poitier was educated, intelligent, spoke "proper" English (as opposed to dialect), dressed conservatively, and had good manners. According to Donald Bogle, Poitier was the black man who met all the standards of white audiences and was also accepted by black audiences as a paragon of black middle-class morals and virtues (175–76). The masculinity that Poitier's characters represented was a step forward from the stereotypes in Hollywood film that had preceded them, but they were always tame men, never impulsive, never a threat to the system, and distinctly asexual. Poitier presented an image of black masculinity that fulfilled Hollywood's criteria, but that criteria belonged to the white mainstream and was not representative of African-American culture.

In the Heat of the Night (Jewison 1967) introduced the first notable black detective-hero, Virgil Tibbs, played by Poitier. The film is a biracial buddy film teaming Poitier's character with a white police chief, Gillespie (Rob Steiger), and is one of the few biracial buddy films that makes race one of the main issues of the narrative. On his arrival in Gillespie's small Southern town, Tibbs, because he is black, is immediately suspected of killing Colbert, a wealthy white businessman. The irony is that the victim was developing opportunities for the oppressed black population of the town with a new factory. Race is merely the most obvious manifestation of the "otherness" in the film as Tibbs represents many kinds of "otherness" to the people of Sparta. Tibbs is not just black but middle class, well educated, well dressed, well spoken, makes more money doing the same job as the local police, and is better at that job than they are. Like the train that brings him into Sparta at the beginning of the film, Tibbs is associated with the modern and urban North. Sparta, on the other hand, is associated with lawlessness and corruption, and the townspeople are portrayed as half-witted and animalistic, following their instincts rather than using any intelligence. The threat Tibbs offers is less based on his being black (for there are other black characters in the film) than on his being the confirmation that the urban North and the civilization it represents are beginning to intrude upon the ways of the rural South.

The film offers an expression of black experience by foregrounding Tibbs as the detective-hero and the character who propels the narrative. Several times the film makes obvious its bias in favor of Tibbs and the Northern attitudes he represents by aligning the camera with his perspective. For example, when Tibbs is accosted by Sam, a local cop, at the beginning of the film, he is frisked and referred to by the derogatory appellation of "boy." While Sam appears to be in control of the situation, the camera offers the viewer a close-up of Tibbs's expression of intelligent annoyance and resolve to indulge Sam's impertinence. The film aligns the viewer with Tibbs's perspective, but this positioning is not motivated by questions of race; it is an alignment with all the other values that Tibbs represents as a middle-class, Northern, urban professional, and the positive representation of his black masculinity then, in many ways, becomes a token one. The film does not address the problems of racism in America as a whole, only in the South where racism has historically always been a problem. Although Tibbs is black and an acclaimed member of his police force, he is devoid of any black community. He is not married, has no children, probably works in a predominantly white police department, and has little connection with the black community of Sparta. He does not identify with the poor blacks of Sparta who pick cotton in the fields or even with the black family that offers him a place to stay while he is in town. But when faced with infiltrating the black community to uncover vital information, Tibbs is able to adopt the local dialect to gain the trust of the black community. The film offers a clear message that "otherness" is not uniform—that being black can embody different meanings. By having to assume a different type of black identity to infiltrate the black community of Sparta, Tibbs is recognized as embodying a different type of black culture.

In fact, Tibbs identifies most closely not with the black community but with Gillespie, a policeman with above-average intelligence and a sense of justice. Gillespie rightly accuses Tibbs also of being prejudiced. "You're just like the rest of us," Gillespie exclaims when Tibbs wants to bring down the local oppressive landowner, Mr. Endicott, because he is a racist. Ultimately the film is about the developing relationship between the two detective-figures—one white and one black, one from the North and one from the South—and it is their resulting friendship and admiration of one another that give the film closure. Because their relationship becomes the central focus of the film, there is a displacement of emphasis on racism as an issue. Although the film only tackles racism in a very contained way by relegating it to a problem that exists in the South, it seems quite progressive even by today's standards because it *does* address race as an issue.

By the end of the 1960s several of the major film companies had hired black publicists or public relations firms in an attempt to capitalize on black audiences, and, as a result, black character actors appeared with more frequency and a few studios promoted black stars, though usually as a more militant kind of black masculinity, such as Calvin Lockhart, Raymond St. Jacques, and Jim Brown (Walker 355). The roles that these black stars played differed from those of Poitier's by bringing with them an emphasis on toughness and sexuality. By the 1970s, Poitier's black gentleman was replaced by a headstrong militant figure who did not just ask for his civil rights, but demanded them, and also by the hypersexual and very nonwhite figure of the "Superspade" embodied by Blaxploitation-heroes like Shaft in Parks's 1971 film of the same name (Bogle 195). This shift from Poitier's black gentleman to a militant and hypersexual masculinity mirrored the shift in African-American culture from an integrationist position to that of a separatist.

A SEPARATIST HERO—THE 1970s

"Who's the black private dick that's a sex machine with all the chicks?"
"Shaft!"

"Damn right! "Who's the man that'll risk his neck for his brother man?"
"Shaft!"

"Can you diggit? Who's the cat that won't cop out when there's danger all about?"
"Shaft!"
—Isaac Hayes, from the theme song "Shaft"

In opposition to *In the Heat of the Night*'s integrationist hero, the Blaxploitation films of the 1970s centered on separatist heroes. Yvonne Tasker argues that Blaxploitation films were an aggressive articulation of black masculinity working through the exaggeration of existing stereotypes and constructing the black hero as a powerful figure but also a hypersexual one (37). The hero of the Blaxploitation film was the Superspade, a term first applied to Poitier, to evoke the image of Humphrey Bogart's Sam Spade but a Spade that was "[i]ndestructable, flippant, romantic, and triumphant in Hollywood's best private-eye tradition" (Leab 4).[5] The Superspade of the 1970s represented a tough, successful, and sexual masculinity, but he was still a caricature. Blaxploitation films have been criticized for effectively substituting one black stereotype for another, creating a "stud" to avoid reproducing the passive, asexual figure. But Blaxploitation films were not concerned with portraying a realistic image of black experience but with exploring black representation to attract white and black audiences alike, and that included the exploitation of stereotyped images of black masculinity in order to debunk them. The Blaxploitation hero may have been hypersexualized but he was not shown as such in a negative way; in fact, it was almost comical how women—white and black—were powerlessly attracted to him.

In *Shaft* (Parks 1971) Richard Roundtree's detective-hero offers a shift in the representation of black masculinity because he is very much constructed in the tradition of white American heroes. In fact, MGM publicists billed Shaft as the new James Bond, being able to bounce back after being shot and irresistible to women—in other words, a cartoon-like hero (Leab 251). Like the hardboiled detective, he is the tough guy who works alone, knows the streets, is successful with women, and uses violence when necessary. But unlike the hardboiled detective, he rules the mean streets rather than being dominated by them; he is able to maintain a relationship with a woman, Ellie, who loves him (despite his having sex with other women); and he has the respect and understanding of at least some members of the police force, most notably Vic Androzzi. Shaft offers an updated version of the *noir*-detective for the 1970s, representing black masculinity at the center of the narrative and a hero whose actions drive the narrative forward. He also represents a shift from the internally divided hero, who disguised his trauma beneath a mask of tough masculinity, to a transparent hero who is as tough as he seems. Shaft stands up to the police, not divulging any information to them despite their threats to suspend his detective's licence; he stands up to Bumpy, the gang boss, calling him on his private phone line and demanding $20,000 for the services Bumpy wishes to be performed; and he stands up to the Mafia, toying with them while they wait for him to arrive home and then calling the police to come and arrest them. Not only is Shaft tough, but he is cool—well-dressed, wise-cracking, and successful with women. He gets the job done, always outwitting the villains and the cops and coming out on top.

Unlike the integrationist heroes that Poitier portrayed in the 1960s, Roundtree's Shaft represents the shift to a separatist hero. Shaft does not work with the police and, instead, does the job they are incapable of doing as an independent private detective. It is his knowledge and connections on the street that makes him successful where the police fail. They are white and part of mainstream culture and, therefore, do not respect the reality of life in Harlem or understand the rules of the street. The police represent white mainstream culture in the film and, by not fearing the police or wishing to gain their approval, Shaft represents a separatist standpoint. Although he is not portrayed as an active supporter of the Black Power movement, he did a lot of "street-time" with those who were. Shaft is a tough, sexualized, and empowered black man that maintains his ties to the black community and rejects opportunities to embrace ties to the mainstream. He represents black masculinity that is not passive or impotent and is an expression of black experience at the center of a Hollywood film narrative. This representation of black masculinity all but disappeared by the late 1970s and, other than with Eddie Murphy in the 1980s, failed to reemerge until the mid-1990s. With the rise of several black actors to star status in Hollywood in the 1990s, particularly Denzel Washington, Samuel L. Jackson, and Morgan Freeman, mainstream cinema began to explore black masculinity once again, including the resurrection of Shaft.

In the remake of *Shaft* (Singleton 2000), Samuel L. Jackson takes up the role of the Superspade's nephew, with the original Shaft, Richard Roundtree, appearing briefly as his uncle. In the 1970s Shaft was a lone law fighter who was positioned between the black community and the police: he was on the side of the law but also a step away from it with his allegiance to the black community, and it was his knowledge of that community that made him a more effective force than the police. Roundtree's Shaft was a hero of the 1970s who represented a desire for black power without necessarily having to be integrated into the dominant culture at the expense of his own culture. But the fight for civil rights is long over by the time Shaft's nephew (Jackson) appears on the scene, and race is not a central issue in the 2000 film despite the few token racist comments being thrown at the hero. The film initiates an address of race as an issue with the demonizing of the racist villain, who is white and hates blacks, but subsequently reinscribes the issue of race along stereotyped lines as villainy is then relocated to the Hispanic gang and to the Italian narcotics officer (Dan Hedaya). Yet the film is less about race than it is about bringing the very cool and very tough Shaft back to the screen to stride along in time to Isaac Hayes's famous theme song. Even Shaft's trademark 1970s brown leather jacket is given a contemporary twist as Jackson sports a handful of designer Armani leather coats. Despite being a vigilante hero (he throws in his badge in order to pursue the case), Jackson's Shaft enlists the help of his police colleagues to catch the villain whereas his uncle would have worked alone. And despite being descended from the hypersexual Blaxploitation heroes of the 1970s, Jackson's Shaft sees little sexual action. The updated version of *Shaft* focuses on Jackson as a vengeful vigilante. The original film seems a more potent representation of black masculinity as Roundtree's Shaft was an intelligent, sexual, and funky black hero in a time when such portrayals in Hollywood film were uncommon.

WITH A WHITE HERO—THE 1980s

Mainstream detective cinema of the 1980s and 1990s was not completely void of black detectives, but most of them were merely the sidekicks to a central white hero. The biracial buddy film emerged in Hollywood films with the teaming of Poitier with white stars in *The Defiant Ones* (Kramer 1958) and *In the Heat of the Night*. As I have already discussed in relation to the cop action film *Lethal Weapon* (Donner 1987), it is the black man who is civilized and the white man who is "savage" in the biracial buddy film of the 1980s. Why does Hollywood feel the need to pair the black character up with a white one? As Guerrero notes, there is a reluctance in mainstream cinema to place a black star in a film without a white costar and/or a white context to allow a point of identification for the white spectator ("Black" 239). If the representation of black masculinity on the screen is so problematic, then why does Hollywood attempt it all? It comes down to maximizing box-office profits. A large part of the American population is nonwhite, and a significant portion of that nonwhite population is African American. For the film industry the biracial buddy movie attracts the broadest audience by appealing to white and black audiences. The biracial buddy film is a proven winning formula for meeting the ideological needs of its audience, appealing to the black audience by offering black subjectivity and to a white audience by offering a token liberalism (ibid. 240). But these films do not truly address problems of racism and black experience in American culture because they simplify the issues and resolve them within the narrative, effectively presenting audiences with an escapist fantasy.

A NEW EQUALITY—THE 1990s

As Christopher Ames notes, the transformations of the black/white buddy relationship in popular culture—from the traditional pairing up of a civilized white man and a savage black man to the reverse in 1980s biracial buddy films—revealed a great deal about contemporary attitudes toward race and sexuality (54). Since the mid-1990s, other intriguing transformations have occurred within the subgenre of the biracial buddy film. The black man has been reframed from the position of the white man's sidekick to being the central hero with his own sidekick—often a white woman. The black hero, has also occasionally found himself reframed from being the sidekick to being the main hero, with a white man as an assistant or equal. The shift has echoed the movement of the biracial buddy film from the genre of the cop-action film to that of the criminalist detective film and the movement in Hollywood film in general to sensitive, thinking heroes. The shift in the representation of black masculinity to the center of the narrative and in the hero also demonstrates the ascendancy of many black stars in Hollywood, including Morgan Freeman and Samuel L. Jackson. In *Seven* (Fincher 1995), Morgan Freeman plays Detective Somerset, who offered audiences a new kind of hero—a black sleuth—who uses his intelligence, knowledge, and wits to solve the mystery and remain unaffected by the villain. Similarly, Samuel L. Jackson played Danny Roman in *The Negotiator* (Gray 1998), a "wrong man" story of a cop who must prove his innocence of embezzling police funds. In both cases they are paired with white buddies.

Seven begins its story following the activities of its black detective, Somerset (Freeman), not its white detective, Mills (Brad Pitt), and these initial scenes offer the audience a more intimate identification with him. In the first scene, the camera follows Somerset as he performs his daily routine that he has down to a science: methodically, he lays out the tools of the trade—his gun, holster, pen, badge, keys, and switchblade. The pen may seem like an odd element, but, as will be revealed later in the film, Somerset is a thinking detective who relies on his intellect more than his muscle or his gun. Somerset is called into a homicide investigation, where his first action is to gather information rather than physical clues. As the story unfolds, the first of Doe's victims is discovered, and Mills is sent in to work with Somerset because he will replace Somerset, who is set to retire the following week. Somerset is old and experienced and, as is obvious by the way he handles the case of John Doe's (Kevin Spacey) killings, he is a breed apart from the other detectives: he is a modern-day sleuth. Unlike his fellow officers, epitomized by Mills, who rely on street smarts and physical violence to handle a case, Somerset relies on his knowledge and insight into the criminal mind accumulated from much reading and years of experience. It is his recognition of Doe's literary allusions to Dante and his recognition of Doe's capacity for evil that help Somerset track down Doe.

Somerset is portrayed as an excellent detective and a good partner. He is also black, but his skin color is never made an issue in the film. No racist comments are ever made; no one ever suggests that he is an inferior detective because he is black; no recognition of his "otherness" occurs. Somerset lives in a predominantly white world and has no intimate connections to the black community. He also lacks any romantic interests in the story. As he explains to Mills's wife, Tracy (Gwyneth Paltrow), he was in love once but a terminated pregnancy ended their relationship and he has never been married or had children. Now facing retirement and loneliness, Somerset seems to regret his lack of intimate relationships. In fact, he chooses at the end of the film not to retire because he realizes that he has nothing to retire to: his job is his life and his identity. Somerset is good at his job and takes pride in upholding the law and in trying to make the world a better place. He sacrifices his personal happiness for that of the society in which he lives, and that makes him a hero. One could argue that he represents the service of black masculinity to aid mainstream culture in the solution of its problems, but this does not take away from the fact that Somerset is a likeable, admirable, heroic, and central figure. *Seven* is colorblind in the sense that it does not matter if Somerset is black or white because color is never an issue. As Barry Keith Grant notes,

> Many, perhaps even most, new genre movies are traditional or reactionary in terms of their representation of race and gender. Often these films merely plug in, or substitute, blacks, women, or gay characters for white male heroes but do little or nothing to challenge the sexist or racist assumptions that inform the myths by which they operate. ("Strange" 196)

That race is not an issue means that the film, rather than offering a representation of black experience, merely ignores it—and, thus, contains it. Instead, *Seven* focuses on the relationship that forms between the two detectives—one white, one black—and that is why, although the film initially places Somerset in a position at the center of the narrative, the film is ultimately a biracial buddy film rather than a film about black experience.

The Negotiator begins with Lieutenant Danny Roman (Jackson) at work, negotiating a difficult hostage situation. Following his successful negotiation, Danny is given a party to celebrate his birthday, the significance of which is to illustrate how much he is respected within his department for doing his job well and also how much he is liked by his peers. This respect of his peers rapidly dissipates when Danny is accused of killing his partner and of being responsible for the embezzlement of police funds. The fact that his fellow police officers, who have known and respected him for years, could turn against him so quickly, although this is never explicitly stated, seems to be related to the fact that he is black. To prove his innocence, Danny takes hostages, including Nebaum (J. T. Walsh) of Internal Affairs, a man who might be responsible for the embezzlement. Danny's fellow officers are brought in to handle the negotiation, and Danny is regarded as the enemy. He demands to talk to Chris Sabian (Kevin Spacey), a renowned negotiator, and the film follows Sabian's attempt to negotiate with Danny while Danny himself tries to discover the truth about the embezzlement and the murder to clear his name. Eventually, he convinces his hostages of his innocence and Sabian helps him gather the evidence he needs to prove it. The film ends with him happily reunited with his wife, his friends, and his badge.

As with Somerset, Danny's color is never explicitly made an issue. The opening credit sequence of the film shows black and white photographs of the police department. The photos show Danny, a black officer, accepted by and bonded with his fellow white police officers, not at the level of ethnicity but at that of masculinity: they are an all-male department. Danny is not shown as having connections to a black community but he does have a new bride who is also black. Her presence functions to sexualize Danny but she also fulfills the role of the cop's wife. Through her obvious fear that Danny will not escape alive from the situation he has got himself into, the audience recognizes the danger of Danny's job and his position as an accused cop killer. Traditionally, when a cop film raises the wife's fear of her husband's job as an issue, the film concludes with the cop retiring for the sake of his family. *The Negotiator*, on the other hand, concludes with his badge returned to him once his innocence is proven, suggesting that, through his misadventure, Danny has had the chance to prove his manliness to his new wife and himself.

Danny is presented as sexually potent, as successful at his profession (one dominated by white men), and as a great friend to his fellow officers. But this "positive" representation is, unfortunately, marred by the fact that Danny seems to be on the verge of cracking up due to the pressure of his job and responsibilities. His wife supports this implication when she warns him not to go out and do anything "crazy"—which is, of course, what he does. Fortunately for him his plan works out but only because of the presence, trust, and assistance of the white negotiator, Sabian. The film suggests that Danny is only happily reintegrated into the dominant white community thanks to the help of a white man who does the same job he does. The film initially seems to be about Danny as the detective-figure and the wrong man, but ultimately the film is about the two negotiators and their relationship, and so the film concludes as a biracial buddy film, with the black man sharing the center with a white man.

WITH A FEMALE SIDEKICK—
THE 1990s AND 2000s

The hypersexuality of Shaft in the 1970s represented the assumed threat that black masculinity posed to white society. This "threat" of black masculinity is contained in the biracial buddy film by replacing a romantic relationship between the hero and a woman with that between the hero and his buddy. But the 1990s saw not only the proliferation of black heroes with white male buddies but also those with white *female* buddies. So what happens to the threat of the black male's sexuality? It is similarly ignored because the criminalist detective narrative, like the classical, is centered on the investigation, and, despite the presence of a woman, the buddy relationship is still just that—one that forms between two "buddies." The threat of the black detective's sexuality can be neutralized by having him happily married to a black woman, as is Danny in *The Negotiator*. John Orr argues that Hollywood has created a "mythic black male professional, devoted father and husband within the cherished nuclear family copied from models of conservative white America," as embodied in Denzel Washington's character in Jonathan Demme's 1993 film *Philadelphia* (190). Or his sexuality can also be defused by denying the black man romantic involvement with any woman. In *The Pelican Brief* (Pakula 1993), Gray Grantham (Denzel Washington) does not get the girl—played by Julia Roberts—despite the fact that he does so in the novel.[6] And, notably, the hot interracial sex scenes of several novels are deleted in their adaptions to the big screen—including that of *Devil in a Blue Dress* (Mosley 1990), *Kiss the Girls* (Patterson 1995), *Along Came a Spider* (Patterson 1993), and *The Bone Collector* (Deaver 1997).

Like *Seven* and *The Negotiator*, the film *Kiss the Girls* (Fleder 1997) begins with its detective-hero, Alex Cross (Morgan Freeman), shown on the job. He is a forensic psychologist and "talks down" a woman, Diane, who has just shot her abusive husband and is about to kill herself. Like the other two detective-heroes, Alex is an educated, professional man and very good at his job. Like Danny and Somerset, Alex works in an almost all-white world and enjoys a very successful career according to mainstream standards. But unlike Danny and Somerset, Alex is given a black community to which he is connected beyond the environment of his work. When Alex is called in to talk down Diane, he is at a local boxing club where he coaches children, the majority of whom are black. The suggestion is that before becoming a psychologist Alex was a boxer—a skill he probably learned in the community where he grew up. Not only is he given a sense of a black community, he also has a family. It is his sister who pleads with Alex to go to North Carolina to help find her daughter, who has gone missing. But for the course of the film he is removed from his community and family, and goes off to North Carolina to do his job in a predominantly white community.

FIGURE 19. Denzel Washington and Angelina Jolie in *The Bone Collector*. Role reversal: In *The Bone Collector* (1999), it is the white female buddy (Angelina Jolie) who performs the traditional male feats of action, killing, and seduction while the disabled hero (Denzel Washington) is bedridden. Photo from author's collection.

Alex is black and goes to work in a part of the United States renowned for racist conflict; he is warned by Detectives Sikes and Ruskin that their chief, who is in charge of the investigation, will not treat him with respect. And yet despite the suggestion of racial tension, none emerges. No racially motivated comments or violence occurs and there is no suggestion that Naomi, Alex's niece, has been a victim of a racially motivated crime. In fact, Casanova, the kidnapper, purposely collects girls of different talents and different backgrounds. The film introduces many possibilities for race as an issue and then acts on none of them. In the novel, however, race is explicitly made an issue as Alex and his partner Sampson are not welcome in Durham, North Carolina. As Alex describes their arrival in the Durham Police Department:

> "Feel like we just landed on Mars," Sampson says. [. . .] "Don't like the feeling I get from the Martians. Don't like their beady little Martian eyes. Don't think I like the new South."
>
> "You think about it, we'd fit in the same anywhere," I told Sampson. "We'd get the same reception, same cold stares, at Nairobi Police Headquarters."
>
> "Maybe. [. . .] But at least they'd be black Martians. At least they'd know who John Coltrane is." (Patterson, *Kiss* 52)

In Patterson's novel, Alex meets his niece's friend—Florence Campbell, a law student. Florence is a young black woman; her cousin, Seth Taylor, is Naomi's boyfriend, and the three of them are very outspoken about racism. Naomi had taken to wearing an old sharecropper's straw hat, and Seth a hardhat with "Slave Labor" written on it, in an attempt to raise awareness about racism (Patterson, *Kiss* 112). Florence tells Alex that she feels racism has influenced the police's progress on Naomi's case: "They didn't seem to think Naomi was in any real trouble. [. . .] Because Naomi's an Afro-American woman" (ibid. 111). In one scene in the novel, Sampson and Alex are themselves victims of racial injustice. Two Durham cops, looking for the serial killer whom they know is white, pull Sampson and Alex over and then physically assault them when they try to explain that they are police detectives. As Alex explains: "Why were we suspects? Because we were a couple of black males riding on the side streets of Chapel Hill at ten o'clock in the goddamn morning" (ibid. 325). Race is repeatedly made an issue in Patterson's Cross novels, but these instances are absent in their adaptation to the screen, as are the scenes of Alex with his family and within his community.

In the films of both *Kiss the Girls* and *Along Came a Spider* (Tamahori 2001),[7] Alex is taken out of his milieu—southeast Washington, D.C.—and placed in white communities. But in both of Patterson's novels Alex is often shown at home with his family and dealing with crime in his troubled neighborhood in D.C. In both films, Alex has no wife or children and, other than entertaining the notion of a relationship with Kate in *Kiss the Girls*, he lacks romantic love interests. But in the novels Alex has a family: his wife, Maria, is dead and he lives with his grandmother and his two children, Damon and Janelle. In the novel *Along Came a Spider*, Alex has not had a relationship since Maria died but falls in love, and has a sexual relationship, with his detective partner Jezzie Flanagan; in the film, Alex does not have any romantic involvement with Jezzie (as played by Monica Potter). In the novel *Kiss the Girls*, Alex, although traumatized from the betrayal of Jezzie, finds love again with Kate. They fall in love and spend one night of sexual intimacy together; on the other hand, in the film, Alex and Kate (Ashley Judd) are mutually attracted to one another but nothing physical comes of that attraction.

Alex is presented as sexualized in Patterson's novels and both Jezzie and Kate describe Alex as looking like Muhammed Ali. As Kate thinks to herself: "He was strong, smart, funny, kind. He loved children, and was even in touch with the child in himself. He had a sculpted body, fabulous bone structure, a sensational torso, also. Yes, she had a crush on Alex Cross" (Patterson, *Kiss* 290). Not only does Alex have a lot of contact with his black community and family, but he also receives a lot of grief from them for his interest in these white women. His grandmother has always warned him not to trust white people. This sexualizing and racializing of Alex Cross in the novels makes him a very powerful representation of black masculinity, but these elements are all but eradicated in the adaptations of Patterson's novels to the screen.

Along with his sexuality, the black hero's opportunities to perform heroically are also contained. The black sidekick of the 1980s biracial buddy film was often an action-oriented man, offering his black energy to save the white hero. But one of the shifts that has occurred with the black man becoming the central hero is that he is often denied the displays of action associated with heroic masculinity. Instead, the white female buddy gets to be the body of spectacular action and the black hero gets to flex his brains rather than his brawn. The result of this relationship between body and action-oriented spectacle means that the female body becomes somewhat masculinized and, by implication, the black body somewhat feminized. In

Kiss the Girls, Kate becomes Alex's most useful detective ally and she works side by side with him to find Casanova. In many ways she is portrayed in a stereotypical role—as one of Casanova's victims and a potential love interest for Alex. But she is also presented as physically tough and an intelligent Watson to Alex's Sherlock Holmes. The black detective in a buddy film, as secondary to the white hero, had his sexuality subverted into violent action (Guerrero, "Black" 251)—leaving the white buddy to be constructed in terms of sexualized display. So what occurs when the black detective is the main hero and he is given a female buddy? Although it would be logical that the female buddy would somehow leave the black hero free to be put on sexual display, especially with the potential for her to fall in love with the hero, in fact, the opposite happens.

The female body is constructed in mainstream cinema almost always in terms of sexual display for the male gaze, but in many of the detective films of the 1990s the female body is presented less as an erotic object and more as spectacular—either in action as the female buddy or in death as the female corpse. In *Kiss the Girls*, Kate becomes the body of action. Her physical strength (for example, her prowess at kickboxing) and strength of character are what prevent her from becoming one of Casanova's more unfortunate victims whom he kills. She uses her strengths to gain not only her freedom from his dungeon, but also the ability to face him again. As such a strong and admirable character, Kate defies the traditional representation of a woman in this type of film, where women tend to be the helpless victims. There is no physical confrontation between Alex and Casanova until the final scene of the film, when Kate lies helpless on the floor and even then Alex only has to shoot the villain. On the other hand, the film indulges in several spectacular instances of Kate physically attacking Casanova or defending herself against him with her kickboxing techniques. Thus, Kate's presence as Alex's buddy frees his body from the burden, and potential threat, of being specularized and potentially sexualized, leaving Alex in much the same position as if he had been given a white male buddy after all.

In *The Bone Collector*, Denzel Washington plays Lincoln Rhyme, a police detective who is a quadriplegic due to an accident while on the job. A young beat-patrol cop, Amelia Donaghy (Angelina Jolie) discovers the body of a dead man and clues, which, when examined by Rhyme, suggest another victim will follow. Working together—Amelia doing all the "legwork" while the bedridden Rhyme uses his brain—they unravel the clues left behind by the killer and get close to figuring out his identity, but not before he attacks his ultimate target: Rhyme himself. Amelia is masculinized: in the film's introduction of her, her lover is shown in bed and a police officer's tools of the trade strewn on the floor—boots, belt, gun, etc.—the implication being that they belong to Amelia's manly lover. But it is she who is the cop and her boyfriend who complains that she is commitment phobic and that he feels like the night they just spent together was "another slam bam thank you ma'am." This role reversal establishes Amelia as masculinized, and, therefore, it is not surprising that she turns out to be a tough and competent cop, only balking from her duty when she is told to cut off the hands of a dead victim for a forensic examination.

Rhyme, on the other hand, appears feminized. Bedridden, helpless, depressed, and planning what he calls his "final transition"—in other words, his suicide—Rhyme is depicted as passive and only regains his masculinity through his mental pursuit of the serial killer and his emotional pursuit of Amelia. But Rhyme has a chance to prove his masculinity despite his seeming impotence—being paralyzed—and he is able to defend himself against the killer's attack, albeit in rather unorthodox ways. Rhyme discovers that the killer is Richard Thompson (Leland Orser), the technician who is in charge of his heart monitor, who was once a cop convicted of an offence based on the evidence of a report that Rhyme had produced. Before Richard attempts to kill Rhyme, he breaks Rhyme's one mobile extremity—his finger—and tries to turn him into a "vegetable" with electric charges from his heart stimulator. In retaliation, Rhyme activates his bed mechanism with his mouth controller, collapsing the heavy hospital bed onto Richard's hand, crushing it. The fight culminates with the two men on the floor and Richard threatening to cut Rhyme open. But Rhyme whispers softly to him, luring him toward the only mobile part of his body (his head and neck). He suddenly bites Richard's neck, hitting an artery and causing him to bleed copiously. Despite his paralysis, Rhyme is able to reassert his masculinity by warding off the killer's attack. But it is ultimately Amelia who saves him. As Richard, in one last desperate attempt to kill him, aims a scalpel at Rhyme's heart, Amelia arrives to shoot Richard. Rhyme is stripped of his sexuality and the possibility of action, despite the fact that he recovered his will to live, fought off the killer, and has won the girl. The threat that his masculinity might pose is contained because at the end of the film he is still paralyzed and unable to perform his masculinity in the traditional ways of sex and action.

WITH NO BUDDY AT THE CENTER

The narrative of a film is constructed in terms of time and space, and, according to Diawara, both are only occupied in mainstream cinema by white people: in Hollywood film, whites occupy the center of the narrative space and blacks occupy the periphery constructed only in relation to the white protagonists ("American" 11–12). Space is related to power, and those at the center, white, have power, and those on the periphery, "other," do not. Diawara argues that the narrative expression of black experience, where the spectator is placed in a position of identification with a black subjectivity, is usually celebrated by blacks but debunked by whites as controversial (ibid. 12). This can be seen as a reason why Hollywood places the black experience so infrequently at the center—for fear of alienating the dominant audience. But that does not mean that it never happens. In *Devil in a Blue Dress* (Franklin 1995), Easy Rawlins (Denzel Washington) is the character who drives the narrative forward and also the voice that tells the story, literally, in a voice-over narration. This film, compared to the others I have discussed, in terms of black masculinity is the closest a mainstream film has come to dealing with black experience in any way to rival American black independent cinema. Easy is a fully rounded character who is realistic, sexual, and vulnerable. He is not highly educated, but he is intelligent; he is not wealthy, but he owns his own house and car; he is not married, but he is sexually attractive and active; he is not a professional detective, but he gets the job done. This film offers a realistically complex representation of black masculinity, so why is it that Hollywood feels that it can present such an image of black masculinity in this film but not in others? Because this film is a retrospective one.

As E. Ann Kaplan suggests, Hollywood cannot deal with social criticism without some strategy of containment to protect itself (*Looking* 123). In *Devil in a Blue Dress*, the strategy of containment is the past, the narrative and the issues raised in it being ascribed to the society of 1948. By attributing the racism, the segregation of the black community from the white, and the mainstream society's condemnation of interracial relationships to a previous period in history, the film does not have to acknowledge these problems as belonging to the present. Although making the film retrospective is used to relegate the issues of black experience to the past, the film does explore black experience: Easy *is* a black man and *is* at the center of the narrative. As Kelly Oliver and Benigno Trigo note, *Devil in a Blue Dress* brings the color line that was invisible in classic *noir* to the surface as the main issue and identifies the source of anxiety in 1940s society: not violence, but racism (165–66). So ultimately what does the film say about this black man's story and his experience? As Oliver and Trigo suggest, the film is about self-determination and seeing behind the façade of the American dream (166)—that is, the American dream of *white* culture.

Easy is an optimist and has a plan for a stable future, but he gets caught up in a web of white people's deceit and corruption. At the beginning of the film he loses his job working for white employers because he is black. But by the end of the film he has started his own detective agency and is self-employed. He is admirable for making himself a success in a time when few black men would have had their own business, home, and car. Although the detective-hero usually has to rely on weapons or muscle to defeat the villains, Easy relies on his wits and avoids violence. Mouse (Don Cheadle) is a character introduced from Easy's troubled past to assist his investigation, but also to commit the violence that Easy cannot. Easy sends Mouse packing at the end of the film because he does not want to do business at the level of the thugs he had been up against; this constructs Easy as a detective-figure reminiscent of Raymond Chandler's Philip Marlowe (as embodied by Humphrey Bogart)—a chivalrous figure who follows his own code of morality and justice.

Easy is also a sexualized figure. He has been hired to find Daphne, a white woman who likes to frequent black clubs. While on his quest to find Daphne, Easy meets up with Coretta, who accuses him of being interested only in white women. "Colored women aren't good enough anymore?" she asks him. The irony is, of course, that Daphne has black parentage and is "passing" for white. Easy and Coretta do have sex, but it is less about love or romance than it is about power. Easy thinks that by having sex with Coretta he will discover the information he wants regarding Daphne. But as the sexual act occurs we see that Easy is desperate for sex and at Coretta's mercy, quite literally, giving her information in return for sexual gratification. His sexuality then becomes a weakness rather than a strength, and he admits as much in his voice-over. But unlike the novel, the screen version of Mosley's story denies Easy his torrid romance with Daphne. It seems that even though the film of *Devil in a Blue Dress* can offer a sophisticated portrayal of black experience at the center, the representation of interracial relationships in mainstream cinema is still a sensitive subject.

As Guerrero notes, despite being based on the popular novel by Mosley, directed by an outstanding filmmaker, praised uniformly by critics, and featuring a major Hollywood star, the film was a flop at the box

FIGURE 20. Denzel Washington in *Devil in a Blue Dress*. No buddy: In *Devil in a Blue Dress* (1995), Easy Rawlins (Denzel Washington) is left alone at the center to be the master of his own fate—and that of the film's. The film updates the history of *noir* by bringing to the genre the black subjectivity its label implies but ignores. Photo from author's collection.

office ("*Devil*" 41). Guerrero suggests that the reason for its disappointing return at the box office is the issue of race: the film was released closely on the heels of the O. J. Simpson trial, and racial tensions were running high across the country. Leon Lewis suggests the reason for the film's lack of commercial success was that it was missing a white sidekick (137)—precisely because it was *not* a biracial buddy movie. Whatever the reasons for its box office failure, *Devil in a Blue Dress* remains an important film in the history of *film noir*. Unlike many of the neo-*noirs* of the last two decades, *Devil in a Blue Dress* captures the mood of classic *film noir*. The director, Carl Franklin, recognizes that "the psychological attitude of the *noir* era, which was built on a lingering hangover from the Depression, a post-war malaise, cold war anxiety and nuclear trauma, has its ongoing analogue in the black community throughout the twentieth century" (Lewis 135). The film is thus a successful revisiting to the *noir* form because, not only does it authentically recreate the postwar mood, but it also applies it to a more contemporary issue. Unlike his *noir* predecessors, like Marlowe, Easy is able to walk into the world of *noir* at the beginning of the film and walk back out of it again at the end. He leaves the dark, smoky, jazz-filled clubs of the city to walk in the sunshine on his palm tree-lined suburban street filled with a sense of community and hope, something that the classic *noir*-hero could never experience. The film's most important contribution to the *noir* form is its rewriting of *noir* history, bringing to *noir* the black subjectivity its label implies but ignores. The film reveals the voice of an entire section of the population that was silenced in original *film noir*. The film not only follows Easy's story, the story of a black man, but it is told by Easy himself in his own voice and thus offers black experience at the center of a film's narrative that is not contained.

CLASS AND CULTURE: ISOLATING THE HERO

Diawara states that the white spectator can only make a film with a black subject, like a Blaxploitation film, intelligible if he/she suspends his/her critical judgment and identifies with the black hero ("Spectatorship" 68). Mainstream cinema avoids this problem of identification by placing the black character in a white context. This allows the white spectator a familiar point of identification, and, for all intents and purposes, the film basically ignores the fact that the character is black. He could easily be white without altering the plot or thematics of the film, and, therefore, avoids any issue of race completely. Class thus can offer a strategy of containment, with black characters being presented in line with middle-class sensibilities and offering identification on the level of values, profession, or lifestyle. By placing black characters within white mainstream definitions of middle-class values, lifestyle, and profession, they are made more familiar, identifiable, and "unthreatening." Valerie Smith argues that the black middle class has become "a space of pure compromise and capitulation, from which all autonomy disappears once it encounters hegemonic power" (67). White hegemonic power thus occupies the middle class and defines it as the ideal to which to aspire. The middle class then becomes a space that cannot be redefined with specificity for black culture and meaning for the "other"; instead it can align the "other" with the mainstream. Hollywood, thus, uses the space of the middle class to contain the black detective-hero by aligning him with mainstream values and hegemonic power.

In *Beverly Hills Cop* (Brest 1984), the detective Axel Foley (Eddie Murphy) is displaced; he is taken from Detroit and transplanted to Beverly Hills. The juxtaposition of Axel's working-class cop in upper-class Beverly Hills functions to illicit laughs from the audience as well as to "mainstream" the black detective. This displacement of the black character into isolation in white culture is illustrated as the story moves from Detroit to Los Angeles. The opening scene depicts Detroit as a city of smoke and industry, car manufacture, and boarded-up buildings; the people of the city—black *and* white—belong to the underclass but they have a sense of community and gather around cars and homes to socialize. This is the milieu from which Axel hails, and it is sharply contrasted with his arrival in Beverly Hills. Mirroring the "Nice to have you in Detroit" sign are the signs of Beverly Hills: the Beverly Hills Hotel, Rodeo Drive, Cartier, Ricci, and Fendi. Detroit's industrial wasteland and stacks spewing smoke are replaced by palm trees and blue skies; small run-down family homes and boarded-up buildings are replaced by movie-star mansions; junked cars and pick-up trucks are replaced by Porsches, convertibles, and Rolls-Royces. Axel is transplanted from his almost all-black, and certainly working-class, community to isolation in an almost completely white and upper-middle-class one.

The film establishes that there will be tension between Axel and this new world to which he is an outsider, but race is never made the issue. Instead the issue is the difference in his background, attitude, and class. Axel's Beverly Hills counterparts—Taggart (John Ashton) and Rosewood (Judge Reinhold)—sport suits while Axel dresses "like a hoodlum," according to his friend Jenny, in jeans, runners, and a hooded-sweatshirt. The Beverly Hills cops drive pristine cars while he drives an old and dilapidated junker; they follow procedure and go by the book while he ignores the rules if it means getting the job done. The issue of race is replaced in the film with the issues of background, class, and attitude in relation to their common profession as police officers. By the end of the film, Axel has won the respect of his fellow cops: he has solved the case because he followed his own methods even when it meant breaking the rules. Axel is isolated, having been removed from his home and community in Detroit, but he is also aligned with mainstream sensibilities because the film makes fun of the community and culture into which he is transplanted. Beverly Hills does not represent average American society—it is an extreme identified with the rich and famous—and much of the film's comedy stems from poking fun at the eccentric nature of its inhabitants through Axel's experiences there: he is identified as normal and average—like the audience—in the face of the extremely rich, vain, and feminized. Even the Beverly Hills cops are presented as "soft" due to their area of jurisdiction being one where "real" crime—in other words, violent crime—like that found in Detroit, is absent. When this kind of crime does penetrate the community, the cops, due to their lack of experience with such crime, are ineffectual.

Thus, the threat of difference and disruption that Axel poses to Beverly Hills is eradicated because at the end of the film he is sent home. This seems to undermine any serious message that the film might be making about black masculinity as well as the fact that the film is in many ways a comedy. On the other hand, Axel—like Easy in *Devil in a Blue Dress*—is sexual, intelligent, good at his job, a team player, and has a black community to go home to. He is also at the center of the narrative, allowing the film to be concerned with black subjectivity and have a laugh at the expense of white American culture. The popularity of Eddie Murphy with white and black audiences is evident, with *Beverly Hills Cop* (Brest 1984) and *Beverly Hills Cop II* (Scott 1987) being the top grossing films of their respective years (Guerrero, "Black" 243).

Guerrero sees the isolation of the black figure from a community as a strategy of containment; regardless, in the case of the contemporary detective film, it is one of the genre's codes—no matter what the hero's race. Like the Western, the detective is defined by the lone hero who enters a social space to restore order but does not remain in that social space. If he stays, he will no longer be an effective law enforcer because the skills he is required to possess in order to defeat the enemy—violence, toughness, lack of emotional involvement—are qualities deemed antisocial. The black detective is tested and must prove his masculinity not because he is black but *because he is a detective*. This generic convention, as well as those of a lack of sexuality and lack of action, is exploited by Hollywood to bring black stars to the screen—cashing in on their fame and appeal to both white and black audiences without having to tackle the issues that the representation of America's black community might entail. The black detective of contemporary film tends to be isolated from a black community and family and, therefore, from potential issues of race and culture. He also tends to be a thinking detective (rather than an action hero) and, therefore, middle class, well dressed, well mannered, and well educated. The black hero is thus made identifiable for the dominant, white, middle-class audience through class and profession, not unlike Sidney Poitier's characters were in the 1960s. Race is often relegated to being a nonissue in the Hollywood detective film, and the hero could as easily be played by a white star as he is by a black one, especially considering that many of these films were originally written for white stars. For example, Eddie Murphy's role in *Beverly Hills Cop* and Samuel L. Jackson's in *The Negotiator* were both originally intended for Sylvester Stallone, and Danny Glover's role in *Lethal Weapon* was meant for Nick Nolte (Guerrero, *Framing* 126; Welsh 165). Thus, the issue of race is displaced onto one of class, and the "threat" that the black detective, according to Hollywood, poses for white audiences is neutralized because he is placed within a white, middle-class, mainstream context.

Contemporary mainstream cinema is not completely void of black protagonists, but it does seem to offer black experience to its audiences only when that "otherness" can be contained and regulated. The contemporary detective film offers Hollywood the ideal space for the presentation but also the containment of a black protagonist because one of its main codes is the isolation of the hero. Perhaps that is why when black actors are at the center of a Hollywood narrative, it is often in a detective film. Hollywood can offer subjectivity to a black character without having to delve into the specificity of black experience as an issue. The detective is, by nature, an outsider and alone, and the black detective is isolated or separated from a black community or family. But he is rarely—even in recent films—left to stand alone because the white costar is seen by the film industry to offer a greater crossover appeal than the black star on his own. Hollywood still tends to pair the black detective up with a white buddy—whether a white hero at the center as in films of the 1980s, or a white women at his side as in films of the 1990s and 2000s.

CHAPTER EIGHT

Investigating the "Other": Women and Youth

NEW KINDS OF HEROES FOR A NEW ERA

The early 1990s saw the introduction of kinder, gentler men on screen, mirroring a social shift to the valuing of more sensitive and vulnerable masculinity. But this move away from the hypermasculine action hero also included the proliferation of feminine or "feminized" heroes: women and youths. The youth—male and female—has taken over the role as action hero since the mid-1990s, replacing the hard-body hero of the 1980s as the new body of spectacle. And, with a decrease in emphasis on hard bodies and violence as the defining features of heroism and an increase in education, intelligence, and work-related experience as the keys to successful crime investigation, the female detective became a more prevalent figure in the detective genre.

The female detective was not new to the detective film in the 1990s. The 1930s and 1940s had seen film series following the exploits of female detectives like Torchy Blane, Hildegard Withers, and Nancy Drew. In the 1980s television offered the groundbreaking series *Cagney and Lacey* (1982–88), starring Tyne Daly and Sharon Gless as two female police officers; *Moonlighting* (1985–89), starring Cybill Shepherd, and *Hart to Hart*

(1979–84) starring Stephanie Powers as female private investigators paired with male partners and comedic overtones; and the long-running series *Murder, She Wrote* (1984–96) starring Angela Lansbury as sleuth Jessica Fletcher.[1] Female detectives on the big screen in the 1980s tended to be lawyers, but by the 1990s there was a growing number of films like *The Silence of the Lambs* (Demme 1991), *V. I. Warshawski* (Kanew 1991), *The Pelican Brief* (Pakula 1993), *The Client* (Schumacher 1994), *Copycat* Amiel 1995), and the celebrated British television series *Prime Suspect* (1990–96) that offered many kinds of female investigators, from lawyers to FBI agents to hardboiled private eyes. As the decade wore on, the female detective became a staple of the genre—for example, in films like *Kiss the Girls* (Fleder 1997), *Murder at 1600* (Little 1997), *The Bone Collector* (Noyce 1999), *The Thomas Crown Affair* (McTiernan 1999), *Hannibal* (Scott 2001), *Along Came a Spider* (Tamahori 2001), *High Crimes* (Franklin 2002), *Murder by Numbers* (Schroeder 2002), and *Taking Lives* (Caruso 2004), and in television series like *Crossing Jordan* (2001–), *Law and Order: Special Victims Unit* (1999–), and *CSI: Crime Scene Investigation* (2000–). While detective films with a male protagonist focus on investigating the masculinity of the hero, these films and shows have concerned themselves with examining the heroine's struggle as a woman in a man's world trying to balance a professional and personal life. This struggle is most intense with the serial killer narrative as the detective—as a female—often has the potential to become a victim of the man she hunts.[2]

The emphasis on education and experience has all but excluded the youth from the criminalist narrative: young men have not had the time, opportunity, or inclination to gain investigative experience and develop honed observational and deductive skills. In the contemporary detective film, it is the wisdom of age and experience that succeeds where the folly of youth fails, and, other than the occasional appearance in the genre to act as a foil for the older, more experienced detective, the youth is absent. The detective is seldom seen as youthful, vulnerable, and inexperienced; his/her success as an investigative hero comes from years on the job, learning his/her profession, and understanding criminal behavior. Experience comes with age, not youth, and the contemporary crime world is inhabited by the clever criminal who can outwit and outsmart a hero who relies on muscle to get the job done. Just as the old-fashioned tough-guy detective—for example, Agent Kujan of *The Usual Suspects* (Singer 1995)—cannot compete with the clever criminal, nor can Hollywood's young hero, despite his success and popularity as an action hero. The youth is not a predominant hero in the detective genre in general; therefore, his occasional appearance is notable and for effect: Detective Mills (Brad Pitt) in *Seven* (Fincher 1995), Ichabod Crane (Johnny Depp) in *Sleepy Hollow* (Burton 1999), Inspector Abberline (Johnny Depp) in *From Hell* (Hughes Bros. 2001), and Detective Calden (Josh Hartnett) in *Hollywood Homicide* (Shelton 2003). The appeal of the youth as the contemporary criminalist is, in many ways, to watch him struggle and fail. In *Seven*, Mills fails by shooting the killer instead of apprehending him; in *Sleepy Hollow*, Crane literally does not have the stomach for the job, being sick at the sight of a corpse; and in *From Hell*, Abberline is more confident and experienced than Crane but he is also plagued by the excesses of youth, including an opium habit and being in love with a prostitute and one of the killer's intended victims. But the youth did appear as the predominant hero of a series of lawyer films throughout the 1990s, where his youthful exuberance serves him well in the dogged pursuit of political corruption.

WOMEN, YOUTH, AND THE LAW

Nicole Rafter argues that the courtroom or lawyer film explores the tension between immutable, natural law and fallible, man-made law, and the hero of such films is a "justice figure" who attempts to close the gap between the two—from man-made law to the ideal (93–94). The female lawyer dominated the genre in the 1980s and was the product of the same male anxieties that informed the erotic thriller: the result was a group of films that offered a feminist but simultaneously reactionary politic. The focus of the films was on women trying to attain success in the male-dominated world of the law and tended to be played by actresses who carried associations of feminist empowerment: Glenn Close in *Jagged Edge* (Marquand 1985), Cher in *Suspect* (Yates 1987), Theresa Russell in *Physical Evidence* (Crichton 1989), Jessica Lange in *Music Box* (Costa-Gravas 1989), Kelly McGillis in *The Accused* (Kaplan 1988), Mary Elizabeth Mastrantonio in *Class Action* (Apted 1991), Barbara Hershey in *Defenseless* (Campbell 1991), Sean Young in *Love Crimes* (Borden 1992), Demi Moore in *A Few Good Men* (Reiner 1992), and Rebecca DeMornay in *Guilty as Sin* (Lumet 1993). But as lawyers, they were also presented as incompetent, unethical, and overly emotional.

As Cynthia Lucia explains, the female lawyer *appeared* to be a feminist model—as a professional, powerful, central female character—but her representation was really a result of the glossing over of reactionary impulses to feminism. Despite her alliance with the law, the female lawyer, like the *femme fatale* of the erotic thriller, was presented as "dangerously ambitious," but this masculine trait and her independence were denied by her presentation as "personally and professionally deficient" (Lucia 33). In terms of their professional lives, they were not necessarily competent as lawyers: they were often forced to defer to male authority or proved wrong by their male colleagues. In terms of their personal lives, they were not whole but flawed characters; they were married to their jobs and could not attain happiness or fulfillment until children and/or love interests entered into their personal lives. Thus, while the female lawyer of the late 1980s and early 1990s presented an image of central female protagonist in the detective genre, it was an image that also contained the independent women through presenting her as incompetent, incomplete, and one who caved in to patriarchal authority in her personal and professional life. Just like the *femme fatale* who died at the end of the film or was brought to justice, the female lawyer experienced a neutralization of her power as she gave up her independence to embrace the socially prescribed roles of wife and mother.

The female lawyer or law student has made only a few appearances since the early 1990s—for example, in *The Pelican Brief* (Pakula 1993) starring Julia Roberts, *The Client* (Schumacher 1994) starring Susan Sarandon, and *High Crimes* (Franklin 2002) starring Ashley Judd—but in these films she is presented as a much more competent, intelligent, and successful woman and lawyer than her 1980s counterparts. Perhaps one of the most successful female "lawyer" films of the last decade has been *Erin Brockovich* (Soderberg 2000), except that technically the protagonist is not a lawyer—but that is exactly the film's point.

The heroine and title's namesake Erin Brockovich (Julia Roberts) is not a lawyer but a victim—literally, the victim of a car accident—and she seems to be a victim of life and men. As she says to her neighbor, George (Aaron Eckhart), when she begins to fall in love with him, "Are you gonna be something else I have to survive?" But rather than allow herself to be a victim, she chooses to be a survivor and uses her looks, wiles, and—most importantly—her brains to become a success. She forces her lawyer, Ed (Albert Finney), to give her a job, chases hunches and leads in a case, and turns a lost-cause case into a success story when she comes across a cover-up by a large company that has inadvertently poisoned an entire community. By the end of the film, she has cracked the case, helped hundreds of victimized people, and earned two million dollars—and she did so without a law degree or the help of a man. In fact, when the big-time lawyers step in to help out with the case, they actually hinder it. Because they are out of touch with the working-class people who are the victims of the contaminated water cover-up, the hotshot lawyers Kurt and Theresa threaten the case by alienating the clients of the lawsuit. In the end, it is Erin who is the mediator between the high-class lawyers and the lower-class clients. When signatures are needed, Erin goes door-to-door to convince all 634 plaintiffs to sign. Kurt and Teresa are shocked and ask how she managed it. She managed it through the trust she has gained from the victims by taking a personal interest in them and their families over the years. But she knows exactly what they think of her and plays with their preconceptions of her— she tells them she performed 634 blow jobs.

Presented as hyperfeminine, in small, tight, flashy clothes that reveal a lot of leg and cleavage, Erin looks like a woman who invites the wrong kind of attention and has been defined by the men with whom she has had relationships—and, to a point, she has. She was a small-town beauty queen who married young, has two ex-husbands, three kids, and a lot of debt. Despite her appearance of femininity, Erin is not unlike her 1980s predecessors as a "masculinized" woman who suffers from the inability to have a successful career *and* a great home life. She is portrayed as tough, independent, and ambitious and jeopardizes her relationship with her kids and her boyfriend George because of the time and dedication she devotes to the case rather than to them. A role reversal occurs: George stays at home minding the kids while Erin is the career-minded breadwinner of the family. Erin's appearance is deceiving: her hyperfemininity does mask an intelligent, hard-working, and caring person. But this is only a result of society's preconceptions about women: dressing to highlight your body suggests a corresponding low IQ. The fact that the film is based on a real-life case, and Roberts's character on a real person, complicates this assumption that a woman who *looks* "cheap" is, in fact, worthless. The film plays off the spectacle of Roberts—Hollywood's biggest box-office female star—playing a working-class, single mother with a foul mouth, bad attitude, and poor fashion sense. And just as the film plays on the disparity between the star and the role she plays—a disparity that critics and audiences noted and for which she won an Oscar—so too does it play on that between the protagonist's appearance and her character. The spectacle of the female body so apparent in *Erin Brockovich* is rare for the detective film as it is most often in the contemporary action film that the female hero's body is placed on spectacular display.

The female lawyer all but disappeared from the screen by the early 1990s. Instead it was the youth who repeatedly appeared as the lawyer in the courtroom in what some critics have dubbed the "Grisham cycle."[3] In the majority of the films adapted from John Grisham's best-selling novels, the detective-hero is the young male lawyer at the start of his career—for example, *The Firm* (Pollack 1993) starring Tom Cruise, *The Chamber* (Foley 1996) starring Chris O'Donnell, *A Time to Kill* (Schumacher 1996) starring Matthew McConaughey, and *The Rainmaker* (Coppola 1997) starring Matt Damon. The youth can fulfill the role of the lawyer-detective because he is young, inquisitive, and looking to make his mark and, unlike his older and jaded superiors, is more likely to charge headlong in pursuit of an investigation rather than leave it to the police— the official investigators of crime. With the shift from the woman as lawyer to the youth, the debate of the courtroom film also shifted from the woman trying to juggle her personal and professional life unsuccessfully to a debate about American moral and political corruption. Images of lawyers as self-serving—defending wealthy criminals, despite their guilt, for money and glory—and courtroom justice as a three-ring circus for big-time lawyers to "sell" their version of the "truth" at the expense of the innocent circulated in the popular imagination. As Keith Bartlett notes, the youth lawyer films tended to "pitch a 'David' versus a corporate, criminal or political 'Goliath'" (273). A generational debate also arose as older men were portrayed as jaded and the betrayers of justice and the law, and the youth as idealistic and determined to bring natural/ideal—vs. man-made—justice back to the system. The youth offered audiences a sense of hope that the law was not corrupt and that the system still worked.

FEMINIZED BODIES AND ACTION

The Youth in Action

The "youth movement" of the last decade introduced young actors as the heroes in popular film, replacing the older, more physical actors who carried over from the 1980s—action men like Harrison Ford, Mel Gibson, and Bruce Willis. Actors like Leonardo DiCaprio, Johnny Depp, Brendan Fraser, Keanu Reeves, Ben Affleck, and Josh Hartnett—independent of their age—are young, boyish, and/or androgynous in appearance.[4] Nevertheless, they have become the new male stars of Hollywood portraying action heroes, roles that in the 1980s would have been played by more manly actors such as Ford, Gibson, or Willis. For example, Leonardo DiCaprio plays the leading man in *Titanic* (Cameron 1997) while the more manly looking actor, Billy Zane, plays the supporting role. Brendan Fraser has twice played the action-hero archaeologist Rick O'Connell in *The Mummy* films (Sommers 1999 and 2001), a role similar to Harrison Ford's archaeologist Indiana Jones of the 1980s. Despite Fraser's pumped-up body, he too is a sensitive youth, weeping uncontrollably over the dead body of his young wife and acting less mature than his young son in *The Mummy Returns*. Johnny Depp, despite being over forty, continues to play youthful action heroes in films like *Pirates of the Caribbean: The Curse of the Black Pearl* (Verbinski 2003). Josh Hartnett has also played youth heroes in *Pearl Harbor* (Bay 2001), *Black Hawk Down* (Scott 2002), and opposite Harrison Ford in *Hollywood Homicide*.

The replacement of manly action men with youth heroes is most apparent with Affleck's succession to the role of CIA agent Jack Ryan in the film based on Tom Clancy's best-selling novel *The Sum of all Fears* (Robinson 2002). The role was portrayed throughout the 1990s by Harrison Ford, and before him by Alec Baldwin. Will Smith has also become a major box-office star with *Independence Day* (Emmerich 1996), the *Bad Boys* films (Bay 1995 and 2003), and the *Men in Black* films (Sonnenfeld 1997 and 2002). As Geoff King notes, Smith has crossover appeal as both an African American who attracts black and white audiences and as a star in both film and music ("Stardom" 62). There is also the association of youth with his persona, as television critic Matt Roush notes in an episode of *Biography*, "There is an optimism to Will Smith; there's this true freshness to him." When trying to cast the hero for *Independence Day*, film producer Dean Devlin said that they asked themselves, "Who is the all-American young man?" and the answer they arrived at was Will Smith.[5] What is interesting is that they specifically were thinking of their hero as "young" not as simply "the all-American hero." Even Tom Cruise has remained a youthful hero, despite his age, and has played the youth lawyer in *The Firm* (Pollack 1993) and *A Few Good Men* and the spy/action hero in *Mission: Impossible* (De Palma 1996), *Mission: Impossible 2* (Woo 2000), and *Minority Report* (Spielberg 2002). As Mark Simpson argues, Tom Cruise is the ideal model for men in our century, because "Cruise looks younger every year. It's his greatest achievement. He is still a boy at forty" (qtd. in

FIGURE 21. Tom Cruise. "Still a boy at 40": Tom Cruise has been called the ideal model for men because he continues to look so young. The contemporary ideal of masculinity has come to incorporate many feminine elements, including narcissism and attention-seeking. Photo from author's collection.

Field 2). Since the 1980s, the male body has become a new target for consumerism and the beauty industry. Because of changing gender roles and the increasing cult of celebrity, the male body is identified as the site where masculinity is located and defined and thus where masculinity can be performed and enhanced. In his book *Sex Terror: Erotic Misadventures in Pop Culture* (2002), Simpson notes,

> Now that women are more independent and assertive, straight men have to compete more to attract their attention. Narcissistic isn't something they could have been before. They supported the family as fathers and in exchange they were nurtured. Now we live in a world where there are women bosses who are likely to favour something cute. It's a market place, and being a nice bloke isn't enough. It's a big advantage if you can attract attention by the way you look. Celebrity culture and glossy magazines have shown that you have to brand yourself if you want to get on. (qtd. in Field, 1-2)

The last decade has seen the proliferation of the feminized body—whether that of a woman or the slighter, slimmer, more androgynous body of a youth—that can perform different work than the adult male body. It can embody, and offer the expression of, insecurity, passivity, vulnerability, and sexuality without compromising the masculinity of the hero. Instead, the youth and female hero can successfully combine traditional notions of heroism associated with masculinity—like action, strength, courage, and independence—with traits associated with femininity—like insecurity, vulnerability, and sensitivity. The feminized body can also bear the weight of the erotic gaze of the male and female spectator without the implications it would have if that character were a traditional adult male hero. A shift in the representation of masculinity in fashion and advertising occurred in the 1990s as a new, young, more androgynous male was placed in positions of passivity and unawareness of the spectator's gaze—a mode of representation previously reserved for the female body; a similar change has occurred in the representation of masculinity in contemporary cinema. The spectacle of action and objectification—the body as erotic *and* passive—can be indulged in and celebrated without evoking fears of homoerotic identification for the heterosexual male viewer through the youth. The body of the man may be emasculated by being placed in the passive and erotic position of representation, but the body of the youth can be presented as erotic in passivity and be displayed in a mode of representation usually reserved for that of the female body—without his masculinity necessarily being compromised. Youth functions not as a specific age group but a mode of representation that can raise and resolve the problematic issues that challenge masculinity, such as physical and emotional vulnerability. Because the masculinity of the youth is relegated to the realm of adolescence, his vulnerability can be contained by disguising its implications on manliness. The assumption is that his more feminine characteristics of physical and emotional vulnerability will disappear as he grows into a man, yet in the meantime he offers the successful combination of the characteristics of traditional masculinity with more contemporary, somewhat feminized ones in a single representation. Through the youth, popular films can offer audiences a hero who can perform as a man of action but at the same time be sensitive, romantic, confused, and vulnerable—something that America's traditional heroes, like Clint Eastwood and John Wayne, could never do.

Women of Action

The 1990s witnessed the dramatic rise of the youth as action hero, but also that of the woman. Women as action heroes were rare in the late 1980s but increasingly common in the 1990s and presented a transgression of generic codes that dictated that women should be passive and peripheral characters in Hollywood action films. Such a transgression opened up questions about gender identity and changing representations of women. But many critics whose discussions stemmed from psychoanalytic discourse saw these women merely as male heroes masquerading as female (Hills 38–39).

    Blue Steel (Bigelow 1990) was an anomaly—a film before its time—with a female cop-action hero when the majority of cop-action heroes were men, and women tended only to portray lawyers when cast as detective-heroes. Audiences of the 1980s did not seem ready for the woman of action: two television series that were developed and taken as far as the pilot stage but no further were *Lady Blue,* in which Jamie Rose played "Dirty" Harriet—evoking Clint Eastwood's violent vigilante hero—and *Foxfire,* in which Joanna Cassidy played a counterspy (Green 176). *Blue Steel* follows the experiences of its hero, Megan Turner (Jamie Lee Curtis), a female cop who, like the female lawyer, struggles to be successful both in her private life and her career. When men are introduced to Megan, they do not believe her when she tells them she is a cop and they ask why a woman so beautiful would waste her talents on law enforcement. Although most men seem turned off by her occupation, two are not: the man she dates and does not know is the serial killer she seeks—Eugene Hunt (Ron Silver)—and the police detective she works alongside in that pursuit—Nick Mann (Clancy Brown).

The film, not unlike the female lawyer films of the time, offers a deliberation of the problems facing a woman in the man's world of law enforcement. But not unlike the male cop-action film of the time, the subtext of the film is masculine crisis caused by independent women like Megan. Despite the fact that Eugene has a career on the stock exchange, a beautiful apartment, an immaculate wardrobe, success, money, good looks, and charm with which he seduces Megan, he represents masculinity in crisis. He is the New Man, a product of 1980s consumerism, and he is first introduced doing his own grocery shopping after work. At the grocery store, an armed and masked man proceeds to hold it up, and it is Megan who comes to the rescue and shoots the perpetrator. As the shooting takes place, Eugene is mesmerized by the perpetrator's gun, and, when it hits the ground, he takes it. Eugene then commits a series of murders using the .44 Magnum. Whether Eugene has a history of psychosis or the incident at the grocery store merely kick-starts a breakdown is not made clear, but his use of bullets etched with Megan's name and his pursuit of her as a lover clearly aligns his serial killing with her as both a woman and a cop with the authority to kill. As foreplay in their first sexual encounter, Eugene asks Megan to hold her gun in both hands and aim it at him. This link between his attraction to her and her ability to wield a deadly weapon—or her possession of the phallus—and the suggestion that female sexuality holds dangers for men are compounded and confirmed as Eugene only pursues sex with Megan after she shoots him and then rapes her liked a crazed animal. Rape is the only way that Eugene can exert power over the independent woman, highlighting the fact that, despite being a cop, she is still vulnerable because of her gender.

As a film of its time, *Blue Steel* is concerned with gender difference and changing gender roles, and these concerns are brought to the fore. Megan's body becomes a site for the playing out of questions of gender and a spectacle of conflicting conversations about masculinity and femininity. Her uniform as a police officer initially de-genders her, and many moments in the film highlight how the uniform is an equalizer that makes all bodies within them cops rather than men or women. At the beginning of the film, Megan is shown pulling her uniform on over her bra to cover the breasts that "betray" her gender. She and the few other female cops of her graduating class are then shown as almost indistinguishable from the men they stand side by side with in their dress-blues and white caps. Similarly, when her mother comes to the station to find Megan, she asks if this is where Megan works. Megan sarcastically points out that it *is* where she works, that is why all the other people in the building are wearing the same uniform. But the film then plays up the differences between her overtly feminine body when she goes out on dates with Eugene and her somewhat masculinized body when on duty as a detective on Nick's team, where she wears men's shirts, jeans, and shoes. In a nightmare, she returns to her date with Eugene: this time she falls out of his helicopter as they take a nighttime ride over the city, and, while he briefly catches hold of her arm, he then lets her fall. She feels most vulnerable when she appears most feminine—in a dress and on a date with a man; her uniform, on the other hand, invites associations with male paternalist authority, which Megan uses to become empowered. Lying in the hospital after being brutally raped, Megan is treated like a victim: her boss, Stan, pats her awkwardly on the shoulder and a nurse gives her pills to help her sleep. But Megan refuses to play the victim, knocking out her guard, donning his uniform, and going in pursuit of Eugene. The uniform makes her a cop rather than just a woman, and, as she walks down the hall, her silhouette and demeanor are contrasted to that of another woman: Megan looks mannish as she strides down the hall in the opposite direction of the woman whose hair, dress, and walk mark her as distinctly feminine. Empowered by her uniform and despite her ordeal, Megan pursues Eugene, engages him in a shootout, and kills him.

The best-known forerunners to today's action women were Ripley (Sigourney Weaver) in the *Alien* films (1979 [R. Scott], 1986 [Cameron], 1992 [Fincher], 1997 [Jeunet]) and Sarah Connor (Linda Hamilton) in *Terminator 2: Judgment Day* (Cameron 1991). Women can be the body of action, although often as a criminal rather than the hero—for example, in *Thelma and Louise* (Scott 1991), *Femme Fatale* (De Palma 2002), and *Terminator 3: Rise of the Machines* (Mostow 2003). More recently, there has been an explosion of action women in film, including Trinity (Carrie-Ann Moss) in *The Matrix* films (Wachowski Bros. 1999, 2003, and 2003), the Angels (Drew Barrymore, Cameron Diaz, and Lucy Liu) in the *Charlie's Angels* films (McG 2000 and 2003), Lara Croft (Angelina Jolie) in the *Tomb Raider* films (West 2001 and de Bont 2003), and the X-Women (Halle Berry and Famke Janssen) in the *X-Men* films (Singer 2000 and 2003), and on television with Buffy (Sarah Michelle Gellar) in *Buffy the Vampire Slayer* (1997–2003), Xena (Lucy Lawless) in *Xena: Warrior Princess* (1995–2001), Nikita (Peta Wilson) in *La Femme Nikita* (1997–2001), and Sydney (Jennifer Garner) in *Alias* (2001–2006).

The action woman offers an empowered image of women being just as good as the guys—or does she? Is she just another way in which to offer the female body on display for the erotic male gaze but in a codified manner, with action necessitating the spectacle of the female body rather than sexual relations or victimization? Is she also just a politically correct version of violent heroism? Violence perpetrated by men against women—for example, in erotic thrillers like *Fatal Attraction* (Lyne 1987) and *Final Analysis* (Joanou 1992)—fell out of fashion by the early 1990s, so perhaps the action woman offers a way in which to indulge in spectacular violence against and by women while not offending feminist or pro-feminist audiences. As Jeffrey A. Brown notes, the reaction to the action woman, from both the public and critics, was mixed: some regarded the action woman as signalling "a growing acceptance of non-traditional roles for women and an awareness of the arbitrariness of gender traits" while others saw her as recycling the same gender politics of the 1980s action film by having essentially masculine women (52–53). The action heroine can be seen as allowing all of these readings, but she can also be regarded as a very positive shift in Hollywood's representation of women. The action film does put the female body on display but mainly in sequences of action rather than in sex. The female action hero is shown to "kick ass" as effectively as, or moreso than, men, relying on martial arts—made all the more spectacular through digital and stop-motion cinematography, which can literally suspend the body of action in midair—rather than guns and firepower, as in *Charlie's Angels* and *The Matrix*. As the male body was in the action film of the 1980s, so too was the female body in the 1990s: the hero's most effective weapon against evil.

The body of the female heroine and villain, like that of the erotic thriller of the late 1980s and early 1990s, is offered as sexualized and on display for the audience's pleasure and functions as the spectacular body of the films. While in the late 1980s and early 1990s, female action heroes like Ripley of *Aliens* and Sarah Connor of *Terminator 2* were masculinized, wielding big guns and sporting the uniform of action men—a tank top and combat pants—that reveal bulging biceps but obscure breasts, hips, and buttocks. Female action heroes of more recent years embody ultimate fighting capabilities with hyperfemininity. The heroes of *Tomb Raider* (Angelina Jolie), *Charlie's Angels* (Cameron Diaz, Lucy Liu, Drew Barrymore), and *X-Men* (Halle Berry and Famke Jansen), and the villains of *Femme Fatale* (Rebecca Romjin-Stamos), *Terminator 3: Rise of the Machines* (Kristaana Loken), *Charlie's Angels 2: Full Throttle* (Demi Moore), and *X-Men* (Rebecca Romjin-Stamos) are clad in spectacular outfits that reveal or cling to

FIGURE 22. Sandra Bullock in *Murder by Numbers*. In *Murder by Numbers* (2002), Cassie (Sandra Bullock) is presented as more masculine than feminine in her gender nonspecific clothes and armed with her gun. Photo from author's collection.

their bodies, highlighting their femininity—curvaceous breasts, hips, buttocks—and present them through a cartoon-like combination of masculine
and feminine traits. Although, as David Roger Coon points out, films like
Charlie's Angels and television series like *Alias* do explore the physical and
mental abilities of their multifaceted heroines even if their more visible and
pervasive promotional material focuses on her sex appeal (3), a major facet of
the heroines' abilities are their spectacular bodies. As Sherrie Inness explains, "The popular media are still deeply ambivalent about how they depict
tough women so they do not challenge gender conventions too dramatically"
(5). The movement toward science fiction and fantasy evident in *X-Men*,
Terminator 3, *Tomb Raider*, and even to some extent *Charlie's Angels*, with its
slow-motion, unrealistic but spectacular action sequences, moves these
women into the realm of fantasy and out of believable reality. Whether the
action woman defies gender role stereotyping or is simply another version of
it, like the *femme fatale*, she offers an image of empowered and independent
women. But unlike the *femme fatale*, the action heroine survives the film and
is not punished for her transgression of gender roles.

VICTIMS IN A MAN'S WORLD:
THE FEMALE CRIMINALIST

Although the current cycle of thinking detective films did not appear in its
present form until 1995 with the release of *Seven*, Jonathan Demme's 1991
film *The Silence of the Lambs* can be seen as a precursor.[6] As Barry Keith Grant
notes, *Silence of the Lambs* "brought serial killing squarely into the mainstream"
("American" 23). The film is still very much in the vein of the 1980s thriller/
horror film rather than the contemporary trend of the serial killer/criminalist
film with its focus on the pleasure of spectacular and gruesome violence as well
as heightened suspense rather than on the processes of the detective's deductions. The film follows the investigation of Clarice (Jodie Foster), an FBI
agent-in-training, into the deaths and kidnappings attributed to a killer
known as Buffalo Bill. At the beginning of the film, Clarice runs through the
outdoor training course at the FBI academy at Quantico. The manner in
which the scene is filmed plays with the established conventions of the female
as victim. Clarice runs through misty and darkened woods with the camera
following her and then along side her—both shots evoking the idea of the
victim running away from her pursuer. But Clarice defies these conventions,
despite the camera's positioning, and jogs confidently and unperturbed even

when a man runs up behind her and calls her name. He is also from the academy and bears a message for Clarice to see Jack Crawford (Scott Glenn). As Clarice returns to the academy, she jogs in her gray sweatsuit in the opposite direction of groups of male agents training in blue sweatsuits. In the elevator she is again contrasted against a group of male agents in red and towering above her short stature. These opening scenes emphasize the fact that a female presence in the academy in unusual; more importantly, however, it functions to differentiate her from the body of agents-in-training. She is not a run-of-the-mill student, but exemplary; she does not run with the crowd, but is independent. Her position as a student, an outsider, and a woman will give her the advantage of objectivity, emotional detachment, and a fresh perspective in her pursuit of the serial killer Jame Gumb, a.k.a. "Buffalo Bill."

The film is, in many ways, a meditation on gender. Christina Lane argues that Jodie Foster's star persona (specifically the debate over whether or not she is a lesbian) is "liminal"—resting on the threshold between and encompassing the oppositions of masculine/feminine and heterosexual/homosexual rather than submitting to their binary structure (149). The roles she played as a child and teenager were tough rather than "girlie" girls, and her publicity as an adult has presented her in a range of images from nonfeminine to feminine. Mizejewski argues that in *The Silence of the Lambs* Clarice's lack of opportunities to perform her heterosexuality mark her as a potential lesbian, but that such a reading is displaced onto the body of Gumb as a homosexualized man (18). Rather than being masculinized or lesbianized, I would argue that Demme uses Foster's liminal status to explore issues of gender in the film. The film redefines many of the presumed gender roles in society and film of the time; therefore, the female detective is not merely a masculinized woman, or the killer an emasculated male killing to assert his manhood.[7] Clarice is a woman in the male-dominated world of law enforcement and she is tough, self-confident, and ambitious. But she embodies and uses femininity as a weapon and an aid in her investigation. Dr. Chilton suggests that Clarice is sent to talk to Hannibal (Anthony Hopkins) because she is female and he has not seen a woman in eight years. Clarice does occasionally use her female charms on men when she needs to—for example, to placate Dr. Chilton and to procure the help of the entomologist Dr. Pilchar. She also learns to embrace her emotional connections with the victims rather than suppress them, as they eventually lead her to the killer. Ultimately, Clarice is a good agent empowered by her ambition, experiences, her skills in behavioral science, psychology, and profiling. Her femininity, also, makes her successful in tracking down Jame Gumb where the men of the local law enforcement and FBI have failed.

While the female detective has remained a staple of the serial killer genre, and the presence of a women in the role of protagonist (or partner to a male detective) should articulate a positive image of women onscreen, the serial killer film tends to contain or overturn a feminist theme because the female detective presents a problem with her appropriation of the male position in mainstream film. Linda Mizejewski argues that

> the "problem" of the female investigator is most easily resolved through familiar heterosexual strategies: the excessive fetishization and domesticization of the female detective in *V. I. Warshawski* (1991); the imposition of a romantic subplot [. . .] in *The Stranger among Us* (1992); the glamorization in *Impulse* (1990); the heterosexual partnership in Rush (1992). An alternative resolution of the female dick problem in cinema has been to represent her as a Hollywood version of the lesbian, thereby associating her with another kind of "illegitimacy." (6–7)

In *Blue Steel, The Silence of the Lambs*, and *Point of No Return* (Badham 1993), it is apparent that the woman's fear is that through the appropriation of the male position as detective (i.e., "dick") and the male weapon of the gun (i.e., phallus), she suffers a loss of femininity—or at least the ability to perform it successfully. In *Blue Steel*, Megan (Jamie Lee Curtis) looks uncomfortable and out of place in her evening dress when out on a date compared with the confidence she exudes when in her masculine uniform; in *Silence of the Lambs*, Hannibal Lecter undermines Clarice and her self-confidence when he identifies her cheap shoes and perfume; and in *Point of No Return*, while Maggie (Bridget Fonda) is proficient in street-fighting and firing a gun, she needs lessons in how to walk, dress, and present herself convincingly as a woman. This construction of female heroism in the early 1990s through signifiers associated with established notions of male heroism may account for what Mizejewski sees as the "lesbianization" of the female hero—aligning her with "illegitimate" notions of femininity in order to mediate her accession to heroism.

The most common method of dealing with the "problem" of the female detective in the criminalist narrative, however, is to enact an over-identification between the heroine and the victim (and to place her in the position of past or potential victim), and her masculinization (and related problematic relationships with men). Her salvation—i.e., "re-feminization"—occurs by the end of the film, not so much through her pursuit and execution of the killer, but often through her acquiescence to a "healthy"/heteronormative relationship with a male love interest. Hilary Radner argues that the masculinized or de-feminized "psychofemme" of the 1990s—for example, Sarah Connor (Linda Hamilton) of *Terminator 2: Judgment Day* and Margie Gunderson (Frances McDormand) of *Fargo* (Coen 1996)—offered a strong and independent model for women, one not dependent on sacrifice, acceptance, or reeducation demanded in melodramas and comedies (248). In the contemporary criminalist, however, the masculinized or de-feminized detective most often embraces traditional social roles at the end of the film. The male detective tends to be presented as a stable and self-controlled individual—for example, Morgan Freeman's Detective Somerset in *Seven* or Alex Cross in *Kiss the Girls*—or, if presented initially as traumatized or in crisis—for example, Denzel Washington's Lincoln Rhyme in *The Bone Collector*, Al Pacino's Will Dormer in *Insomnia* (Nolan 2002), or Clint Eastwood's Terry McCaleb in *Blood Work* (Eastwood 2002)—then the hunt for the serial killer and his eventual demise at the hands of the detective function to restore and revitalize the hero's self-confidence and prove his masculinity. On the other hand, those films with a female protagonist, echoing the female lawyer film of the 1980s, are concerned with examining their heroes' struggle as women in a man's world trying to balance a professional and personal life—and losing.

Like Clarice, the contemporary female criminalist tends to be presented as a somewhat masculinized woman. In *Murder by Numbers*, Cassie (Sandra Bullock) wears non-gender-specific clothes, most often a turtleneck or T-shirt with trousers and a black "pleather" jacket, little make-up, and her long hair is usually tied back for functionality. Cassie and her new partner, Sam (Ben Chaplin), represent a role reversal: she is the sexual predator in the relationship and he is the one who asks, "What about what I want?" Cassie's nickname, given to her by her male colleagues on the force, is "The Hyena"; the female hyena has a mock penis and Cassie acts as if she possesses a phallus. In *Kiss the Girls*, Kate McTiernan (Ashley Judd) is originally one of the killer's captives but later becomes his hunter and is presented as physically tough. In her kickboxing class, her muscles gleam and flex under the stress of her combat as her fists and feet find their marks, and her body is revealed in a sports top and shorts during these sequences of action rather than in feminine garb and in positions of passivity.

FIGURE 23. Ashley Judd in *Kiss the Girls*. Making a spectacle of herself: In *Kiss the Girls* (1997), Kate's (Ashley Judd's) body is presented as stripped off only when performing action rather than being sexually passive—a cinematic position usually reserved for men. Photo from author's collection.

In fact when she is held captive by the killer—drugged up and tied to the bed—she is covered up in a shapeless sweater. In *Twisted*, Ashley Judd plays a homicide detective, Jessica Shepard, who investigates a string of killings to which she is intimately involved: all the victims are men that she has had sexual relations with. Like Cassie in *Murder by Numbers*, Shepard's uniform is jeans and turtleneck sweaters under a leather jacket. Her hair is short and she is presented as pretty—but also pretty tough. She is also a sexual predator, roaming bars for passionate one-night stands with strangers. *Taking Lives* begins with Special Agent Illeana Scott (Angelina Jolie) portrayed as a smart and skilled behavioral scientist, with her self-control and confidence echoed in her put-together outfits: dark, slim-fitting shirts, dark trousers, and a blazer or leather jacket—and her hair tightly wound back. Even her name—she answers her phone with her surname, "Scott"—and her cool handling of her black Mustang convertible in a car chase suggest she is masculine. Like Shepard and Cassie, Illeana is a highly sexualized woman, and she develops what she describes as a "favorable reaction" to the lead witness, Costa (Ethan Hawke)—eventually having passionate sex with him. Although she wears a wedding ring—suggesting that, unlike the majority of female detectives, she has found a balance between her professional and personal life—she confesses to Costa that it is a prop, worn to ward off male advances.

While *The Silence of the Lambs* was generally regarded as "a profoundly feminist movie" (Taubin, "Grabbing" 129), the reviews of 1995's *Copycat* highlight the possibility of dual readings of the serial killer film with a female protagonist (or two in the case of this film). Lizzie Francke of *Sight and Sound* praised the casting of Holly Hunter and Sigourney Weaver as the film's protagonists—the detective and the potential victim—as "enhancing its status to an instant post-feminist classic" (51); conversely, Kenneth Turan of the *L.A. Times* argued that the casting led the filmmakers "to believe that they'[d] made a significant feminist statement, the movie's two hours-plus of almost continual sadistic abuse of women notwithstanding" (1). As Peter Krämer notes, the success of *The Silence of the Lambs*, as well as Foster's success in Hollywood as a result of the film, was the result of this move to a female hero who was not a marginalized or victimized woman (207–08). But despite this great start to the career of the female hero in the criminalist narrative, the majority of those who followed in Clarice's footsteps tended to be cast as hero but also potential victim. Even Clarice is cast as such in her final showdown with Gumb as he gazes powerfully at her through night-vision goggles (a view the audience shares) and she stumbles blindly through the dark unaware that he is right in front of her. Similarly, more recent serial killer films offer some of Hollywood's toughest and most attractive female stars appearing repeatedly in the genre—for example, Ashley Judd and Angelina Jolie—offering strong female characters while simultaneously undermining their agency through casting them as the former or potential victims of male violence. The female body—of the detective as well as the victim—thus functions as a site of the negotiation of masculine anxieties incited by a female presence in the traditionally masculine profession of law enforcement.

In *Taking Lives*, Illeana is introduced as a very successful and talented profiler from the FBI. The Montreal detectives she has been assigned to assist—Duval and Paquette—find her not at the airport but in the grave where the victim was buried. One of the problems with the film is the fact that this and other aspects of what the film's official Web site identifies as her "intuitive, unconventional approach" and "unorthodox methods" (www.takinglives.warnerbros.com)—like her posting of crime scene photos above her bed, in the bathroom, and on the chair opposite her at dinner— are never developed or explained. But the process of lying in the grave would suggest an attempt to align herself with the victim. Similarly, at Martin's childhood home, Illeana discovers a basement room where it is implied Martin as a child was confined, and she lies in his bed. She tries to identify with Martin, whom she begins to regard as a victim himself (of an obsessive and cruel mother) only to be attacked by Martin, who is hiding under the bed. Her renowned abilities as a profiler are called into question by her fellow detectives, and, to her horror, Illeana discovers that the witness—and the man she has fallen for—is, in fact, the killer she seeks. With her realization that she has been seduced by the killer, she begins to unravel emotionally, a loss of confidence mirrored by her increasingly dishevelled appearance, with her long hair in tangles and her red eyes rimmed with tears. Although she begins the film as a strong character, her inability to identify the killer correctly and his seduction of her portray Illeana as a woman successful in her profession but weak when it comes to men; it is her femininity that makes her vulnerable and almost one of Martin's unfortunate victims. But the usual cause of the female detective's inability to be both professionally and personally successful in the serial killer film is cited as a past trauma involving violence perpetrated by men.

Similarly, in *Murder by Numbers*, Cassie's singleminded pursuit of the killer and her abandonment of a personal life in favor of doing her job are attributed to her past: her abusive ex-husband attempted to kill her, stabbing her seventeen times. This attack haunts every aspect of her life: in her private life, she sabotages any relationship that brings any man too close—"That's Cassie's MO" her ex-boyfriend explains to her new partner Sam. And in her professional life, she overidentifies with the victim. As her boss explains, the detective must identify with the killer in order to catch him, not with the victim. Cassie's close alignment with the murdered woman (indicated by Cassie's referral to her by her first name) leads to her being removed from the case. Cassie must deal with her own victimization in order to move on with her life, but she avoids it at all costs. When Sam asks her why she became a police detective, she lies and says it was because someone she knew was killed. And later, when she recounts her traumatic past, she refers to herself in the third person: she uses a nickname and her maiden name, Cassie Mayweather, to differentiate herself from the victim of the attack, Jessica May Hudson. Although her own baggage does cloud her judgment—she was convinced Richard (the boy who reminds her of her husband) was the real villain, and killer, rather than the loner Justin, with whom she self-identified—by meeting face to face with the killers in this case, fighting them, and bringing them to justice, Cassie rewrites her past with a new sense of herself as a survivor. She concludes her rehabilitation by facing her former husband as a witness at his parole hearing and, when called as "Jessica May Hudson," Cassie answers.

Whereas Cassie used Sam for sexual gratification at the beginning of the film, before literally kicking him out of bed, the film suggests that by coming to terms with her past as victim she will now embrace a normal relationship with Sam. This concern with "deviant" sexuality is also made explicit through the "unhealthy" relationship that emerges between Richard and Justin (Ryan Gosling and Michael Pitt). The real-life killers, Leopold and Loeb, were rich, young men, and also lovers; while *Murder by Numbers* does not suggest that Richard and Justin engage in a homosexual relationship, it does imply that had Justin's teenaged exuberance been channelled in the more usual direction of sexual interest in girls, he would never have turned to murder as a hobby. He says suggestively to Lisa, the girl he likes, "If only I had met you first." She comforts him saying that, left to his own devices, he would not have killed—that Richard "seduced him" into it. Similarly, Jessica's "unhealthily" active and aggressive—i.e., masculine—sexual appetite in *Twisted* is also linked to murder as it is her one-night-stands who turn up dead in the morning.

While Cassie is haunted by her near-fatal experience at the hands of her abusive husband, the masculinization of the heroines of *The Silence of the Lambs, The Bone Collector,* and *Twisted* is blamed on the violent deaths of their policemen fathers at the hands of criminals. In *The Silence of the Lambs,* Clarice successfully navigates the patriarchal men who test or challenge her presence in law enforcement, brings the killer who eludes the male police and agents to justice, and concludes the film without abandoning her career and/or taking a more socially prescribed role as the "significant other" of a man. In the classic horror movie, Diane Dubois notes, the female protagonist is often recovered through being "rescued" from her career by the hero through marriage and motherhood or through her "abandonment of career-based ambition," but *The Silence of the Lambs* demands its protagonist does neither (305). On the other hand, *The Bone Collector* ends with Amelia recouped into this more traditional role: she effects Rhyme's emotional rehabilitation as he does not carry out his plans for his "final transition" (suicide), and he is reunited with his long-estranged friends and family by Amelia. More importantly, Amelia has suppressed her masculine sexual appetites apparent at the beginning of the film to be Rhyme's nonsexual companion: he is a quadriplegic, and sexual intimacy between the two occurs only through the stroking of his one finger that maintains feeling. The conclusion of *Twisted* also sees its heroine's femininity recovered as it is suggests that Jessica will embark on a meaningful and exclusive relationship with her police partner, Mike (Andy Garcia).

New Twists in the Genre

The more recent contributions to the genre, *Taking Lives* and *Twisted,* present a shift from the majority of serial killer films with female detectives that preceded them. Both films present a serial killer who preys on male rather than female victims and this, in turn, *should* present a shift in the representation of the female detective away from being the potential victim of the killer and male violence. In *Twisted,* Jessica is not a potential victim but rather a suspect in the case because the murder victims are men with whom she has had intimate relations. The past trauma that haunts her is that her father—also a police detective—committed a series of murders that concluded with her mother's murder and his own suicide. It is revealed by the end of the film, however, that it was not her father who committed those atrocities when she was a child, but her seemingly benevolent guardian and police commander (Samuel L. Jackson). He did not like the men that her mother was pursuing affairs with and disposed of them; similarly, he does not like the men that Jessica sleeps with and is killing them. Jessica does not suffer from an unhealthy alignment with the victims, fearing that she may become one; instead, she develops an unhealthy alignment with the killer, fearing that she may be the one committing the murders, like her father. Once she discovers the truth that it is her guardian who is the murderer, Jessica is "cured" of her neurosis—and thus her masculinity; she is able to become feminized—i.e., vulnerable—and fall in love with Mike.

In *Taking Lives*, the victims of the killer are men because the killer wants to be someone else with a life different from his own; so he kills in order to take their place and live their lives like a hermit crab, as one of the detectives notes in the film. Illeana does not suffer from a childhood trauma; she appears to be confident and stable. She does not overidentify with the victims and remains professional in her following of the case. But she does form an attraction to the killer—although unbeknownst to her. While she appears somewhat masculinized in the first half of the film, her traumatic realization that her lover is the killer sends her into a self-destructive spiral signalled by her increasingly "feminized" appearance. At the end of the film, she comes to embody hyperfemininity as she appears to be seven months pregnant with Costa's twins. He confronts her in her farmhouse hideaway and viciously attacks her—beating her, kicking her, strangling her, and ultimately stabbing her in the belly. What was interesting about this scene is the effect it had on the audience. At the screening I attended, the audience—myself included—was visibly and audibly disturbed at the sight of a heavily pregnant young woman being beaten so viciously. For Illeana/Jolie to engage in a fight with the killer seems to be acceptable to the audience only when she is masculinized; when she is feminized to this extreme degree, an incompatibility arises between her role as mother-to-be and "manhunter." But this image of the detective as feminized—the horrifying image of a pregnant woman being attacked and beaten—is only a masquerade; Illeana is not pregnant but only pretends to be in order to lure Costa to her so that she may exact justice by killing him in self-defence. Thus, the disturbing nature of the scene dissipates with the realization that Illeana is still a masculine woman merely using the masquerade of femininity to achieve her desire—to kill Martin outside the bounds of the law.

These more recent additions to the serial killer film offered new "twists" in order to attract viewers now familiar with the subgenre's conventions: *Taking Lives* and *Twisted* offer male killers who pursues male—rather than the usual female—victims. *Twisted* also attempts to surprise viewers by directing suspicion onto its female detective-hero who is, of course, revealed to be innocent of the crimes. One film of recent years, however, has broken with the conventions of the trend not only by presenting a serial killer who is a woman but also by making the killer—rather than a detective—the film's protagonist. *Monster* (Jenkins 2003) stars Charlize Theron as real-life killer Aileen Wuornos, and, rather than having a detective's investigation as the driving force behind the narration, the film focuses instead on the desires and crimes of the female killer. The film's critical success—Theron won both the Golden Globe and the Academy Award for Best Actress—and box-office success as an independent film—earning more than $34 million (www.imdb.com)—may cause Hollywood to reconsider the focus and formulation of the recent serial killer film. But much of the interest in the film, no doubt reflected by the awards it won, was in its success at transforming the female body at the center of the narrative. Rather than the bodies of Wuornos's victims, the film offers Theron's as the spectacle of the narrative. Theron—hailed as one of Hollywood's most glamorous actresses—was successfully transformed into the Florida prostitute-turned-killer with the help of make-up, greasy hair, crooked teeth, thirty pounds of weight gain, and a dramatic change in her physical posturing to disguise her years of ballet training. In other words, Wuornos/Theron is masculinized not only because her inattention to her looks, her unfashionable clothes, and her physical carriage are nonfeminine, but also because she commits what is traditionally male violence—serial murder—and engages in a nonheteronormative relationship with another woman. But at the same time, the film presents its killer as sympathetic—and, to some extent, justifies her actions—because she is the victim of male violence herself. Thus, while *Monster* deviates from the current mainstream trend with its focus on the killer—and a female killer at that—it does retain an emphasis on the female body, the masculinization of the female protagonist, and depicting women as the victims of male violence.

Women Can't Have It All

The female detective tends to be presented initially as extremely successful at her job: she is an intuitive and astute observer and tracker. Her failing tends to be in her personal life; she is unable to develop a satisfying and committed relationship with a man because she is married to her job or because she, or her father, was the victim of male violence. But a shift occurs during the film whereby the female detective's inability to form a normal relationship with a man comes to impede her ability to perform her job—as in *Murder by Numbers* and *Twisted*—or she becomes the intended or potential victim of male violence—as in *Kiss the Girls* and *Taking Lives*. Her personal life intersects with the professional and leaves her vulnerable and/or unable to do her job well. In *Murder by Numbers*, Cassie is pulled off the case because she develops an unhealthy identification with the victim and a dislike for Richard; in *Twisted*, Jessica is regarded as the most likely suspect as her father was a killer and she slept with all the victims; in *The Bone Collector*, Amelia is pulled off the case by the police chief as she attempts to play detective instead of keeping to her place as a beat patrol cop; in *Kiss the Girls*, Kate has escaped from the killer once but becomes his target again at the end of the film; and in *Taking Lives*, Illeana misreads the case and embraces the killer as a lover instead of recognizing him as the serial murderer. Like the female lawyer protagonist of the 1980s, the female criminalist is still plagued by the seeming inability to have both a healthy personal life and a strong professional one, most likely because her function in contemporary film is still to process and negotiate male anxieties centered on the proliferation of women in traditionally male spheres of public life.

While these films leave the heroine at a moment of balance—success in both her professional and personal lives—in other words, a happy ending—one cannot help but suspect that, having dealt with the traumatic past event that drove her to be a detective, our heroine may lose her ambitious—and "masculine"—drive in terms of work. Similarly, now that she has found romance and stability with her partner, the female detective will no longer be able to indulge in the singleminded pursuit of the killer. The lone male detective of the serial killer film remains unattached at the end of the narrative; like the Western hero, the detective must remain unencumbered by romantic and familial entanglements if he is to remain effective as the detective that operates on the margins of society on the thin blue line between crime and the law. The female detective, on the other hand, is expected to give up her independence and work with the team—especially her partner. While the female detective may prove her abilities as a "manhunter," she is ultimately contained or her success devalued through a reinscribing and containment of her professional ambition and aggressive sexuality in the contemporary serial killer film.

Or Can They?

The female detective has appeared more often with the proliferation of the criminalist narrative. But she has also appeared frequently in recent years in the detective film comedy. *Charlie's Angels* (McG 2000), *Miss Congeniality* (Petrie 2000), and *Legally Blonde* (Luketic 2001) offer a less serious approach to law enforcement and crime fighting and are a testament to the popularity of the female detective comedy because, unlike their more serious sister films that I have discussed above, they have all produced sequels.[8] Comedy has traditionally been more popular with audiences than with critics and scholars. As Geoff King notes, film comedy is popular but not prestigious, critically acclaimed, or award-winning: "Comedy, by definition, is not usually taken seriously" (*Film* 2). King defines film comedy as embodying one, or sometimes both, of the following impulses: to generate laughter through its disruption of harmony, or the normal state of things; or to move to, and conclude with, a happy ending, or a state of harmony being achieved (ibid 8). Technically, the vast majority of "serious" detective films (dramas vs. comedies) conclude with a happy ending or harmony (order) restored: the detective-hero successfully solves the mystery surrounding the crime and brings the killer to justice. But films like *The Silence of the Lambs*, *Kiss the Girls*, and *Murder by Numbers* would not be termed comedies, with the contemporary connotation of the term being the evocation of laughter and a lack of seriousness. The contemporary female detective film has seen actors like Ashley Judd and Angelina Jolie reprise their roles as the female criminalist in more than one film. But, while Sandra Bullock has similarly appeared in more than one detective film, her roles has differed greatly. In *Murder by Numbers*, Bullock plays your typical female detective: masculine in appearance, manner, and profession and driven to a career in law enforcement because she is haunted by a past in which she was the victim of male violence. Conversely, in *Miss Congeniality* (Petrie 2000) and *Miss Congeniality 2: Armed and Fabulous* (Pasquin 2005) Bullock portrays a comic detective hero. While the latter two films might appear less serious than *Murder by Numbers*, they explore the same core issue: a gender-bending heroine who attempts to balance her personal life while hunting a criminal and attempting to succeed professionally in the male-dominated world of law enforcement.

Although *Miss Congeniality* is comic throughout, with jokes, pratfalls, and unexpected outcomes, there is still a threat at the center of the film to investigate—a killer threatens to explode a bomb during the Miss United States beauty pageant—and a potential killer whose identity must be exposed before he/she has the opportunity to carry out the threat and commit murder and mayhem. To what extent is the film a comedy and to what extent a detective narrative, in the more traditional sense? In detective films like *Murder by Numbers*, there are comic scenes or moments—scenes that evoke laughter. For example, when Cassie explains to her new partner Sam that her nickname is "The Hyena" because she acts as if she thinks she has a penis. But these detective dramas do not offer comedy through the disruption of harmony or the expected way of the world. In these films it is the killer, using horror rather than comedy, who disrupts normalcy. *Miss Congeniality*, on the other hand, does offer comic moments through disruption; for example, early in the film, FBI agent Gracie Hart (Bullock) is on her way to work when she receives a call from her superior. The audience is not privy to the details of the call but understands it to be an emergency, especially when Gracie activates her rooftop light, races through traffic, parks illegally, and pushes her way through a crowd, all the while the dramatic score builds tension. The music comes to a noticeably abrupt stop as she reaches the front of the crowd and promptly orders a dozen coffees from the clerk behind the Starbucks counter. The film's self-conscious disruption of established generic codes marks it as a comedy.

King notes that comedy is not taken seriously, and, indeed, even this study of the detective genre offers only a limited consideration of this other mode (mainly because to do so would be another book in itself).[9] But comedy can be critical, and not just in the more obvious cases of political satire and black comedy. The very fact that comedy is *not* taken seriously can be liberating; as King argues, that fact can "sometimes gives it licence to tread in areas that might otherwise be off-limits" (*Film* 2). Detective film comedies like *Charlie's Angels*, *Miss Congeniality*, and *Legally Blonde* offer, to varying dregrees, a disruption of established gender codes. *Fargo* (Coen 1996), as a black comedy, is perhaps more obviously critical and disruptive than these "lighter" comedies with its presentation of a highly competent, stable, and successful female detective who dresses like a man while simultaneously being visibly pregnant. As a successful detective *and* wife (and mother-to-be), Margie breaks all the rules. But so too does Elle (Reese Witherspoon) of *Legally Blonde*, to an extent, offer the disruption of normal expectations as a ditzy blonde who makes it into Harvard law school and then solves a case. Even Natalie (Cameron Diaz), Dylan (Drew Barrymore), and Alex (Lucy Liu) of *Charlie's Angels*, unlike their serious counterparts, seem to achieve a cohesive feminine identity as successful action heroines who remain feminized. But unlike those other female detectives, the Angels are also highly sexualized and placed on display for the heterosexual male's viewing pleasure, which could be argued to compromise their "girl power" message. But perhaps Gracie of *Miss Congenial-*

ity is the most interesting of these female detectives because she so readily is a send-up and yet simultaneously an expression of the themes of the female detective drama.

The film begins with Bullock's character presented as a parody of the kind of heroine she would play two years later in *Murder by Numbers*, both which are based on a tradition of representation well established by the early 2000s. Gracie is presented not only as unfeminine but unattractive and lacking social graces in her uniform—a white dress shirt, black blazer and trousers, and what one woman points out are "masculine shoes." While these are the preestablished markers of the contemporary female detective, a lone woman working in a man's world, the film takes the stereotype further—and thus into the realm of the comic—by having Gracie walk, talk, and eat "like a man." Her masculinity is highlighted and ridiculed in Victor's (Michael Caine's) attempts to teach her how to be feminine—to transform her from what he calls "Dirty Harriet": she walks with a manly swagger rather than "glides"; she snorts when she laughs and replies "yeah" instead of "yes"; and she talks with her mouth full of burger and/or beer while ketchup drips onto her shirt and paperwork. Whereas the female criminalist of films like *Twisted* and *Taking Lives* represents a seemingly successful integration of the masculine into the feminine (at least at the beginning of the film), Gracie embodies the disparity between the two: she is not cool, competent, and attractive as are the "serious" female detectives, including her own Cassie Mayweather in *Murder by Numbers*, and is repeatedly shown as awkward, even tripping over her own feet.

Gracie is masculinized at the start of the film, and her competence as an agent is called into question when her disobedience gets another agent shot. Over the course of the film, she is feminized, although here it is for a job rather than a natural state of events that occurs as she "heals" herself by coming to terms with herself and her past. But the result is the same: her feminization attracts the attention of her male colleague, Agent Eric Matthews (Benjamin Bratt), and leads her to a "healthy," heteronormative relationship with him. Despite this ending, Gracie is shown to be an empowered woman and a competent agent as she solves the case, in part because of her intelligence and ability to read the clues, and in part because her femininity allows her to masquerade as a pageant contestant and get behind the scenes of the world of the potential crime. Gracie proves to be successful in both of these different worlds—the male world of law enforcement and the female world of beauty pageants. In addition, she proves successful in both her career life of law enforcement, having cracked the

FIGURE 24. Sandra Bullock in *Miss Congeniality*. She cleans up real nice: In *Miss Congeniality* (2000), a tough female FBI agent (Sandra Bullock) is helped to "pass" convincingly as a woman for a beauty pageant with the help of a man (Michael Caine) and an army of beauticians. Photo from author's collection.

case and saved lives, and in her personal life, having gained a close female friend, pageant winner Cheryl (Heather Burns), and a caring boyfriend, Eric. At the beginning of the film, Gracie is presented as a feminist who rejects feminine charms and skills like wearing makeup and cooking in favor of being good at her job. Her criticism of the beauty pageant at the beginning of the film is replaced by an admiration for the women who compete in it. Whether one considers her comment at the end of the film that the beauty pageant was a "liberating" experience as undermining any serious comment about gender roles in the twenty-first century is another point altogether. But the sequel does seem to atone for the "happy"—hetero-coupling and feminization of the heroine—ending.

Miss Congeniality 2: Armed and Fabulous begins with Gracie back at work three weeks after the pageant. Her convincing feminization that helped her infiltrate the pageant and also to gain notoriety for cracking the case have made her a celebrity and unable to do her job successfully; adoring fans recognize her, blowing her cover when she attempts to prevent a bank robbery. At the beginning of the film, she has rejected the hyperfeminization evident at the conclusion of the first film, but she has not completely reverted to her old, masculine ways: she wears muted make-up and presents herself more gracefully than before while sporting a gender-neutral outfit. Her fame, which inhibits her ability to perform in the field, leads her to a new role in the FBI—becoming its "new face" and spokesperson as she makes the talk-show rounds and writes a book. She internalizes her new hyperfeminine identity with her affected manner and speech and is contrasted to the new masculine female detective on the force—Sam Fuller (Regina King)—who is Gracie's bodyguard and echoes how Gracie was once—i.e., masculine. The film follows the movement of the two women's relationship from conflict to friendship through their investigation of the kidnapping of Miss United States, Cheryl, and the pageant's producer, Stan (William Shatner). Sam's masculinity—especially her aggression, inability to work well with others, and tendency to use violence to solve problems—is a running joke in the film. When their assistant from the Nevada office, Jeff (Enrique Murciano), starts to crack under the pressure of their unauthorized covert operation, Sam says to Jeff, "Be a man!" Gracie quips, "Yeah, like Fuller!" The first film ended with Eric coming to Gracie's rescue, while the second has Sam fulfill this role. While both *Miss Congeniality* films highlight the performativity of femininity with Gracie's ability to don and divest herself of it in order to do her job most efficiently, *Armed and Fabulous* takes this theme further. Ironically, Gracie and Sam are dressed most femininely when they infiltrate a gay club as drag performers—women masquerading as men masquerading as women. And, unlike the first film, *Armed and Fabulous* does not end with Gracie's acceptance of hyperfemininity and its related social roles (domesticated and coupled) as the preferred option. Instead, the film ends with her rediscovery of her more masculine self—indicated through her return to her original FBI uniform (white shirt, dark suit, "masculine" shoes) and her reembracing of violence as a necessary means. Also, rather than end with the successful union of a heterosexual couple, the relationship that is celebrated is the official partnering of Sam and Gracie back in New York.

Whether one takes comedy seriously or not, what one must take seriously is that *Armed and Fabulous* is centered on the relationship between two strong female characters who succeed in the male-dominated world of law enforcement where their male counterparts fail, and who consider the most significant relationship in their personal lives to be with each other: these comic detectives achieve the success in their professional and personal lives that their "serious" counterparts cannot. I would argue that while the majority of the female detective dramas offer qualified or even reductive messages about female empowerment, the female detective comedy seems to offer a more positive message. Of course it could be argued that the power of that message is undermined by the dominant comic tone of the film, but it is also that tone that is responsible for allowing these strong female characters and their successes to slip under the radar of writers or producers who do not seem to feel the need to qualify those messages. The comic overtone of these films suggests that the gender-bending issues they tackle are of no "threat" and, therefore, do not need to be taken seriously. Whether or not that makes it less powerful a message is up for debate because it is present nonetheless and audiences seem to appreciate these movies. I would argue that it is time to take these films seriously because, while Jessica, Amelia, Cassie, and Kate—the women of the female detective drama—appear once on the screen and are gone, it is Elle, Alex, Dylan, Natalie, and Gracie—the heroines of the female detective comedy—who are popular and return to the screen in sequels to continue their successes.

THE NEXT GENERATION

The female criminalist has been more prolific in fiction and on television than on the big screen, most likely because youth tends not to have the age and experience to be the thinking detective-hero and mainstream film tends only to present the young and attractive woman in the role of the action hero. Most notable is the absence of Patricia Cornwell's forensic detective Kay Scarpetta from the big screen as the novels centered on her have been bestsellers for more than a decade. Perhaps this is because Scarpetta is middle-aged. While the older male thinking detective—those heroes played by Clint Eastwood, Al Pacino, and Morgan Freeman—have been successful on the big screen, no older women have. Youth—whether the young woman in the criminalist detective film or the young man in the lawyer film—offers a specific kind of heroism: when the older men, aligned with outdated notions of masculinity, have gone bad, the youth is there to take up the reigns of justice. A series of films in the 1990s centered on this issue—exposing corruption within law enforcement—through the relationship between a jaded and/or corrupt veteran and a young and naïve youth. These films have focused predominantly on male youths, including *Training Day* (Fuqua 2001) with Denzel Washington and Ethan Hawke, *Dark Blue* (Shelton 2002) with Kurt Russell and Scott Speedman, and *The Corrupter* (Foley 1999) with Chow Yun-Fat and Mark Whalberg. But one offers a female youth faced with the decision of whether to expose the corruption she has discovered. In the serial killer film *Insomnia* (Nolan 2002) Detective Will Dormer (Al Pacino) encourages Detective Ellie Burr (Hillary Swank) to uncover the truth even though he may find himself under investigation as a result. As he lays dying as a result of a shootout with a killer, Ellie offers to "lose" vital evidence that implicates him in his own partner's death. But he tells her not to "lose [her] way" as he did and to always reveal the truth. She could cover up the fact that Dormer shot his own partner, but instead she keeps hold of the evidence to add to her report of the investigation. Ellie represents hope that, although the older generation of law enforcers made justice happen when they could not prove it, the new generation brings an idealism to law enforcement and also the brains and conviction to see justice done.

BAD BOYS AND GIRLS

The predominant criminals of the Hollywood detective film have always been men—from Sidney Guttman in *The Maltese Falcon* (Huston 1941) to Hans Gruber in *Die Hard* (McTiernan 1988) and Hannibal Lecter in *The Silence of the Lambs*. Especially in the criminalist narrative, the serial killer is almost always male, just as he is in reality. Women and youths do occupy the role of the criminal in Hollywood crime film, but rarely in the detective film. Films with a youth or female criminal tend to focus on the exploits of the criminals rather than the investigation of the detective-hero. But why? What is it about the female or young male body that offers different associations and readings of criminality? The young male embodies notions of social rebellion that will bring about his demise if not checked in time but is potentially recoverable and redeemable because he is young. Women, on the other hand, as the victims of patriarchal males, are allowed to get away with their crimes as long as those that they injure or kill "deserve" it—in other words, are more bad than they are. The youth and female villains have appeared increasingly since the cult of the villain was revived in the 1990s with the popularity of villains like Keyser Soze and Hannibal Lecter. But these young villains carry with them far less sinister associations, and audiences enjoy seeing them getting away with their crimes—mainly because they are perpetrated against dull and impotent older men.

Catch Me If You Can (Spielberg 2002) presents one of Hollywood's leading youth stars, Leonardo DiCaprio, as the criminal Frank Abagnale, Jr., that the detective, Carl Hanratty (Tom Hanks), seeks. But the youth as criminal is not presented as psychotic or murderous; rather, he is enigmatic and exciting. The film does not encourage an alignment with the detective, but instead with the criminal as he goes about his incredible exploits as a con artist and perpetrator of bank fraud. The film, based on the novel by Abagnale, is very much a comedic look at villainy and offers the audience the pleasure of seeing how Abagnale, a teenage con artist, appropriated $4 million and became an airline copilot, a doctor, and a lawyer, all without education or qualification by the age of nineteen. The film also revels in a nostalgia for the 1960s, the time that Abagnale's exploits took place, with lavish décor, costumes, and cars, and a sense that crime was much less prevalent and insidious than it is today.

The film, like the criminalist narrative, does offer an exploration of the relationship between the hunted and the hunter. Abagnale is the son of two fathers, in a manner of speaking: one, his real father taught him to develop his talents to be a crook; the other, his substitute father Hanratty, teaches him to use those talents on the right side of the law. Rather than the detective fearing an overidentification with the criminal on his part, as is usual in the criminalist narrative, in *Catch Me If You Can* it is the criminal who crosses the line through his overidentification with the detective. The final irony of Abagnale's true story is that after being caught, he was brought in by Hanratty to work for the FBI to assist in catching check defrauders, and later he was paid by big companies to design secure checks to prevent fraud. Although the film's criminal-hero was apprehended and brought to justice and, technically, does not get away with his crimes, the pleasure of the film is the excitement generated by Abagnale's exploits that disprove the maxim that crime does not necessarily pay.

Hollywood film has offered women a variety of roles since the 1990s, including the criminal of the erotic thriller—for example, in *The Last Seduction* (Dahl 1994), *Diabolique* (Chechik 1996), *Bound* (Wachowski Bros. 1996), and *Femme Fatale* (De Palma 2002). But these films tend not to be detective films as the focus of the narrative is on the thrilling exploits of the women criminals rather than on the law that would pursue them. *The Last Seduction* offered a revisioning of the themes of the erotic thriller of the late 1980s and early 1990s typified by *Basic Instinct* (Verhoeven 1992) by casting the independent, professional woman as a figure not to be condemned but celebrated. The monstrous female as a product of the paranoid male's imagination is recast as a hero of the contemporary society where men are weak.[10]

Both the youth and woman as criminal allow the audience pleasure of the alignment with the transgressors of the law rather than with the law itself. But why do we like these kinds of criminals and not mind their ultimate elusion of justice but not those of the grown male criminal in general? First, the female and youth criminals in these films are not cruel and sadistic murderers unlike the young serial killer (Brad Pitt) in *Kalifornia* (Sena 1993), who proves violent and cruel. On the other hand, the criminals of *The Last Seduction*, *Diabolique*, *Bound*, *Femme Fatale*, and *Catch Me If You Can* tend to be thieves (rather than murders), or at least they kill people who seem deserving of it—usually cruel and controlling husbands. Second, the bodies of the female and the youth are able to embody conflicting notions of villainy and heroism that the body defined as white, male, and distinctly American cannot. Bruce Willis, Mel Gibson, and Clint Eastwood do not play villains (unless in a comedic role like Willis's as an assassin in *The Whole Nine Yards* [Lynn 2000]) and, even if they did portray them, they would not be allowed to get away with their crimes. The youth criminal is still a boy, and, as in the case of *Catch Me If You Can*, he has the opportunity to go straight when he grows up. The female criminal, on the other hand, is seen as a victim of patriarchy and, thus, as long as her violence is centered on paternalistic and abusive males and not against innocent victims or society in general, then we do not mind if she gets away with her crimes. Similarly, those white, male villains that occupy nontraditional male bodies and commit crimes against those deserving of them are also somewhat redeemable; for example, Hannibal Lecter (Anthony Hopkins) is a European intellectual and aesthete, and Verbal Kint (Kevin Spacey) is diminutive, disregarded, and disabled. Just as the type of man who embodies heroism can imbue that heroism with certain associations, so too can the type of man who embodies villainy offer different kinds of villainy from the invisible killer to the admirable super-criminal.

CHAPTER NINE

Investigating the "Other":
The Cult of Villainy

[T]he psychopath may indeed be the perverted and dangerous front-runner of a new kind of personality which could become the central expression of human nature before the twentieth century is over.

—Norman Mailer, *Advertisements for Myself*

THE UN-AMERICAN VILLAIN

Hollywood has always constructed villains for its heroes to fight, but the villain has rarely received the critical attention that the hero has. Yet without the opposition of villainy there could be no concept of heroism. The villain represents that which is evil and morally wrong in society, but notions of villainy change with the times, just as notions of heroism do. As William Everson states:

> The activities of the bad guys tell us far more about the changing mores and morals of our time than a similar study of the good guys could ever do. From time's beginning, the basic *virtues* have remained unchanged. But social, moral, and legal behavior is forever changing. (*Bad* xi)[1]

253

Although some virtues may come to be seen as old-fashioned, they will never be deemed antisocial; on the other hand, what was once deemed antisocial can come to be seen as socially acceptable. Just as shifting social conceptions of masculinity can affect the constructions of heroes in popular culture, so too do they inform the constructions of villainy. And just as notions of heroism are linked to national myths of American masculinity, so too are those of villainy linked to "otherness" (in other words, un-Americanness) as a product of historically specific fears and anxieties.

Although the cinematic villain can be an American, he is most often made "other"—differentiated from normal society—by being portrayed as racially "other," and meditations on American national identity come into play when discussing the hero's adversary. The conflict between American heroes and "othered" villains can offer insight into the broader situation of international conflict at a specific moment in time: in many films released during and immediately after World War II, the cinematic villains were German or Japanese; during the Cold War, they were often Soviet; and during recent decades, new international villains have appeared, such as the Colombian drug lord and the Middle-Eastern terrorist. There is a long and established history of British actors portraying the villains of Hollywood film, beginning with the horror films of the 1930s and 1940s in which the monsters and/or evil doctors tended to be portrayed by actors such as Claude Rains, Lionel Atwill, Colin Clive, and Boris Karloff. As Everson states, in regard to Classical Hollywood cinema, "it is from England that the steadiest stream of villains has come" (*Bad* 118). The representation of foreignness—collapsed into Britishness either through British actors or the actors' adoption of a British accent—as villainous is the result of trying to define Americanness as heroic.

During the Depression, one of the myths that developed in Hollywood films was that of the gentleman adventurer. The hero—the cavalier—was played by an American actor, and his rival—the cad—was played by an English, or Anglicized, actor. The heroes included American actors like Douglas Fairbanks (senior and junior), John Barrymore, Errol Flynn, and Tyrone Power, whereas their villainous rivals were played by English actors like Basil Rathbone and George Sanders.[2] The films followed the adventures of the cavaliers, who were constructed as nostalgic heroes that perform chivalric deeds, not unlike the knights of old. Knights could not be intellectuals—they were men of action—and, therefore, the English cads were differentiated from the American heroes by their intellect. The most famous archvillains—

criminal masterminds with international empires—are associated with intellectualism. Professor Moriarty, Dr. Mabuse, Dr. Fu Manchu, and Dr. No are all cultured, educated men, which is indicated by their being doctors or professors. Harriet Hawkins suggests that in American culture it is a weak man who displays too much interest in poetry, classical music, art, or the ballet (13). This idea stems from the egalitarian virtues of the frontier and Wild West where the lack of a classical education (associated with the East) was not something to be held against one. The ability to use violence effectively against one's enemies became not only admirable in American film, but also necessary if the hero was to defeat the villain. The ideal of heroic masculinity in Hollywood film has traditionally been a violent one. As Joan Mellen explains, "Film after film has insisted that the masculine male is he who acts—and kills—without a moment's thought. To think is to be a sissy, a bumbling eunuch of a man" (9). Thus, the villain is differentiated from the American hero through his intellect, education, and/or love of the classical arts rather than his ability to be physical and violent. Rather than debasing himself by performing violence, the intellectual villain tends to employ "heavies" to perform that dirty side of his business on his behalf.

The sound era produced its own unique brand of villain—polished, suave, smooth-talking, and cultured—who arrived in the early 1930s just as detective films began to appear on the screen with increasing frequency. There may be differences between the types of heroes that populated the classical and transitional detective films of the 1930s and 1940s and the *noir*-detective film of the 1940s and 1950s, but their villains were similar. There is little to distinguish the wife-murderer of the classical detective film *Love from a Stranger* (Lee 1937) played by Basil Rathbone and the suave murderer of the *noir* film *Laura* (Preminger 1944) played by Clifton Webb. Everson regards Kasper Guttman (Sydney Greenstreet) of *The Maltese Falcon* (Huston 1941) as the definitive example of the mastermind villain of the detective story. He is portrayed as a foreigner and homosexual in opposition to Sam Spade/Humphrey Bogart's Americanness and heterosexuality; similarly, Joel Cairo (Peter Lorre) is also presented in the film as a foil to Spade's American brand of heroism, as a different kind of European overindulgence. Whereas Guttman is obese and cruel, Cairo is slight and effeminate, with his scented cards and perfumed handkerchief—a suave, elegant, dandified foreigner. Robert Corber argues that *noir* developed a distinctive iconography for depicting homosexual characters that stemmed from Classical Hollywood's signifiers of an upper-crust accent, effeminate mannerisms, and impeccable taste (10). These are the signifiers that are normally attributed to the Englishman or European: both Guttman and Cairo represent the extremes and consequences of European living—namely, that civilization has a feminizing effect on masculinity. This association of homosexuality and villainy persisted in Hollywood film: the psychopathic serial killer of *Dirty Harry* (Siegel 1971) is given markers of homosexuality—long hair, mincing run, hippie clothes—despite the fact that he has raped his female victims; similarly, the serial killer in *The Silence of the Lambs* (Demme 1991) is presented as longhaired, made-up, dancing with his genitalia tucked between his legs, and the motivation for his murders is the desire to transform his male body into a female one through the wearing of a "dress" made out of the hides of his female victims.

The construction of American masculinity in contrast to a European one was reinforced in popular culture during World War II. The civilized and cultured villains of detective films, and the British actors who played them, found a new embodiment of expression in the wartime villain. In the war and postwar periods, the hero "personified natural and national virtue, in dialectical opposition to an autocratic, aristocratic, and always well educated Enemy-Alien-Other, who personified un-American vice" (Hawkins 14). American popular culture has always associated intellectualism and cultivation with an ineffectual, homosexual, or even villainous masculinity. As Hawkins explains,

> any knowledge of the "fine arts" such as the opera or the ballet, and certainly any interest in matters intellectual, is virtually bound to mark a male character as either a sissy (by implication a homosexual), an ineffectual intellectual (a wishy-washy liberal), a doomed and damnable Faust-type scientist or a sinister, un-American villain. (13)

For instance, Everson notes that the highest-level Nazi villains in World War II films were portrayed as men of "supreme intellect and culture, placidly listening to Wagner while [their] storm troopers tried to beat a confession out of the hero" (*Bad* 130). These cultured Nazi villains were not played by German actors but by British ones such as Cedric Hardwicke, George Sanders, Herbert Marshall, and Basil Rathbone. The portrayal of the Nazi villain as methodical, regimental, and intellectual established a general stereotype of the cultivated villain for postwar film but was embodied by those same British actors who had played the villains in the wartime films. Thus Britishness came to be firmly associated with villainy in Hollywood film and "by the middle of the twentieth century, a familiarity with the fine arts and a cultivated British accent were all it took to establish a given male character as an enemy of the American way of life" (Hawkins 17).

This still holds true in contemporary Hollywood film as the majority of American film villains pitted against American male action heroes are played by British actors (even if they are portraying villains from other countries). For example, Alan Rickman and Jeremy Irons play the German villains of *Die Hard* (McTiernan 1988) and *Die Hard with a Vengeance* (McTiernan 1993), respectively; David Suchet, the Middle Eastern terrorist of *Executive Decision* (Baird 1996); Nigel Hawthorne, the British-accented villain of *Demolition Man* (Brambilla 1993); Gary Oldman, the Russian terrorist of *Air Force One* (Petersen 1997); and Welsh actor Anthony Hopkins, Hannibal Lecter of *The Silence of the Lambs*, *Hannibal* (Scott 2001), and *Red Dragon* (Ratner 2002). Even American actors like John Lithgow in *Cliffhanger* (Harlin 1993) and American characters like the U.S. Army villain in *Toys* (Levinson 1992) don British accents to appear villainous (J. Dawson 24). This tendency for British actors to portray the villains in American films has become so widespread as to reach comic proportions. An article in *The Guardian* entitled "How to Be a Euro-Villain" invited British people to see if they have what it takes to be an un-American villain, listing the attributes necessary to portray this stereotypical villain—a sneer, tailored suit or uniform, minions, weapon, clever comeback for the hero, etc. (Elias 6).

In Hollywood film, Americanness is thus associated with heroism; "otherness" with villainy. Whether it is the Nazi villain of the 1940s war film or the independent, careerist woman of the 1980s thriller, the villain is a product of a specific time and culture, but more importantly he/she functions as an inverse image of the hero. Whatever qualities the villain possesses, the hero tends to embody the opposite in order to defeat the villain. The villain in contemporary Hollywood film can be marked as "other"—foreign, ethnic, homosexual, or female—because the contemporary threats to American masculinity are perceived as globalization, and the feminist, civil rights, and gay rights movements. They can be foreign, as in *Clear and Present Danger* (Noyce 1994) and *The World Is Not Enough* (Apted 1999); ethnic, as in *The Siege* (Zwick 1998) and *Just Cause* (Glimcher 1995); homosexual, as in *The Silence of the Lambs* and *Hannibal*;

effeminate, as in *The Bone Collector* (Noyce 1999) and *Copycat* (Amiel 1995); or female, as in *Disclosure* (Levinson 1994) and *The Last Seduction* (Dahl 1994). Ultimately, the detective's masculinity is tested and proven heroic and successful in his defeat or capture of the villain that he pursues.

THE SUPER-CRIMINAL

Intelligence as the hero's most effective weapon seemed to die out with the era of the sleuth. With the shift of setting from the classical detective story's British country estate to the hardboiled detective story's American city, brains became a less effective tool when the villains were street thugs and the need for violence and physical strength became necessary attributes for a hero to possess. The master criminal, introduced in the classical detective story, continued to thrive in spy narratives, but he rarely was involved in any physical violence and, instead, had "heavies" to do his dirty work for him. But since the 1980s a new kind of villain has evolved: a hybrid, embodying the violence of the heavy and the intelligence of the master criminal. As introduced in *The Silence of the Lambs* and continued in *The Usual Suspects* (Singer 1995) and *Seven* (Fincher 1995), an emphasis on the detective-hero's need for both brains and brawn to defeat this new clever villain has become the rule.

The super-criminal is intelligent, violent, and often invisible; he commits murder and/or other crimes often for the more traditional motive of revenge, greed, or a misguided sense of justice. The super-criminal is differentiated from his predecessors in the detective film in that he is more intelligent and more violent and thus invokes a more dramatic test of the hero's masculinity because the villain has the ability to outwit the detective. He is highly intelligent like the mastermind criminal of the classical detective variety, such as Professor Moriarty, yet street smart and physically capable of doing harm to the detective like the adversary of the hardboiled variety, such as Guttman. Although he is ruthless and violent to the extreme in his crimes, he is admirable and even justified in some respects in his acts of criminality. The super-criminal embodies contemporary social fears of a criminal who possesses the brutality, cleverness, and power to beat the system—in other words, to get away with his crimes.

In an earlier chapter, I explored the rise of the contemporary criminalist in response to the invisible and dangerous serial killer; in this chapter, I will focus on the cult of villainy that has appeared in the last decade—the villain as evil, psychotic, and murderous but often more popular than the detectives who pursue them. Just as Fu Manchu proved far more appealing than Nayland Smith, Keyser Soze, John Doe, and Hannibal Lecter have developed cult status while their pursuers fade to the background. They are villains who are as enigmatic as they are evil, as admirable as they are terrifying. Hannibal is perhaps the most infamous of the three villains but certainly would not have returned to the screen, as embodied by actor Anthony Hopkins, after *The Silence of the Lambs* without the appearance and popularity of the other two—Keyser Soze and John Doe, both played by Kevin Spacey.

Keyser Soze

Keyser Soze of *The Usual Suspects* is a criminal of mythical stature.[3] Even the people working for him have not seen him, and most often they do not even know that they are working for him. Although Verbal's story turns out to be completely fabricated, the viewer is left to assume that the gist of it is based in truth.[4] Agent Kujan (Chazz Palminteri), however, never even suspects that Verbal (Spacey) is Soze until it is too late because Verbal does not *look* like he could be a criminal mastermind. "The greatest trick the devil ever pulled was convincing the world that he didn't exist," Verbal explains to Kujan. Little does Kujan realize that Verbal is Soze and that he, too, has convinced the world that he does not exist by employing a masquerade of ineffectual masculinity to disguise his true villainous potency.

The audience, like Kujan, assumes that excessive brutality would be embodied in a man with more than average physical strength. There is also the preconception that great intelligence would be embodied in a man who sounds intelligent. We do not expect brutality and cleverness to come packaged in the small, crippled body of a man who talks too much. Physically, Verbal portrays himself with a limp, a twisted arm, and ineffectual hands with which he cannot even light a cigarette. Socially, he portrays himself as one who talks too much, hence his nickname "Verbal," and as inept at conversation. When he is denied a coffee by Agent Kujan, Verbal launches into a story, just like a child would, about how when he was a little boy he used to get so dehydrated that his urine would come out "thick like snot." The effect of this performance is that he seems to have been weak and sickly his whole life, but also that he is very infantile

FIGURE 25. Kevin Spacey in *The Usual Suspects*. Convincing the world he doesn't exist: The audience of *The Usual Suspects* (1995), like the film's detective, assumes that excessive brutality and intelligence would be embodied by a masculine man, not by the small and ineffectual Verbal (Kevin Spacey). Photo from author's collection.

in his behavior and lacks normal social competence. Verbal presents himself as emasculated and presents Soze, throughout his narrative, as a powerful criminal mastermind; it seems impossible to reconcile these two identities in the body/person we are presented. The detective's preconceptions of what a super-criminal should be and the masquerade that Verbal/Soze employs are based on an anticipation of those preconceptions—and how Soze convinces the world that he does not exist. The film concludes with Verbal/Soze convincing the detective that his story is true and the detective's theory that Keaton was Soze; not only does he get away with his crimes, but he does so by confronting his nemesis—the detective-hero. Rather than evade justice by going into hiding, Verbal/Soze chooses to play a game with the detective, giving himself up for questioning to see if he can outsmart the hero. He spins a tale of fabrications and half-truths that the detective believes and walks out the front door, scot-free—game, set, and match for the villain.

John Doe

John Doe in *Seven* is like Verbal Kint—a deceptive and elusive criminal—and is portrayed by the same actor, Kevin Spacey. Not only does he employ a masquerade of weakness but he also remains invisible to the detective for most of the film. He is a serial killer but not a typical one: he demonstrates infinite patience and control, planning and executing his "masterpiece" (his series of killings) for more than a year. He does not kill due to blood lust, but out of a misguided sense of making the world a better place: his "work" is seven killings, each exacted against one who has committed one of the seven cardinal sins, as a warning to society in general. His *Gluttony* victim is a man whose only crime is obesity, and Doe's punishment for him is to force-feed him over a period of twelve hours until he dies. His *Greed* victim is a powerful defence attorney whom Doe forces to cut a pound of flesh off his own body before letting him slowly bleed to death over a period of three days. His *Sloth* victim is a small-time criminal involved in drugs, armed robbery, and assault whom Doe starves, tortures, and fills with drugs for a full year. His *Lust* victim is forced to have sex with a prostitute using a prosthetic phallus that is actually a knife. His *Pride* victim is a model to whom Doe offers the choice of killing herself or surviving with major disfigurement. His *Wrath* victim is Mills, whose wife Doe beheads. And, lastly, Doe is his own victim for *Envy*, his punishment for which is to die at the hand of Mills. His intelligence, cunning, and success make him more of a super-criminal than a run-of-the-mill serial killer, and, like Verbal, he is not the kind of man who immediately strikes one as a super-criminal, physically or mentally. The first images of Doe cast him as a shadowy, faceless, and violent man. When he finds detectives Somerset (Morgan Freeman) and Mills (Brad Pitt) waiting at his apartment door, he stands at the end of the hallway in a long black coat, a brimmed black hat, and holding a large shopping bag. Without warning he walks swiftly but calmly towards them. He drops his shopping bag, pulls out a gun, and shoots at them, all in one smooth movement. The unexpected attack catches the detectives off-guard and he fires repeatedly at them before running away. Mills eventually tracks him to an alley, where Doe knocks him to the ground with a crowbar. As Mills tries to raise himself from where he lays face-first in a puddle, Doe shoves a gun in his face. As Doe confronts Mills, the only image Mills, and the spectator aligned with him, sees of Doe is a blurred one.

In order to identify the killer, the detectives must first piece together his profile from his life and his "work" (his killings). Doe's apartment offers the detectives many clues to the kind of man he is. All his clothes hang in plastic covers, and he has multiple bolts and locks on the front door, revealing an obsessive and paranoid personality. His bed is narrow and bathed in a red light from a large illuminated cross that hangs above it, and his bedside drawer is filled with dozens of aspirin bottles, a rosary, and a Bible, demonstrating a devotion to religion. His study's shelves are filled with more than 2,000 identical notebooks, the pages of which are covered with small and careful handwriting that reveals his disgust with society and the machinations of his psychotic but highly organized mind. The body parts pickled in jars in his kitchen, and his darkroom filled with photos of the tortures he has committed on his victims reveal the horrors he is capable of. Similarly, the opening credit sequence of the film shows a montage of images: a blank book; a sketch on graph paper of two hands—one drawing the other in an infinite conundrum; a razor blade; photos developing; a new journal and boxes full of other journals; small and neat handwriting; the red light of the dark room, with developing photos and cut negatives; an article cut out and a photo being trimmed; an article or book on sexuality being censored; pictures of heads and faces; thread and needles for binding the pages of his journals; tweezers and cotton wool; from a dollar bill he cuts out the word "God"; and over top of this sequence plays the *Nine Inch Nails* song "Closer to God." As will be revealed later in the film, Doe feels that his "work" will bring him closer to God. These scenes establish Doe as possessing the same skills and interests as the criminalist: he is methodical, organized, and precise; he catalogues, preserves, and analyzes. These images of photos, writing, and instruments could just as easily be the tools of the criminalist attempting to find the villain, as they are the "art" of the villain himself. The artifacts in Doe's apartment support Somerset's impression of him, as Somerset explains to Mills: "Imagine the will it takes to keep a man bound for a full year—to sever his hand and use it to plant fingerprints—to insert tubes into his genitals. This guy is methodical, exacting, and—worst of all—patient."

The detectives and the audience feel they know John Doe before they even see him: they have seen his crimes; they have seen him in action; and they have seen his home. Yet he is not immediately recognized when he walks into the police station on the heels of Somerset and Mills, despite the fact that his hands and shirt are covered in blood. He is a small, unprepossessing man with a limp who does not look like he is capable of extreme and brutal violence. His manner of speaking is soft and, to attract the attention of Mills and Somerset, he has to raise his voice insistently. He does not look like a super-criminal capable of the horrendous crimes he has committed, which is one of the reasons why, if he had not turned himself in, the police would never have found him. As he says to Mills: "Realize, Detective—the only reason that I'm here right now is because I wanted to be." Doe represents a villain whose evil does not need to be performed for the camera to be effective; in fact, it is not until near the end of the film that he is seen clearly and speaks. As Kevin Spacey explained in an interview:

> When I saw the movie I saw the havoc my character had wreaked, and I understand why people responded the way they did. But you have to realize that the audience is doing half of my work at this point. Everything built up to that scene [in the car at the end of the film] and so you don't have to be drooling in the back seat—you just have to talk. (qtd. in Salisbury 52)

In *Seven*, Doe is invisible but his profile is evident—assembled through his victims and the information Somerset uncovers. When Doe is finally revealed to the audience, the audience experiences a powerful reaction and shock at the sight of him: a diminutive, intelligent man capable of such horror. His physical presence does not correspond with the gravity of his crimes, and that makes him an even more terrifying, and enigmatic, villain.

Like Verbal, Doe also does not seem to match Mills's preconceptions of the super-criminal. Mills cannot accept that the man who committed these terrible crimes could be anything but a raving lunatic. Somerset explains that it would be a mistake to be so dismissive of their criminal. Doe is highly intelligent, well read, and has the highest of moral standards: his crimes arise out of a desire to preach the word of God to the deaf ears of modern society. Somerset can comprehend the intelligence and brutality that Doe embodies in committing these crimes as well as the misguided morality that motivates him, whereas Mills has no ability to see insanity as anything worthy of respect. Doe is a combination of a brutal and insane serial murderer from the underbelly of urban society and the classical criminal masterminds like Conan Doyle's Professor Moriarty. Doe is capable of excessive violence but also of winning the game he plays with the detectives: Mills actually fulfils the villain's "work" rather than stopping it. The detective fails to be the worthy adversary of John Doe, a modern-day Moriarty.

THE VILLAIN AND METAPHYSICS

Patricia Merivale and Susan Elizabeth Sweeney define the metaphysical detective story as

> a text that parodies or subverts traditional detective-story conventions—such as narrative closure and the detective's role as surrogate reader—with the intention, or at least the effect, of asking questions about mysteries of being and knowing which transcend the mere machinations of the mystery plot. (2)

The metaphysical detective story does not follow the structures of the traditional detective story, whether the story is one centered on a sleuth, private eye, or other type of detective-figure. Instead it subverts those structures in anticipation of audience expectations, altering the focus of the story away from solution of the mystery to addressing unanswerable questions about identity, reality, and knowledge. One of the most dramatic shifts from the traditional detective story to the metaphysical is that of the ending: it is unsolvable. Merivale defines the metaphysical ending as one where the detective becomes the murderer he has sought. But Merivale and Sweeney argue that in other stories it may be that the sleuth fails to solve the crime or he only does so by accident (2). William V. Spanos characterized this type of story as the "anti-detective story"—a narrative that evokes the impulse to detect "in order to violently frustrate it by refusing to solve the crime" (qtd. Merivale and Sweeney 2–3).

Merivale and Sweeney argue that some films are metaphysical detective narratives, including *Angel Heart* (Parker 1987) because at the end the detective discovers the identity of the killer to be himself, and *Face/Off* (Woo 1997) because the detective has to literally take over the villain's identity to catch him (5). Just as Merivale and Sweeney see *Angel Heart* and *Face/Off* as examples of the metaphysical detective narrative in film, so too does Stanley Orr see *Pulp Fiction* (Tarantino 1994) and *The Usual Suspects* as examples of a similar trend—a deconstructive recasting of the traditional *noir* vision (65). He argues that these films, as well as others released in the past several years, invoke the conventions of *noir* only to subvert its fundamental assumptions and, in the case of *The Usual Suspects*, to move beyond the existentialist dilemma of the *noir*-heist formula and focus on the process of fiction-making itself (68). He agrees that as critics recognize "anti-detective" fiction, these films demonstrate that there is also "anti-*noir*." I would argue that *The Usual Suspects* and *Seven* are metaphysical detective films that subvert the success of detection, order, and heroism in favor of an exploration of questions about knowledge, truth, and evil. Both films are concerned with many of the themes that Merivale and Sweeney attribute to the metaphysical detective story.[5]

First, the detective of the metaphysical detective narrative is not heroic and does not restore order but is defeated. In *The Usual Suspects*, Agent Kujan believes he has solved the mystery—namely, that Keaton is Soze. But he is wrong, and the villain gets away. Rather than successfully protecting society from villainy, Kujan has aided its continuation. Similarly, in *Seven*, Mills and Somerset may solve the mystery of the killer's identity, but Doe is only brought to justice because he turns himself in. He also proceeds to go unpunished—at least in terms of the law—as he convinces Mills to execute him. Somerset may survive Doe's defeat and continue to be a detective, but Mills's career as a detective is over.

Second, the world or city is a labyrinth. In *The Usual Suspects*, the world is an empire to be conquered by Soze (and a strong sense of the geographical relations of those places is not made), but also a riddled maze of criminal activity. The film suggests that the labyrinth is so extensive and complicated—a web of lies, half-truths, and false signifiers—that Kujan will never be able to find the start of it to unravel and destroy it. In *Seven*, it is the city that becomes the labyrinth—it is nameless, timeless, and seemingly endless. The only image of the city not presented as the wet, dark, sepia-toned mass of concrete and tall buildings is that of the edge of the city presented in the last scene. The scene is full of light and color in contrast to the dullness of the city center. Nevertheless, one cannot help but feel that the city is inescapable, as the country road on which the final showdown takes place is riddled with wires and pylons, and still accessible by car and helicopter. The labyrinth of the city is characterized not only by maze-like alleys, but also by the feeling that there is no escape from it.

Third, the clues and evidence are ambiguous, ubiquitous, eerily meaningful, or utterly meaningless. In *The Usual Suspects*, the only clues—Verbal's narrative and the sketch of Soze—become meaningless. Verbal's narrative turns out to be a story of lies and misinformation founded on random signifiers—names, ideas, and images on the police notice board. Similarly, the artist's sketch of the Hungarian's description of Soze arrives too late to assist the detective, and instead only compounds his failure. On the other hand, in *Seven*, the clues and evidence are eerily meaningful. Doe's use of the seven cardinal sins to name his crimes and his references to classical literature not only test the intelligence of the detectives, but also provide the clues to stop him if the detectives can anticipate his next move.

Fourth, there is the idea of the missing person, the double, or the lost, stolen, or exchanged identity. In *The Usual Suspects*, Soze is the missing person/identity that becomes the basis for Kujan's investigation, and Verbal disguises his true identity as the villain who is sought. The film's story of detection ultimately becomes an investigation of identity. In *Seven*, the identity of the villain is the prime objective of the detective, constructed through an examination of clues and his crimes. But once the villain is apprehended, he functions more as a double for the detectives, challenging their notions of right and wrong, good and evil. He is intelligent and methodical—just like the detectives—and he wants to rid the world of evil—just like the detectives.

And finally, there is an absence, falseness, circularity, or self-defeating nature of closure to the investigation. In *The Usual Suspects*, the scene of revelation—the first montage of images and Kujan's explanation of Keaton as Soze—is exploded by the subsequent disclosure that Verbal is the villain. This disrupts the expectation for a traditional ending with order restored at the hand of the detective. But the film does give the audience a sense of closure with the surprise revelation of the villain's true identity. On the other hand, *Seven* ends with a self-defeating sense of closure. The villain may have been caught and killed, but there is no sense that order has been restored or that society is safe from evil. During the course of the film notions of good and evil are challenged, and the question is raised of whether or not contemporary society is fundamentally evil. There is no possibility for the triumph of good or the restoration of order because society is potentially evil and no order existed in the first place. Both *The Usual Suspects* and *Seven* depart from the conventions of the traditional detective story— whether this can be attributed to the films being anti-detective, metaphysical, or *noir*—especially with their enigmatic villains that manipulate and defeat their traditional heroes.

Manipulating the Detective/Audience

The detective narrative follows the investigation of a detective-hero— a semiotician who reads and interprets the signs left behind by the villain in order to identify and bring him to justice. In *Seven*, Doe deliberately leaves behind signs for the detectives to read and decipher: the chips of linoleum floor in the obese man's stomach; *Gluttony* written on the wall in grease; and the quotation from *Paradise Lost* pinned to the wall. The signs in Doe's apartment also can be read and understood, from the pickled body parts in his kitchen to the illuminated red cross over his single bed as well as the literature he reads. By decoding these signs the detectives can discover the psychology of the killer and the motives behind his murders. Similarly, in *The Usual Suspects*, Verbal's narrative offers the detective and the viewer a network of information and clues to be unravelled and understood. Like the traditional detective story, both films encourage the audience to recognize the clues, piece together the evidence, and reconstruct the story of the crime alongside the detective in order to identify the criminal.

Both *Seven* and *The Usual Suspects* follow this preconceived pattern of mystery, clues, and solution. But both films conclude with the subversion of these expectations. The series of clichés that begins *Seven*—the old cop on the verge of retirement, the hot-headed rookie on the rise, and the psychopathic serial killer—is then transformed into something interesting (Reynolds 61). The ending of the film is bleak and "subverts the ingrained Hollywood cliché whereby the cop [. . .] shoots the psycho" (Wrathall 50).

Instead of the heroic showdown between detective and villain or the taking into custody of the villain at the end of the film, Mills shoots Doe in cold blood and "lowers" himself to Doe's level. For Mills to act as hero, according to the conventions of the detective genre, he would have had to put his duty as a police officer above his personal feelings of anguish and brought Doe to justice to be punished by the law. Similarly, *The Usual Suspects* subverts the generic conventions by exposing Verbal's narrative as fabricated. Verbal's power lies in his ability to manipulate recognizable signs and play on the meanings associated with those signs—from his appearance to the tale that he weaves from everyday items in the room. In terms of character, Kujan and the viewer assume that there is a stability and reliability in the construction of character: Verbal is a "gimp" and Keaton is a sophisticated criminal. But this stability is subverted as Verbal turns out to be the criminal mastermind who gets away with his evil plan.

Merivale and Sweeney state that the metaphysical detective narrative, whether by intention or effect, asks questions about mysteries of being and knowing above and beyond the machinations of the plot (2). Although *The Usual Suspects* and *Seven* seem to be posing questions about the elusiveness of villainy (*The Usual Suspects*) and the prevalence of evil in society (*Seven*), ultimately these films seem less about addressing the fundamental questions of existence and more about subverting the rules of the genre or creating new rules. Surprise endings and super-criminals are presented to jaded audiences, rejuvenating a familiar genre and thereby offering new pleasures to the audience. These films with their super-criminals and unresolved endings may be the product of a desire to explore some of the unsolvable questions of existence, knowledge, and good and evil at the turn of a new millennium. Or they could simply be a renovation of the genre that offers the thrill of seeing cool villains finally beat the boring detective at his own game.

HANNIBAL "THE CANNIBAL"

The most infamous and unstoppable serial killer of the past decade has been Thomas Harris's creation: Hannibal "The Cannibal" Lecter. Hannibal's screen appearances began with *Manhunter* (Mann 1986), a film based on Harris's first Hannibal Lecter (then spelled Lecktor) novel *Red Dragon* (1981), starring Brian Cox as the villain. But Lecter's resonance for film audiences began with Anthony Hopkins's portrayal of the enigmatic killer in *The Silence of the Lambs*. It was a result of his overwhelming popularity that a sequel and prequel came to the screen a decade later with *Hannibal* (sequel) and *Red Dragon* (prequel), following on the heels of the popular success of *The Usual Suspects* and *Seven*. Although *Manhunter* did not, at the time of its release, garner the attention that the films starring Hopkins have since, critics and audiences alike have returned to the film and reclaimed it as a sophisticated thriller and a precursor to the contemporary trend of serial killer narratives. While *The Silence of the Lambs* was an Academy Award-winning film, *Hannibal* was considered a mediocre film at best. David Thomson describes the film as camp and self-parodic; he argues that if one takes Demme's film and Harris's novels seriously as receptacles for intelligence, ideas, and arguments, then *Hannibal* can be nothing but regretted (20). But what this series of films demonstrates is the changing themes of the detective film from the mid-1980s to the early 2000s. *The Silence of the Lambs* marked the beginning of the trend of the contemporary serial killer film but also a redefinition of heroism, with a female criminalist detective, and *Hannibal* cashed in on the cult of the villain that *The Usual Suspects* and *Seven* had made popular. What is interesting about the return of the story of *Red Dragon* to the screen is how it updates the themes of the story from *Manhunter* with its hero's crisis of masculinity in keeping with the themes of 1980s neo-*noir* and cop-action films to a focus on the game of cat-and-mouse played between the contemporary criminalist and the serial killer he or she seeks.

The Beginning of the Trend: The Silence of the Lambs

The contemporary serial killer is often portrayed as a less than manly type of masculinity. Jame Gumb (Ted Levine)—the killer at the center of *The Silence of the Lambs*—is a feminized man who desires to shed his manhood and literally to become a woman: he is a transvestite who wishes to be a transsexual. He kills women not out of sexual desire as many male serial killers do, but out of the desire to be like them; their deaths are merely the by-product of his main objective: to skin the women to make a woman's "suit" to wear. Gumb gets the nickname Buffalo Bill from the police because "he skins his humps," but he embodies neither the traditional manly masculinity his nickname evokes nor the sexual deviant the description implies. But *The Silence of the Lambs* is less interested in its transvestite killer than its enigmatic Hannibal

FIGURE 26. Jodie Foster and Anthony Hopkins in *The Silence of the Lambs*. A New Man for the New Woman: In *The Silence of the Lambs* (1991), Hannibal Lecter (Anthony Hopkins) has a worthy adversary (Jodie Foster) with which to match wits—unlike in *Hannibal* (2001). Photo from author's collection.

Lecter. Whereas Bill is understandable, Hannibal is the enigma of the story. He is the intelligent and twisted mind that Clarice (Jodie Foster) must understand and identify with in order to catch Gumb.

Hannibal is extremely cultured—well-educated and passionate about the arts—but at the same time he may be the ultimate savage: a cannibal. Julie Tharp argues that just as Lecter challenges the cultural boundaries between the civilized and the savage, he also challenges those between masculinity and femininity because he is cultured: "The epicurean, classical music aficionado, and artist capable of rendering a Florence street scene from memory is already dangerously feminine" (111). Tharp suggests that Hannibal is a New Man to Clarice's New Woman, talking to her about feelings and discussing perfume and fashion with her—unlike the traditional male. This representation of Hannibal as the cultured gentleman is not, however, intended to relegate him to the feminine, but to the villainous. In keeping with the tradition of American film villains, Hannibal is both intelligent—as a doctor of psychiatry—and cultured—as a lover of classical music. But despite being played by a British actor (Hopkins), Hannibal is presented as American. He regards his killings as works of art and "conducts" music in his cell after he violently attacks two security officers. Hannibal is admirable and in many ways even sympathetic; the audience grows to like the charming and gentlemanly Hannibal and is not displeased to see him get away at the end of the film, even though we know that he will be "having an old friend for dinner"—Dr. Chilton. Dr. Chilton is not a sympathetic character; he sexually harasses Clarice and torments Hannibal in a manner not in keeping with his profession. Hannibal's freedom is not seen as threatening because the audience knows that he admires and identifies with Clarice. As he says to her in the final scene, "I have no plans to call on you, Clarice. The world's more interesting with you in it." The adversary worthy of the detective is left to go free at the end of the film and to get away with his crimes, much to the audience's pleasure as it means he can return for more exploits in a sequel—*Hannibal*.

The Villain Takes Over: Hannibal

Ten years after Demme's *The Silence of the Lambs*, Hannibal Lecter returned to the screen in Ridley Scott's *Hannibal*, based on Thomas Harris's 1999 novel of the same name. But both the novel and the film seem to have come into existence merely to satiate the public's desire for more exploits of the monstrous cannibal rather than to advance the themes and characters of Harris's first two novels, *Red Dragon* (1981) and *The Silence of the Lambs* (1988). As Rachel Johnson notes, "*Hannibal*'s evident popularity reveals the cult power of Lecter as a cinematic monster. Charismatically identified with Hopkins, Lecter has become a cultural fact" (30). But instead of remaining the enigmatic anti-hero of *The Silence of the Lambs*, Hannibal becomes a sadistic and exaggerated villain, and, rather than being Demme's intriguing and maturing detective-hero, Clarice (this time played by Julianne Moore) all but disappeared from the narrative. Rather than being a meditation on gender and a well-crafted thriller like *The Silence of the Lambs*, *Hannibal* simply functions to resurrect the charming villain and to let him loose on the world to commit gruesome executions with little rhyme or reason. More importantly, he dominates the narrative with his killings and exploits but is given no true adversary with which to match wits—the winning formula for a satisfying serial killer film.

Between Demme's *The Silence of the Lambs* and Scott's *Hannibal*, Hannibal Lecter achieved a cult status as cinematic villain, so in the second film he—the villain—becomes the star of the narrative while the protagonist of the first film, Clarice—the detective—is pushed to the background, thus shifting the film from hero-centered to villain-centered. A detective film, by definition, follows the investigation of a detective-hero to discover who the perpetrator of the crime is and to bring them to justice. But in *Hannibal* the viewer knows the identity of the villain and the film focuses on his gruesome exploits rather than on the detective's investigation. Hannibal's identity is known and his whereabouts are known, but Clarice does not pursue him. Instead, it is Hannibal who tracks her. This is not a story of detection but of criminal violence, and the film shifts completely from the genre of the detective film to that of the horror film without sophistication or significant contemplation.

The attraction and repulsion of Hannibal's character in *The Silence of the Lambs* derived from his *potential* for gory violence, of which the film revealed little. Demme recognized the power to terrify through *not* showing Hannibal's killings and, instead, he allowed viewers to let their imaginations conjure up the worst images of violence. In *Hannibal*, Ridley Scott did the opposite. Rather than suggest horror, he exhibited it as often and as graphically as possible. For example, in *The Silence of the Lambs*, Dr. Chilton shows Clarice a photo of Hannibal's one female victim—a nurse he disfigured in the asylum—in order to impress upon her how dangerous Hannibal is. The viewer is not allowed to see this image, only Clarice's reaction of shock and horror at the sight of it. In *Hannibal*, however, Clarice—and the audience—view the surveillance video of this attack on the nurse from the previous story—a savage assault in which Hannibal tries to eat the woman's face. In Demme's film, none of Gumb's killings or mutilations of his victims are shown, and even Hannibal's attack on the security guards is only partially revealed—the viewer does not witness the removal of one man's face or the stringing up of the other into a crucifixion. On the other hand, Scott seemed to take great pleasure in visually recounting Hannibal's violence, offering his attack on Mason Verger (Gary Oldman) in a psychedelic flashback where Verger, in a drug-induced state, is persuaded by Hannibal to cut off his own face to be fed to his dogs; similarly, Hannibal's serving up of Paul Krendler's (Ray Liotta) brains to the victim while he is still alive is also offered in gruesome detail to the film's audience. The power of *The Silence of the Lambs* was the creation of a villain who has the ability to instill dread in audiences without having to be seen committing any violence. Hannibal is portrayed as the ultimately dangerous killer who must be caged behind a wall of glass—not approached, not come into contact with—because, given an inch of opportunity, Hannibal will kill and do so most violently. The result is a shift from a criminalist narrative with a meditation on the relationship between the killer and the detective to a horror one with an emphasis on gory violence. Hannibal is reduced from being a villain renowned for his cleverness to being known for his cruelty, from being a worthy adversary to a sadistic killer, and with this reduction he is less admirable.

From Crisis to Criminalist: Manhunter *to* Red Dragon

If audiences were worried that Hannibal, once free, might never return to the screen, their fears have been laid to rest with the release of *Red Dragon*. The film is the prequel to both *Hannibal* and *The Silence of the Lambs* and introduces a younger Hannibal Lecter before his capture and incarceration in Dr. Chilton's Baltimore institution. Jude Law was originally in talks to play the villain's younger self (Medicoff 14), but it is unlikely that audiences would have taken pleasure in seeing Hollywood's most popular villain recast. Instead, Hopkins, with the aide of a workout regime that helped him lose twenty pounds and computer graphic effects that erased facial wrinkles, took up the role once again. The film announces its relationship to the previous installments in the Hannibal franchise with an in-joke at the beginning of the film, opening with Hannibal attending a concert of the Baltimore Philharmonic Orchestra and his obvious distaste for the poor playing of one of the flautists. Later on that evening he serves dinner to the members of the Philharmonic's Board, the suggestion being that "dinner" is in fact Benjamin Raspell, the mediocre flautist that Hannibal is credited with killing in his last film.

In Harris's novel *Red Dragon*, the capture of Hannibal was never related other than in passing. Similarly, *Manhunter* began with Special Agent Will Graham (William Petersen) being called upon to assist in the "Tooth Fairy" case and eventually turning to his nemesis Hannibal Lecktor (Brian Cox) for help, but his previous dealings with the villain are not shown. Ratner's *Red Dragon*, on the other hand, prefaces Graham's return to duty with his preceding clash with Hannibal. Hannibal had been assisting Graham (this time played by Edward Norton) in tracking a killer, but Graham realizes that it is Hannibal who is, in fact, the killer at the same moment that he attempts to make Graham his next victim. Able to defend himself, Graham is badly wounded, but Hannibal is as well, and both go into retirement. This creation of an initial interaction between the detective and the killer is necessary for the film to develop a relationship between the two, a relationship that is left mainly undeveloped by *Manhunter*. Rather than an emphasis on an intellectual game played between Graham and Dolarhyde (Ralph Fiennes), *Red Dragon*—like *The Silence of the Lambs* and *Hannibal*—establishes Hannibal as the adversary of the hero. In *The Silence of the Lambs*, Clarice is on the case of a killer known as "Buffalo Bill," and, in *Red Dragon*, Graham pursues the "Tooth Fairy"; both detectives are forced to seek out the help of Hannibal, a noted forensic psychologist despite his psychosis. It is Hannibal who is the worthy adversary with whom they must match wits in order to unravel their cases, rather than the killers that they seek.

But in *Manhunter*—Michael Mann's adaptation of Harris's novel— the doctor is notable by his absence. While *Dragon*'s Graham (Norton) carries with him a deep-seated sense of fear because of his experiences with Hannibal, *Manhunter*'s Graham (Petersen) is outright traumatized, and the film explores his crisis of masculinity brought about by hunting another killer. In the past *Dragon*'s Graham came too close to Hannibal, which almost cost him his life. But *Manhunter*'s Graham came so close as to think like the doctor—to transform his mind into that of a killer's. Both Grahams had to spend time in the psychiatric ward of a hospital after their initial dealings with Hannibal, but whereas *Dragon*'s is able to face his demons, *Manhunter*'s runs away—and *never comes back*. As the manhunter of the film's title, Graham explains to his son, "It's only my job to find them." But as he hunts the Tooth Fairy, Graham proves once more that to catch a killer the hero must first be able to think like one—to pick up the scent of the trail. At the beginning of the film, he chooses to visit Lecktor (Cox) in order to "recover the mindset" of a killer. Although *Dragon*'s Graham displays fear in the presence of Hannibal, this seems to stem from a lack of maturity on the part of the detective—he seems somewhat naïve and intimidated by the power he sees in the killers he faces. On the other hand, *Manhunter*'s is traumatized by his visit to Lecktor, who pushes the right buttons to set him off. At the end of their visit, Lecktor suddenly asks: "Do you know how you caught me, Will?" Graham does not wish to hear the answer and tries to make a hasty retreat from Lecktor's cell, but the door is locked. Lecktor repeats: "You know how you caught me? The reason you caught me, Will, is we're just alike." As Graham charges out the door, Lecktor adds: "You want the scent? Smell yourself." Graham bolts from the cell and then down a seemingly neverending series of ramps in a sterile, airless, white space until he finally reaches fresh air and the world slowly comes back into focus—quite literally. He leans against the railing and stares at the lawn, which is at first a blur of color and then comes into focus as he calms down. In his dealings with Lecktor before, Graham crossed the fine line between trying to understand the mindset of a killer and possessing one himself. This encounter with his old adversary has pushed him close to the edge of insanity once again and this is the danger his wife later reiterates: "You'll make yourself sick or get yourself killed."

Manhunter presents the overidentification with the killer taken to its limit. From his first visit to the home of the killer's latest victims, the Leeds family, Graham is cinematically identified with the killer. The opening scene of the film is dominated by a subjective shot from the killer's point of view as he shines a flashlight onto his victim, Mrs. Leeds, as she sleeps and then wakes. Similarly, when Graham comes to investigate the house it is nighttime and the camera offers the viewer a subjective shot from his point of view as he walks up the stairs to the bedroom with a flashlight guiding his way. As his investigation proceeds, Graham begins to carry on a one-sided dialogue with the killer as if he were present. Graham has already begun to overidentify with the killer (spelled Dollarhyde in this film) and as he waves goodbye to his family at the airport, he turns to his own reflection in the window and speaks—as if to Dollarhyde—"Just you and me now, sport." Later, Graham returns to the Leeds's home for another look and now speaks in the first person *as* the killer rather than *to* him. He looks at the bed in the master bedroom and declares: "I see you there." Then he conjures up the image of the victim once more in her bed and then imagines her eyes as reflective, just as Dollarhyde would have seen them with pieces of mirror inserted into them. In his confrontation of the killer, Graham does not wait for backup, and, instead, he attacks the killer alone. A fight ensues and, in a shoot-out, he kills Dollarhyde. By destroying the killer, Graham has, in fact, "cured" his own psychosis, which was brought about through an overidentification with the killer and his mindset. Whereas *Dragon*'s detective was merely scared into retirement through his earlier dealings with Hannibal and must catch the Tooth Fairy in order to prove himself, for *Manhunter*'s hero it is his very sanity that is on the line, and his defeat of the killer is necessary for his own salvation. *Manhunter* offers a hero in crisis, and the film's investigation becomes centered on his masculinity. By confronting and defeating Dolarhyde, Graham proves his masculinity and thus his crisis ends. On the other hand, *Red Dragon* offers a much greater proportion of screen time to both Dolarhyde (Fiennes) and Hannibal and the masculine crisis suffered by the former and the game of cat-and-mouse played by the latter. *Red Dragon*, like *The Silence of the Lambs* and unlike *Manhunter*, offers a division of labor between the two killers.

Red Dragon increases the emphasis on Hannibal, but its mistake is to also increase the presence of the film's other killer—Dolarhyde. In *Manhunter*, Lecktor (Cox) appears once during Graham's visit with him and is later heard in a phone call; in *Red Dragon*, on the other hand, Hannibal (Hopkins) is in several scenes, including those depicting multiple visits by Graham and the important first and final scenes of the film. The consequence of these frequent meetings between the detective and Hannibal is that, unlike in *Manhunter*, where the detective is so traumatized by his one visit with the killer that he cannot go back, the viewer sees *Dragon*'s hero overcome his fears. This Graham is able to build up his resistance to Hannibal with each meeting and regains his confidence enough to manipulate Hannibal into helping him, and, thus, undo any residual damage that Hannibal had inflicted upon the mental health of the hero. Dolarhyde is also much more fully developed than his *Manhunter* counterpart. He is introduced to the viewer in the credit sequence through his scrapbook containing newspaper clippings on Hannibal but also images of child abuse and Dolarhyde's past, offering an early insight into the mind of the killer. The crisis of masculinity in this film is experienced by the killer, not the hero, as Dolarhyde is the victim of traumatic childhood abuse at the hands of his grandmother, represented by the abandoned Victorian sanatorium in which he resides. When out of the house, he is able to resist the "call" of the Red Dragon (the poster of Blake's painting up in the attic) and act relatively normal; only at home does he begin to feel the affect of "Him," and, in the end, he destroys his house in an effort to free himself from the Dragon's power. In *Manhunter*, Dollarhyde is an unknowable character; the only motive offered for his crimes is the fantasy of being desired and wanted. In *Red Dragon*, a much fuller profile is drawn of the killer, and the viewer is moved to sympathy for him.

It is the other killer, however, who steals the show: the film begins and ends with Hannibal/Hopkins. Just as the film begins with tying the narrative back to *Hannibal* with the Doctor's murder of Benjamin Raspell, it also concludes with tying the narrative forward to *The Silence of the Lambs*. Chilton announces to Hannibal that he has a visitor in a repetition of the scene from *The Silence of the Lambs* where Hannibal's next adversary, Clarice Starling (unseen here), arrives at the asylum to consult with him on the Gumb case. *Hannibal* and *Red Dragon* are very much showcases for Hollywood's most charming and notorious villain—Hannibal "The Cannibal" Lecter.

GETTING AWAY WITH IT

The characteristics of villainy change over time because what society deems socially deviant changes with time. Villains are the individuals that indulge in the activities and behavior that society finds unfit, illegal, and morally wrong; they also represent our fears about social decay. Just as American society in the 1930s feared that gangsters were running the city streets, or in the 1950s that organized crime was taking over the city, so too does contemporary society have its own fears about crime in the city. However, the crimes committed by Soze, Doe, and Hannibal are not new. The 1980s saw dozens of films about drug lords, criminals betraying their friends, and serial killers on the rampage. So what makes these villains different from their predecessors? The real fear addressed—or attraction offered—by these films is that these criminals are violent, intelligent, and getting away with their crimes, and the law seems powerless to stop them.

In *The Usual Suspects*, Soze represents an elusive power of villainy. The story of Soze's past sounds like an urban myth. As Verbal tells Kujan, the story of Soze is that of the Bogey Man, a spook story that criminals tell their kids at night to make them behave. The reality of Soze is in some ways so mundane: he is the small, seemingly crippled, innocuous man seated before

Kujan. But part of Verbal's ability to keep his true identity undetected is to perpetuate the myth of Soze. No one knows what his parentage is, although it is thought that he is Turkish with a German father. This might be true, as *soz* is Turkish for "word" and would suggest Verbal is Soze. Foreigners as villains have always been a common trope, and not just of the detective film. Allen Woll and Randall Miller argue that the racial images present in American film do not exist to make a racist statement but to serve as metaphors for those film characters who are outsiders or "other" (7). The different kinds of people represented by these characters become inter-changeable since they all represent the same theme: namely, that the ene-mies of America are un-American. By presenting evil or criminality as something foreign, one can protect the sanctity of American culture and heroism. But the comfort in thinking that Soze is foreign and a myth is overturned when it is revealed that Soze is, in fact, Verbal. Not only is he an American, but he can also masquerade as a small, ineffectual "Mr. Nobody"—like the serial killer. Gwendoyn Audrey Foster notes that science fiction and horror films of the 1950s featured unstable white bodies—out of control, invisible, visibly monstrous, and abnormal ("Monstrosity" 39); today's "monsters," such as the serial killer, are frighteningly unassum-ing and *apparently* normal. Soze is an interesting example of a powerful man who masquerades as abnormal in order to sneak under the detective's radar, and the fear that he represents is that criminals are more powerful than the law, invisible, and getting away with their crimes. The chief of police, the mayor, and the governor all give protection to Soze because he has that kind of power; no one knows who he really is before it is too late. He has not been and will not be stopped.

John Doe, similarly, represents specific social fears about contempo-rary crime. He is a brutal serial killer who tortures victims of all levels of society (from lawyers to prostitutes) in horrifying ways. Christopher Shar-rett has remarked that *Seven* exemplifies the "exhaustion" of film at the turn of the millennium because it is neo-conservative and recycles mainly Hollywood clichés—including the unsettling *mise-en-scène* of the horror film and the older man-young acolyte archetypal relationship of the action film—under the guise of being a "provocative, risk-taking" film ("End" 321 and 329). While I agree with Sharrett that the film certainly relies on these recognizable tropes, it does use them in a manner that breathed new life into the detective genre—redefining the cop-action film with the shift toward the criminalist narrative. Rather than the turn toward comedy that defined the cop-action film in the 1990s (and still does today), *Seven* offered a more serious meditation on the cop-hero and his fraught relationship with his partner, partly through this much darker and more horrific world within which the heroes worked. Sharrett argues that the film is conservative in terms of how it presents and resolves the battle between good and evil and yet also suggests that the film does not provide easy answers for its metaphysical deliberations. He notes that Somerset's reading of the classical texts referenced in Doe's "work" is less about finding clues to the killer's logic and more about

> valorizing pre-Enlightenment thought and recovering a philosophy that will restore stability to the off-kilter world. The film insists on the notion that crime is rooted in an unknowable "evil" rather than social causes, and is therefore beyond the remedy of science and reason as marshaled by modern institutions. ("End" 321)

The film does suggest that we cannot combat today's evil with our contemporary methods and attitudes toward crime. But what Sharrett does not address is the fact that the film essentially offers up Doe as the law-enforcing hero. This is a step further than what Linnie Blake explores—the serial killer as the last American hero. While Blake and others (as previously discussed) see the serial killer as embodying the independence, violence, and freedom from the law that the frontier hero evokes, *Seven*, although only somewhat tentatively, suggests that it takes evil to combat evil and that only someone like Doe can rid the world of sin. The contemporary city is the new Wild West, and, in our savage world, we need a savage hero who feels no remorse in exacting punishment for those who sin against the system but which the system is incapable of stopping. As Somerset points out, Doe is invisible to the law; otherwise he would not have been able to torture his victims for such long periods of time without getting caught. If he had not turned himself in as part of his fanatical plan, he could have stayed at large and been able to commit more crimes because the police were unable to find him. Like Soze, he has the power and intelligence to beat the system—but the greatest fear Doe represents is that he might be right. Somerset and Mills accuse him of killing innocent people, but he responds vehemently, "Only in a world this shitty could you even try to say these people were innocent and keep a straight face. But that's the point." So maybe Doe is right: contemporary society regards these people as innocent and that is what is wrong with society. Despite the brutality of his actions, Doe's forced attrition on his victims is an answer since the law seems incapable of stopping the crime and vice of contemporary society.

At the end of *Manhunter* and *Red Dragon*, Hannibal is safely locked away in a Baltimore psychiatric hospital. But at the end of both *The Silence of the Lambs* and *Hannibal*, he escapes to freedom. Although he is supposedly an unstoppable killer and a violent criminal, the escape of Hannibal does not strike fear in the hearts of viewers. He may kill violently and continually elude capture by society's toughest law enforcers, but he is not the typical serial killer that society loves to fear. The serial killer is a frightening figure because he seems to prey randomly on the innocent of society: we are not safe from his attacks. Hannibal, however, does not prey on the innocent, and there is no fear that he will kill us. He kills those who threaten him, who cage him or attempt to capture him, or who threaten Clarice. As Barney (Frankie Faison), the former guard at Chilton's asylum, explains, Hannibal only kills those who are "rude" to him—the vulgar, the disrespectful, those who try to exert their authority over him. Hannibal tends only to kill—and consume—the guilty: Dr. Chilton (*Silence*) sexually harasses Clarice and torments Hannibal; similarly, Krendler (*Hannibal*) is homophobic, corrupt, and sexually harasses Clarice despite being married. Hannibal is not a random and senseless killer, which is why the audience does not mind that he escapes rather than being captured by the law.

The super-criminal is the product of contemporary society: a combination of the characteristics of different types of villains from different social and cinematic moments. Verbal and Doe embody the incredible intellect of the criminal mastermind like Dr. No or Fu Manchu, but unlike them Doe and Soze are not foreign villains but American ones. In Hollywood film, Doe and Soze represent a fear that excessive evil, which was once possessed only by "others" like the wartime Nazi villain, now exists within American society. Doe, Soze, and Hannibal also possess the excessive brutality evoked by the serial killer of detective fiction of the last two decades by authors like Patricia Cornwell, James Patterson, Jeffrey Deaver, and Thomas Harris. But the representation of villainy embodied by the contemporary super-criminal—violent but intelligent, evil but enigmatic—does represent a shift from the "othered" villain that preceded the 1990s and still continues in action films concerned with international affairs. How is the national myth of heroism worked through in the narratives and characters of the contemporary detective film? The villain has become elusive and invisible; he wears the mask of normalcy and appears to be an average

American. The myth of national heroism has taken an inward turn, recognizing that evil is not readily discernable from good and that it resides within society as well as without. That said, there is a level of reassurance offered by these films. In *The Usual Suspects*, the sympathies of the audience are aligned with Verbal as a victim of Kujan's self-importance and vanity; in *Seven*, a pattern and motivation is discernable even with Doe's killings; and in the Hannibal films, Hannibal only kills those who "deserve" it. After all, Soze's victims, and to some extent Doe's and Hannibal's, were not innocent people, which makes the villains killing them seem less culpable. Why are we obsessed with villains in film at the moment? Because, as Murray Pomerance notes, "Calling Hannibal Lecter an epitome of evil is a way to help people organize themselves morally" ("Bad" 7). But because we are given an insight into the villains' minds, an understanding of the motivation of their crimes, and a sense of the ineptitude of the detective-heroes, we do not necessarily mind that the villains are getting away with it.

CHAPTER TEN

End of the Investigation: Case Closed

The detective genre has had a long history on the big screen, appearing almost as soon as the medium was born and becoming popular in the sound era as its many characters, complicated plots, suspense, and intrigue were developed. Each decade has seen the dominance and proliferation of at least one trend in the genre: the classical sleuth and softboiled detective in the 1930s and 1940s, the *noir* private eye in the 1940s and into the 1950s, the procedural police detective of the late 1940s and the 1950s, the vigilante cop of the late 1960s and early 1970s, the neo-*noir* hero in the 1970s and 1980s, the cop-action hero in the 1980s, and the criminalist of the 1990s and 2000s. These trends have often mirrored what was popular in fiction, and later on television, but broader social, cultural, and political change have had an impact on the detective narrative and the evolution of the investigative hero. Americans escaped the Depression through the Classical Hollywood detective film, and postwar American society was critiqued by *film noir*; Vietnam was refought and often won, and Reaganite politics were embodied in the triumphs of the cop action hero; and today's fears of violent crime and technology are placated by the criminalist's use of the latter to eradicate the former. At moments over the last century when gender roles were being redefined in society, Hollywood detective films have expressed, explored, and often resolved masculine anxieties through highlighting sexual difference with violent heroes and dangerous women. The genre has evolved and altered in a negotiation of social attitudes and anxieties toward the law, crime, gender, and heroism—and the genre will continue to do so.

I remember being asked by a *noir* critic in the spring of 2002 what I thought was going to happen to the detective genre now that the serial killer/criminalist narrative was over. My response was that I did not think it was over: I argued that more female and black criminalists would grace the screen before the trend finally petered out, and that the criminalist would proliferate in television shows. In 2002 *Insomnia* and *Blood Work*, with older detectives (Al Pacino and Clint Eastwood), were released, along with *Murder by Numbers* and *High Crimes*, with female detectives (Sandra Bullock and Ashley Judd partnered with Morgan Freeman); 2004 saw *Twisted* and *Taking Lives*, both featuring female detectives (Ashley Judd and Angelina Jolie) and serial killers who kill men in another twist of the conventions of the genre. And just as I thought that the trend might be coming to an end on the big screen in 2004, new serial killer films appeared, including *Suspect Zero* (Merhige 2004) starring Aaron Eckhart as an FBI agent hunting a serial killer (Ben Kingsley) who hunts serial killers; *Hostage* (Siri 2004) starring Bruce Willis as a former LAPD hostage negotiator faced with a serial killer (Ben Foster) who might kill his family; *Mindhunters* (Harlin 2004) starring an ensemble cast, including Val Kilmer, Christian Slater, and Jonny Lee Miller, as a group of FBI agents in training who discover that one of them is a killer; and *Saw* (Wan 2004) about a serial killer who plays games with his victims, getting them to kill each other to survive. The criminalist and serial killer genres seem to be going strong in the fiction of Patricia Cornwell, Jeffrey Deaver, and James Patterson, and on television, with the criminalist still dominating the police drama, including spin-offs from *CSI* (*Miami* [2002–] and *NY* [2004–]) and *Law & Order* (*Special Victims Unit* [1999–], *Criminal Intent* [2001–], and *Trial by Jury* [2005–]). But while the criminalist narrative is still popular in fiction and on television, the cool reception of *Twisted* and *Taking Lives* and the almost complete disregard of *Suspect Zero* suggests the serial killer narrative may soon disappear from the big screen. It will be interesting to see how a new series like *The Inside* (2005) will fare as a series centered on a female investigator (Rachel Nichols) who hunts serial killers because of a traumatic encounter when she was a child. What kind of narrative will be the next trend and what kind of detective will be the new hero?

We will have to wait and see. But recent political events like 9/11, the war in Afghanistan, and the war in Iraq will no doubt have an impact on Hollywood's representation of heroism as such events have altered the conception of the hero in the public imagination—for example, the new-found respect for policemen and firefighters in the wake of 9/11 that is finding its way to the big screen in films like *Ladder 49* (Russell 2004) starring Joaquin Phoenix and John Travolta. The events of 9/11 and the War on Terror are still being filtered through American culture, and it is likely that they will find their reflection in Hollywood's imagination. With the identification of evil as being the foreign "other" once more, perhaps the criminalist narrative will be replaced by more action films starring youth heroes as American agents fighting international terrorism. The serial killer as an invisible and American enemy may be replaced once again with the more visible foreign terrorist, and Hollywood's exploration of crime may move from the domestic to the external. Whatever the next step in the evolution of the detective genre, it will likely involve a redistribution of emphasis between brawn and brains, vigilanteism and teamwork, justice and procedure, and a reconception of the relationship of men and women to the law. But at the moment this investigation comes to a close: the contemporary detective narrative offers an intelligent, experienced, and professional hero who can be male or female, black or white, old and sometimes young, able bodied or not, and who fights crime through observation, deduction, and technology. The modern-day sleuth uses science and teamwork to make the law effective in the fight against crime, offering audiences the reassurance that, while violent crime may be on the rise in contemporary America, we have a hero that can successfully detect evil and catch today's most elusive—and often enigmatic—criminals.

NOTES

CHAPTER 1.
INTRODUCTION: THE CASE

1. The only two early examples of critical examinations of masculinity in film were Joan Mellen's *Big Bad Wolves* (1977) and Donald Spoto's *Camerado* (1978). More recently there have appeared many more, including Steven Cohan and Ina Rae Hark's *Screening the Male* (1993), Peter Lehman's *Running Scared* (1993), Pat Kirkham and Janet Thumim's *You Tarzan* (1993), Yvonne Tasker's *Spectacular Bodies* (1993), Dennis Bingham's *Acting Male* (1994), Susan Jeffords's *Hard Bodies* (1994), Fred Pfeil's *White Guys* (1995), Gaylyn Studlar's *This Mad Masquerade* (1996), Steven Cohan's *Masked Men* (1997), Neal King's *Heroes in Hard Times* (1999), Murray Pomerance's *Ladies and Gentlemen, Boys and Girls* (2001), Ashton D. Trice and Samuel A. Holland's *Heroes, Antiheroes and Dolts* (2001), and Chris Holmlund's *Impossible Bodies* (2002), among others.

2. They include Spencer Selby's *Dark City: The Film Noir* (1984), Jon Tuska's *Dark Cinema: American Film Noir in Cultural Perspective* (1984), Foster Hirsch's *The Dark Side of the Screen: Film Noir* (1986), Ian Cameron's *The Book of Film Noir* (1992), Joan Copjec's *Shades of Noir: A Reader* (1993), R. Barton Palmer's *Hollywood's Dark Cinema: The American Film Noir* (1994), Alain Silver and James Ursini's *Film Noir Reader* (1996), James Naremore's *More than Night: Film Noir in Its Contexts* (1998), and Kelly Oliver and Benigno Trigo's *Noir Anxiety* (2003).

3. Exceptions include William Everson's *The Detective in Film* (1972), Jon Tuska's *The Detective in Hollywood* (1978), Michael R. Pitts's *Famous Movie Detectives* (1979), and James Robert Parish and Michael R. Pitts's *The Great Detective Pictures* (1990); however, these books are in many ways tributes to the genre or a detailing of specific characters and adaptations of detective fiction rather than critical commentaries on the genre.

4. The exception is Frank Krutnik's *In a Lonely Street: Film Noir, Genre, Masculinity* (1991).

5. Dates are often debated but most critics agree that the Studio Era began to form in the 1910s and was defunct by the 1960s. The term "Classical Hollywood" is used by critics to describe the dominant style of filmmaking during the Studio Era. The Production Code will be discussed in detail in a later chapter.

6. Although I will explore the proliferation of the female detective-hero in contemporary film, in my discussions of the detective film in which the male hero is dominant I will use the pronouns "he" and "him" to refer to *only* male detectives rather than "he/she" or "her/him" to refer to detective figures in general.

7. According to Steve Neale, during the Classical Hollywood era the use of the term "melodrama" to describe women's films was rare ("Melo" 74). As Neale demonstrates, the film industry used the term "melodrama" not for describing the films directed at female audiences but for "war films, adventure films, horror films, and thrillers, genres traditionally thought of as, if anything, 'male'" (ibid. 69).

8. Elizabeth Peters's Amelia Peabody mysteries are a good example of this original classical structure: the narrative is related through a series of manuscripts and letters as a retrospective treatment of the story of the crime.

9. In the first telling, Verbal says that he saw Keaton's murderer approach Keaton as he lay on the ground, a few words were exchanged, and then Keaton was shot. This scene is composed mainly of medium shots of the two characters. In the second telling, Verbal claims he saw the murderer shoot Keaton from the second deck of the boat while Keaton was standing. This scene is composed mainly of long shots from Verbal's distanced standpoint. There are similar moments in other scenes when the camera's association with Verbal's subjective narration is made explicit. At the New York police station, the five criminals meet for the first time and are held together in a cell. The scene progresses for several minutes, with discussions between four of the criminals—Keaton, Fenster, Mc-Mannis, and Hockney. The camera moves to many positions in the cell, following the movements of the different characters. An insightful viewer asks him/herself how Verbal can relate this information in his narrative if he was not present to witness it. Suddenly Verbal's name is mentioned and it is only at this point that the camera pans to the left to reveal him sitting on the other side of the room. He has been there all along, yet the camera did not reveal him until he is mentioned within the narrative. A similar delayed revelation occurs when Keaton speaks to his girlfriend outside of the jail. They converse for a minute or two, and the viewer again questions Verbal's knowledge of the event, until he walks out of the shadows and continues past them. He has been eavesdropping on their conversation.

10. This shift has, no doubt, occurred in a reaction to the growing fascination with criminal psychology that has proliferated since the mid-twentieth cen-

tury. Classical detective criminals tended to commit murder for the old-fashioned motives of greed and lust, but contemporary audiences are fascinated with sociopaths and psychopaths who kill for seeming unmotivated reasons. Like the criminalist, we want to get inside the head of the contemporary killer to make sense of his/her seemingly senseless violence.

11. Similar scenes can be found in *The Boondock Saints* (Duffy 1999), in which the detective, Paul Smecker (Willem Dafoe), explains how a crime was perpetrated after he examines the evidence. His oral account of the crime is accompanied by a flashback sequence in which he, in some places, enters the space of the past to narrate the moment—or to partake in it. For example, in one scene, Smecker demonstrated that the evidence can be read in two ways: the seemingly obvious answer is that the "Saints" (Sean Patrick Flanery and Norman Reedus) were fired upon by six different shooters. But the correct reading is that there was only one shooter armed with six guns. As Smecker explains this, the six shooters of the first reading are replaced by Smecker miming the shooting, standing in for the killer armed with six guns.

12. See Rick Altman's *Film/Genre* (1999) and Steve Neale's *Genre and Hollywood* (2000) and *Genre and Contemporary Hollywood* (2002).

13. This accounts for the growing number of sequels and series in recent film, especially as budgets are progressively larger and the need to recoup costs becomes increasingly important to guarantee. Sequels and series, like the four *Lethal Weapon* films or *The Lord of the Rings* trilogy, promise audiences "more of the same" but slightly different—the same *kind* of movie rather than the exact same movie. Film producers hope that as such these films will guarantee larger audiences than an original film that has no previously established audience.

CHAPTER 2.
THE MYTHS OF MASCULINITY

1. While the individuals may be said to perform their gender through these acts, gestures, etc., Butler stresses that the idea of performativity should not be confused with that of performance. It is the representation that enables the subject (performativity) rather than the subject enabling the representation (performance). See Judith Butler, *Bodies that Matter* (1993): 95.

2. See Tania Modleski, *Feminism without Women* (1991): 96; and Chris Holmlund, "Masculinity as Multiple Masquerade," in *Screening the Male* (1993): 213.

3. Mellen examines masculinity in film from the 1920s through the 1970s and Studlar matinee idols of the Jazz Age.

CHAPTER 3.
INVESTIGATING NATIONAL HEROES:
BRITISH SLEUTHS AND AMERICAN DICKS

1. The term "hardboiled" hails from a variety of meanings. According to Wendy Haslem, the term originally referred to the fact that a hardboiled story only took as long to read as it did to hard boil an egg; alternatively, she suggests that the term refers to the snappy dialogue and romance that can reach the boiling point between the hero and his love interest (Haslem). However, it would seem that the most common interpretation of the term is that the hero of the narrative is tough, like a hardboiled egg is compared to a normal egg. I, thus, use the term "softboiled" to refer to the transitional detective in order to differentiate him from the kind of hero that populated hardboiled stories, even if he hails from that fiction himself.

2. The classical detective refers to the character and associated set of traits created by Poe and popularized by Doyle, Christie, Sayers, and other authors: the sleuth. On the other hand, the popular detective of the period of Classical Hollywood film was the transitional detective and later the hardboiled detective of *film noir* that represented a subversion of Classical Hollywood realist films. Therefore, the classical Hollywood detective is the transitional detective rather than the classical detective.

3. Agatha Christie was criticized for *The Murder of Roger Ackroyd* (1926) because the narrator is revealed at the end of the novel to be the murderer.

4. The Production Code (also known as the Hays Code) was used in conjunction with a policy of self-censorship within the film industry. The Code laid out what was or was not considered moral content or themes, and it was left to a film's producers to ensure that the film did not challenge the Code. The vicarious treatment of sex and violence and the glorification of lawless and amoral behavior would have been regarded as challenging the Code.

5. See William Stowe, "Hard-boiled Virgil" and Richard Slotkin, "The Hard-boiled Detective Story," in *The Sleuth and the Scholar* (1988), and Paul Bernard Plouffe, *The Tainted Adam* (1979).

6. The following information on specific detective film series can be found in Tuska's *The Detective in Hollywood* (1978) or on the Internet Movie Database (www.IMDb.com).

7. That series has been re-run a number of times, and Raymond Burr and Barbara Hale (who played Perry Mason and Della Street, respectively, in the television series) were brought back in the 1980s to do a new series of feature-length episodes for television that ran from 1985 to 1995. Raymond Burr, sadly, passed away in 1993. The Perry Mason television series was continued with friends of Mason "filling in" to defend a case: Paul Sorvino played Anthony Caruso in one 1993 episode, and Hal Halbrook played "Wild Bill" McKenzie in three episodes from 1994 to 1995.

8. See Ron Lackmann's *The Encyclopedia of American Radio* (2000).

9. The series featuring Dick Tracy ran from 1935 to 1948, Charlie Chan from 1932 to 1948, Nero Wolfe from 1943 to 1951, Philip Marlowe from 1947 to 1951, Sam Spade from 1946 to 1951, The Thin Man from 1941 to 1950, Boston Blackie from 1944 to 1950, Bulldog Drummond from 1941 to 1954, The Saint from 1945 to 1951, The Falcon from 1943 to 1954, and Perry Mason from 1943 to 1955.

10. The majority of Classical Hollywood detective films of the 1930s did tend to have this dual nature as both comedy and detective narrative, but the comedy, and the inciting of laughter in the audience, was not the primary focus of the films—the mystery was. Nor was the comedy derived from foiling audience and generic expectations as in the case of *The Pink Panther* films of the 1960s and 1970s, featuring the bumbling Inspector Clouseau (played by Peter Sellers) and spoof films like *Without a Clue* (Eberhardt 1988), in which it is suggested that Watson was the real brains behind the more media-friendly Holmes. See chapter 3 of Peter Lehman and William Luhr's *Blake Edwards* (1981) for a close discussion of the Inspector Clouseau films.

11. The "Yellow Peril" incited by Chinese immigration and then the Immigration Act in 1924 that denied Asian immigration into the States resulted in a virtual absence of Chinese characters on the screen and then the appearance of the "Oriental" villain that, by the 1920s, was well-established through the characters of Long Sin and Wu Fang from the serials starring Pearl White, and Sax Rohmer's Fu Manchu.

12. Just like Oland, both Karloff and Lorre had a reputation for playing "bogeymen." Karloff (a Eurasian actor of East Indian and English descent) played horror monsters and villains, including Fu Manchu for MGM in 1932, before he was chosen to play Mr. Wong. Lorre saw his career launched on an international level with his portrayal of the psychopathic child killer in Fritz Lang's *M* (1931) before landing the role of Mr. Moto.

13. An example of this displaced mode of representation is in *Casablanca* (Curtiz 1942), in the scene when Rick and Isla meet alone in his apartment. They kiss passionately; the camera cuts to the spotlight tower then back to the apartment where Rick smokes a cigarette. The ellipsis of time implied and the psychoanalytic phallic connotations attached to the tower and cigarette can be interpreted as suggesting that Rick and Ilsa have had sexual relations during that time ellipsis. The scene does not overtly suggest that sexual relations have taken place; thus, it could get past the censors. But for the viewer with knowledge of popular psychoanalysis, the scene becomes sexualized.

14. Similarly, Foster Hirsch identifies three types of *noir*-hero: the sleuth, the victim, and the criminal (*Dark* 13). Although I disagree with Hirsch's use of the term "sleuth" because of its connotations of the classical detective, I agree that this type of *noir*-hero is indeed a detective but a hardboiled detective, rather than the cultured gentleman sleuth.

15. For example, the narrative of *The Big Sleep* (Hawks 1946) is notoriously complicated, and the conclusion of the film does little to wrap up the plot's loose ends. But the film offers a satisfying ending, with the detective and leading lady (Bogart and Bacall) coming together.

CHAPTER 4.
INVESTIGATING CRISIS:
NEO-*NOIR* HEROES AND *FEMMES FATALES*

1. See Raymond Borde and Etienne Chaumeton's *Panorama du Film Noir Américáin* (1955); or the new edition translated by Paul Hammond (San Francisco: City Lights Publishers, 2002).

2. Second-wave feminism emerged in most Western countries in the late 1960s and early 1970s. The term "second-wave" arises in reference to "first-wave" feminism—the feminism of the nineteenth and early twentieth centuries, which is usually associated with the demand for women's suffrage (Jackson and Scott 26 ff2). In conjunction with the publication of several important feminist texts, including Betty Friedan's *The Feminine Mystique* (1963), Kate Millet's *Sexual Politics* (1969), and Germaine Greer's *The Female Eunuch* (1971), was the rise of a militant feminism in reaction to the virulent antifeminism that had thrived from the end of World War II through the 1950s and the domestic role it prescribed for women. There were two related but different strands of second-wave feminism: a critical and academic movement as well as an activist one.

3. Emphasis in original.

4. Rick Altman points out that the basis of genre is the idea of binary oppositions: "Constantly opposing cultural values to counter-cultural values, genre films regularly depend on dual protagonists and *dualistic* structures" (24, emphasis in original). The hero never exists in isolation in a film, and his role is always complemented by that of a woman, villain, or buddy. For the binary structure of genre to work, oppositions are necessary, and genres like the detective film rely on the difference between good and evil—difference that is often drawn along the lines of gender. For a detailed discussion of how heroism and villainy can be drawn along gender lines in an all-male genre like the war film, see Jeffords's *Remasculinization of America* (1989). These oppositions can also be established through race and class; these will be addressed in the following chapter.

5. The "How fast was I going?" exchange in *Double Indemnity* (Wilder 1944):

PHYLLIS: Why don't you drop by tomorrow evening about eight-thirty. He'll be in then.

NEFF: Who?

PHYLLIS: My husband. You were anxious to talk to him weren't you?

NEFF: Yeah, I was, but I'm sort of getting over the idea, if you know what I mean.

PHYLLIS: There's a speed limit in this state, Mr. Neff. Forty-five miles an hour.

NEFF: How fast was I going, officer?

PHYLLIS: I'd say around ninety.

NEFF: Suppose you get down off your motorcycle and give me a ticket.

PHYLLIS: Suppose I let you off with a warning this time.

NEFF: Suppose it doesn't take.

PHYLLIS: Suppose I have to whack you over the knuckles.

NEFF: Suppose I bust out crying and put my head on your shoulder.

PHYLLIS: Suppose you try putting it on my husband's shoulder.

NEFF: That tears it.

6. Although *Body Heat* predates *Fatal Attraction*, Matty is not presented as a professional woman but the spoiled housewife of a professional man.

7. Episode aired on *A&E* June 15, 2003.

8. See www.IMDb.com/Trivia?0093010; and Leitch 323 ff 8.

9. Stables gives a concise and thorough explanation of the development of postclassical/postmodern cinema and its relationship to shifting industrial factors—the breakdown of the studio system, the rise of the blockbuster, etc. (165–66).

CHAPTER 5.
INVESTIGATING CRISIS:
THE SPECTACLE OF "MUSCULINITY"

1. Dirty Harry is the protagonist of *Dirty Harry* (Siegel 1971), *Magnum Force* (Post 1973), *The Enforcer* (Fargo 1976), *Sudden Impact* (Eastwood 1983), and *The Dead Pool* (Van Horn 1988).

2. The character appears in *First Blood* (Kotcheff 1982), *Rambo: First Blood Part II* (Cosmatos 1985), and *Rambo III* (MacDonald 1988).

3. Emphasis in the original.

4. Six of the top ten-grossing films of the decade in terms of box-office receipts featured hard-body heroes. The hard-body hero film proved to be a

healthy earner in general: *Rambo* made $80 million in 1985, *Top Gun* $82m in 1986, and *Lethal Weapon 2* $79.5m in 1989 (see Jeffords, *Hard Bodies*, 197–98 ff 60).

5. *Die Hard* (1988), *Die Harder* (1990), *Die Hard with a Vengeance* (1993), *Lethal Weapon* (1987), *Lethal Weapon 2* (1989), *Lethal Weapon 3* (1992), *Lethal Weapon 4* (1998), *Terminator* (1984), *Terminator 2: Judgment Day* (1991), *Terminator 3: Rise of the Machines* (2003).

6. The following are the domestic box-office takings for selected Schwarzenegger films (figures are from www.IMDb.com):

Film	Domestic Takings	Estimated Budget
Terminator 3 (2003)	$150,350,192	$175,000,000
Collateral Damage (2002)	$40,048,332	$85,000,000
The 6th Day (2000)	$34,543,701	$82,000,000
End of Days (1999)	$66,862,068	$83,000,000
Eraser (1996)	$101,228,120	$100,000,000
True Lies (1993)	$146,261,000	$100,000,000
Terminator 2 (1991)	$204,843,350	$100,000,000

While *Eraser*, *True Lies*, and *Terminator 2* were big successes, earning their money back in domestic box-office sales alone, *Collateral Damage* and *The 6th Day* did not fair so well, in each case making back less than a half their budget.

CHAPTER 6.
INVESTIGATING THE HERO:
THE CRIMINALIST

1. The majority of serial killer narratives have criminalist investigators either as the main character whose investigations drive the narrative or as the adversary who hunts, and successfully stops, the killer. But not all detective narratives starring criminalists have serial killers as their criminals. Often the criminalist will investigate single murders, especially in the television versions of the narrative. Thus, I use the term "serial killer narratives" to refer to narratives that follow the exploits of a serial killer with a criminalist as the protagonist, and "criminalist narrative" to refer to the broader subgenre in which the criminalist is the detective-hero, but he/she is not necessarily pursuing a serial killer.

2. For further discussion about the dramatization of real-life serial killers see Christian Fuchs's *Bad Blood* (2002). For further discussion of the fictional serial killer in film see Carl Goldberg and Virginia Crespo's "A Psychological Examination of Serial Killer Cinema: The Case of *Copycat*" (2003).

3. Ronald and Stephen Holmes explain the classification of different kinds of "multicide," of which one is serial killing (2).

Classification:	Mass Murder	Spree Murder	Serial Murder
Victims	At least three	At least three	At least three
Events	One event	At least three	At least three
Location	One location	At least three	At least three
Cool-off	No	No	Yes

What differentiates the serial killer from the other kinds of multicide murderers is the cooling-off period. While the mass murder and spree murder may kill many people, they tend to do so at one point in time—they "snap" and kill rather than calculate to do so. The serial killer has time to reflect upon his/her killings and makes a choice to commit more. This lack of remorse for murder that allows him/her to kill again and over long periods of time is often indicative of a psychopathic or sociopathic personality.

4. Emphasis in the original.

5. Both *CSI* and *Law & Order* have produced multiple successful spin-offs focused on criminalist investigators: *CSI: Miami* (2002), *CSI: New York* (2004), *Law & Order: Special Victims Unit* (1999), *Law & Order: Criminal Intent* (2001), and *Law & Order: Trial by Jury* (2005).

6. Upon a second viewing, the audience identifies with Verbal—the criminal—and takes pleasure in his ability to outwit the pompous detective, Kujan. But it is important to remember that in the initial viewing of the film, the viewer is conditioned to identify with the detective due to their foreknowledge of the generic structures. Once the trick ending of the film is known, however, the viewer will tend to align him/herself with Verbal in an attempt to unravel the "truth" from the yarn he spins.

7. Martin Norden argues that the early history of disability in film was most often drawn along gender lines with the portrayal of the disabled as either "obsessive avengers," who were usually male, and "sweet innocents," who were usually female (86). The representation of disability in Hollywood film tends to fall into two categories: those that seem to appear out of a desire to win Academy recognition with plots that center on disability, often with a big star as the main character—for example, *Rain Man* (1988) and *Forrest Gump* (1995)—and those that "mainstream disability into the plot" (Bondi). This second group of films portrays disability without issues of disability being central to the plot—for example, a brother who is deaf in *Four Weddings and a Funeral* (Newell 1994) and a friend that is wheelchair-bound in *Notting Hill* (Michell 1999)—and offer token representations of the disabled, and the character's disability is not addressed as an issue. The first group of films, including *Rain Man* (Levinson 1988), *Awakenings* (Marshall 1990), *Forrest Gump* (Zemeckis 1994), *I Am Sam* (Nelson 2001), and

A Beautiful Mind (Howard 2001), present big stars in the role of the disabled, many garnering Oscars for their efforts, but are not played by disabled actors. The Screen Actors Guild insists that producers audition actors with disability for characters with disability, but the producers are not obliged to hire them (Bondi).

8. The decision to cast Ironside as a disabled detective is rumored to have been due to the fact that the show's star, who had previously played Perry Mason in a long-running series, had undergone knee surgery or his weight was causing mobility problems. The wheelchair was therefore more a question of necessity for the star than based on a desire to present a disabled hero.

CHAPTER 7.
INVESTIGATING THE "OTHER":
RACE AND THE DETECTIVE

1. The exception is the Asian detective of classical Hollywood as discussed in chapter 3. In Classical Hollywood film, the Asian detective was the great exception: he was the only example of a nonwhite hero in the genre (although he was portrayed by white actors). He all but disappeared from the genre until the last decade, where we have seen the return of the Asian hero. But unlike Charlie Chan and Mr. Wong, the contemporary Asian detective is less a cerebral investigator and more a man of action. Hong Kong action-star Jackie Chan and Chinese action-stars Jet Li and Chow Yun-Fat star in Hollywood action film and offer the exotic hero who performs spectacles of martial arts action. While the cop-action hero as white, male, and muscular has decreased in size and number in the 1990s, films starring the Asian detective as action hero have increased as another kind of feminized body—smaller, slimmer, and "other" than the traditional American action hero. The "otherness" of the Asian star/detective is a complex set of associations because, while his being foreign makes him "other," audiences tend to interpret him as a somewhat "American" hero. As Julian Stringer demonstrates, fans do not necessarily consider stars like Chow Yun-Fat as Chinese but as Asian American (229–30). Yun-Fat's presence at the center of a Hollywood film, battling America's enemies, aligns him with conceptions of American heroism, but ones different from those aligned with white cop-action heroes.

Like the African-American detective, the Asian hero tends to be accompanied by a buddy rather than left in the spotlight on his own—typically, either women or African-American men: Jackie Chan with Chris Tucker in *Rush Hour* (Ratner 1998) and *Rush Hour 2* (Ratner 2001), Jennifer Love Hewitt in *The Tuxedo* (Donovan 2002), and Owen Wilson in *Shanghai Noon* (Dey 2000) and *Shanghai Knights* (Dobkin 2003); Jet Li with Aaliyah in *Romeo Must Die* (Bartkowiak 2000), Bridget

Fonda in *Kiss the Dragon* (Nahon 2001), and DMX in *Cradle 2 the Grave* (Bartkowiak 2003); and Chow Yun-Fat and Mira Sorvino in *The Replacement Killers* (Fuqua 1998) and Mark Whalberg in *The Corrupter* (Foley 1999). In the 1980s, the buddy was used to highlight the white working-class hero but also to draw larger audiences with two stars at the center of the narrative; similarly, the buddy of the Asian hero—whether black and/or female—functions to attract larger ethnic audiences as well as to allow mainstream audiences a point of identification with the American buddy, as it seems that producers are concerned that the Asian hero may be too "other" to allow such an identification.

The Asian detective is not a criminalist. But rather than relying on big guns or his fists, the Asian hero uses martial arts to defeat the enemy. These films are known, and sold to audiences, on the basis of their spectacular action sequences. Jackie Chan's fame stems from the fact that he does all his own stunts, to the point that most of his films conclude with outtakes of stunts gone wrong as the credits role. The body of the Asian hero is often smaller and slimmer than that of the 1980s male action hero, but it is placed very much on display in choreographed balletic action sequences. But it has only been the hard-body action stars like Yun-Fat that have gained contracts in Hollywood, not the softer, more sensitive stars like Yun-Fat's frequent costar Leslie Cheung (Stringer 234). The Asian star in Hollywood also offers a fluidity of identity in terms of culture as American films and audiences do not necessarily recognize the variety of different Asian cultures; instead, Hollywood offers a generic image of "Asianness," and stars like Jason Scott Lee appear as Chinese, Filipino, and Japanese in different films (ibid. 236–37). Similarly, the Asian action hero in Hollywood film, like the black detective, is denied sexuality: Stringer notes how one is hard-pressed to recall any film in which Chow Yun-Fat has sexual relations with his costar (229). The Asian detective has, thus, proliferated as a Hollywood action hero, one that can be put on display for audiences in amazing martial arts sequences without compromising notions of American masculinity. In American culture, duking it out with one's fists is seen as more primal, spontaneous, and natural than the skill and devotion that martial arts require; thus, while the American hero is expected to be a "natural" fighter (in other words, born with the ability to be violent and victorious), the Asian hero is accepted—and respected—as a trained fighter. And while the Asian detective appears frequently in action films, he is notably absent from the criminalist narrative, no doubt because his "otherness" puts him at a disadvantage in understanding the particularly American phenomenon of the serial killer.

2. The 1980s and 1990s witnessed the proliferation of black independent cinema. In these films, black characters are placed in positions of articulation and subjectivity, and their experience is the dominant concern of the narrative. I will not address the representation of black experience in black independent films but will instead focus on that put forth in Hollywood films. This is because black independent

cinema has produced no detective films and produces films from the perspective of African-American culture; in other words, it does not reflect Hollywood's mainstream ideology concerning ethnicity and race.

3. For a comprehensive history of the representation of African Americans in film, see Donald Bogle, *Toms, Coons, Mulattoes, Mammies, and Bucks* (1973).

4. Guerrero uses the term "strategies of containment" as Fredric Jameson defines it in *The Political Unconscious* (New York: Cornell University Press, 1981): 52–53.

5. Of course, the term "Superspade" is also a play on the use of "spade" as a racial slur.

6. This was not necessarily the decision of the film's producers, as supposedly a kiss was filmed between Washington and Roberts; it was Washington's decision to have the scenes edited out of fear of alienating his core black female audience. See Akin Ojumu's "Will Talent Out This Time?" (2002).

7. *Along Came a Spider* is the first of the Cross novels but is the second Cross film.

CHAPTER 8.
INVESTIGATING THE "OTHER":
WOMEN AND YOUTH

1. These series also were briefly reprised with TV-movie specials: *Cagney and Lacey*, with four between 1994 and 1996; *Hart to Hart*, with eight between 1993 and 1996; and *Murder, She Wrote*, with four between 1997 to 2003.

2. In *Twisted* and *Taking Lives* the serial killer's victims are men. This seems to be the newest evolution of the genre, and this gender twist enacts a shift in the relationship between the detective and the killer but also the victims and is a theme I will explore later in the book.

3. See Bartlett's "Grisham Adaptations and the Legal Thriller" (2003).

4. While Josh Hartnett (b. 1978) is in his twenties, Brendan Fraser (b. 1968), Ben Affleck (b. 1972), and Leonardo DiCaprio (b. 1974) are in their thirties, and Johnny Depp (b. 1963) and Keanu Reeves (b. 1964) are in their forties (see www.IMDb.com).

5. Episode aired on *A&E* July 23, 2003.

6. *The Silence of the Lambs* was not the first film adaptation of Thomas Harris's novels. Michael Mann directed *Manhunter* (1986) based on *Red Dragon*, the first of the novels featuring Hannibal Lector/Lektor. But *Manhunter* was not as commercially successful or widely seen as *The Silence of the Lambs*, and it is with the latter that most audiences are familiar.

7. Gumb is a man who wants to be a woman, not one who feels that society has emasculated him. He kills women not for the traditional motives of sexual desire or a troubled childhood, but because he wants to be a woman himself: murder is merely the by-product of his main intention to remove their skin.

8. *Charlie's Angels 2: Full Throttle* (McG 2003), *Legally Blonde 2: Red, White and Blonde* (Herman-Wurmfeld 2003), and *Miss Congeniality 2: Armed and Fabulous* (Pasquin 2005).

9. King notes that defining comedy as a *mode* rather than a *genre* is a more useful way of understanding how it functions because it is not made up of a set of conventions (like a genre) but as a manner of representing a genre (*Film* 2). The comedy is often generated from the parody or spoof of that genre through a play with its recognizable and familiar conventions.

10. Some of these contemporary films offer lesbians or bisexual women as their villains. According to Lynda Hart, lesbianism represents the enemy within— the normative female rendered unreproductive and, therefore, unnatural (116). Unlike *Basic Instinct* and *Single White Female* (Schroeder 1992), which vilified lesbianism, *Bound* celebrates its heroines' relationship as being one in which trust and love are possible when it is not in a heterosexual one. But the film still exploits its sexually "othered" protagonists in graphic sex scenes intended to titillate and/or shock mainstream audiences.

CHAPTER 9.
INVESTIGATING THE "OTHER":
THE CULT OF VILLAINY

1. Emphasis in the original.

2. See Tony Thomas's *Cads and Cavaliers* (1973).

3. Verbal Kint is not necessarily Keyser Soze. Since the story he tells Kujan is a fabrication, the audience's and Kujan's final assumption that Kint is Soze could also be false. Verbal is the man who shot the Hungarian on the boat, most likely the man who orchestrated the heist, and could be an all-powerful criminal, but that does not mean that the identity of Soze is his: Soze could just be a myth.

4. The five criminals, after all, do work and commit specific crimes together. Kobayashi's name may be a fabrication taken from Kujan's coffee mug, but as a person he does exist. He drives Verbal away to freedom at the end of the film, an action that occurs outside of Verbal's narrative. Verbal's explanation of the final heist as an act of revenge on those who have crossed him is the only logical explanation for the crime since no drugs were involved. If the entire story that Verbal tells were completely false then there would be no basis from which the spectator

can comprehend Soze as a clever and evil villain. Even the director, Bryan Singer, says that some parts of Verbal's story are real—for example, the deaths of the other four criminals (Nathan, *The Sequel* 93).

5. See Merivale and Sweeney (1993): 8. They list six themes, including the idea of "The Purloined Letter," which exists as embedded text, *mise en abyme*, textual constraint, or text as object. The idea of the purloined letter as a literary technique will function in this way only in the detective novel, so I do not address it here in my discussion of the detective film.

SELECTED FILMOGRAPHY

Absolute Power. Dir. Clint Eastwood. Perf. Clint Eastwood, Gene Hackman, and Ed Harris. Columbia Pictures, 1997.

The Accused. Dir. Jonathan Kaplan. Perf. Kelly McGillis and Jodie Foster. Paramount Pictures, 1988.

Agatha Christie's Poirot. Perf. David Suchet, Hugh Fraser, and Philip Jackson. London Weekend Television, 1989–.

All the President's Men. Dir. Alan J. Pakula. Perf. Dustin Hoffman, Robert Redford, and Jack Warden. Warner Bros, 1976.

Along Came a Spider. Dir. Lee Tamahori. Perf. Morgan Freeman, Monica Potter, and Michael Wincott. Paramount Pictures, 2001.

American Beauty. Dir. Sam Mendes. Perf. Kevin Spacey, Annette Bening, and Thora Birch. DreamWorks, 1999.

American Psycho. Dir. Mary Harron. Perf. Christian Bale, Willem Dafoe, and Jared Leto. Universal Pictures, 2000.

Anatomy of a Murder. Dir. Otto Preminger. Perf. James Stewart, Lee Remick, and Ben Gazzara. Columbia Pictures, 1959.

And Then There Were None. Dir. Peter Collinson. Perf. Oliver Reed, Elke Sommer, and Richard Attenborough. Embassy Pictures, 1974.

Angel Heart. Dir. Alan Parker. Perf. Mickey Rourke, Robert De Niro, and Lisa Bonet. TriStar Pictures, 1987.

Appointment with Death. Dir. Michael Winner. Perf. Peter Ustinov, Lauren Bacall, and Carrie Fisher. Cannon Films, 1988.

Arrest in Chinatown, San Francisco, Cal. Dir. Thomas Edison. Edison Manufacturing Company, 1897.

Bad Day at Black Rock. Dir. John Sturges. Perf. Spencer Tracy and Robert Ryan. Metro–Goldwyn–Mayer, 1955.

Basic Instinct. Dir. Paul Verhoeven. Perf. Michael Douglas, Sharon Stone, and George Dzundza. TriStar Pictures, 1992.

The Beach. Dir. Danny Boyle. Perf. Leonardo DiCaprio, Tilda Swinton, and Virginie Ledoyen. Figment Films, 2000.

The Best Years of Our Lives. Dir. William Wyler. Perf. Fredric March, Dana Andrews, and Harold Russell. Samuel Goldwyn Company, 1946.

Beverly Hills Cop. Dir. Martin Brest. Perf. Eddie Murphy, Judge Reinhold, and John Ashton. Paramount Pictures, 1984.

Beverly Hills Cop II. Dir. Tony Scott. Perf. Eddie Murphy, Judge Reinhold, and Jürgen Prochnow. Paramount Pictures, 1987.

Beverly Hills Cop III. Dir. John Landis. Perf. Eddie Murphy, John Tenney, and Joey Travolta. Paramount Pictures, 1994.

The Big Clock. Dir. John Farrow. Perf. Ray Milland, Charles Laughton, and Maureen O'Sullivan. Paramount Pictures, 1948.

The Big Easy. Dir. Jim McBride. Perf. Dennis Quaid, Ellen Barkin, and Ned Beatty. Kings Road Entertainment, 1987.

The Big Sleep. Dir. Howard Hawks. Perf. Humphrey Bogart, Lauren Bacall, and John Ridgley. Warner Bros, 1946.

The Big Sleep. Dir. Michael Winner. Perf. Robert Mitchum and Sarah Miles. Winkast Film Productions, 1978.

The Bill. Perf. Mark Wingett, Trudie Goodwin, Eric Richard, et al. Thames Television, 1984–.

A Black Sherlock Holmes. Dir. R. W. Phillips. Perf. Sam Robinson, Rudolf Tatum, and George Lewis. Ebony Film Group, 1918.

Black Widow. Dir. Bob Rafelson. Perf. Debra Winger, Theresa Russell, and Sami Frey. Twentieth Century Fox, 1987.

Blade Runner. Dir. Ridley Scott. Perf. Harrison Ford, Rutger Hauer, and Sean Young. The Ladd Company, 1982.

Blind Justice. Perf. Ron Eldard, Marisol Nichols, Reno Wilson, et al. Paramount Television, 2005–.

Blood Work. Dir. Clint Eastwood. Perf. Clint Eastwood and Jeff Daniels. Warner Bros, 2002.

The Blue Dahlia. Dir. George Marshall. Perf. Alan Ladd, Veronica Lake, and William Bendix. Paramount Pictures, 1946.

Blue Steel. Dir. Kathryn Bigelow. Perf. Jamie Lee Curtis and Ron Silver. Mack–Taylor Productions, 1990.

Body Heat. Dir. Lawrence Kasdan. Perf. William Hurt, Kathleen Turner, and Richard Gere. The Ladd Company, 1981.

The Bone Collector. Dir. Phillip Noyce. Perf. Denzel Washington, Angelina Jolie, and Queen Latifah. Universal Pictures, 1999.

The Boondock Saints. Dir. Troy Duffy. Perf. Willem Dafoe, Sean Patrick Flanery, and Norman Redus. B. D. S. Productions, 1999.

Bound. Dir. Andy and Larry Wachowski. Perf. Jennifer Tilly and Gina Gershon. Dino De Laurentiis Productions, 1996.

Bullitt. Dir. Peter Yates. Perf. Steve McQueen, Robert Vaughn, and Jacqueline Bisset. Solar Productions, 1968.

Cagney and Lacey. Perf. Tyne Daly, Sharon Gless, Al Waxman, et al. CBS Television, 1982–88.

Call Northside 777. Dir. Henry Hathaway. Perf. James Stewart, Richard Conte, and Lee J. Cobb. Twentieth Century Fox, 1948.

The Canary Murder Case. Dir. Malcolm St. Clair and Frank Tuttle. Perf. William Powell, Louise Brooks, and Jean Arthur. Paramount Pictures, 1929.

Casablanca. Dir. Michael Curtiz. Perf. Humphrey Bogart, Ingrid Bergman, and Paul Henreid. Warner Bros, 1942.

Casualty. Perf. Derek Thompson, Catherine Shipton, et al. British Broadcasting Corporation, 1986–.

Catch Me if You Can. Dir. Steven Spielberg. Perf. Leonardo DiCaprio and Tom Hanks. DreamWorks, 2002.

The Chamber. Dir. James Foley. Perf. Chris O'Donnell, Gene Hackman, and Faye Dunaway. Universal Pictures, 1996.

Charlie Chan and the Curse of the Dragon Queen. Dir. Clive Donner. Perf. Peter Ustinov, Lee Grant, and Angie Dickinson. A. C. I., 1981.

Charlie Chan at the Circus. Dir. Harry Lachman. Perf. Warner Oland, Keye Luke, George Brasno, and Olive Brasno. Twentieth Century Fox, 1936.

Charlie Chan at the Opera. Dir. H. Bruce Humberstone. Perf. Warner Oland, Boris Karloff, and Keye Luke. Twentieth Century Fox, 1937.

Charlie's Angels. Dir. McG. Perf. Cameron Diaz, Drew Barrymore, and Lucy Liu. Columbia Pictures, 2000.

Charlie's Angels 2: Full Throttle. Dir. McG. Perf. Cameron Diaz, Drew Barrymore, and Lucy Liu. Columbia Pictures, 2003.

Chicago Hope. Perf. Mandy Patinkin, Christine Lahti, Adam Arkin, et al. Twentieth Century Fox Television, 1994–2000.

The China Syndrome. Dir. James Budges. Perf. Jane Fonda, Jack Lemmon, and Michael Douglas. ICP Films, 1979.

Chinatown. Dir. Roman Polanski. Perf. Jack Nicholson, Faye Dunaway, and John Huston. Paramount Pictures, 1974.

The Chinese Parrot. Dir. Paul Leni. Perf. Sojin, Marian Nixon, and Florence Turner. Universal Pictures, 1927.

Citizen X. Dir. Chris Gerolmo. Perf. Stephen Rey and Donald Sutherland. Home Box Office, 1995. (TV movie).

Class Action. Dir. Michael Apted. Perf. Gene Hackman and Mary Elizabeth Mastrantonio. Twentieth Century Fox, 1991.

The Client. Dir. Joel Schumacher. Perf. Susan Sarandon, Tommy Lee Jones, and Mary-Louise Parker. Warner Bros, 1994.

Cliffhanger. Dir. Renny Harlin. Perf. Sylvester Stallone and John Lithgow. Carolco Pictures, 1993.

Closer and Closer. Dir. Fred Gerber. Perf. Kim Delaney. Power Pictures, 1996. (TV movie).

Cobra. Dir. George P. Cosmatos. Perf. Sylvester Stallone and Brigitte Neilsen. Warner Bros, 1986.

Cold Squad. Perf. Julie Stewart, Jay Brazeau, et al. Alliance Atlantis, 1998–.

Columbo. Perf. Peter Falk. Universal Television, 1967–.

Coogan's Bluff. Dir. Don Siegel. Perf. Clint Eastwood, Lee J. Cobb, and Susan Clark. Universal Pictures, 1968.

Cop Land. Dir. James Mangold. Perf. Sylvester Stallone and Harvey Keitel. Miramax Films, 1997.

Copycat. Dir. John Amiel. Perf. Sigourney Weaver, Holly Hunter, and Dermot Mulroney. Warner Bros, 1995.

The Corrupter. Dir. James Foley. Perf. Chow Yun-Fat and Mark Wahlberg. New Line Cinema, 1999.

Crash Donovan. Dir. William Nigh. Perf. Jack Holt, John 'Dusty' King, and Nan Guy. Universal Pictures, 1936.

Crossing Jordan. Perf. Jill Hennessy, Miguel Ferrer, et al. National Broadcasting Corporation, 2001–.

CSI: Crime Scene Investigation. Perf. William L. Petersen, Marg Helgenberger, et al. CBS Productions, 2000–.

Dark Blue. Dir. Ron Shelton. Perf. Kurt Russell, Scott Speedman, and Michael Michele. Intermedia Films, 2002.

Dark Passage. Dir. Delmer Daves. Perf. Humphrey Bogart, Lauren Bacall, and Bruce Bennett. Warner Bros, 1947.

Da Vinci's Inquest. Perf. Nicholas Campbell, Donnelly Rhodes, Gwynyth Walsh, et al. Canadian Broadcasting Corporation, 1998–.

Dead Again. Dir. Kenneth Branagh. Perf. Kenneth Branagh, Andy Garcia, and Emma Thompson. Paramount Pictures, 1991.

The Dead Pool. Dir. Buddy Van Horn. Perf. Clint Eastwood, Patricia Clarkson, and Liam Neeson. Warner Bros, 1988.

Death on the Nile. Dir. John Guillermin. Perf. Peter Ustinov, Jane Birkin, and Mia Farrow. EMI Films, 1978.

Defenseless. Dir. Martin Campbell. Perf. Barbara Hershey and Sam Shepard. New Visions Pictures, 1991.

Demolition Man. Dir. Marco Brambilla. Perf. Sylvester Stallone and Wesley Snipes. Warner Bros, 1993.

Detective Story. Dir. William Wyler. Perf. Kirk Douglas, Eleanor Parker, and William Bendix. Paramount Pictures, 1951.

The Detectives of the Italian Bureau. Dir. Edwin S. Porter. Edison Manufacturing Company, 1909.

Devil in a Blue Dress. Dir. Carl Franklin. Perf. Denzel Washington, Jennifer Beals, and Tom Sizemore. TriStar Pictures, 1995.

Diagnosis Murder. Perf. Dick Van Dyke, Barry Van Dyke, Victoria Rowell, et al. CBS Television, 1993–2001.

Die Hard. Dir. John McTiernan. Perf. Bruce Willis, Bonnie Bedelia, and Reginald Veljohnso. Twentieth Century Fox, 1988.

Die Hard 2. Dir. Renny Harlin. Perf. Bruce Willis, Bonnie Bedelia, and Reginald Veljohnson. Twentieth Century Fox, 1990.

Die Hard with a Vengeance. Dir. John McTiernan. Perf. Bruce Willis, Jeremy Irons, and Samuel L. Jackson. Twentieth Century Fox, 1993.

Dirty Harry. Dir. Don Siegel. Perf. Clint Eastwood, Harry Gaudino, and Reni Santoni. Warner Bros, 1971.

Disclosure. Dir. Barry Levinson. Perf. Michael Douglas and Demi Moore. Warner Bros, 1994.

Double Indemnity. Dir. Billy Wilder. Perf. Fred MacMurray, Barbara Stanwyck, and Edward G. Robinson. Paramount Pictures, 1944.

Dragnet. Perf. Jack Webb, Barton Yarborough, et al. National Broadcasting Company, 1951–59.

ER. Perf. Anthony Edwards, Noah Wyle, Laura Innes, et al. Warner Bros Television, 1994–.

Eraser. Dir. Chuck Russell. Perf. Arnold Schwarzenegger and James Caan. Warner Bros, 1996.

Erin Brockovich. Dir. Steven Soderbergh. Perf. Julia Roberts and Albert Finney. Jersey Films, 2000.

Evil under the Sun. Dir. Guy Hamilton. Perf. Peter Ustinov, Jane Birkin, and Colin Blakely. EMI Films, 1982.

Eye of the Beholder. Dir. Stephan Elliott. Perf. Ewan McGregor and Ashley Judd. Village Roadshow Pictures, 1999.

The Eyes of Laura Mars. Dir. Irvin Kershner. Perf. Faye Dunaway, Tommy Lee Jones, and Brad Dourif. Columbia Pictures, 1978.

Face/Off. Dir. John Woo. Perf. John Travolta, Nicholas Cage, and Joan Allen. Paramount Pictures, 1997.

The Falcon's Brother. Dir. Stanley Logan. Perf. Tom Conway, George Sanders, and Jane Randolf. RKO Radio Pictures, 1942.

Falling Down. Dir. Joel Schumacher. Perf. Michael Douglas and Robert Duvall. Warner Bros, 1993.

Fantômas. Dir. Louis Feuillade. Perf. René Navarre and Edmond Bréon. Gaumont, 1913.

Farewell, My Lovely. Dir. Rick Richards. Perf. Robert Mitchum, Charlotte Rampling, and John Ireland. Incorporated Television Company, 1975.

Fargo. Dir. Joel Coen. Perf. Frances McDormand and William H. Macy. PolyGram Filmed Entertainment, 1996.

Fatal Attraction. Dir. Adrian Lyne. Perf. Michael Douglas, Glenn Close, and Anne Archer. Paramount Pictures, 1987.

A Few Good Men. Dir. Robert Reiner. Perf. Tom Cruise and Jack Nicholson. Columbia Pictures, 1992.

Fight Club. Dir. David Fincher. Perf. Brad Pitt, Edward Norton, and Helena Bonham Carter. Fox 2000 Pictures, 1999.

The Firm. Dir. Sydney Pollack. Perf. Tom Cruise, Jeanne Tripplehorn, and Gene Hackman. Paramount Pictures, 1993.

48 Hrs. Dir. Walter Hill. Perf. Nick Nolte and Eddie Murphy. Paramount Pictures, 1982.

The French Connection. Dir. William Friedkin. Perf. Gene Hackman, Fernando Rey, and Roy Scheider. Twentieth Century Fox, 1971.

From Headquarters. Dir. William Dieterle. Perf. George Brent, Margaret Lindsay, and Eugene Pallette. Warner Bros, 1933.

Getting Evidence, Showing the Trials and Tribulations of a Private Detective. Dir. Edwin S. Porter. Edison Manufacturing Company, 1906.

Gilda. Dir. Charles Vidor. Perf. Rita Hayworth, Glenn Ford, and George Macready. Columbia Pictures, 1946.

Gladiator. Dir. Ridley Scott. Perf. Russell Crowe, Joaquin Phoenix, and Connie Nielsen. DreamWorks, 2000.

The Glass Key. Dir. Stuart Heisler. Perf. Alan Ladd, Veronica Lake, and Brian Donlevy. Paramount Pictures, 1942.

Guilty as Sin. Dir. Sidney Lumet. Perf. Rebecca De Mornay and Don Johnson. Hollywood Pictures, 1993.

The Hand that Rocks the Cradle. Dir. Curtis Hanson. Perf. Annabella Sciorra and Rebecca De Mornay. Hollywood Pictures, 1992.

Hannibal. Dir. Ridley Scott. Perf. Anthony Hopkins, Julianne Moore, and Gary Oldman. Dino De Laurentiis Productions, 2001.

Harper. Dir. Jack Smight. Perf. Paul Newman, Lauren Bacall, and Julie Harris. Warner Bros, 1966.

Hart to Hart. Perf. Robert Wagner, Stephanie Powers, and Lionel Stander. Columbia Pictures Television, 1979–84.

High Crimes. Dir. Carl Franklin. Perf. Ashley Judd and Morgan Freeman. New Regency Pictures, 2002.

Hill Street Blues. Perf. Daniel J. Travanti, Michael Conrad, Michael Warren, et al. National Broadcasting Company, 1981–87.

Hollywood Homicide. Dir. Ron Shelton. Perf. Harrison Ford and Josh Hartnett. Revolution Studios, 2003.

The Hound of the Baskervilles. Dir. Sidney Lanfield. Perf. Richard Greene, Basil Rathbone, and Nigel Bruce. Twentieth Century Fox, 1939.

The House on 92nd Street. Dir. Henry Hathaway. Perf. William Eythe, Lloyd Nolan, and Signe Hasso. Twentieth Century Fox, 1945.

The House without a Key. Dir. Spencer Gordon Bennet. Perf. William Bailey, John Webb Dillon, and George Kuwa. Pathé, 1926.

Identity. Dir. James Mangold. Perf. John Cusack and Amanda Peet. Columbia Pictures, 2003.

In the Heat of the Night. Dir. Norman Jewison. Perf. Sidney Poitier and Rod Steiger. The Mirisch Corporation, 1967.

In the Line of Fire. Dir. Wolfgang Petersen. Perf. Clint Eastwood, John Malkovich, and Rene Russo. Columbia Pictures, 1993.

Insomnia. Dir. Christopher Nolan. Perf. Al Pacino and Robin Williams. Buena Vista International, 2002.

Ironside. Perf. Raymond Burr, Don Galloway, et al. Universal Television, 1967–75.

Ivy. Dir. Sam Wood. Perf. Joan Fontaine, Patric Knowles, and Herbert Marshall. Universal International Pictures, 1947.

The Jackal. Dir. Michael Caton-Jones. Perf. Bruce Willis, Richard Gere, and Sidney Poitier. Universal Pictures, 1997.

Jagged Edge. Dir. Richard Marquand. Perf. Jeff Bridges, Glenn Close, and Peter Coyote. Columbia Pictures, 1985.

Junior. Dir. Ivan Reitman. Perf. Arnold Schwarzenegger and Danny DeVito. Universal Pictures, 1994.

Just Cause. Dir. Arne Glimcher. Perf. Sean Connery, Lawrence Fishburne, and Kate Capshaw. Warner Bros, 1995.

Kindergarten Cop. Dir. Ivan Reitman. Perf. Arnold Schwarzenegger and Penelope Miller. Universal Pictures, 1990.

Kiss Me Deadly. Dir. Richard Aldrich. Perf. Ralph Meeker, Albert Dekker, and Paul Stewart. Parklane Pictures, 1955.

Kiss the Girls. Dir. Gary Fleder. Perf. Morgan Freeman, Ashley Judd, and Cary Elwes. Paramount Pictures, 1997.

L.A. Confidential. Dir. Curtis Hanson. Perf. Kevin Spacey, Russell Crowe, Guy Pearce, and James Cromwell. Warner Bros, 1997.

The Lady in the Lake. Dir. Robert Montgomery. Perf. Robert Montgomery, Audrey Totter, and Lloyd Nolan. Metro–Goldwyn–Mayer, 1947.

Last Action Hero. Dir. John Mc Tiernan. Perf. Arnold Schwarzenegger and F. Murray Abraham. Columbia Pictures, 1993.

The Last of the Mohicans. Dir. Michael Mann. Perf. Daniel Day-Lewis, Madeleine Stowe, and Russell Means. Morgan Creek Productions, 1992.

The Last Seduction. Dir. John Dahl. Perf. Linda Fiorentino, Peter Berg, and Bill Pullman. Incorporated Television Company, 1994.

Laura. Dir. Otto Preminger. Perf. Gene Tierney, Dana Andrews, and Clifton Webb. Twentieth Century Fox, 1944.

Law & Order. Perf. Jerry Obach, Jesse L. Martin, et al. NBC Universal Television, 1990–.

Law & Order: Criminal Intent. Perf. Vincent D'Onofrio, Kathryn Erbe, et al. NBC Universal Television, 2001–.

Law & Order: Special Victims Unit. Perf. Christopher Meloni, Mariska Hargitay, et al. NBC Universal Television, 1999–.

Legal Eagles. Dir. Ivan Reitman. Perf. Robert Redford, Debra Winger, and Daryl Hannah. Universal Pictures, 1986.

Legally Blonde. Dir. Robert Luketic. Perf. Reese Witherspoon and Luke Wilson. Metro–Goldwyn–Mayer, 2001.

Legally Blonde 2: Red, White and Blonde. Dir. Charles Herman–Wurmfeld. Perf. Reese Witherspoon and Sally Field. Metro–Goldwyn–Mayer, 2003.

Lethal Weapon. Dir. Richard Donner. Perf. Mel Gibson, Danny Glover, and Gary Busey. Warner Bros, 1987.

Lethal Weapon 2. Dir. Richard Donner. Perf. Mel Gibson, Danny Glover, and Joe Pesci. Warner Bros, 1989.

Lethal Weapon 3. Dir. Richard Donner. Perf. Mel Gibson, Danny Glover, and Joe Pesci. Warner Bros, 1992.

Lethal Weapon 4. Dir. Richard Donner. Perf. Mel Gibson and Danny Glover. Warner Bros, 1998.

The Long Goodbye. Dir. Robert Altman. Perf. Elliott Gould, Nina Van Palland, and Sterling Hayden. Lions Gate Films, 1973.

Love Crimes. Dir. Lizzie Borden. Perf. Sean Young and Patrick Bergin. Miramax Films, 1992.

Love from a Stranger. Dir. Rowland V. Lee. Perf. Ann Harding, Basil Rathbone, and Binnie Hale. United Artists, 1937.

The Maltese Falcon. Dir. Roy Del Ruth. Perf. Ricardo Cortez, Bebe Daniels, and Dudley Digges. Warner Bros, 1931.

The Maltese Falcon. Dir. John Huston. Perf. Humphrey Bogart, Mary Astor, and Sydney Greenstreet. Warner Bros, 1941.

Manhunter. Dir. Michael Mann. Perf. William L. Petersen, Kim Greist, and Brian Cox. De Laurentiis Entertainment Group, 1986.

Marlowe. Dir. Paul Bogart. Perf. James Garner, Gayle Hunnicutt, and Carroll O'Connor. Metro–Goldwyn–Mayer, 1969.

McCallum. Perf. John Hannah, Zara Turner, et al. Scottish Television Enterprises, 1995–98.

Memento. Dir. Christopher Nolan. Perf. Guy Pearce, Carrie-Anne Moss, and Joe Pantoliano. Newmarket Capital Group, 2000.

Mercury Rising. Dir. Harold Becker. Perf. Bruce Willis, Alec Baldwin, and Miko Hughes. Universal Pictures, 1998.

Miami Vice. Perf. Don Johnson, Philip Michael Thomas, et al. Universal Television, 1984–89.

Mildred Pierce. Dir. Michael Curtiz. Perf. Joan Crawford, Jack Carson, and Zachary Scott. Warner Bros, 1945.

The Mirror Crack'd. Dir. Guy Hamilton. Perf. Angela Lansbury, Wendy Morgan, and Margaret Courtney. EMI Films, 1980.

Miss Congeniality. Dir. Donald Petrie. Perf. Sandra Bullock and Michael Caine. Castle Rock Entertainment, 2000.

Miss Congeniality 2: Armed and Fabulous. Dir. John Pasquin. Perf. Sandra Bullock and Regina King. Castle Rock Entertainment, 2005.

Monster. Dir. Patty Jenkins. Perf. Charlize Theron and Christina Ricci. Newmarket Films, 2003.

Moonlighting. Perf. Cybill Shepherd, Bruce Willis, et al. ABC Circle Films, 1985–89.

Mr. Moto's Gamble. Dir. James Tinling. Perf. Peter Lorre, Keye Luke, and Dick Baldwin. Twentieth Century Fox, 1938.

Murder Ahoy. Dir. George Pollock. Perf. Margaret Rutherford, Lionel Jeffries, and William Mervyn. Metro–Goldwyn–Mayer, 1964.

Murder at 1600. Dir. Dwight H. Little. Perf. Wesley Snipes, Diane Lane, and Daniel Benzali. Warner Bros, 1997.

Murder at the Gallop. Dir. George Pollock. Perf. Margaret Rutherford, Stringer Davis, and Robert Morley. Metro–Goldwyn–Mayer, 1963.

Murder by Numbers. Dir. Barbet Schroeder. Perf. Sandra Bullock and Ryan Gosling. Warner Bros, 2002.

Murder Most Foul. Dir. George Pollock. Perf. Margaret Rutherford, Ron Moody, and Charles 'Bud' Tingwell. Metro–Goldwyn–Mayer, 1964.

Murder, My Sweet. Dir. Edward Dmytryk. Perf. Dick Powell, Claire Trevor, and Anne Shirley. RKO Radio Pictures, 1944.

Murder on the Orient Express. Dir. Sidney Lumet. Perf. Albert Finney, Lauren Bacall, and John Gielgud. EMI Films, 1974.

The Murder Rooms. Perf. Ian Richardson and Robert Laing. British Broadcasting Corporation, 2000–01.

Murder She Said. Dir. George Pollock. Perf. Margaret Rutherford, Arthur Kennedy, and Muriel Paulow. Metro–Goldwyn–Mayer, 1961.

Murder, She Wrote. Perf. Angela Lansbury, William Windom, Ron Masak, et al. Universal Television, 1984–96.

Music Box. Dir. Costa-Gavas. Perf. Jessica Lange and Armin Mueller-Stahl. Carolco Pictures, 1989.

The Naked City. Dir. Jules Dassin. Perf. Barry Fitzgerald, Howard Duff, and Dorothy Hart. Universal International Pictures, 1948.

The Negotiator. Dir. F. Gary Gray. Perf. Samuel L. Jackson, Kevin Spacey, and David Morse. Warner Bros, 1998.

Nowhere to Run. Dir. Robert Harmon. Perf. Jean-Claude Van Damme and Rosanna Arquette. Columbia Pictures, 1993.

N.Y.P.D. Blue. Perf. Dennis Franz, Jimmy Smits, David Caruso, et al. Twentieth Century Fox Television, 1993–2005.

Out of the Past. Dir. Jacques Tourneur. Perf. Robert Mitchum, Jane Greer, and Kirk Douglas. RKO Radio Pictures, 1947.

The Paper. Dir. Ron Howard. Perf. Michael Keaton, Robert Duvall, and Glenn Close. Universal Pictures, 1994.

The Parallax View. Dir. Alan J. Pakula. Perf. Warren Beatty, Hume Cronyn, and William Daniels. Paramount Pictures, 1974.

Passenger 57. Dir. Kevin Hooks. Perf. Wesley Snipes, Bruce Payne, and Tom Sizemore. Warner Bros, 1992.

The Pelican Brief. Dir. Alan J. Pakula. Perf. Julia Roberts, Denzel Washington, and Sam Shephard. Warner Bros, 1993.

Perry Mason. Perf. Raymond Burr, Barbara Hale, William Hopper, et al. CBS Television, 1957–66.

Persons in Hiding. Dir. Louis King. Perf. Lynne Overman, Patricia Morison, and J. Carrol Naish. Paramount Pictures, 1939.

Physical Evidence. Dir. Michael Crichton. Perf. Burt Reynolds and Theresa Russell. Columbia Pictures, 1989.

Pitfall. Dir. André De Toth. Perf. Dick Powell, Lisabeth Scott, and Jane Wyatt. United Artists, 1948.

Point of No Return. Dir. John Badham. Perf. Bridget Fonda and Gabriel Byrne. Warner Bros, 1993.

The Postman Always Rings Twice. Dir. Tay Garnett. Perf. Lana Turner and John Garfield. Metro–Goldwyn–Mayer, 1946.

The Postman Always Rings Twice. Dir. Bob Rafelson. Perf. Jack Nicholson and Jessica Lange. Paramount Pictures, 1981.

Presumed Innocent. Dir. Alan J. Pakula. Perf. Harrison Ford, Greta Scacchi, Brian Dennehy, and Raul Julia. Warner Bros, 1990.

Prime Suspect. Perf. Helen Mirren, et al. Granada Television, 1990–96.

The Private Life of Sherlock Holmes. Dir. Billy Wilder. Perf. Robert Stephens, Colin Blakely, and Geneviève Page. United Artists, 1970.

Pulp Fiction. Dir. Quentin Tarantino. Perf. John Travolta, Samuel L. Jackson, and Uma Thurman. Miramax Films, 1994.

Quincy, M.E. Perf. Jack Klugman, Val Bisoglio, Robert Ito, et al. Universal Television, 1979–83.

The Rainmaker. Dir. Francis Ford Coppola. Perf. Matt Damon, Danny De Vito, and Claire Danes. American Zoetrope, 1997.

Rambo: First Blood Part II. Dir. George Cosmatos. Perf. Sylvester Stallone and Richard Crenna. Carolco Entertainment, 1985.

Rear Window. Dir. Alfred Hitchcock. Perf. James Stewart and Grace Kelly. Paramount Pictures, 1954.

Rear Window. Dir. Jeff Bleckner. Perf. Christopher Reeve, Daryl Hannah, and Robert Forster. Hallmark Entertainment, 1998. (TV movie).

Red Dragon. Dir. Brett Ratner. Perf. Anthony Hopkins and Edward Norton. Dino De Laurentiis Productions, 2002.

Red Rock West. Dir. John Dahl. Perf. Nicholas Cage, Dennis Hopper, and Lara Flynn Boyle. PolyGram Filmed Entertainment, 1992.

Regarding Henry. Dir. Mike Nichols. Perf. Harrison Ford and Annette Bening. Paramount Pictures, 1991.

The Return of Perry Mason. Perf. William Burr, Barbara Hale, and William Katt. Viacom Productions, 1985–95.

Rope. Dir. Alfred Hitchcock. Perf. James Stewart, John Dall, and Farley Granger. Warner Bros, 1948.

Rush Hour. Dir. Brett Ratner. Perf. Jackie Chan and Chris Tucker. New Line Cinema, 1998.

Rush Hour 2. Dir. Brett Ratner. Perf. Jackie Chan and Chris Tucker. New Line Cinema, 2001.

The Saint in New York. Dir. Ben Holmes. Perf. Louis Hayward, Kay Sutton, and Jonathan Hale. RKO Radio Pictures, 1938.

The Saint's Double Trouble. Dir. Jack Hively. Perf. George Sanders, Helene Withey, and Jonathan Hale. RKO Radio Pictures, 1940.

The Saint Strikes Back. Dir. John Farrow. Perf. George Sanders, Wendy Barrie, and Jonathan Hale. RKO Radio Pictures, 1939.

Satan Met a Lady. Dir. William Dieterle. Perf. Bette Davis and Warren William. Warner Bros, 1936.

Scarlet Street. Dir. Fritz Lang. Perf. Edward G. Robinson, Joan Bennett, and Dan Duryea. Universal Pictures, 1945.

The Science of Crime. "Psychopaths." Equinox. December 7, 2000.

The Science of Crime. "Criminal Evidence." Equinox. December 14, 2000.

Sea of Love. Dir. Harold Becker. Perf. Al Pacino, Ellen Barkin, and John Goodman. Universal Pictures, 1989.

Second Sight. Perf. Clive Owen. British Broadcasting Corporation, 1999–2000.

Serial Killer. Dir. Pierre David. Perf. Kim Delaney, Gary Hudson, and Tobin Beel. Republic Pictures Corporation, 1995.

Seven. Dir. David Fincher. Perf. Morgan Freeman, Brad Pitt, and Kevin Spacey. New Line Cinema, 1995.

Shaft. Dir. Gordon Parks. Perf. Richard Roundtree, Moses Gunn, and Charles Cioffi. Metro–Goldwyn–Mayer, 1971.

Shaft. Dir. John Singleton. Perf. Samuel L. Jackson, Vanessa Williams, and Jeffrey Wright. Paramount Pictures, 2000.

Sherlock Holmes. Dir. Albert Parker. Perf. John Barrymore and Roland Young. Goldwyn Pictures Corporation, 1922.

The Silence of the Lambs. Dir. Jonathan Demme. Perf. Anthony Hopkins, Jodie Foster, and Scott Glenn. Orion Pictures, 1991.

Silent Witness. Perf. Amanda Burton, William Armstrong, et al. British Broadcasting Corporation, 1996–.

Simon & Simon. Perf. Gerald McRaney and Jameson Parker. Universal Television, 1981–88.

The 6th Day. Dir. Roger Spottiswoode. Perf. Arnold Schwarzenegger and Michael Rapaport. Phoenix Pictures, 2000.

The Sixth Sense. Dir. M. Night Shyamalan. Perf. Bruce Willis, Toni Collette, and Haley Joel Osment. Hollywood Pictures, 1999.

Sleepy Hollow. Dir. Tim Burton. Perf. Johnny Depp, Christina Ricci, and Miranda Richardson. Paramount Pictures, 1999.

So Evil My Love. Dir. Lewis Allen. Perf. Ray Milland, Ann Todd, and Geraldine Fitzgerald. Paramount Pictures, 1948.

Spellbound. Dir. Alfred Hitchcock. Perf. Ingrid Bergman, Gregory Peck, and Michael Chekhov. Selznick International Pictures, 1945.

Stage Fright. Dir. Alfred Hitchcock. Perf. Jane Wyman, Marlene Dietrich, and Michael Wilding. Warner Bros, 1950.

Stakeout. Dir. John Badman. Perf. Richard Dreyfuss, Emilio Estevez, and Madeleine Stowe. Touchstone Pictures, 1987.

Sudden Death. Dir. Peter Hyams. Perf. Jean-Claude Van Damme and Powers Boothe. Universal Pictures, 1995.

Sue Thomas: F.B.Eye. Perf. Deanne Bray, Yannick Bisson, Enuka Okuma, et al. Pebblehut Productions, 2002–.

The Sum of All Fears. Dir. Phil Alden Robinson. Perf. Ben Affleck, Morgan Freeman, and Jamie Harrold. Paramount Pictures, 2002.

Suspect. Dir. Peter Yates. Perf. Cher, Dennis Quaid, and Liam Neeson. TriStar Pictures, 1987.

The Sweeney. Perf. John Thaw, Dennis Waterman, et al. Euston Films, 1975–78.

Taking Lives. Dir. D. J. Caruso. Perf. Angelina Jolie and Ethan Hawke. Warner Bros, 2004.

Tango & Cash. Dir. Andrei Konchalovsky and Albert Magnoli. Perf. Sylvester Stallone and Kurt Russell. Warner Bros, 1989.

Taxi Driver. Dir. Martin Scorsese. Perf. Robert De Niro, Cybill Shepherd, and Harvey Keitel. Columbia Pictures, 1976.

Tears of the Sun. Dir. Antoine Fuqua. Perf. Bruce Willis, Monica Bellucci, and Cole Hauser. Revolution Studios, 2003.

The Terminator. Dir. James Cameron. Perf. Arnold Schwarzenegger and Michael Biehn. Orion Pictures, 1984.

Terminator 2: Judgment Day. Dir. James Cameron. Perf. Arnold Schwarzenegger and Linda Hamilton. Carolco Pictures, 1991.

Terminator 3: Rise of the Machines. Dir. Jonathan Mostow. Perf. Arnold Schwarzenegger and Nick Stahl. Intermedia Films, 2003.

The Thin Man. Dir. W. S. Van Dyke. Perf. William Powell, Myrna Loy, and Maureen O'Sullivan. Metro–Goldwyn–Mayer, 1934.

Think Fast, Mr. Moto. Dir. Norman Foster. Perf. Peter Lorre, Thomas Beck, and Virginia Field. Twentieth Century Fox, 1937.

This Gun for Hire. Dir. Frank Tuttle. Perf. Veronica Lake, Alan Ladd, and Robert Pres-ton. Paramount Pictures, 1942.

The Thomas Crown Affair. Dir. John McTiernan. Perf. Pierce Brosnan and Rene Russo. United Artists, 1999.

A Time to Kill. Dir. Joel Schumacher. Perf. Matthew McConaughey, Sandra Bullock, and Samuel L. Jackson. Warner Bros, 1996.

Touch of Evil. Dir. Orson Welles. Perf. Charlton Heston, Janet Leigh, and Orson Welles. Universal International Pictures, 1958.

A Touch of Frost. Perf. David Jason, Bruce Alexander, et al. Yorkshire Television, 1992–.

Traffic in Souls. Dir. George Loane Tucker. Perf. Jane Gail and Matt Moore. Independent Moving Picture Company, 1913.

Training Day. Dir. Antoine Fuqua. Perf. Denzel Washington and Ethan Hawke. Warner Bros, 2001.

True Confessions. Dir. Ulu Grosbard. Perf. Robert DeNiro, Robert Duvall, and Charles Durning. United Artists, 1981.

True Crime. Dir. Clint Eastwood. Perf. Clint Eastwood, Isaiah Washington, and Denis Leary. Malpaso Productions, 1999.

True Lies. Dir. James Cameron. Perf. Arnold Schwarzenegger and Jamie Lee Curtis. Twentieth Century Fox, 1994.

Twisted. Dir. Philip Kaufman. Perf. Ashley Judd and Samuel L. Jackson. Paramount Pictures, 2004.

The Two Jakes. Dir. Jack Nicholson. Perf. Jack Nicholson, Harvey Keitel, and Meg Tilly. Paramount Pictures, 1990.

Unbreakable. Dir. M. Knight Shyamalan. Perf. Bruce Willis, Samuel L. Jackson, and Robin Wright Penn. Touchstone Pictures, 2000.

Under Suspicion. Dir. Stephen Hopkins. Perf. Morgan Freeman, Gene Hackman, and Thomas Jane. Revelations Entertainment, 2000.

Unfaithful. Dir. Adrian Lyne. Perf. Diane Lane and Richard Gere. Fox 2000 Pictures, 2002.

Universal Soldier. Dir. Roland Emmerich. Perf. Jean-Claude Van Damme and Dolph Lundgren. Carolco Pictures, 1992.

The Usual Suspects. Dir. Bryan Singer. Perf. Gabriel Byrne, Kevin Spacey, and Chazz Palminteri. Polygram Filmed Entertainment, 1995.

Les Vampires. Dir. Louis Feuillade. Perf. Musidora, Edouard Mathé, and Marcel Lévesque. Gaumont, 1915.

Vertigo. Dir. Alfred Hitchcock. Perf. James Stewart, Kim Novak, and Barbara Bel Geddes. Paramount Pictures, 1958.

V. I. Warshawski. Dir. Jeff Kanew. Perf. Kathleen Turner, Jay O. Sanders, and Charles Durning. Warner Bros, 1991.

When the Bough Breaks. Dir. Michael Cohn. Perf. Ally Walker, Martin Sheen, and Ron Perlman. Osmosis Productions, 1993.

Witness. Dir. Peter Weir. Perf. Harrison Ford, Kelly McGillis, and Josef Sommer. Paramount Pictures, 1985.

Young Sherlock Holmes. Dir. Barry Levinson. Perf. Nicholas Rowe, Alan Cox, and Sophie Ward. Paramount Pictures, 1985.

WORKS CITED

Altman, Rick. *Film/Genre*. London: BFI Publishing, 1999.

Ames, Christopher. "Restoring the Black Man's Lethal Weapon: Race and Sexuality in Contemporary Cop Films." *Journal of Popular Film and Television* 20:3 (1992): 52–60.

Athanasourelis, John Paul. "Film Adaptation and the Censors: 1940s Hollywood and Raymond Chandler." *Studies in the Novel* 35:3 (Fall 2003): 325–39.

Bailey, Cameron. "Nigger/Lover—The Thin Sheen of Race in 'Something Wild.'" *Screen* 29:4 (1988): 28–43.

Barker, Martin. "The First and Last Mohicans." *A Sight and Sound Reader*. Ed. José Arroyo. London: BFI Publishing, 2000. 96–100.

Bartlett, Keith. "Grisham Adaptations and the Legal Thriller." *Genre and Contemporary Hollywood*. Ed. Steve Neale. London: BFI Publishing, 2003. 269–80.

Belton, John. *American Cinema/American Culture*. New York: McGraw-Hill Inc., 1994.

Bernardi, Daniel. "Introduction: Race and the Hollywood Style." *Classic Hollywood, Classic Whiteness*. Ed. Daniel Bernardi. Minneapolis: University of Minnesota Press, 2001. xiii–xxvi.

Blake, Linnie. "Whoever Fights Monsters: Serial Killers, the FBI and America's Last Frontier." *The Devil Himself: Villainy in Detective Fiction and Film*. Eds. Stacy Gillis and Philippa Gates. Contributions to the Study of Popular Culture Ser. 73. Westport, CT: Greenwood Press, 2002. 197–210.

Blum, John Morton. *V Was for Victory: Politics and American Culture during World War II*. New York: Harcourt Brace Jovanovitch Publishers, 1976.

Bogle, Donald. *Toms, Coons, Mulattoes, Mammies and Bucks: An Interpretative History of Blacks in American Films*. New York: Viking Press, 1973.

Bondi, Nicole. "Hollywood portrayals of disability improve, but some still miss the mark." *iCan News Service* (March 22, 2001) <www.ican.com/news/fullpage.cfm/articleid/E357B6A7-E30A-47C6-917675653101AA6A/cx/news.features/article.cfm> June 24, 2003.

Bone Collector Official Web Site <http://www.thebonecollector.com> February 15, 2001.

Boozer, Jack. "The Lethal Femme Fatale in the Noir Tradition." *Journal of Film and Video* 51:3/4 (1999): 20–35.

Borde, Raymond and Etienne Chaumeton. *Panorama du Film Noir Americáin* (1941–53). Paris: Les Editions de Minuit, 1955.

Bordo, Susan. *The Male Body: A New Look at Men in Public and in Private*. New York: Farrar, Straus and Giroux, 1999.

Bordwell, David. *Narration in the Fiction Film*. 1990 ed. London: Routledge, 1990.

Branston, Gil. ". . . Viewer, I Listened to Him. . . . Voices, Masculinity, *In the Line of Fire*." *Me Jane: Masculinity, Movies and Women*. Eds. Pat Kirkham and Janet Thumim. New York: St. Martin's Press, 1995. 37–50.

Breathwaite, John. "Morgan Freeman . . . *Along Came a Spider*." *New African* (September 2001): 38.

Brittan, Arthur. "Masculinities and Masculinism." *The Masculinities Reader*. Eds. Stephen M. Whitehead and Frank J. Barrett. Cambridge, UK: Polity Press, 2001. 51–55.

Britton, Andrew. "Stars and Genre." *Stardom: Industry of Desire*. Ed. Christine Gledhill. London: Routledge, 1991. 198–206.

Brod, Harry. "The Case for Men's Studies." *The Making of Masculinities: The New Men's Studies*. Ed. Harry Brod. Boston: Allen & Unwin, 1987. 39–62.

———. "Introduction: Themes and Theses of Men's Studies." *The Making of Masculinities: The New Men's Studies*. Ed. Harry Brod. Boston: Allen & Unwin, 1987. 1–18.

———. "Masculinity as Masquerade." *The Masculine Masquerade: Masculinity and Representation*. Eds. Andrew Perchuk and Helaine Posner. Cambridge, MA: MIT Press, 1995. 13–19.

Brown, Jeffrey A. "Gender and the Action Heroine: Hardbodies and the *Point of No Return*." *Cinema Journal* 35:3 (Spring 1996): 52–71.

Brown, Royal S. "*Seven*." Rev. of *Seven*, dir. David Fincher. *Cineaste* 22:3 (1996): 44–46.

Browne, Nick. "Preface." *Refiguring American Film Genres: History and Theory*. Ed. Nick Browne. Berkeley, CA: University of California Press, 1998. xi–xiv.

Buscombe, Edward. "The Idea of Genre in the American Cinema." *Film Genre Reader II*. Ed. Barry Keith Grant. Austin, TX: University of Texas Press, 1995. 11–25.

Butler, Judith. *Bodies that Matter: On the Discursive Limits of Sex*. New York: Routledge, 1993.

———. *Gender Trouble: Feminism and the Subversion of Identity*. London: Routledge, 1990.

California Association of Criminalists (CAC) <http://www.cacnews.org> August 22, 2001.

Caputi, Jane. "Small Ceremonies: Ritual in *Forrest Gump, Natural Born Killers, Seven*, and *Follow Me Home*." *Mythologies of Violence in Postmodern Media*. Ed. Christopher Sharrett. Detroit: Wayne State University Press, 1999. 147–74.

Caputi, Jane and Diana E. H. Russell. "Femicide: Sexist Terrorism against Women." *Femicide: The Politics of Killing Women*. Eds. Jill Radford and Diana E. H. Russell. New York: Twyane Publishers, 1992: 13–21.

Cawelti, John G. *Adventure, Mystery, and Romance: Formula Stories as Art and Popular Culture*. Chicago: University of Chicago Press, 1976.

Chapman, Rowena. "The Great Pretender: Variations on the New Man Theme." *Male Order: Unwrapping Masculinity*. Eds. Rowena Chapman and Jonathan Rutherford. Male Order Series. London: Lawrence & Wishart, 1988. 225–48.

Clarke, Eric and Mathew Henson. "Hot Damme! Reflections on Gay Publicity." *Boys: Masculinities in Contemporary Culture*. Ed. Paul Smith. Cultural Studies Series. Boulder, CO: Westview Press, 1996. 131–50.

Clay, Andrew. "Men, Women and Money: Masculinity in Crisis in the British Professional Crime Film 1946–1965." *British Crime Cinema*. Eds. Steve Chibnall and Robert Murphy. New York: Routledge, 1999. 51–65.

Cocchi, John. "The 2nd Feature: A History of the B Movies—Detectives and Mysteries." *Classic Images* 132 (1986): 19–22, C13.

———. "The 2nd Feature: A History of the B Movies—Detectives and Mysteries 2." *Classic Images* 133 (1986): 43–46, 63.

Cohan, Steven and Ina Rae Hark. "Introduction." *Screening the Male: Exploring Masculinities in Hollywood Cinema*. Eds. Steven Cohan and Ina Rae Hark. London: Routledge, 1992. 1–8.

Cole, Stephen. "Outside the Box." *Globe Television* (February 15–21, 2003): 3.

Collier, Aldore. "Why Hollywood Ignores Black Love and Intimacy: Black Stars Challenge Race and Market Fears that Limit On-Screen Romance." *Ebony* 44:6 (1989): 41.

Collins, Gerard. "Contagion and Technology in Patricia Cornwell's Scarpetta Novels." *The Devil Himself: Villainy in Detective Fiction and Film.* Eds. Stacy Gillis and Philippa Gates. Contributions to the Study of Popular Culture Ser. 73. Westport, CT: Greenwood Press, 2002. 159–69.

Coltrane, Scott. "Theorizing Masculinities in Contemporary Social Science." *Theorizing Masculinities.* Eds. Harry Brod and Michael Kaufman. Research on Men and Masculinities Ser. 5. Thousand Oaks, CA: Sage Publications, 1994. 39–60.

Concise Oxford Dictionary of Current English. Eds. H. W. Fowler and F. G. Fowler. 9th ed. Oxford: Clarendon Press, 1995.

Connell, Robert W. *Masculinities.* Cambridge, UK: Polity Press, 1995.

Cook, Pam. "Masculinity in Crisis? Pam Cook on Tragedy and Identification in *Raging Bull.*" *Screen* 23: 3–4 (September/October 1982): 39–46.

Coon, David Roger. "Two Steps Forward, One Step Back: The Selling of *Charlie's Angels* and *Alias.*" *Journal of Popular Film and Television* 33:1 (Spring 2005): 2–11.

Cooper, James Fenimore. *The Last of the Mohicans: A Narrative of 1757.* Leather-stocking ed. London: George Routledge, 1826.

Cooper, Stephen. "Sex/Knowledge/Power in the Detective Genre." *Film Quarterly* 42:3 (1989): 23–31.

Corber, Robert J. *Homosexuality in Cold War America: Resistance and the Crisis of Masculinity.* Durham, NC: Duke University Press, 1997.

Cornwell, Patricia. *Portrait of a Killer: Jack the Ripper—Case Closed.* New York: G. P. Putnam's Sons, 2002.

———. *Post Mortem.* New York: Avon Books, 1990.

Craib, Ian. "Masculinity and Male Dominance." *Sociological Review* 35:4 (1987): 721–43.

Craik, Jennifer. *The Face of Fashion: Cultural Studies in Fashion.* London: Routledge, 1994.

Daly, Sean. "Kinder, Gentler Willis." *Toronto Star* (Arts and Entertainment Section, March 3, 2003): E1 and E4.

Dargis, Manohla. "*Devil in a Blue Dress.*" Rev. of *Devil in a Blue Dress,* dir. Carl Franklin. *Sight and Sound* 6:1 (1996): 38.

Dawson, Jeff. "The Worst of the British." *Empire* 49 (1993): 24.

DeAndrea, William L. *Encyclopedia Mysteriosa: A Comprehensive Guide to the Art of Detection in Print, Film, Radio, and Television*. Paperback ed. New York: Macmillan, 1997.

Deaver, Jeffrey. *The Bone Collector*. New York: Viking, 1997.

Deleyto, Celestino. "The Margins of Pleasure: Female Monstrosity and Male Paranoia in *Basic Instinct*." *Film Criticism* 21 (Spring 1997): 20–42.

Diawara, Manthia. "Black American Cinema: The New Realism." *Black American Cinema*. Ed. Manthia Diawara. AFI Film Readers. New York: Routledge, 1993. 3–26.

———. "Black Spectatorship—Problems of Identification and Resistance." *Screen* 29:4 (1988): 66–79.

Dickson, Kevin. "Crime Story." *TV Guide* (February 1, 2003): 11–13.

Dittman, Earl. "Man of Mettle." *Famous* 4:7 (July 2003): 20–22.

Dittmar, Linda and Gene Michaud. "Introduction." *From Hanoi to Hollywood: The Vietnam War in American Film*. Eds. Linda Dittmar and Gene Michaud. New Brunswick, NJ: Rutgers University Press, 1990. 1–15.

Doane, Mary Ann. *Femmes Fatales: Feminism, Film Theory, Psychoanalysis*. New York: Routledge, 1991.

Douglas, Wayne J. "The Criminal Psychopath as the Hollywood Hero." *Journal of Popular Film and Television* 8:4 (1981): 30–39.

Dove, George. *The Police Procedural*. Bowling Green, OH: Bowling Green University Popular Press, 1982.

Dyer, Richard. *Heavenly Bodies: Film Stars and Society*. New York: St. Martin's Press, 1986.

———. "Kill and Kill Again." *Sight and Sound* 7:9 (1997): 14–17.

———. *Stars*. London: BFI Publishing, 1979.

———. "White." *Screen* 29:4 (Autumn 1988): 44–65.

Easthope, Antony. *What a Man's Gotta Do: The Masculine Myth in Popular Culture*. London: Paladin Grafton Books, 1986.

Edwards, Tim. *Men in the Mirror: Men's Fashion, Masculinity, and Consumer Society*. London: Cassell, 1997.

Ehrenreich, Barbara. *The Hearts of Men: American Dreams and the Flight from Commitment*. Garden City, NY: Anchor Books, 1983.

Elias, Justine. "How to Be a Euro-Villain." *The Guardian* (Screen July 21, 2000): 6.

Everson, William K. *The Bad Guys: A Pictorial History of the Movie Villain*. New York: Citadel Press, 1964.

———. *The Detective in Film: A Pictorial Treasury of the Screen Sleuth from 1903 to the Present*. 3rd paperbound ed. Secaucus, NJ: Citadel Press, 1980.

Faludi, Susan. *Backlash: The Undeclared War against Women*. London: Vintage, 1992.

———. *Stiffed: The Betrayal of the Modern Man*. London: Chatto and Windus, 1999.

Feschuk, Scott. "Geezer Pleasers from Over the Hill." *The National Post* (August 3, 2000): B3.

Fiedler, Leslie. *What Was Literature? Class Culture and Mass Society*. New York: Simon & Schuster, 1982.

Field, Marcus. "The New Narcissism." *The Independent on Sunday* (Life Etc. December 8, 2002): 1–2.

Fleck, Patrice. "Looking in the Wrong Direction." *Postscript* 16:2 (1997): 35–43.

Foster, Gwendolyn Audrey. "Monstrosity and the Bad-White-Body Film." *Bad: Infamy, Darkness, Evil, and Slime on Screen*. Ed. Murray Pomerance. Albany, NY: State University of New York Press. 2004. 39–53.

———. *Performing Whiteness: Postmodern Re/Constructions in the Cinema*. The SUNY Series in Postmodern Culture. Albany, NY: State University of New York Press, 2003.

Foucault, Michel. *Discipline and Punish: The Birth of the Modern Prison*. Trans. from the French by Alan Sheridan. London: Penguin Books, 1977.

Fox, Terry Curtis. "City Knights." *Film Comment* 20:5 (1984): 30–36.

Francke, Lizzie. "Review of *Copycat*." *Sight and Sound* 6:5 (1996): 51–52.

Fuchs, Christian. *Bad Blood: An Illustrated Guide to Psycho Cinema*. Trans. Otmar Lichtenwoerther. Creation Cinema Collection, Vol. 18. New York: Creation Books, 2002.

Gallagher, Mark. "I Married Rambo: Spectacle and Melodrama in the Hollywood Action Film." *Mythologies of Violence in Postmodern Media*. Ed. Christopher Sharrett. Detroit: Wayne State University Press, 1999. 199–225.

Gledhill, Christine. "Rethinking Genre." *Reinventing Film Studies*. Eds. Christine Gledhill and Linda Williams. London: Arnold, 2000. 221–43.

Goldberg, Carl and Virginia Crespo. "A Psychological Examination of Serial Killer Cinema: The Case of *Copycat*." *Post Script: Essays in Film and the Humanities* 22.2 (2003): 55–63.

Goulden, Joseph C. *The Best Years: 1945–1950*. New York: Atheneum, 1976.

Grady, Frank. "Arnoldian Humanism, or Amnesia and Autobiography in the Schwarzenegger Action Film." *Cinema Journal* 42:2 (2003): 41–56.

Grant, Barry Keith. "American Psycho/sis: The Pure Products of America Go Crazy." *Mythologies of Violence in Postmodern Media*. Ed. Christopher Sharrett. Detroit: Wayne State University Press, 1999. 23–40.

———. "Strange Days: Gender and Ideology in New Genre Films." *Ladies and Gentlemen, Boys and Girls: Gender in Film at the End of the Twentieth Century*. Ed. Murray Pomerance. SUNY Series in Cultural Studies in Cinema/Video. Albany, NY: State University of New York Press, 2001. 185–99.

Green, Philip. *Cracks in the Pedestal: Ideology and Gender in Hollywood*. Amherst: University of Massachusetts Press, 1998.

Grieveson, Lee. "Review Article." Rev. of *Screening the Male* by Steven Cohan and Ina Rae Hark, *Clint Eastwood* by Paul Smith, and *Spectacular Bodies* by Yvonne Tasker. *Screen* 35:4 (1994): 400–406.

Griffith, Richard. *The Movie Stars*. Garden City, NY: Doubleday, 1970.

Grisham, John. *The Pelican Brief*. New York: Doubleday, 1992.

Grist, Leighton. "Moving Targets and Black Widows: Film Noir in Modern Hollywood." *The Book of Film Noir*. Ed. Ian Cameron. New York: Continuum, 1992. 267–85.

Guerrero, Ed. "The Black Image in Protective Custody: Hollywood's Biracial Buddy Films of the Eighties." *Black American Cinema*. Ed. Manthia Diawara. AFI Film Readers. New York: Routledge, 1993. 237–46.

———. "*Devil in a Blue Dress*." Rev. of *Devil in a Blue Dress*, dir. Carl Franklin. *Cineaste* 22:1 (1996): 38–41.

———. *Framing Blackness: The African American Image in Film*. Philadelphia: Temple University Press, 1993.

Gunning, Tom. "The Exterior as *Intérieur*: Benjamin's Optical Detective." *Boundary 2* 30:1 (2003): 105–29.

———. "A Tale of Two Prologues: Actors and Roles, Detectives and Disguises in Fantomas, Film and Novel." *The Velvet Light Trap* 37 (Spring 1996): 30–36.

———. "Tracing the Individual: Photography, Detectives, and Early Cinema." Eds. Leo Charney and Vanessa R. Schwartz. *Cinema and the Invention of Modern Life*. Berkeley: University of California Press, 1995. 15–45.

Gutterman, David S. "Postmodernism and the Interrogation of Masculinity." *Theorizing Masculinities*. Eds. Harry Brod and Michael Kaufman. Research on Men and Masculinities Ser. 5. Thousand Oaks, CA: Sage Publications, 1994. 219–38.

Hall, Stuart. "New Ethnicities." *Black British Cultural Studies: A Reader*. Eds. Houston A. Baker Jr., Manthia Diawara, and Ruth H. Lindeborg. Chicago: University of Chicago Press, 1996. 163–72.

Hantke, Steffen. "Monstrosity without a Body: Representational Strategies in the Popular Serial Killer Film." *Post Script: Essays in Film and the Humanities* 22.2 (2003): 34–54.

Harmon, Jim. *Radio Mystery and Adventure and Its Appearance in Film, Television and Other Media*. Jefferson, NC: McFarland and Co., Inc., 1992.

Harris, Thomas. *Hannibal*. London: Heinemann, 1999.

———. *Red Dragon*. 1981. London: Bodley Head, 1982.

———. *The Silence of the Lambs*. London: Heinemann, 1988.

Hart, Lynda. *Fatal Women: Lesbian Sexuality and the Mark of Aggression*. Princeton, NJ: Princeton University Press, 1994.

Haslem, Wendy. "Romance and Paranoia in *The Big Sleep* (1946)." *Australian Screen Education* 29 (Winter 2002): 164–68.

Hatty, Suzanne E. *Masculinities, Violence, and Culture*. Sage Series on Violence against Women. Thousand Oaks, CA: Sage Publications, Inc., 2000.

Haut, Woody. *Neon Noir: Contemporary American Crime Fiction*. London: Serpent's Tail, 1999.

Hawkins, Harriet. *Classics and Trash: Traditions and Taboos in High Literature and Popular Modern Genres*. New York: Harvester Wheatsheaf, 1990.

Heilbrun, Carolyn G. "Keynote Address: Gender and Detective Fiction." *The Sleuth and the Scholar: Origins, Evolution, and Current Trends in Detective Fiction*. Eds. Barbara A. Rader and Howard G. Zettler. Contributions to the Study of Popular Culture Ser. 19. New York: Greenwood Press, 1988. 1–8.

Higham, Charles and Joel Greenberg. *Hollywood in the Forties*. International Film Guide Series. London: A. Zwemmer Ltd., 1968.

Hills, Elizabeth. "From 'Figurative Males' to Action Heroines: Further Thoughts on Active Women in the Cinema." *Screen* 40:1 (Spring 1999): 38–50.

Hirsch, Foster. *The Dark Side of the Screen: Film Noir*. 3rd paperback ed. San Diego: A. S. Barnes & Co., Inc., 1986.

———. *Detours and Lost Highways: The Map of Neo-Noir*. New York: Limelight Editions, 1999.

Hoggart, Paul. "Yesterday's Viewing." *The Times* (February 2, 2001): 31.

Holmes, Ronald M. and Stephen T. Holmes. "Part I—What Is Serial Murder? The Character and the Extent." *Contemporary Perspectives on Serial Murder.* Ed. Ronald M. Holmes and Stephen T. Holmes. Thousand Oaks, CA: Sage Publications, 1998. 1–4.

Holmlund, Chris. *Impossible Bodies: Femininity and Masculinity at the Movies.* London: Routledge, 2002.

———. "Masculinity as Multiple Masquerade: The 'Mature' Stallone and the Stallone Clone." *Screening the Male: Exploring Masculinities in Hollywood Cinema.* Eds. Steven Cohan and Ina Rae Hark. London: Routledge, 1993. 213–29.

———. "Reading Character with a Vengeance: The *Fatal Attraction* Phenomenon." *The Velvet Light Trap* 27 (Spring 1991): 25–36.

hooks, bell. *Reel to Real: Race, Sex, and Class at the Movies.* New York: Routledge, 1996.

Inness, Sherrie. *Tough Girls: Women Warriors and Wonder Women in Popular Culture.* Philadelphia: University of Pennsylvania Press, 1999.

Internet Movie Database (IMDb) <http://www.imdb.com> February 15, 2001.

Jackson, Stevi and Sue Scott. "Sexual Skirmishes and Feminist Factions: Twenty-Five Years of Debate on Women and Sexuality." *Feminism and Sexuality: A Reader.* Eds. Stevi Jackson and Sue Scott. New York: Columbia University Press, 1996. 1–29.

Jeffords, Susan. "The Big Switch: Hollywood Masculinity in the Nineties." *Film Theory Goes to the Movies.* Eds. Jim Collins, Hilary Radner, and Ava Preacher Collins. AFI Film Readers. New York: Routledge, 1993. 196–208.

———. "Can Masculinity Be Terminated?" *Screening the Male: Exploring Masculinities in Hollywood Cinema.* Eds. Steven Cohan and Ina Rae Hark. London: Routledge, 1993. 245–62.

———. *Hard Bodies: Hollywood Masculinity in the Reagan Era.* New Brunswick, NJ: Rutgers University Press, 1994.

———. *Remasculinization of America: Gender and the Vietnam War.* Bloomington: Indiana University Press, 1989.

Johnson, Rachel. "Playing Fathers and Monsters: The Classical Appeal of Anthony Hopkins." *CineAction!* 55 (2001): 24–30.

Kane, Kathryn. *Visions of War: Hollywood Combat Films of World War II.* Studies in Cinema Ser. 9. Ann Arbor, MI: UMI Research Press, 1982.

Kaplan, E. Ann. "Introduction to the New Edition." *Women in Film Noir*. Ed. E. Ann Kaplan. Revised ed. London: BFI Publishing, 2001. 1–14.

———. *Looking for the Other: Feminism, Film, and the Imperial Gaze*. New York: Routledge, 1997.

Karimi, Amir. *Toward a Definition of American Film Noir (1941–1949)*. New York: Arno Press, 1976.

Karnick, S. T. "The Bourgeois Detective." *The Weekly Standard* 7:16 (December 31, 2001): 40–42 <charliechangfamily.tripod.com/id80.html> June 5, 2004.

Kaufman, Michael. "Men, Feminism, and Men's Contradictory Experiences of Power." *Theorizing Masculinities*. Eds. Harry Brod and Michael Kaufman. Research on Men and Masculinities Ser. 5. Thousand Oaks, CA: Sage Publications, 1994. 142–63.

Keller, James R. "'Like to Chaos': Deformity and Depravity in Contemporary Film." *Journal of Popular Film and Television* 23:1 (Spring 1995): 8–14.

Kellner, Douglas. "Film, Politics, and Ideology: Reflections on Hollywood Film in the Age of Reagan." *The Velvet Light Trap* 27 (Spring 1991): 9–24.

Kimmel, Michael. "The Contemporary 'Crisis' of Masculinity in Historical Perspective." *The Making of Masculinities: The New Men's Studies*. Ed. Harry Brod. Boston: Allen & Unwin, 1987. 121–53.

———. *Manhood in America: A Cultural History*. New York: The Free Press, 1996.

———. "Masculinity as Homophobia: Fear, Shame, and Silence in the Construction of Gender Identity." *Theorizing Masculinities*. Eds. Harry Brod and Michael Kaufman. Research on Men and Masculinities Ser. 5. Thousand Oaks, CA: Sage Publications, 1994. 119–41.

King, Geoff. *Film Comedy*. London: Wallflower Press, 2002.

———. "Stardom in the Willennium." *Contemporary Hollywood Stardom*. Ed. Thomas Austin and Martin Baker. London: Arnold, 2003. 62–73.

King, Neal. *Heroes in Hard Times: Cop Action Movies in the U.S*. Philadelphia: Temple University Press, 1999.

Kirkham, Pat and Janet Thumim. "Me Jane." *Me Jane: Masculinity, Movies and Women*. Eds. Pat Kirkham and Janet Thumim. New York: St. Martin's Press, 1995. 11–35.

———. "You Tarzan." *You Tarzan: Masculinity, Movies and Men*. Eds. Pat Kirkham and Janet Thumim. London: Lawrence & Whishart, 1993. 11–26.

Kleinhans, Chuck. "Class in Action." *The Hidden Foundation: Cinema and the Question of Class*. Eds. David E. James and Rick Berg. Minneapolis: University of Minnesota Press, 1996. 240–63.

Krämer, Peter. "'A Woman in a Male-Dominated World': Jodie Foster, Stardom and Nineties Hollywood." *Contemporary Hollywood Stardom.* Ed. Thomas Austin and Martin Baker. London: Arnold, 2003. 201–14.

Krutnik, Frank. *In a Lonely Street: Film Noir, Genre, Masculinity.* London: Routledge, 1991.

Kutner, C. Jerry. "Beyond the Golden Age: Film Noir since the '50s." *Bright Lights* 12 (1994): 23–32.

Lackmann, Ron. *The Encyclopedia of American Radio: An A-Z Guide to Radio from Jack Benny to Howard Stern.* Updated ed. New York: Facts on File Inc., 2000.

Lane, Anthony. "The Big Round-Up." *The New Yorker* (August 14, 1995): 85–87.

Lane, Christina. "The Liminal Iconography of Jodie Foster." *Journal of Popular Film and Television* 22:4 (Winter 1995): 149–53.

Lane, Christina, Sue Murray, and Connie Shortes. "Introduction." *The Velvet Light Trap* 38 (1996): 1–3.

Langman, Larry and Daniel Finn. *A Guide to American Crime Films of the Forties and Fifties.* Biographies and Indexes in the Performing Arts Ser. 19. Westport, CT: Greenwood Press, 1995.

———. *A Guide to American Crime Films of the Thirties.* Biographies and Indexes in the Performing Arts Ser. 18. Westport, CT: Greenwood Press, 1995.

———. *A Guide to American Silent Crime Films.* Biographies and Indexes in the Performing Arts Ser. 15. Westport, CT: Greenwood Press, 1994.

Lawrence, Amy. "Jimmy Stewart Is Being Beaten: *Rope* and the Postwar Crisis in American Masculinity." *Quarterly Review of Film and Video* 16:1 (1995): 41–58.

Leab, Daniel J. *From Sambo to Superspade: The Black Experience in Motion Pictures.* London: Secker & Warburg, 1975.

Lee, Susanna. "The Menace of the Post-Hardboiled Maverick: Jim Thompson's *Pop. 1280* and Modern Television Detective Drama." *Journal of Popular Culture* 37:1 (August 2003): 43–55.

Lehman, David. *The Perfect Murder: A Study in Detection.* Ann Arbor: The University of Michigan Press, 2000.

Lehman, Peter. *Running Scared: Masculinity and the Representation of the Male Body.* Culture and the Moving Image. Philadelphia: Temple University Press, 1993.

Lehman, Peter and William Luhr. *Blake Edwards.* Athens: Ohio University Press, 1981.

Leitch, Thomas. *Crime Films*. Cambridge: Cambridge University Press, 2002.

Lewis, Leon. "*Devil in a Blue Dress*." Rev. of *Devil in a Blue Dress*, dir. Carl Franklin. *MCA 1996: A Survey of the Films of 1995*. Eds. Beth A. Fhaner and Christopher P. Scanlon. Detroit: Gale, 1996. 135–37.

Livingstone, Jay. "Crime and the Media: Myths and Reality." *USA Today* 122:2588 (1994): 40–42.

Lucia, Cynthia. "Women on Trial: The Female Lawyer in the Hollywood Courtroom." *Cineaste* 19:2–3 (1992): 32–37.

MacInnes, John. *The End of Masculinity: The Confusion of Sexual Genesis and Sexual Difference in Modern Society*. Buckingham, UK: Open University Press, 1998.

MacKinnon, Kenneth. *Uneasy Pleasures: The Male as Erotic Object*. London: Cygnus Arts, 1997.

Mailer, Norman. *Advertisements for Myself*. New York: G. P. Putnam's Sons, 1959.

Maltby, Richard. *Hollywood Cinema: An Introduction*. Oxford: Blackwell Publishers, 1995.

Mandel, Ernest. *Delightful Murder: A Social History of the Crime Story*. London: Pluto Press, 1984.

McCann, Graham. *Rebel Males: Clift, Brando and Dean*. London: Hamish Hamilton, 1991.

Medicoff, Zack. "Preview: *Red Dragon*." *Tribute* 19:7 (October 2002): 14.

Mellen, Joan. *Big Bad Wolves: Masculinity in the American Film*. London: Elm Tree Books, 1978.

Melling, John Kennedy. *Murder Done to Death: Parody and Pastiche in Detective Fiction*. Lanham, MD: The Scarecrow Press Ltd., 1996.

Merivale, Patricia and Susan Elizabeth Sweeney. "The Game's Afoot: On the Trail of the Metaphysical Detective Story." *Detecting Texts: The Metaphysical Detective Story from Poe to Postmodernism*. Eds. Patricia Merivale and Susan Elizabeth Sweeney. Philadelphia: University of Pennsylvania Press, 1999. 1–24.

Messent, Peter. "Introduction: From Private Eye to Police Procedural—The Logic of Contemporary Crime Fiction." *Criminal Proceedings: The Contemporary American Crime Novel*. Ed. Peter Messent. London: Pluto Press, 1997. 1–21.

Mizejewski, Linda. "Picturing the Female Dick: *The Silence of the Lambs* and *Blue Steel*." *Journal of Film and Video* 45: 2–3 (Summer/Fall 1993): 6–23.

Modleski, Tania. *Feminism without Women: Culture and Criticism in a "Post-Feminist" Age*. New York: Routledge, 1991.

Molden, David. "African Americans in Hollywood: A Black-on-Black Shame." *Black Issues in Higher Education* 12:23 (1996): 112.

Morrison, Ken. "The Technology of Homicide: Constructions of Evidence and Truth in the American Murder Film." *Mythologies of Violence in Postmodern Media*. Ed. Christopher Sharrett. Detroit: Wayne State University Press, 1999. 301–16.

Morrow, Daniel J. "Radio Detectives." *Encyclopedia of Mystery and Detection*. Eds. Chris Steinbrunner and Otto Penzler. New York: McGraw-Hill, 1976. 333–35.

Mosley, Walter. *Devil in a Blue Dress*. New York: W. W. Norton & Co., 1990.

Mulvey, Laura. "Afterthoughts on 'Visual Pleasure and Narrative Cinema' Inspired by *Duel in the Sun*." *Framework* 15–17 (1981): 12–15.

———. "Visual Pleasure and Narrative Cinema." *Screen* 16:3 (1975): 6–18.

Naremore, James. "American Film Noir: The History of an Idea." *Film Quarterly* 49:2 (1995/1996): 12–28.

Neale, Steve. *Genre and Hollywood*. London: Routledge, 2000.

———. "Masculinity as Spectacle: Reflections on Men and Mainstream Cinema." (1983) *Screening the Male: Exploring Masculinities in Hollywood Cinema*. Eds. Steven Cohan and Ina Rae Hark. London: Routledge, 1993. 9–20.

———. "Melo Talk: On the Meaning and Use of the Term 'Melodrama' in the American Trade Press." *The Velvet Light Trap* 32 (1993): 66–89.

Neibaur, James L. *Tough Guy: The American Movie Macho*. Jefferson, NC: McFarland & Company, 1989.

Norden, Martin F. and Madeleine A. Cahill. "Violence, Women, and Disability in Tod Browning's *Freaks* and *The Devil Doll*." *Journal of Popular Film and Television* 22:3 (Summer 1998): 86–94.

Official NYC Website <http://www.ci.nyc.ny.us/html/nypd/html/misc/crimlst.html> August 22, 2001.

Ojumu, Akin. "Will Talent Out This Time?" *The Observer* (March 24, 2002) <observer.guardian.co.uk/comment/story/0,6903,673041.00.html> October 12, 2005.

Oliver, Kelly and Benigno Trigo. *Noir Anxiety*. Minneapolis: University of Minnesota Press, 2003.

Orr, John. *Contemporary Cinema*. Edinburgh: Edinburgh University Press, 1998.

Orr, Stanley. "Postmodernism, Noir, and the Usual Suspects." *Literature/Film Quarterly* 27:1 (1999): 65–73.

Parish, James Robert, and Michael R. Pitts. *The Great Detective Pictures*. Metuchen, NJ: The Scarecrow Press, Inc., 1990.

Parshall, Peter F. "*Die Hard* and the American Mythos." *Journal of Popular Film and Television* 18:4 (Winter 1991): 134–44.

Pascall, Jeremy. *Hollywood and the Great Stars: The Stars, the Sex Symbols, the Legends, the Movies and How It All Began*. New York: Crescent Books, 1976.

Patterson, Jim. *Along Came a Spider*. Boston: Little, Brown, & Co., 1993.

———. *Kiss the Girls*. Boston: Little, Brown, & Co., 1995.

Peek, Wendy Chapman. "Cherchez la Femme: *The Searchers*, *Veritgo*, and Masculinity in Post-Kinsey America." *Journal of American Culture* 21:2 (1998): 73–87.

Pfeil, Fred. *White Guys: Studies in Postmodern Domination and Difference*. London: Verso, 1995.

Pidduck, Julianne. "The 1990s Hollywood Fatal Femme: (Dis)Figuring Feminism, Family, Irony, Violence." *Cineaction* 38 (1995): 64–72.

Pitts, Michael R. *Famous Movie Detectives*. Metuchen, NJ: The Scarecrow Press, 1979.

Pleck, Joseph and Elizabeth Pleck. "Introduction." *The American Male*. Eds. Joseph Pleck and Elizabeth Pleck. Englewood Cliffs, NJ: Prentice-Hall Inc., 1980. 1–49.

Plouffe, Paul Bernard. *The Tainted Adam: The American Hero in Film Noir*. Ann Arbor, MI: University Microfilms International, 1979.

Pollard, Tom. "Postmodern Cinema and the Death of the Hero." *Cineaction* 53 (2000): 40–48.

Pomerance, Murray. "Introduction: From Bad to Worse." *Bad: Infamy, Darkness, Evil, and Slime on Screen*. Ed. Murray Pomerance. Albany, NY: State University of New York Press. 2004. 1–18.

———. "Introduction: Gender in Film at the End of the Twentieth Century." *Ladies and Gentlemen, Boys and Girls: Gender in Film at the End of the Twentieth Century*. Ed. Murray Pomerance. SUNY Series in Cultural Studies in Cinema/Video. Albany, NY: State University of New York Press. 2001. 1–15.

Pratt, Ray. *Projecting Paranoia: Conspiratorial Visions in American Film*. Lawrence, KS: University Press of Kansas, 2001.

Radner, Hilary. "New Hollywood's New Women: Murder in Mind—Sarah and Margie." *Contemporary Hollywood Cinema*. Eds. Steve Neale and Murray Smith. London: Routledge, 1998. 247–62.

Rafter, Nicole. *Shots in the Mirror: Crime Films and Society.* New York: Oxford University Press, 2000.

Regency Enterprises. "Media Release for *L.A. Confidential.*"

Reiner, Robert. "Keystone to Kojak: The Hollywood Cop." *Cinema, Politics, and Society in America.* Eds. Philip Davies and Brian Neve. Paperback reprint, 2nd ed. Manchester, UK: Manchester University Press, 1985. 195–220.

———. *The Politics of the Police.* Brighton, UK: Wheatsheaf Books Ltd., 1985.

Reynolds, Scott. "Taking Chances." *Sight and Sound* 8:2 (1998): 61.

Rimoldi, Oscar. "The Detective Movies of the 30s and 40s: Part I." *Films in Review* 44:5/6 (1993): 164–73.

———. "The Detective Movies of the 30s and 40s: Part II." *Films in Review* 44:7/8 (1993): 204–33.

———. "The Detective Movies of the 30s and 40s: Part III." *Films in Review* 44:9/10 (1993): 308–13.

Rosen, David. *The Changing Fictions of Masculinity.* Urbana, IL: University of Illinois Press, 1993.

Rubin, Martin. "The Grayness of Darkness: *The Honeymoon Killers* and its Impact on Psychokiller Cinema." *Mythologies of Violence in Postmodern Media.* Ed. Christopher Sharrett. Detroit: Wayne State University Press, 1999. 41–64.

———. *Thrillers.* Genres in American Cinema Series. Cambridge, UK: Cambridge University Press, 1999.

Rutherford, Jonathan. *Men's Silences: Predicaments in Masculinity.* London: Routledge, 1992.

———. "Who's That Man?" *Male Order: Unwrapping Masculinity.* Eds. Rowena Chapman and Jonathan Rutherford. Male Order Series. London: Lawrence & Wishart, 1988. 21–67.

Ryan, Michael and Douglas Kellner. *Camera Politica: The Politics and Ideology of Contemporary Hollywood Film.* Bloomington, IN: Indiana University Press, 1990.

Salisbury, Mark. "Kevin Spacey." *Empire* 83 (1996): 52–53.

Schatz, Thomas. *Hollywood Genres: Formulas, Filmmaking, and the Studio System.* Philadelphia: Temple University Press, 1981.

Schrader, Paul. "Notes on Film Noir." *Film Genre Reader.* Ed. Barry Keith Grant. Austin: University of Texas Press, 1986. 169–82.

Segal, Lynne. "Look Back in Anger: Men in the Fifties." *Male Order: Unwrapping*

Masculinity. Eds. Rowena Chapman and Jonathan Rutherford. Male Order Series. London: Lawrence & Wishart, 1988. 68–96.

———. *Slow Motion: Changing Masculinities, Changing Men*. London: Virago Press Ltd., 1990.

Self, Robert T. "Redressing the Law in Kathryn Bigelow's *Blue Steel*." *Journal of Film and Video* 46:2 (Summer 1994): 31–43.

Seltzer, Mark. *Serial Killers: Death and Life in America's Wound Culture*. New York: Routledge, 1998.

Shadoian, Jack. *Dreams and Dead Ends: The American Gangster/Crime Film*. Cambridge, MA: MIT Press, 1977.

Sharrett, Christopher. "End of Story: The Collapse of Myth in Postmodern Narrative Film." *The End of Cinema as We Know It: American Film in the Nineties*. Ed. Jon Lewis. New York: New York University Press, 2001. 319–31.

———. "Introduction." *Mythologies of Violence in Postmodern Media*. Ed. Christopher Sharrett. Detroit: Wayne State University Press, 1999. 9–20.

Shipman, David. *The Great Movie Stars: Vol. 1—The Golden Years*. New revised ed. London: Angus and Robertson, 1979.

Silver, Alain and Elizabeth Ward. *Film Noir: An Encyclopedic Reference Guide*. Revised and expanded ed. London: Bloomsbury Publishing Ltd., 1988.

Silverman, Kaja. *Masculinity at the Margins*. New York: Routledge, 1992.

Simpson, Philip L. "The Politics of Apocalypse in the Cinema of Serial Murder." *Mythologies of Violence in Postmodern Media*. Ed. Christopher Sharrett. Detroit: Wayne State University Press, 1999. 119–44.

———. *Psycho Paths: Tracking the Serial Killer through Contemporary American Film and Fiction*. Carbondale, IL: Southern Illinois University Press, 2000.

Sklar, Robert. *City Boys: Cagney, Bogart, Garfield*. Princeton: Princeton University Press, 1992.

Slotkin, Richard. "The Hard-Boiled Detective Story: From the Open Range to the Mean Streets." *The Sleuth and the Scholar: Origins, Evolution, and Current Trends in Detective Fiction*. Eds. Barbara A. Rader and Howard G. Zettler. Contributions to the Study of Popular Culture Ser. 19. New York: Greenwood Press, 1988. 91–100.

Smith, Valerie. *Not Just Race, Not Just Gender: Black Feminist Readings*. New York: Routledge, 1998.

Sobchack, Vivian. "Lounge Time." *Refiguring American Film Genres: History and Theory*. Ed. Nick Browne. Berkeley, CA: University of California Press, 1998. 129–70.

Southam, Andrew. "Special K." *Empire* 99 (1997): 92–98.

Spicer, Andrew. "The Emergence of the British Tough Guy: Stanley Baker, Masculinity and the Crime Thriller." *British Crime Cinema.* Eds. Steve Chibnall and Robert Murphy. London: Routledge, 1999. 81–93.

Stables, Kate. "The Postmodern Always Rings Twice: Constructing the *Femme Fatale* in 90s Cinema." *Women in Film Noir.* Ed. E. Ann Kaplan. Revised ed. London: BFI Publishing, 2001. 164–82.

Stowe, William W. "Hard-boiled Virgil: Early Nineteenth-Century Beginnings of a Popular Literary Formula." *The Sleuth and the Scholar: Origins, Evolution, and Current Trends in Detective Fiction.* Eds. Barbara A. Rader and Howard G. Zettler. New York: Greenwood Press, 1988. 79–90.

Straayer, Chris. "*Femme Fatale* or Lesbian Femme: *Bound* in Sexual *Différance.*" *Women in Film Noir.* Ed. E. Ann Kaplan. Revised ed. London: BFI Publishing, 2001. 151–63.

Stringer, Julian. "Scrambling Hollywood: Asian Stars/Asian American Star Cultures." *Contemporary Hollywood Stardom.* Ed. Thomas Austin and Martin Baker. London: Arnold, 2003. 229–42.

Studlar, Gaylyn. "Cruise-ing into the Millennium: Performative Masculinity, Stardom, and the All-American Boy's Body." *Ladies and Gentlemen, Boys and Girls: Gender in Film at the End of the Twentieth Century.* Ed. Murray Pomerance. SUNY Series in Cultural Studies in Cinema/Video. Albany, NY: SUNY Press, 2001. 171–83.

———. *This Mad Masquerade: Stardom and Masculinity in the Jazz Age.* Film and Culture Series. New York: Columbia University Press, 1996.

Symons, Julian. *Criminal Practices: Symons on Crime Writing 60s to 90s.* London: Macmillan, 1994.

Taking Lives Official Website <takinglives.warnerbros.com> March 23, 2004.

Tasker, Yvonne. *Spectacular Bodies: Gender, Genre and the Action Cinema.* Film, Media, and Cultural Studies; Popular Fiction Series. London: Routledge, 1993.

Taubin, Amy. "Death and the Maidens—A Series of Serial Killers: The Loss of Innocence, Mobility, and Air." [Review of *Felicia's Journey, The Bone Collector,* and *Oxygen*] *Village Voice* (November 16, 1999): 136.

———. "Grabbing the Knife: *The Silence of the Lambs* and the History of the Serial Killer Movie." *Women and Film: A Sight and Sound Reader.* Eds. Pam Cook and Philip Dodd. London: Scarlet Press, 1991. 123–31.

Telotte, J. P. "Rounding up *The Usual Suspects*: The Comfort of Character and Neo-Noir." *Film Quarterly* 51:4 (1998): 12–20.

Tharp, Julie. "The Transvestite as Monster: Gender Horror in *The Silence of the Lambs* and *Psycho.*" *Journal of Popular Film and Television* 19:3 (1991): 106–13.

Thomas, Ronald R. *Detective Fiction and the Rise of Forensic Science.* Cambridge, UK: Cambridge University Press, 1999.

Thomas, Tony. *Cads and Cavaliers: The Gentlemen Adventurers of the Movies.* South Brunswick, NJ: A.S. Barnes & Co., 1973.

Thomson, David. "The Riddler Has His Day." *Sight and Sound* 11:4 (2001): 18–21.

Tietchen, Todd F. "Samplers and Copycats: The Cultural Implications of the Postmodern Slasher in Contemporary American Film." *Journal of Popular Film and Television* 26:3 (1998): 98–107.

Todorov, Tzvetan. *The Poetics of Prose.* Trans. Richard Howard. Ithaca, NY: Cornell University Press, 1977.

Travers, Peter. "Movies Crime Fiction." *Rolling Stone* (October 5, 1995): 75–79.

Tudor, Andrew. "Genre." *Film Genre Reader II.* Ed. Barry Keith Grant. Austin: University of Texas, 1995. 3–10.

Turan, Kenneth. "Review of *Copycat.*" Rev. of *Copycat,* dir. John Amiel. *Los Angeles Times* (October 27, 1995): Calendar 1.

Tuska, Jon. *The Detective in Hollywood.* New York: Doubleday & Co., Inc., 1978.

TV Guide 27:28, issue 1385 (July 12–18, 2003).

VanDerBeets, Richard. *George Sanders: An Exhausted Life.* London: Robson Books, 1990.

Vasey, Ruth. *The World According to Hollywood, 1918–1939.* Exeter, UK: University of Exeter Press, 1997.

Vernet, Marc. "*Film Noir* on the Edge of Doom." *Shades of Noir: A Reader.* Ed. Joan Copjec. London: Verso, 1993. 1–31.

Walker, Alexander. *Stardom: The Hollywood Phenomenon.* London: Michael Joseph, 1970.

Wardell, Jane. "London Audience Flocks to Public Autopsy." *Toronto Star* (November 21, 2002): A16.

Waugh, Hillary. *Hillary Waugh's Guide to Mysteries and Mystery Writing.* Cincinnati: Writer's Digest Books, 1991.

Weaver, Michael. "The New Science of Policing: Crime and the Birmingham Police Force, 1839–1842." *Albion* 26:2 (1994): 289–308.

Welsh, James M. "Action Films: The Serious, the Ironic, the Postmodern." *Film Genre 2000: New Critical Essays.* Ed. Wheeler Winston Dixon. The SUNY

Series in Cultural Studies in Cinema/Video. Albany: State University of New York Press, 2000. 161–76.

Werner, James V. "The Detective Gaze: Edgar A. Poe, the Flaneur, and the Physiognomy of Crime." *The American Transcendental Quarterly* 15:1 (March 2001): 5–21.

White, Susan. "T(he)-Men's Room: Masculinity and Space in Anthony Mann's *T-Men*." Ed. Peter Lehman. *Masculinity: Bodies, Movies, Culture.* New York: Routledge, 2001. 95–114.

Whitt, Jan. "The 'Very Simplicity of the Thing': Edgar Allan Poe and the Murders He Wrote." *The Detective in American Fiction, Film, and Television.* Eds. Jerome Delamater and Ruth Prigozy. Contributions to the Study of Popular Culture Ser. 62. Westport, CT: Greenwood Press, 1988. 111–21.

Wilkinson, Rupert. *American Tough: The Tough-Guy Tradition and the American Character.* Contributions in American Studies Ser. 69. Westport, CT: Greenwood Press, 1984.

Williams, Carol Traynor. *The Dream Beside Me: The Movies and the Children of the Forties.* London: Associated University Press, 1980.

Williams, Linda. "Film Bodies: Gender, Genre, and Excess." *Film Quarterly* 44:4 (1991): 2–13.

Wilson, Ron. "The Left-Handed Form of Human Endeavor: Crime Films during the 1990s." *Film Genre 2000: New Critical Essays.* Ed. Wheeler Winston Dixon. SUNY Series in Cultural Studies in Cinema/Video. Albany: State University of New York Press, 2000. 143–59.

Woll, Allen L. and Randall M. Miller. *Ethnic and Racial Images in American Film and Television: Historical Essays and Bibliography.* Garland Reference Library of Social Science Vol. 308. New York: Garland Publishing, Inc., 1987.

Wong, Eugene Franklin. "The Early Years: Asians in the American Films Prior to World War II." *Screening Asian Americans.* Ed. Peter X. Feng. New Brunswick, NJ: Rutgers University Press, 2002. 53–70.

Wrathall, John. "*Seven*." Rev. of *Seven*, dir. David Fincher. *Sight and Sound* 6:1 (1996): 49–50.

Wyatt, Justin. "Identity, Queerness, and Homosocial Bonding: The Case of *Swingers*." Ed. Peter Lehman. *Masculinity: Bodies, Movies, Culture.* New York: Routledge, 2001. 51–65.

Young, Lola. *Fear of the Dark: "Race," Gender and Sexuality in the Cinema.* Gender, Racism, Ethnicity Series. London: Routledge, 1996.

INDEX